HIDDEN
RIVALRIES
in
VICTORIAN
FICTION

HIDDEN RIVALRIES

in

VICTORIAN FICTION

*Dickens,
Realism, and
Revaluation*

JEROME MECKIER

THE UNIVERSITY PRESS OF KENTUCKY

This book was published with the assistance of the
Hyder E. Rollins Fund of Harvard University.

Editorial and Sales Offices: Lexington, Kentucky 40506-0024

Library of Congress Cataloging-in-Publication Data
Meckier, Jerome.
    Hidden rivalries in Victorian fiction.

    Bibliography: p.
    Includes index.
    1. English fiction—19th century—History and
criticism. 2. Realism in literature. 3. Social problems
in literature. 4. Dickens, Charles, 1812-1870—Criticism
and interpretation. 5. Literary quarrels—Great Britain.
I. Title.
PR878.R4M4   1987   823'.8'0912   87-6177
ISBN 0-8131-1622-8

For my mother and father,
and for my daughter,
Alison

Contents

. . . twofold Always. May God us keep
From Single vision . . .

—WILLIAM BLAKE

Acknowledgments

While subeditor of *Dickens Studies Annual*, review editor of *Dickens Studies Newsletter*, and trustee of the Dickens Society, I met and befriended many eminent Dickensians upon whom I have subsequently relied for information and example. A partial listing includes Michael Slater, Harry Stone, Robert B. Partlow, William F. Axton, Robert L. Patten, George Ford, David Paroissien, James Kincaid, Albert D. Hutter, and Duane DeVries. I am permanently indebted to Edgar Rosenberg and Jerome Hamilton Buckley for supporting my interest in Dickens when I was at Harvard. I must also thank my colleagues, former and present, for their counsel: Thomas Ashton, Joseph Bryant, Steven Manning, Donald Ringe, and, in particular, John Clubbe.

My thanks go to the editors of the following journals for publishing earlier versions of several essays in this book: *Ariel*, the *Journal of British Studies*, *Dickens Studies Newsletter*, and *Studies in the Novel*. Chapter 1, in its original form titled "Hidden Rivalries in Victorian Fiction: The Case of the Two Esthers," was included in *The Changing World of Charles Dickens* (London: Vision, 1983), edited by Robert Giddings. Those journals in which I published essays bearing upon this study, whether as harbinger or by-product—the *Dickensian*, *Dickens Studies*, *Contemporary Literature*, *Novel*, and the *Journal of Narrative Technique*—receive fuller acknowledgment in notes to the chapters into which the essays have been incorporated or on which they shed light.

Staffs at the Huntington Library and Art Gallery, the Widener Library, UCLA Special Collections, and the M.I. King Library at Kentucky (in particular those who manage the inter library loans and Susan Allen in Special Collections), have invariably been courteous and dependable. I am grateful for fellowship support from the National Endowment for the Humanities and the Huntington Library. I am especially thankful to President Otis Singletary and the Board of Directors at the University of Kentucky for an appointment as Research Professor; having a year off enabled me to complete the research for this project.

Finally, I applaud the many critics with whom I argue throughout the following pages. Coming to terms with other ideas so as to express one's own is not only the major excitement to be found in intellectual endeavor; it is also another way of defining revaluation as several of the greatest Victorian novelists understood it.

Chapter One

The Victorian "Multiverse"

Bleak House

Felix Holt

THIS BOOK grows out of a three-stage progression. The sequence began with Humphry House's *The Dickens World* (1941) and continued through J. Hillis Miller's *Charles Dickens: The World of His Novels* (1958) to Jerome Hamilton Buckley's anthology *The Worlds of Victorian Fiction* (1975).[1] House equated Dickens's world with the real Victorian society in which the novelist lived and attempted to trace the "connexion" between the writings ("historical documents") and the times in which Dickens wrote. Miller capitalized on House's admission that Dickens "made out of Victorian England a complete world with a life and vigour and idiom of its own." The Dickens world for Miller is largely in the novels, which reflect a social milieu refashioned by the writer's spirit. Buckley's title suggests that one should expect as many worlds as there were novelists. While remaining faithful to Victorian contexts, the modern revaluator must acknowledge almost as much turmoil and diversity in the nineteenth-century novel as in modern fiction.

The old-fashioned critic, such as G.M. Young, who envisioned the Victorian ethos as a monolithic structure more sustaining than our own, may soon be about as relevant to the pace of modern scholarship as a hackney cab on an interstate. Scholars dealing with the nineteenth century ought to borrow a word from Aldous Huxley (and Henry Adams) and speak of the Victorian "multiverse." Buckley divides his anthology into four parts—"Views of the Dickens World," "George Eliot and the World of *Middlemarch*," "Private Worlds," and "Other Worlds"—to endorse the multiplicity hailed by his title; he contends that the essays in his volume "chart routes of discovery to some of the many worlds in the galaxy of

Victorian fiction." It becomes harder to frame the Victorian mind if one must deal with a *galaxy*. This space-age metaphor posits a constellation of minds, a series of island universes in which the planet Thackeray and the planet Trollope may be as foreign to one another as Virginia Woolf's description of Mrs. Ramsay's world is to D.H. Lawrence's of Constance Chatterley's. The subsidiary meaning of *galaxy*, an assemblage of brilliant persons, permits an excellent pun: the splendor of the writers in question makes journeying from one island universe to another worthwhile.

The story that remains to be told is how Victorian novelists deliberately created competing worlds, each with its own vigorous idiom. Not only does the planet Trollope or the planet George Eliot differ substantially *from* the planet Dickens, but each differs *with* it as well. Each insisted that he (or she) had fashioned the more credible historical document, the more realistic depiction of actual Victorian society, and took steps to discredit the competition as a way of proving it. One may still look for connections between a fictive world and the times in which it was created or for the peculiar structural form that entitles readers to call the world of a given novel Trollopian or Dickensian. But the modern revaluator must also study the revaluative links between rival Victorian novels.

Hidden Rivalries in Victorian Fiction argues that nineteenth-century British fiction should be seen as a honeycomb of intersecting networks. Within and between these networks, novelists rethink and rewrite other novels as a way of enhancing their own credibility. In a world increasingly relative (thanks mostly to the triumph of a scientific secularity), the goal was to establish one's credentials as a realist, hence a reliable social critic, by taking away someone else's—generally Dickens's. Trollope, Mrs. Gaskell, and especially George Eliot attempted to make room for themselves in the 1850s and '60s by pushing the preeminent Dickens aside. At the same time but from the opposite flank, Wilkie Collins tried a different form of revaluation: he strove to outdo Dickens at the kind of novel Dickens thought he did best, the kind his other rivals tried to cancel, tone down, or repair. Dickens replied to all of his rivals by redoing *them* as spiritedly as they had reused his characters and situations to make their own statements and discredit his.

This is a study of what could be called the "realism wars." Reexamining Victorian fiction as a series of revaluative responses and replies, it changes the way Victorian novels should be read by suggesting a new way that the novelists themselves—professed realists all—read and reread one another.

If one rereads with hidden rivalries in mind, Victorian novelists can be overheard challenging one another's veracity, arguing among themselves to determine whose version of the truth most closely reflects the actual world. Many of the classic Victorian novels were double-barreled documents, written not just for their own sakes but to revise another novelist's views; their authors wrote to pass judgment on society and, at the same time, to offer systematic revaluations (revaluative parodies) of the ideas, characters, and techniques of an established competitor. Major writers-to-be consolidated—sometimes first discerned—their own positions by rewriting a rival's work.

The revaluating novelist wanted to substitute a truer rendition of the way people behave or things happen for what he or she considered another author's misconceptions. A counterpoint soon developed that was genre-wide. The Victorian novelist measured a rival's perception of reality against conclusions reached as a consequence of his own temperament, experiences, and expectations, then refashioned a rival's materials to suit his own philosophy while simultaneously revising the fallacies he claimed to have detected in the other writer's imitations of reality.

In *Oliver Twist* (1837-38), Dickens announced his arrival as a serious novelist by redoing the "Newgate" novels of William Harrison Ainsworth and Edward Lytton Bulwer: instead of offering an outlaw's life-style as an escapist fantasy, he captured the actual squalor of the criminal world, which others romanticized. No stranger to the uses of revaluative parody, however, Dickens was himself the primary target of competitive revaluation and thus remains one's best index to the breadth and intensity of this Victorian phenomenon. Dickens's rivals tried to calm him down, replace his forebodings with brighter forecasts, or disallow his novels outright as total impossibilities. They thought of Dickens as an exaggerator, an alarmist who would damage the era's good name.

Thackeray's declaration of war against "Boz" could have been proclaimed much more justifiably by George Eliot, Trollope, or Mrs. Gaskell: Dickens "knows," Thackeray wrote, "that my books are a protest against his—that if one set are true, the other must be false."[2] In the process of disagreeing with Dickens, however, novelists tacitly allied against him did more than certify his centrality: they also discovered differences of opinion separating them from one another. Moreover, as Dickens's detractors grew in number, they goaded him into counterattacking.

Revaluing the Victorians whose texts double as pretexts means paying more attention to their propensity for revaluing one another.[3] Five examples of hidden rivalry only begin to suggest the breadth and variety of the double-purpose novel-writing they inspired.

1. The first match pits *Felix Holt* against *Bleak House*. George Eliot rewrites Dickens in order, she hopes, to erase him entirely. His world view

is an obstacle she must remove from her path if her more sanguine depiction of change in an evolving social system is to gain credence. *Felix Holt* deserves pride of place in this study because it confirmed the efficacy of parodic revaluation as a major factor in Victorian realism. It also embodied George Eliot's decision that previous anti-Dickens activity, on the part of Trollope and Mrs. Gaskell, had seldom gone far enough.

2. When *The Warden* took on *The Almshouse*, Anthony Trollope concocted an imaginary Dickens novel so that he could modify its extravagances. Dickens's social criticism was absurd, Trollope tried to demonstrate, because that undeservedly popular novelist painted even relatively minor social imperfections in glaring colors.

3. Mrs. Gaskell resolved to restore or rebuild in *North and South* the factory system Dickens labored to knock down in *Hard Times;* consequently, these two novels undercut each other. Mutual recrimination resulted from Mrs. Gaskell's response to what she saw as Dickens's attempt to preclude her favorable treatment of industrialization.

4. Set amid other adjoining and interconnecting rivalries, the Dickens-Collins relationship inevitably manifests itself as a contest, not just an alliance that both relished in the struggle against less sensational, less satirical contemporaries. Throughout *The Woman in White, No Name,* and *The Moonstone,* Wilkie Collins threatened to devalue Dickens by outdoing him at the kind of melodramatic social realism his mentor regarded as *his* prerogative. A beleaguered Dickens retaliated in *Great Expectations, Our Mutual Friend,* and especially the unfinished *Mystery of Edwin Drood.* He tried to outclass the novels that had attempted to supersede *Bleak House* and *A Tale of Two Cities;* his uncompleted novel, besides correcting Trollope and George Eliot, was expected to show Collins who was the real master of suspense and the better delineator of the workings of a superintendent providence.

5. Thanks to the creative stimulus Collins and Dickens gave each other, George Eliot was still working to prove her case against the latter: *Middlemarch* reaffirmed her parodic treatment of *Bleak House* and expanded the attack to cover *The Mystery of Edwin Drood.* But Dickens's bitter irony, sharp satire, and firm sense of the apocalyptic—qualities that George Eliot considered old-fashioned, unrealistic, and counterproductive—have persisted to become compelling, modern-looking traits that enhance his artistry.

Struggles between Dickens and Mrs. Gaskell are typical in that they coruscate with modern parallels. Their quarrel on the subject of the future of human relationships in a world increasingly reliant on technology was a forerunner of D.H. Lawrence's argument with the Bloomsbury Group.

Like Dickens, Lawrence mistrusted industrialization for the dehumanizing impact it appears to have on men and women, not to mention
masters and men; he found Bloomsbury's fostering of connection, its
celebration of better human relationships, unrealistic as a modern surrogate religion. Dickens's use of separation and divorce as a paradigm for the
future indicates that he was skeptical of Mrs. Gaskell's propensity for
marrying her personifications of opposing social forces; Mrs. Gaskell's
admiration for a technocrat like Thornton (in *North and South*), her enthusiasm for the improved machinery he envisions, and her approval of the
factory owner as a social planner seem intended to redress Dickens's
caricature of Thornton's type in the rascal Bounderby (in *Hard Times*).
Their differences on this score look forward to Aldous Huxley's parody,
throughout *Brave New World*, of the managerial scientists whom H.G.
Wells idolized in *A Modern Utopia* and *Men Like Gods*.

"The novel," John Fowles notes, has always been "a kind of self-feeding
form, a cannibal form," so that one "cannot conceive of a writer not
breaking down the material he admires in past novelists and reusing it in his
own work."[4] Victorian novelists are certainly cannibalistic, but seldom so
out of admiration; they break down material to subvert and replace it.
Feeding on the effusions of their rivals, they write the first anti-novels.
Since novelist after novelist hopes to displace a work he distrusts by redoing
it more honestly in one of his own, Victorian realism needs redefining.
This chapter and those that follow pay tribute to the richness and variety of
the rival realisms that flourished during the Victorian era. Every novelist
discussed tried to render an "authentic report of human experience,"[5] yet
each was just as concerned to prove his or her report more authentic than a
rival's. Polyphonic and dialectical, Victorian realism was not so much an
entity as a multiplicity of competing authorial voices.

Consequently, the modern revaluator must attend to the merits of each
perspective that equated itself with realism. He cannot allow any party to
call its outlook *the* scientific or sociological approach. Indeed, the major
varieties of competing Victorian realisms—George Eliot's and Dickens's—
each had both a scientific and a poetic component. Pro-Darwin, George
Eliot and Mrs. Gaskell were also strongly imbued with Wordsworth.
Dickens and Collins had grave reservations about the positive implications
George Eliot drew from the biological sciences; they preferred a perspective colored by Coleridge.

Each strand of Victorian realism also had a bias toward the utopian or
the dystopian. Much depends on the author's assessment of the impact that
social process, considered progress by many, was having on human nature.

The increasing interiority of George Eliot's characters is counter-balanced by Dickens's sense of a deepening interiority of evil. Differences of opinion developed over society's eagerness and capacity for sustained periods of self-improvement. Whenever one novelist recycled another's materials, that ostensibly aesthetic activity underscored fundamental disagreements in their philosophies.

At stake throughout the 1850s and '60s was the position that Victorian England was slated to occupy in history. George Eliot and her supporters hoped that it would be recognized as the apex of civilization to date and the harbinger of a brighter future through secular, scientific evolution. Dickens aroused her ire because temporal existence in his novels, no matter how vociferous their calls for radical reform, seemed destined to remain a vale of suffering, disappointment, and tears. The myth of steady progress, Dickens argued, was historically incorrect; it minimized man's fallen nature, overlooked the problems that such a condition continued to pose for community, and ignored the unparalled pressures polite society was placing upon human fallibility.

Revaluation manifests itself as a program of tireless revision and correction. Victorian novelists turned satire and parody upon their rivals as enthusiastically as some moderns later unlimbered similar weapons against them. But Victorians were generally more serious as parodists and perhaps more subtle. It was gross misrepresentation in the Dickensian mode that they felt needed readjustment through affirmative or reaffirmative parodies, not errors that could be ridiculed by exaggerating them. Still, if undercutting the false, the exaggerated, or the improbable by an account held to be of greater validity is seen as a kind of parody, the Victorian period was not the wholly earnest, nonsatiric age that literary historians once accepted it to be.[6] On the contrary, earnestness regularly expresses itself in the clearing away of descriptions and occurrences deemed irresponsible, misleading, or unscientific.

Rivalries in Victorian fiction have not remained hidden simply because critics have ignored them, though the novelists made it easy for them to do so. On the surface, as good Victorians, they maintained cordial relationships, no matter how acrimonious the exchanges in their fiction. They expected revaluative parody to work surreptitiously, like an agent in the enemy's camp or, in effect, by bringing the enemy into one's own camp, where he is neutralized and absorbed—one might even say, with Fowles, devoured. That Dickens was never eaten alive by his many competitors is one of the strongest testimonies ever recorded to the magnitude of his genius.

Rivalries between Victorian novels have been difficult to uncover because a Victorian novel always does its own job, too, while less directly—one could say surreptitiously—undoing someone else's. The intention behind the re-use of character and theme is always contradiction, but permutations are reconstructive as well as deconstructive; they are never plagiarisms. Competing Victorian fictions are assertions as well as rebuttals, offerings as well as substitutions or cancellations; their proposals are simultaneously counterproposals and vice versa.

The antipathy between *Felix Holt* and *Bleak House* resembles the hostility that *Brave New World* shows for *Men Like Gods*. One crucial difference is that Aldous Huxley's parody of H.G. Wells "got out of hand" to become a full-scale production of its author's fears for the future,[7] whereas a Victorian novel responding to a rival work was planned from the start to be both a separate entity and a revaluative substitution. Whenever George Eliot reshapes Dickens toward her own ends, the reformulation not only becomes sufficiently engrossing to stand alone by virtue of its internal logic, but the restatements are intended to displace—in effect to hide—the novels they reformulate.

Recognizing that many nineteenth-century novels are both integral statements and dependent artifacts redefines the shape and intent of Victorian fiction. Whenever variables begin to replace absolutes, as happened with increasing frequency during the Victorian period, a novelist has to convince readers that he or she possesses the necessary grasp before presuming to draw conclusions. Inaccurate description, the implied rule goes, precludes effective prescription—hence the obsessive concern with establishing the sheer physical reality of the novelist's chosen scene, whether it be Tom-all-alone's in *Bleak House* or a workingman's home in *North and South*.

Moderns remain separated from the Victorians by time but share with them a growing sense of life's astonishing multiplicity and the increasing challenge of a militantly secularized world. Victorian novelists played an insufficiently recognized role in the search for new frameworks, a search that continues to this day; they were professed realists whose contribution was actually the multiplication of realisms. They inhabited a Victorian world that believed strongly in the possibility of an accurate representationalism, but they also created a proto-modern forum for conflicting philosophical perspectives, each as partial, relative, and partisan as the next.

One cannot fully isolate "The Victorianism of Victorian Literature"[8] by characterizing it as a literature of engagement that exhibits little of the modern *angst* as it does confident battle with the world. Part of the Victorianism of major Victorian novels is their intimation of oncoming modernity. During the realism wars of the 1850s and '60s, as aesthetic differences became vehicles for philosophical argument, the novelists resembled an informal debating society rather than participants in an organized crusade. Their battles of words can also be called a war of the worlds.

Unlike Buckley's anthology, Peter K. Garrett's *The Victorian Multiplot Novel* puts the format it investigates strictly within a postmodern context.[9] This unexamined thesis—that literature has always been postmodern or, easier yet, can be treated as though it were—distorts the Victorian novel's role as a battleground for competing philosophies of life during a critical phase in the secularization of Western culture. Structuralist in origin and deconstructionist by inclination, methodology in this kind of study ultimately makes different novels alike. Gone is the heightened critical reception that attends equally to proto-modern and essentially Victorian components in a novelist's personality; instead, one regards multiplot novels as myopically self-absorbed in their own internal contradictions. Were such a single-minded approach legitimate, Victorian fictions could not be mutually revaluative and semimodern; each would be too busy scuttling itself to worry about doing in the competition.

Victorian multiplot novels, says Garrett, are the product of the "double logic" operating within them. Discordant structural principles in such works as *Bleak House, Middlemarch, Vanity Fair,* and *Can You Forgive Her?* collide to generate "unresolved tensions" that become the real meanings, even though their authors never conceived them intentionally. In the deconstructionist scheme of things, *Bleak House* becomes an irresolvable thematic and structural tension: Esther Summerson's subjective view of her maturation contradicts—and is contradicted by—a less optimistic prognosis that has society sliding backward. Thus Victorian multiplot novels are used to exemplify a problem allegedly germane to all works of literature: they are unexpectedly and hopelessly contrapuntal because their parts say different things. Contrary to the author's expectations, the parts work at cross-purposes instead of for the good of the whole.

Dickens's finest novel, one objects, is not a contest between speakers. It does not end in a standoff similar to the impasse Mustapha Mond and John Savage reach when arguing over the merits of the Brave New World; instead, it pieces together an individual's account of her sufferings with a satirist's survey of the larger causes behind them. Double narrative in *Bleak House* is used contrapuntally, but not dialogically, to explore variations on the book's central themes. The thing perceived, the bleakness of life in London at midcentury, is similar throughout both narratives. General conditions that the unidentified third-person narrator deplores impinge without mercy on the difficult life Esther reports. Autobiographical reflection reinforces the social criticism which, in turn, explains Esther's struggle. Instead of trying to silence one another, Esther's narrative and her unnamed partner's add up to a sweeping indictment of social conditions and human behavior that less pessimistic Victorian novelists found infuriating and repeatedly strove to discount.

The modern conflict that Garrett rightly identifies in the Victorian multiplot novel is between perspectives. Unfortunately, he confines this clash to the individual's perspective against society's, with some plots in a given novel allegedly endorsing the person and others the group, each plot taking its turn as the center. But Victorian novelists were generally able to resolve these local contests without confusing themselves or their readers. Esther Summerson, Thackeray's Becky Sharp, Trollope's Alice Vavasor, and George Eliot's Dorothea Brooke, to take a handful of examples, experience society as restraint. None of these instances, however, leaves the contest between individual and group unsettled. Dickens and Thackeray are more critical of society than Trollope or George Eliot, but none of the four is unable to give the individual's viewpoint and the community's what he or she considers due to each. *Hard Times* teems with clashes between individual and group perspectives, yet Dickens is never uncertain whose side he is on. He supports the men as a group against their unjust master, but this does not contradict his preference for individual freedom over tyranny from confederation or intellectual system. Thus he chooses Stephen Blackpool over the union, Sissy Jupe rather than Gradgrind's Utilitarianism.

More problematic than the individual's difficulties with the group are larger altercations, ignored by deconstructionists, that pit one Victorian novel's perspective on such difficulties against another's. Competitions *between* Victorian novels were often severer than those that postmodernist critics attempt to locate *within* them. Novelists who believe that private desires and the public interest can readily be made to coincide feel compelled to refute those who fear that changing social conditions make it less feasible than before. It is precisely a difference of opinion on this matter that causes Dickens and Mrs. Gaskell to fall upon each other and that keeps Dickens and George Eliot worlds apart.

Throughout *Vanity Fair*, Garrett charges, Thackeray exaggerates differences between Becky and Amelia. Simultaneously, the novel's communal voice, apparently also Thackeray, talks in the opposite direction to make their contrasted histories illustrate the ubiquitous *vanitas*. This, one objects, would be an instance of the whole working against the parts, contrary to the structuralist conception of parts working against the whole. Like most multiplotters, Thackeray seems modern and contrapuntal, not postmodern and self-contradictory.

Realizing that all is vanity does not mean that it hardly matters whether one is Amelia or Becky, Dobbin or George Osborne. The novelist studies dissimilar characters who encounter misfortunes that are variant forms of man's universal predicament. It is this predicament that makes the characters similar despite their differences. To perceive this requires *double vision*, not *double logic:* the novelist has two perceptions from two different angles, which do not cancel out. The mental process is compound and unifying, not self-divided or self-confuting. Thackeray's double perspective discriminates between cases without losing sight of the common fate. When critics the likes of Roland Barthes, Claude Lévi-Strauss, Jacques Derrida, and M.M. Bakhtin are invoked, individual Victorian novels become "dialogical" or "polyphonic"; they allegedly contain a "plurality of independent and unmerged voices and consciousnesses." Such a description, the modern revaluator counters, better fits the Victorian novel seen collectively, one author's perspective against another's. A mind full of Bakhtin and Derrida is no substitute for a historical sense. When imposed on specific Victorian fictions, the concept of dialogy makes the multiplot novel a victim of the oncoming modern condition it was designed to address.

Victorian multiplot novels deserve a better fate. Despite being multidimensional, they are complex and unified. In masterpieces like *Bleak House*, Esther's experiences and the third-person narrator's commentary are not contradictory but complementary, mutually illuminating, as are Dorothea's success and Lydgate's failure in *Middlemarch*. Multiplotting signals the dawn of the modern age of experimentation; it must be reexamined as the nineteenth-century novelist's ambitious reaction to a new awareness of secular life's multiplying possibilities. *Bleak House, Middlemarch, Vanity Fair,* and *Can You Forgive Her?* all came out within a twenty-five-year period. That the impulse to multiply story lines overcame major novelists within the same quarter of a century cannot be coincidental. It was a response to life's quickening capacity for diversity, a recognition that employing one center of consciousness or a single story line has affinities with a disappearing era of orthodoxy.

Multiplot novelists, finding themselves in an increasingly secular multiverse, were among the earliest to realize that different outlooks, whether of rival novels or within the interrelated stories of a single fiction, stand or fall by comparison with one another. This was not an eruption of the dialogical. It was conscious acknowledgment of a relativism that seems premodern. It was not an admission that the novel is self-contradictory but a premonition that the format would prove uniquely open to a new sense of life as pluralism. A "plurality of independent and unmerged voices and consciousnesses," to repeat the formula Garrett borrows from Bakhtin, is the vision of modern life and the competitive nature of novel-writing in the Victorian era that multiplot novels were designed to deal with.

The multiplot novel did not vacillate between taking the individual's perspective and society's, but it did make a further concession to the growing importance of individual cases, a phenomenon that the rise of the novel can be said to have first abetted a century earlier. A lot depended on the Victorian novelist's ability to draw conclusions from diversification, to build up consensus piece by piece, story by story. Enumerating patterns of provincial life (*Middlemarch*) requires Bulstrode's downfall along with Dorothea's apotheosis. The third-person narrator's fulminations against the judicial system (*Bleak House*) would seem incredible were it not for Esther's personal encounters with Chancery and several of its dupes. Nineteenth-century multiplot novels are about the need for more ways of looking, the necessity for more eyes, more aspects, additional angles of vision, as a means to greater authenticity.

Narrative techniques as disparate as Conrad's impressionistic rendering, Virginia Woolf's interior monologues, the alternating streams of consciousness in *Ulysses*, and Huxley's vision of society as a contrapuntist's nightmare, a "human fugue" in which each instrument insists on being central or soloist, are all consquences, in part, of the corporate failure of Victorian novelists to shore up or reinvent community view. Ironically, clashes between the competing realisms of novels antagonistic toward one another aggravated the need for sweeping generalization that each purported to be addressing. The widening division of opinion between Victorian novelists, existing voice against voice, is an even stronger indication of oncoming decommunalization than the proliferation of story lines in some of their best novels. Nevertheless, behind the variations on a theme within specific Victorian fictions or the counterpoint between rival Victorian novels lies the assumption that expanded narrative structures can control, if not explain, the "bagginess" now recognized as a major facet of modern chaos: life's constantly accelerating diversity. A deconstructionist approach makes smaller the books Henry James incorrectly thought baggy, as though one would multiply story lines to undercut oneself, thereby saying less.

"Double vision" involves having two (or more) interrelated perceptions at the same time about the same thing. "Double logic" or "Seeing Double"—the latter phrase the title of Garrett's chapter on Thackeray—implies impaired eyesight. Seeing double connotes an undesired lack of clarity, a confusion of mind or doubleness of image whereby one exposure gets in another's way, obscuring both. Seeing double is the postmodern parody of double vision. It is as if Thackeray, unable to decide whether Becky and Amelia are more alike or unlike, proceeds via "double logic" until the ability to tell one case from the other—and the reason for doing so—begins to disappear. When the speaker in Samuel Beckett's *The Unnamable* concludes: "I can't go on, I'll go on," one seems to be seeing and hearing double.[10] Once the deconstructionist, adopting the postmodern novel's techniques, imposes dialogical formulas on *Bleak House*, Esther says she has grown up, but the third-person narrator responds that she cannot.

Point Counter Point—not *Vanity Fair* or *Bleak House* or deconstructionist misreadings of them—turns the multiplot novel against itself and virtually exhausts the form. Huxley explodes this format with a society so fragmented that nearly every one of its eccentric characters, no two being sufficiently alike to establish a positive norm, demands his own story line; there is no group perspective. If multiplotting survives Huxley's parody, it returns best as an anachronism conscientiously updated in the multivolume or sequence novel. Thanks to C.P. Snow's underrated *Strangers and Brothers* sequence and Anthony Powell's *A Dance to the Music of Time*, Huxley's notion of an anthology novel is given some practical extension.

The great Victorian multiplotters cultivated a flexibility of mind almost mandatory in a world where truth was becoming plural: one had to rely on a variety of case histories and challenge another's vision to promulgate one's own. The multiplot novelist had to think of more than one instance or variation of his theme. He also had to think of situations that would express his attitude toward life at the same time that they presented a rethinking of a rival novelist's perspective. Multiplot novels of the Victorian era are not just important because of their quest for additional angles of vision or their uses of double narrative and multiple story line. They also encourage the modern revaluator to develop some double visions of his own: that is, to see a work as both Victorian and modern, or complex yet unified, or as a declaration per se as well as a refutation of another work.

Taking the period from Victoria to the present as a whole, one asserts that revaluation, art interrogating itself, *is* the modern. Ultimately, the interrogation process asks whether life has meaning and, if so, how art can accurately discern it. Postmodernism, extending this inquiry to the point of self-parody, employs art to question the very idea of art, a development in which contexts vanish, texts deconstruct, and artists entertain the possibility that art itself—not just the output of a rival—is a delusion. If defined as the assumption that reality can be represented without idealization or detraction, realism has always been a fiction. Talented Victorians did not always fully articulate this discovery for themselves, but they found it conducive to the proliferation of their disputative artistry. Pinpointing the shortcomings of a rival is a form of parody, but doing so with art itself, a form of self-parody, cannot succeed except as absolute silence. This is less demanding than trying to silence or rephrase someone else. Victorian novelists relished making statements that were simultaneously counterstatements aimed at quashing competitors but knew better than to turn their ability against itself. [11]

Hidden Rivalries in Victorian Fiction aspires to encourage reappraisal of the idea of revaluation as it bears upon the nineteenth-century novel, using the following chapters as variations on a theme. The "great revaluation" of art, moral values, and the relationships between the two did not begin suddenly in 1880, when writers thought the age of certainty, so-called, finally at an end; nor did revaluation stop in 1920. [12] The 1880s did bring a second, possibly less exciting phase during which revaluation ceased to be quite so subterranean a process, and by the 1920s it had become a way of life. But the 1850s and '60s were a veritable training ground for the modern era (more pivotal for nineteenth-century British fiction than the 1840s). [13] Revaluation started with the great Victorians themselves, as they reexamined their Romantic inheritance. The process continues with this book, beginning with the case of the two Esthers.

None of Dickens's detractors rewrote him more diligently than George Eliot. This major novelist made a second career out of parodying his novels to promulgate her own ideas. *Felix Holt* (1866) is the classic instance of Victorian revaluation: a systematic revision, a complete redoing, of Dickens's *Bleak House* (1852-53). Using the same matter to reach different conclusions, George Eliot wanted her more optimistic conception of existing social conditions to supersede Dickens's view. Tensions develop between his bleak perspective and her affirmation of life's organic soundness; every readjustment of a character, incident, or theme from Dickens results in a satiric counterpoint between her book and his.

Dickens's masterwork was a stumbling block for the would-be Victorian sibyl. She had to neutralize its anti-evolutionary satire before her own more hopeful vision of England's prospects for gradual improvement could gain acceptance. Even though she shared Dickens's contempt for most existing political and economic procedures, she found his brand of radicalism destructive rather than ameliorative. An exasperated Dickens invoked spontaneous combustion as a veiled metaphor for revolution and seemed half in love with his own scare tactic. But George Eliot feared that a clean sweep, a disruptive upheaval, would carry with it ideals better preserved; the more painstaking task for a radical was to sift the outmoded and cumbersome in order to isolate the perennially valuable. One must guarantee, in addition to eradicating abuses, that worthwhile tradition will be passed on.

Felix Holt is the first of George Eliot's three principal examinations of society's evolutionary potential. Along with *Middlemarch* and *Daniel Deronda*, it explores the reformer's calling as a secular apostolate, the supreme individual response to energies already at work in life's flow but in need of expert direction. None of this makes sense if Esther Summerson's maturation is as perilous as Dickens contends or as limited. The reformer's vocation seems quixotic as long as the third-person narrator's Juvenalian satire in *Bleak House* remains the accredited estimate of the human situation. *Felix Holt* is George Eliot's most anti-Dickensian novel because it had to create room for itself and two subsequent studies of reformist endeavor.14

The plot of *Felix Holt* teems with Dickensian importations employed slightly askew. For instance, George Eliot parodies the device of hidden parentage. First she doubles Dickens's reliance upon it; then she decides that being the progeny of sexual transgression—a melodramatic metaphor for the restraining power of the past—cannot be taken seriously as divine punishment: it does not predetermine one's fate. Rufus Lyon initially lacks the courage to inform his daughter Esther that he is not her real father, but Matthew Jermyn avoids prosecution from the Transomes by telling Harold that he is his. The identity crisis that Esther and Harold each undergo is not caused or resolved by sensational disclosures. Harold realizes on his own that he is not truly an English radical—by inclination, in fact, not English at all. Esther Lyon learns that her status depends on the mission she and the man she decides to marry choose to undertake, not on who her father was or how much money he left her.

Both novels feature a virtually interminable law case: for Jarndyce versus Jarndyce, read Bycliffe versus Transome as its parody. In *Felix Holt*, the lawsuit is not quite so endless; lawyers do work things out. Nevertheless, Esther Lyon, rightful heir to Transome Court, declines to inherit. A labyrinthine law case, one of Dickens's depressing images of life, turns out to be as inconsequential in George Eliot's novel as belated discovery of one's true parentage. Contrary to the tenets of sensation novels, legacies are not essential for social salvation. Esther Lyon's birthright, and later Dorothea Brooke's, is (to paraphrase Matthew Arnold) the best that man has thought and said.

Having inherited the ongoing cultural process in the world's foremost country, Esther can bequeath as well as receive, a feat seemingly beyond Oliver Twist or David Copperfield. Thanks to Felix's advice, Esther need only commit herself to the evolutionary flux, the forward march of life and mind, in order to save and be saved. Thus she must avoid the deathly fixity that comes from desiring position and a legally certified but unearned identity. The outcome of Jarndyce versus Jarndyce, George Eliot suggests, is not only highly improbable and grossly unfair to the legal profession but more immaterial to any reasonable person's welfare than Dickens realized.

Mrs. Transome, like Lady Dedlock in *Bleak Houses*, has a sexual sin in her past to conceal. Guiltily, she paces the corridors of Transome Court as if it were the walk at Chesney Wold and she its ghost, but Mrs. Transome is no Gothic figment; in George Eliot's novel she is required to survive revelation of her shame. Only if a community is not continually advancing can the lives of individuals, like law cases and governing bodies, reach false climaxes or come to dead ends. Otherwise, life goes on.

Another survivor is Job Tudge. For this sickly, neglected child, Felix makes, without fanfare, the sensible provision George Eliot believes Dickens's Woodcourt ought to have hit upon for Jo. Truth again discredits fantasy when Jermyn replaces Tulkinghorn, whose misogyny George Eliot thinks is unmotivated. Jermyn has had the sexual encounters with Mrs. Transome that Dickens's lawyer only approximates by toppling Lady Dedlock. Both villains excel at keeping secrets for profit, but Jermyn— again more realistically, says George Eliot—discloses a major secret to preserve himself, not to destroy another person.

One finds almost as many secrets in *Felix Holt* as in *Bleak House* and Wilkie Collins's *The Woman in White* combined. Yet George Eliot despises secrecy more vehemently than her more sensational rivals did and deprives these melodramatic materials of the social significance that Dickens taught Collins to give them. Characters maintain secrets in *Bleak House* to avoid responsibility, just as society does by prolonging a law case or driving its unfortunates into out-of-the-way places; Collins shows oppressive moral codes compelling individuals to lead secret lives; in short, secrecy results from and satirically mirrors larger societal failures. A more sanguine George Eliot cannot allow this if her thesis that social process is an often invisible but generally orderly progression is to prevail. She revalues Dickens's position by defining secrets as a wedge a person unwisely drives between his private life and the ongoing public good.

Secrets in *Felix Holt* are counter-evolutionary and therefore of shorter duration than in Dickens. They are futile attempts to put self before community, to interrupt life's incessant unfolding by a folding in of the self. Secrets impede that beneficial interaction through which George Eliot's characters overcome egotism and exchange the personality traits each needs to acquire new abilities. They prevent the improving world displayed in her novel from reaching forward to the least partial good. As a consequence, Eliot portrays secretives as exceptions to life's rule, not extensions of it as in Dickens and Collins; they are individual aberrations, entertaining to read about yet tangential in any scientific analysis of the way life moves forward.

Whenever the moral order is sufficiently outraged, revelations in Dickens and Collins come with Old Testament ferocity to shake an entire society. By contrast, disclosure invariably saves in *Felix Holt*. When Jermyn basely delivers himself from criminal proceedings by telling Harold, "*I am your father,*"[15] he also lifts a burden from Mrs. Transome, preparing the way for a stronger bond between her and her son. For the first time, a considerate Harold, consoling and forgiving his mother, puts another's feelings before his own.

Esther Lyon's "inward revolution" (FH, 591) is of greater consequence in *Felix Holt* than the election riot at Treby Magna. The revolution takes her from an idle young lady's existence to a full life as Felix's wife and partner in educating England's workers. Similarly, Holt's decision to become a worker-teacher, a cultural missionary to his own class, is a more significant event for George Eliot than the resolution of a long-standing law case. She borrows incidents from Dickens to help her put things in proper perspective.

Revelations of parentage, the resolution of a legal matter, and an election outcome are crucial in some theories of what constitutes history and in most melodrama. But, says George Eliot, they generally do not improve society. The unimportance of the pyrotechnics stolen from Dickens is what Eliot's multiplot novel is carefully designed to emphasize at his expense.

Felix and Esther risk forfeiting the reader's sympathies only when they become entangled in the novel's Dickensian apparatus. Esther's involvement in Bycliffe versus Transome is a trap; so is her stay at Transome Court, during which she recognizes that she can possess it and Harold too. Felix unwisely gets caught up in a mob scene that could have originated in *Barnaby Rudge*; he participates in confusion to head off greater disaster but seems out of his element and is later justly punished, one feels, not for inadvertent manslaughter but for endangering his leadership abilities in a pointless melee.

Those who complain about gratuitous complications in the plotting of *Felix Holt* miss the point of George Eliot's parody. Her novel is said to be "unlike *Little Dorrit* or *Bleak House*" because its "complexity" is "unrelated to the central areas of what the novel is saying. There is nothing being said *through* the complexity."[16] This argument sounds fashionably deconstructionist. But it is Dickens whom George Eliot is deconstructing so that she can substitute the missing center, the vital point that she thinks his complications lack. She reuses events dear to melodramatic realism in order to turn them against themselves, to defuse them. (At the same time, of course, they enhance her chances for popular success.) Dickens's complexities, Eliot contends, falsify the social process; they divert attention from events that may appear less exciting but are truly momentous. In *Felix Holt* she tries to reverse this effect. She decenters Dickensian material, driving out his sort of sensational irrelevancies with really significant occurrences that she believes will both reflect and influence the actual world. Displacement, revaluative substitution of the real and the desirable for the unreal and the meretricious—that is what is being said *through* the novel's complexity.

The union of Felix and Esther gradually emerges to replace all else as the novel's climax and goal. When Esther and Felix consecrate themselves to one another and to a better future for society, they substantiate their author's conception of progressive evolution, a program which the real or central plot opposes to the ultimately peripheral histrionics lifted from Dickens. Esther's maturation and her marriage to a social reformer as intelligent as Felix attest to "the wonderful slow-growing system of things," which Holt himself celebrates as a major theme in his "Address to Working Men" (FH, 616).[17] Growth, slow but wondrous, is life's first principle, George Eliot claims—for individual lives, for culture in England, and for all societies.

At first Esther confuses elegant social surfaces at Transome Court with moral content and vitality. Similarly, George Eliot charges, admirers and practitioners of Dickens's kind of novel invariably mistake life's superficial confusion, "the abuses of society," for the "natural order" that Felix insists still lies "beneath" (FH, 609). To clarify the difference between basic integrity and surface malfunction, Eliot offers her rural novel in place of Dickens's metropolitan nightmare. The implication is that a Londoner's realism misapprehends urban blight, which is superimposed, for the real order of things, which is Romantic and organic, agricultural rather than municipal, more like a crop or slowly aging tree than a clogged sewer.

Dickens, one might object, parallels the Chancellor in London with Sir Leicester in the country, Chancery with Chesney Wold, as complementary obstacles to progress. But George Eliot recreates Chesney Wold at Transome Court to rewrite Dickens's parallelism. As the name implies, Transome Court is an illusion, readily seen through, rather than an immovable object. True parallelism renders it a holdover, as negligible to the future of society as the law case determining its ownership, as outmoded politically as a sovereign's retinue, which its name also suggests. George Eliot renames Sir Leicester's estate to deny it any connection with a forest, which, like society, is an extension of the living past and an illustration of a "slow-growing system." Transome Court anticipates H.G. Wells's Bladesover, not E.M. Forster's Howard's End. Unlike Lady Dedlock, who dies attempting to escape from Chesney Wold, Esther Lyon simply walks away from the prison that Transome Court represents. The house is not connected to life's core.

The perpetual stoppages and suppressed human relationships in *Bleak House* offer a false perspective on social problems, says George Eliot, a pessimistic misreading of the evolving nature of things. The realism of *Felix Holt* opposes that of *Bleak House*. Each purports to explain the world, but the result is a debate between a modern Juvenal and a modern Lucretius. The novels become philosophical poems in disguise. As did the Greek scientist and epic poet, George Eliot calms fears: despite Dickens's epic indictment, life is not deteriorating; divine punishments are not imminent; mankind, like Esther Lyon, is in charge of its own development, a situation that continues to offer an exciting challenge.

In both books the heroine is named Esther, and her parentage is obscured, but George Eliot asks readers to decide that Esther Lyon better represents a maturity to model oneself upon. Both novelists rewrite the Book of Esther for Victorian audiences, but Eliot considers her heroine more entitled to the illustrious name. Esther Summerson is not the savior of her race; Esther Lyon could be.

George Eliot's Esther is middle class, with the pretensions of an aristocrat. Felix, resorting to the novel's abundant animal imagery, initially calls her a "squirrel-headed thing" and a "long-necked peacock" (FH, 153, 151). When this would-be lady marries into a class beneath hers, she unites her new-found strengths and her inherent grace with an intellectual working man's indomitable spirit. More than Connie Chatterley, Esther Lyon will have a social as well as a sexual role to play. She will help to save the classes she and Felix represent from destroying each other in upcoming labor disputes or on future election days.

The improved Esther of *Felix Holt* is provided with a more spacious arena for reformist activity and a profounder helpmate than is her counterpart. Harold Transome, for a time a dangerously attractive suitor, regards public matters in terms of his own private needs. Fortunately, Holt schools Esther to regulate her personal life so as to serve the general necessity, to redeem the future. Esther Lyon's mission as cultural ambassador to England's workers brings opportunities that are absent from the narrower round of primarily domestic duties reserved for the Esther in *Bleak House*.

Dickens's Esther reports that she never walks out with her husband, Alan Woodcourt, without hearing the people "bless" him: "I never lie down at night but I know that in the course of that day he has alleviated pain. . . . The people even praise Me as the doctor's wife," she adds. "They like me for his sake."[18] No doubt Dickens's heroine modestly omits her own good deeds. Nevertheless, hers is largely a reflected glory as "the doctor's wife." By contrast, Esther Lyon, Felix's ideological ally as well as the mother of his children, enjoys a fuller partnership. Transome's son behaves like an untutored savage; his father is not a conduit for civilization's values. But Esther Lyon's progeny, one presumes, will be splendid hybrids in the front rank of an organic process of cultural and biological evolution, the syllabus for which would read like a blend of Darwin, Arnold, and Marx.

Together, Felix and Esther will begin to educate the masses so that, besides getting the vote eventually, their minds will be enfranchised with England's cultural tradition, a richness they can only carry in their heads. The "current of ideas" that Arnold found essential among the intelligentsia for the appearance of great poets must be made to flow toward the illiterate and poorly educated, George Eliot is saying. They pose the biggest threat to the cultural transmission they also stand to gain from most.

As an apostle of culture to the amorphous consciousness of the workers, Esther Lyon will participate in what her father calls "the transmission of an improved heritage" (FH, 341). This utopian undertaking is parental in the broadest sense and seems an appropriate task for a heroine whose parentage was once confused. The poorly instructed, George Eliot argues, are the only true illegitimates. Esther Summerson, after all, was properly schooled by a mysterious guardian who turns out to be Jarndyce, but the workers to whom Felix is drawn have been cut off from their country's finest things. Transmitting "an improved heritage" to working men and their children is George Eliot's answer in advance to Carlyle's 1867 anxieties that new reform measures will speed up life's flow until it turns into Niagara's rapids.[19]

The process of cultural transmission is described, fittingly, by a clergyman, Esther's stepfather, for it is a question of passing on the new religion. Yet Felix Holt is the successor to men like Rufus Lyon. The eloquence of this good-natured clergyman is tellingly archaic in syntax and substance, and his religion seems to have made a minimal impression upon Esther. It remains for Felix to put her in touch with her "best self," to awaken "the finest part of [her] nature" (FH, 366, 418). As tutelage leads to betrothal, it becomes virtually a religious experience. Although Esther Lyon is a clergyman's daughter, she is Felix's first convert.

George Eliot projects for her Esther the "difficult blessedness" found only in "beings who are conscious of painfully growing into the possession of higher powers" (FH, 327). Esther Lyon is commissioned as a preserver of traditions and a veritable agent of the life force. Such "higher powers" combine the political and the progenitive, the sacred and the sociological. They are clearly beyond Esther Summerson's reach or desire. Esther Lyon's growth is more arduous than Esther Summerson's because it takes her further. It apparently designates George Eliot's heroine the superior life form. Woodcourt and Esther Summerson form a saving remnant, whereas Holt and Esther Lyon, seemingly left behind by the political whirl of "the memorable year 1832," are actually in the vanguard. A sign of new beginnings, they are "a little leaven spread within us" (FH, 327).

Consequently, disdain for Exodus 34:7 in *Felix Holt* reads like a parody of Dickens's exegesis in *Bleak House* and Collins's reuse of the same text in *The Woman in White*. Dickens rewrites the passage about "the sins of the fathers" to warn that each generation pays for the inadequate reforms instituted by its predecessors. Collins takes it to mean that new improprieties are often committed as the only way of keeping the father's original trespass secret. George Eliot tries to disprove the biblical admonition that each of her rivals modifies to suit his own social concerns. She rejects the antiprogressive contention that individuals suffer directly a revenge that life exacts for actions not their own. The enlightened individual is absolved of the dead past as a restriction, a determinant, or a source of guilt and punishment; the deconstructive past is definitely not part of the heritage one must improve and transmit.

The message of George Eliot's novel, contrary to that of *Bleak House*, is that secularized Victorian life is liberation, not imprisonment. One is free to disregard the Old Testament rumblings that hyperbolic novelists rely on to bolster their authority. In fact, Eliot implies that the Old Testament itself is a sensationalist document whose principle of inexorability, a relentless providence, must be replaced by a sense of continuity that is more of a marvel yet scientifically—that is, biologically—verifiable.

Walter Hartright's retrospective on events in *The Woman in White* relies heavily on "Scripture denunciation." Following Dickens, Collins had Walter reflect: "But for the fatal resemblance between the two daughters of one father, the conspiracy of which Anne had been the innocent instrument and Laura the innocent victim could never have been planned. With what unerring and terrible directness the long chain of circumstances led down from the thoughtless wrong committed by the father to the heartless injury inflicted on the child!"[20] Like Felix Holt, George Eliot puts her trust in "the wonderful slow-growing system of things" rather than in something as punitive as "the unerring and terrible directness" of a "long chain of circumstances" over which individuals have slight control. It takes Esther

Summerson thirty-six chapters to realize she is as "innocent" of her birth, though illegitimate, as a queen is of hers. Coincidentally, Esther Lyon's true identity and her right to the Transome estates are discovered in Chapter 35, but she has already been "growing into the possession of higher powers" for more than one hundred pages.

Esther Summerson, in the course of surviving her trials, develops a fuller appreciation for providence: "I saw very well how many things had worked together, for my welfare." Dickens decides that the warning about the father's sins being visited upon the children applies to irresponsible societies. Nevertheless, Esther helps to keep secret for a time her mother's past, which gives Collins his cue for interpreting Exodus 34:7 in relation to pressures from the proprieties to perpetuate sins. Esther must accept some of the punishment, if not the guilt, for her parents' clandestine love. To varying degrees, she will always be Esther Hawdon or Esther Dedlock as well as Esther Woodcourt. This multiple identity, rather than her many nicknames, prevents a perfect maturation.

On the other hand, Esther Lyon realizes that becoming Esther Bycliffe or Esther Transome (as Harold's wife) would be "to abandon her own past" (FH, 496): that is, to downgrade those acts and decisions of her own that have made her who she is. She rebuts Esther Summerson when she discerns "no illumination" in her stepfather's theory of a "providential arrangement" behind her sudden inheritance (FH, 505). For a passive Esther Summerson, "reserved" by providence "for a happy life," George Eliot substitutes an activist Esther Lyon, committed to influencing the future. Esther Lyon matures not by providential intervention but by social interaction. The exchange of love and ideas between Felix and Esther demonstrates "the effect of one personality on another" (FH, 327).

George Eliot wrote *Felix Holt: The Radical*, as the subtitle indicates, to explain true radicalism and, in the process, to revise Dickens's faulty concept of it. She redefined this phenomenon to mean change continuing organically via careful evolution *from the root*, center, or fundamental source of life, an energy perceived as positive and good. Radicalism, she says, does not mean sudden or sweeping reform and therefore is not the stark opposite of conservatism, as Dickens would designate it; rather, continuity—orderly transition—is a goal that both conservatives and radicals can profitably adopt. If society is an organic continuum, as Eliot's supposedly scientific assessment says it is, only culture—knowledge and wisdom transmitted from one era to the next—keeps it so.

When Harold Transome is defeated in an election for Parliament, as was Sir Leicester Dedlock, George Eliot evens the score by bringing in a conservative for the one Dickens tosses out. However, conservatism and radicalism in *Felix Holt*—or Tory and Benthamite—are two equally disruptive misconstruings of the life process. Dickens's Tories are self-serving protectors of privilege, but George Eliot cautions also against unprincipled reformers who either see a chance for power in the advocacy of quick change (as Harold Transome does) or, more likely, will throw out good with bad from a lack of education.

Felix Holt, who, unlike Trollope or Dickens, would never think of standing for Parliament, has the only feasible social agenda in George Eliot's novel. Moreover, he personifies the prospectus he recommends. This model radical aspires to become a learned artisan, a practical man of the people, equipped for the future as a self-supporting craftsman but with an intelligent appreciation of the past, a sense of "the wealth that is carried in men's minds" (FH, 622). He wants to be "a demogogue of a new sort; an honest one, if possible, who will tell the people they are blind and foolish, and neither flatter them nor fatten on them" (FH, 366).

Long before G.B. Shaw, H.G. Wells, or C.P. Snow, George Eliot had a clear idea of what the new man should be like: Felix Holt is "a man of this generation" who "will try to make life less bitter for a few within [his] reach" (FH, 367), chiefly by broadening their minds. The phrase "less bitter" indicates how modest a radicalism George Eliot prefers. Holt's program, she contends, is more realistic than "the formulas of [Esther's] father's beliefs" and thus provides Esther with "the first religious experience of her life" (FH, 369). It is also more practical than the master plans of England's rival political parties and thus gives the workers Felix addresses their first taste of sensible reform. Parties think in terms of leaps, Eliot implies, because they do not know how to take the first steps. Reform can be entrusted only to enlightened, public-minded individuals who forgo all connection with officialdom.

Holt is a compromise between Mr. Rouncewell and Sir Leicester; consequently, he is also an alternative to Dickens's juxtapositioning of new man and old. George Eliot finds both as unbelievable as they are undesirable: the ironmaster is an impossible ideal, too Carlylean to be of real service to the masses; the baronet is a mere caricature, whereas the civility and refinement of a well-educated aristocracy is too valuable to discard. One can also interpret Felix as a reply to such epitomes, respectively, of compliancy and cunning as Stephen Blackpool and Slackbridge in *Hard Times* and to Mrs. Gaskell's portrait of Nicholas Higgins in *North and South*. Eventually, Holt will be qualified to supervise the transference of authority from a moribund elite, the world of Transome Court and Chesney Wold, to the as yet uncouth proletariat to be found not so much in Tom-all-alone's as in places like Sproxton.

In the workable world George Eliot both describes and foresees, individuals complete one another by exchanging needed characteristics. The
patient tutorial Felix administers for Esther awakens her to the beauties of a
purposeful life. At the same time, however, Esther modifies Felix's resolution never to marry by teaching him, as Adam Bede did for Dinah, that
purposiveness increases in power when suffused with love. Felix's cultivation of Esther, part of his difficult "knighthood" (FH, 419), is an upgrading
of Mr. Knightly's attempts to improve Emma in that the education of
Esther by Felix not only deals with matters George Eliot considers more
important than Jane Austen's but proves reciprocal. The "inward revolution" Felix stirs up in Esther revalues—parodies and eclipses—the elaborate seminar in values John Harmon arranges for Bella Wilfer in *Our Mutual
Friend*, published a year before George Eliot's novel.

Throughout *Felix Holt*, the author advances her claim always to have
been a fomenter of internal, moral revolutions seismically superior to the
changes of heart for which Dickens's novels were famous. No transformation in Esther Summerson quite matches the rapid improvement in Esther
Lyon once she begins to think like George Eliot; she develops a missionary
zeal more level-headed and far-reaching than Mrs. Jellyby's. George Eliot
deflates Dickens's excesses and disarms his caricatures to remind readers
that the most meaningful kind of social change begins quietly and internally, though not without prodding from an outside agent. She submits
Esther Lyon's "inward revolution" to desensationalize Krook's incredible
travesty of revolt.

Dickens uses Krook's spontaneous combustion to stand for the inevitable demolition of Chancery by its irate victims if reforms are not forthcoming. George Eliot's sensible parody of Dickens replaces the satirical but
grotesquely improbable with the positive and more plausible. Revolution
from within, Dickens warns, is what society must at all costs avoid;
"inward revolution," Eliot counters, is what individual members of society
need most. Above all, she wants to show that reciprocity, the mutual
exchange of character traits, works politically for classes as well as personally between individuals. If one personality can be efficacious for another
in a manner beneficial to society, then Felix the learned artisan and Esther
the genteel middle-class lady will create an intermediary class of cultured
workmen—as hypothetical, unfortunately, as Carlyle's captains of industry.

The competing realisms of Dickens and George Eliot are thus simultaneously competing idealisms. Arguments over what is realistic or accurately depicted lead to disagreements about the way things should be if
they were to change for the better. Rivalries between Victorian multiplot

novels extend to conceptions as well as perceptions. Is the real world an organic continuity that sifts itself as it evolves and improves? Or is it discontinuous, a labyrinthine parody of interconnectedness, a place torn between darkness and light so that periodical upheavals become necessary to get the recalcitrant reform process back on course?

The argument on this score, a crucial matter for Victorian realism, is by no means over. Julian Huxley updated the case for secular evolutionary humanism in *Religion without Revelation* (1957) and *Man in the Modern World* (1948). A religious perspective on evolution was reintroduced by Teilhard de Chardin in *The Phenomenon of Man* (1959), and a sophisticated scientific approach to an organic vision of life informs Fritjof Capra's *The Tao of Physics* (1976). On the other hand, bleaker elements in Dickens's dystopian vision cater to antilinear theories of history; they have excited moderns like Franz Kafka and are carried to metaphysical extremes in postmoderns like Samuel Beckett.

Throughout *Felix Holt*, George Eliot sounds more like Julian Huxley than like his grandfather. *Felix Holt* appeared close on the heels of *Man's Place in Nature* (1865) and the six lectures that T.H. Huxley published under the title *On Our Knowledge of the Causes of Organic Nature* (1862). But Eliot's novel, taking a more optimistic view of Darwin, disputes the Huxleyan hypothesis that Evolution and Ethics can proceed in opposite directions; it seems more in accord with *Essays of a Humanist* in which Julian Huxley, a modern expert on evolution, explains his belief that man's body, mind, and soul were not supernaturally created but are products of evolution.[21] George Eliot's evolutionary humanism seems designed to discredit Dickens's weakening or perhaps warier humanistic tendencies by asserting that humanity's destiny is to be sole agent for the future improvement of this planet, with all forms of supernatural intervention excluded.

The unfolding that unites Felix and Esther transpires inevitably, despite such volcanic plot eruptions as the election riot. Melodramatic events crowd the novel's surface but, says George Eliot, never touch its essence: an allegedly truer rendition of life as an underlying process of gradual growth, for communities as well as individuals, is substituted for the melodramatic but superficial events that make radicalism and sensationalism in many Victorian fictions—especially those of Dickens—roughly equivalent and equally unreal.

Felix Holt is the classic instance of hidden rivalries in Victorian fiction. Managing to appear aggressive rather than defensive, it excelled its predecessors in stipulating that Dickens's novels were overwrought. It signaled the arrival of a full-fledged, major adversary whose idea of realism had shaped itself directly contrary to Dickens's. It announced that parodic reconstruction of a rival's world was now to be an indispensable ingredient in the nineteenth-century British novel. Owing to the importance *Felix Holt* attached to parodic revision, one can rediscover opening gambits in *The Warden* and *North and South*, preliminary attacks in the mid-1850s on Dickens's steadily mounting preeminence.

Revaluation in *Felix Holt* is both subject and technique. The revaluative substitutions that characters make throughout the novel reinforce those George Eliot introduces out of disdain for Dickens. Esther Lyon, for example, refuses to take the place of the Transomes at Transome Court but willingly substitutes England's cultural heritage for Harold's wealth, social service for private comfort, and Felix Holt for idle fantasies about Byron. Similarly, Felix elects marriage to Esther instead of the celibate apostolate he originally planned, and the novel endorses his ideas about radicalism in place of Harold Transome's self-serving interest in reform and Dickens's extremism. Alerted to the practice, one seems to be observing George Eliot as she invents and inserts her revaluations. Modern reviewers of hidden rivalries in Victorian fiction can watch process in *Felix Holt*, not just end result; they behold revaluative substitution actively in progress.

Although the argument that Dickens reincorporated into Victorian fiction everything Jane Austen threw out explains the need for another purging, *Felix Holt* is more than George Eliot's *Northanger Abbey*. Austen openly satirized the cult of the Gothic for having little bearing upon real life, but neither she nor the Gothicists believed that life resembles *Vathek* or *The Romance of the Forest*. That quarrel was not over whose novels better represented reality; it was about the novelist's obligation invariably to do so. Dickens was always prepared to defend the fidelity of his melodramatic realism, its capacity to isolate and emphasize existing abuses, if not flaws, in the nature of life itself. He was more dangerous to George Eliot than Walpole or Mrs. Radcliffe to Austen because his stories, even when they used far-fetched incidents, were never escapist. He mimicked popular diversions, including the Gothic mode, but invested them with skillfully constructed moral judgments designed to make a verifiable point about society.

Austen's protest in *Northanger Abbey*, like a Thomas Peacock novel, was primarily literary parody. George Eliot's strategy is to give the impression that hers is too.[22] But the scope and seriousness of her attack indicate otherwise. Obliged to discredit an accomplished social satirist whose less cheerful world view seemed a premeditated barrier to her own, Eliot engaged Dickens in a mid-century dialogue. At stake was not just the way the world works but whether it could be said to work for good or ill. It was Eliot, not the third-person narrator in *Bleak House*, who revalued the maturity of Dickens's Esther, and not by undercutting it but by awarding her own heroine broader prospects.

Despite the recurring anxiety of clouded parentage (FH, 287), Esther proves doubly legitimate—Maurice Christian Bycliffe's daughter and rightful owner of Transome Court—unlike Harold Transome, who is false thrice over (not a true radical, not his father's son, not the legal heir). These changes in status, however, seem trivial compared to the improvement Esther and Felix Holt occasion in each other. A profligate Thomas Transome sold his rights to the estate entailed upon him and the Bycliffes; but when a drunken Tommy Trousem is trampled during the election riot, his death revives the Bycliffe claim to a property that Jermyn, Harold's real father, has mismanaged for personal gain. Since Esther decides not to inherit and the Transomes stay put, sins in the past and a bequest from it turn out to be equally irrelevant to George Eliot's real theme: a celebration of character formation in Felix and Esther that bodes well for the future. The pair leave Treby Magna, which may never return a radical candidate, just as Dorothea Brooke and Will Ladislaw later move on from a largely unchanged Middlemarch; nevertheless, George Eliot has perfected her tone at Dickens's expense: cautious but good-natured, she adopts a moderately hopeful outlook on life and human nature.

Instead of letting plots alternate inconclusively at her novel's center, George Eliot disputes the legitimacy of Dickens's social realism. The only "double logic" that *Felix Holt* manifests is a novelist thinking like a rival in order to rethink him; as one Esther was substituted for another and melodramatic plot devices were parodied into insignificance by a plot more reflective of the life process as a "slow-growing system," it became a question of Eliot's philosophical perspective, her world overtaking and correcting Dickens's in order, finally, to displace it.

Chapter Two

The Cant of Reform

The Warden

THE WARDEN (1855) deserves special recognition as the only Victorian novel to parody a Dickens novel that Dickens never actually wrote. Trollope pretends to be answering an imaginary broadside entitled *The Alms-house*. Chapter 15 of *The Warden* is often celebrated for its dismissal of Dickens as "Mr. Popular Sentiment,"[1] author of the broadside, but a dislike for Boz's latest polemic colors the entire novel. The anti-Sentiment section forms part of a comprehensive reconsideration of Dickens as realist and social critic, especially his use of Juvenalian satire to promote a radical politics and encourage reform.

Trollope's book finds Dickens's outbursts unacceptable as topical realism. This demanding mode, the author contends, ought not to be confused with the inferior productions of sensational journalists. Thesis-novelists like Dickens are merely biased advocates, one-sided proponents in a controversy, hence no more fair-minded than lawyers arguing a case or a Member of Parliament sponsoring a bill. Trollope charges that Dickens's satiric novels resemble Carlyle's pamphlets: they are "condemnatory of all things,"[2] too negative and indiscriminate to be relied upon as depictions of what life is. The assault on Mr. Popular Sentiment, which occurs at the novel's three-quarter mark, epitomizes Trollope's view of Dickens throughout *The Warden* as an exaggerator, unduly famous for magnifying society's short-term failings into serious abuses impossible to overcome.

Trollope's fourth novel was the first in which he found his true style, subject, and milieu.[3] The key to this breakthrough was Trollope's realization that he could best define himself—formulate his own attitude toward life—by writing in opposition to the most successful novelist of the age.

Dickens's ideas not only displeased Trollope but helped him to clarify his own. Opposition to Dickens's darkening vision was just beginning to mount in 1855, when Trollope published *The Warden*. In 1866 George Eliot revised Dickens in *Felix Holt* in hopes of silencing *Bleak House*, replacing the satiric depiction of society in process of devolution with her notion of progress as inevitable organic unfolding; she opted for replacement because the mollifying methods of Trollope and Mrs. Gaskell had proved insufficient.

Determined to earn a hearing for himself in *The Warden* simply by quieting Dickens down, Trollope chose revaluative substitution through reduction, as opposed to George Eliot's outright cancellations. His strategy was to tone down Dickens's hyperbole lest his excesses obscure the real problems that his fictions oversimplified. If Boz's social satire enlarges upon the truth, Trollope argued, one can disregard pressure from vociferous radicals demanding that society be restructured immediately. Provided things are never as bad as they seem in *Oliver Twist* or *Nicholas Nickleby*, social change can be trusted to continue without help from the kind of ardent reformers George Eliot later canonized as the Victorian period's secular saints. In the great debating society of the Victorian novel, Trollope separates Dickens from George Eliot—all three claiming to be realistic—the way Thomas Love Peacock might insert a supporter of the status quo between a deteriorationist and an ameliorist.

An article in *Household Words* (12 June 1852) asserted that in the well-known London refuge of Charterhouse, thousands of pounds intended for the refugees were being spent to support their caretakers. This article proved a godsend for Trollope, not just because he sometimes experienced difficulty inventing plots but because it allowed him to launch his career as a social critic by exposing Dickens's investigative journalism with an exposé of his own. Actually, as Lionel Stevenson points out, Henry Morley wrote the piece on Charterhouse,[4] but Trollope, thinking Dickens had done it, resolved to tell the story of a crisis in Barchester's almshouse as a parodic gainsaying of the overblown tale his foremost rival might have constructed from the journal article. Trollope wrote *The Warden* to compare his own evenhanded treatment of an alleged crime against the poor with the melodramatic overstatement he thought Dickens would have made of it.

The fuss at Hiram's Hospital is plausible, Trollope's novel contends, because the creator of Barchester knows the workings of institutions and their politics from inside. Dickens, by contrast, is portrayed as an intemperate outsider, a marauding journalist eager for copy to support his overly critical opinion of society. *The Warden* rewrites Dickens by challenging the needlessly low estimate of human nature and social responsibility that lay behind a famous competitor's conception of fidelity to actualities.

R.B. Martin insists that Trollope "did not have *Household Words* in mind when writing" *The Warden*. He rejects Stevenson's identification of the Charterhouse episode as Trollope's source, pointing instead to the ecclesiastical scandals throughout the 1850s at Rochester Cathedral and St. Cross Hospital, Winchester, as "the inspiration for the first of [the] Barsetshire novels."[5] Martin confuses *origin*, the term he should have used, with *inspiration*, which better fits Stevenson's argument.

Trollope contemplated the story for *The Warden* on an evening in midsummer of 1851 while wandering "round the purlieus" of Salisbury Cathedral. Yet he did not start writing until 9 July 1852, nearly a year later.[6] Lord Guilford's problems as master of St. Cross and Dr. Whiston's lawsuit against the Dean and Chapter at Rochester provided material for the initial conception; Trollope mentions both incidents prominently at the start of Chapter 2. The Charterhouse piece, however, and the chance to score against Dickens inspired Trollope to begin. Dickens became his effigy for the misguided reformist drive behind all three scandals and for misused creative energy as well. It was the need to defend Victorian life and the province of art from Dickens's brand of realism that finally got Trollope going; he commenced the novel thirty-one days after the essay in *Household Words* appeared.

The Warden is a parody of topical Victorian fiction and of Dickens as its leading exponent. In Trollope's opinion, Dickens's topicality stands to more considered presentation as cant does to sincerity. Thanks to the impetus from *Household Words*, Trollope's novel not only reconsiders current affairs of the Charterhouse variety but stipulates the appropriate manner for dealing with them in fiction. The result is a critique of society that is simultaneously a critique of Dickens's opinions and methods. According to Trollope, Dickens's hasty fabrications create a false impression of Victorian life, which, though imperfect, hardly resembles the hell that Popular Sentiment makes of his almshouse. Church abuse of endowment funds and Dickens's misuse of art's resources become topics that Trollope parallels as dishonest, sacrilegious activities. By inflaming the popular consciousness, Dickens is said to divert the Victorian novel from its judicial functions even more surely than money intended for the upkeep of unfortunates in places like Charterhouse was being squandered on their supervisors.

All of the scandals that gave rise to *The Warden*, including the flap at Charterhouse, occurred between 1849 and 1853. Both the *Daily News* and the *Times* compared Lord Guilford's annual income from multiple livings with the less splendid state of the thirteen inmates he was master of at St. Cross. The seventy-seven-year-old Guilford tried unsuccessfully to resign but had to suffer through a Chancery suit that took four years to settle. On the same day (1 August 1853) that judgment went against him, the House passed the Charitable Trusts Act to ensure greater superintendence of lay and ecclesiastical charities. Also in 1853, Robert Whiston won his suit against Rochester Cathedral. He had disclosed that funds intended for boys in the Cathedral Grammar School, of which he was headmaster, were finding their way into the pockets of the Dean and Chapter. The point for the modern revaluator to stress is not that Guilford provided a model for Septimus Harding and Whiston for John Bold—though of course they did—but that disturbances at Rochester and St. Cross began dying down and the government acted two years before *The Warden* was published. Indeed, Whiston's *Cathedral Trusts and Their Fulfilment* had reached its fifth printing before Trollope issued his verdict.[7]

Although conceived in 1851, *The Warden*, Trollope notes with surprise, was not concluded until "autumn of 1853" and did not appear in print until 1855,[8] when Dickens had already moved on to the weavers' strike at Preston. The need to digest the resolutions of the two law suits contributed to the delay. Trollope's method of going about the preparation of his book is as much a parody of the less meticulous Dickens as the completed work is of Sentiment's *Almshouse*. A desire to rebuke Dickens inspired Trollope to begin writing in 1852, and a similar urge to teach the topical novelist ethical restraint prolonged work on the novel until matters at St. Cross and Rochester were concluded. Once possessed of all the facts, Trollope could revaluate the seriousness of the crisis, making it a test case of the extent to which existing social evils required the kind of sweeping reforms Dickens and Carlyle had been demanding.

As Popular Sentiment's name and his imaginary novel indicate, Dickens's method was to arouse public indignation so that crooked beadles, heartless schoolmasters, and callous industrialists would be shamed into altering course or at least prevented from doing additional damage. Trollope's procedure was to humanize Dickens's caricatures with a more sympathetic analysis of the internal pressures they face, to soften the hearts of officialdom not by instilling fear of reprisals from an angry public but by supplying an attractive role model in the unassuming Harding. The realistic novelist who delays publishing until the heat of the moment passes, Trollope believed, is better able to extract a moral—the historical lesson—from his tale. Trollope's warden was not simply based on actual clergymen involved in the ecclesiastical misdoings of the 1850s; he also personified the novelist's idea of how those men ought to have behaved when attacked.

The Warden was designed to be nearly as current as *Oliver Twist* or *Bleak House* yet more deliberate. One should not rush into print, Trollope's book cautions Dickens, as if in competition with the daily press. Journalists excite public opinion, and legislators try to react to it, but Trollope holds that topical novelists serve as a check on all three. They put crises into better perspective by working out some of the effects they will have on character and community. True topical realists adjust and refine popular sentiment, as Trollope does with Dickens, its incarnation; they ought never to write quickly enough actually to try to form it.

Trollope equated Boz's highly touted topicality, a source of strength regularly attributed to him by modern critics,[9] with exploitation and opportunism. These were not just characteristics an as yet unsuccessful author assigned to the popular writer and popularizer; they were part of a complex exercise in repudiation and self-realization, part of Trollope's reconsideration of the genuine topical realist as a crucial buffer or mediating stage between impetuous journalists and the slower-moving judgments of history.

Of the "two opposite evils" that Trollope said he wrote *The Warden* to expose, only the second seems, in retrospect, suitably Trollopian. Excoriating the misapplication of "funds and endowments" as "income for idle Church dignitaries" is Dickensian stuff. But Trollope's cooler head soon noticed an aspect that more precipitate novelists were likely to miss: "the undeserved severity of the newspapers toward the recipients of such incomes who could hardly be considered to be the chief sinners in the matter."[10] In Trollope's finished novel, the antiseverity theme, congenial to a cautious reformer, parodies Dickens's imaginary diatribe. If a bad practice involves exculpable practitioners, Trollope can modify the alleged extent of corruption in the world without denying its existence or shoving it totally aside. When Trollope demonstrates the advisability of a calmer, fuller perspective on recent crises over the "malversation" of charitable funds, he informs readers and rivals alike that the sensationalist errs with first impressions, whereas the reliable topical novelist benefits from second thoughts.

The Warden is not the victim of the kind of double logic or divided mind that deconstructionists savor. Trollope's declaration that the "two objects" he sought to accomplish in this novel "should not have been combined" is clearly tongue-in-cheek, a continuation of his parody of Dickens. Thanks to novelists like Popular Sentiment, Trollope implied, a corrupted reading public could not manage the subtlety of a novel that endorsed reform in principle yet exonerated Harding in order to disagree with overly zealous measures that were being called for in the interests of change. "Honesty" prevented Trollope from taking up "one side" of the case like "an advocate" and clinging to it as simplistically as a less ethical Dickens would have done. Trollope contended that the topical realist should be even less a lawyer than he is a journalist or a reformer from Parliament.[11] As Popular Sentiment, Dickens is made to resemble all three.

Trollope's novel reduces the thousands of pounds misused by numerous attendants, according to the essay Dickens received from Morley, to Harding's modest salary of eight hundred pounds. The controversial stipend he draws, perhaps wrongly, as warden originates from rents on lands that John Hiram, a successful wool-stapler, bequeathed to the almshouse he endowed. The rents had been intended to support a residence for "twelve superannuated wool-carders" (W,10). With the eventual disappearance of the wool trade from Barchester, the hospital was thrown open by the bishop to "worn-out gardeners, decrepit grave-diggers, or octogenarian sextons"—in short, to the ecclesiastical debris of the diocese. As a deflation of scandalmongering in Dickens's weekly, Trollope's account of the hospital's history is intentionally ludicrous: in place of a major crime or national disgrace, he readies a teapot for a small tempest—from which, however, he extrapolates far-reaching conclusions about the professional behavior of public administrators and of novelists presuming to criticize them.

Murmurs arise that the proceeds from John Hiram's property are not being divided fairly because the income of successive wardens has improved over the years while the daily dole for each of their charges has not. The increase, however, has come about as the result of added value of the almshouse land. After previous wardens laid aside the money due their dependents, more was left over; thus their salary, once almost nonexistent, increased. This, says Trollope, is the quiet way social problems develop. They are not invariably the consequence of villainy, contrary to what one might gather from Mr. Bumble and Mrs. Mann; nor do they always result from hopelessly corrupt institutions, like Chancery or a Yorkshire school. They are not infallible signs of man's fallen nature or proof of an essentially debased world. Rather, they present moot questions, gray areas, unanticipated embarrassments. Cases like Harding's stem from oversight and ossification, which Trollope reduces to temporary imperfections in a social pattern otherwise mostly satisfactory.

Through no fault of Harding's, the post of warden has become "one of the most coveted of the snug clerical sinecures attached to our church" (W,12), the religious equivalent, perhaps, of a rotten borough. Once recognized as such, the useless benefice, Trollope concedes, must go.[12] Yet eradication requires tact, for Harding has not calculatingly enriched himself at the expense of others; in fact, he has tried to compensate for unintentional unfairness "by adding" from his own pocket "twopence a day to each man's pittance" (W, 12). He has also been a kind and compassionate friend to the beadsmen. Thus he resents having "his quiet paths . . . made a battlefield" (W, 54). If he is to be "ruined"—that is, turned out of a situation his predecessors created—he professes a wish that it be done "in quiet" (W, 49), a request for restraint with which the reserved reformer in Trollope sympathizes.

Regrettably, as local discussion of Harding's case mounts, the first number of an imaginary Dickensian novel, *The Almshouse*, is already being published in London to dramatize the situation. As the reformer John Bold reads its first two chapters, one is able to compare *fact*, the unembellished account of life's workings that Trollope contends he is composing, with *fiction*, Popular Sentiment's bloated version. Thus Trollope revalues a crisis and Dickens's evaluation of it simultaneously. Accurate presentation of recent events, neither sensational nor sentimental, is Trollope's equivalent of scientific truth, superior to Dickens's popular journalism. Trollope expects readers to identify the caustic incrimination of Charterhouse in Dickens's periodical with Sentiment's new novel and to recognize that Dickens's darkening world view cannot be trusted, because Sentiment exaggerates compulsively. His reality, no matter how topical its references, is always mostly a fiction.

Dickens's prefaces usually declare that "everything set forth in these pages" is "substantially true."[13] But Trollope maintains that many targets in Dickens's articles and satirical novels can be located only in his overly inventive brain, which colors real life beyond recognition. Consequently, one cannot tell the difference between Dickens's journalistic investigations and his wildly creative novels. Due to the fatal interchangeability of Dickens's periodical essays and the social criticism in his fiction, the article in *Household Words* might as well be the opening number of another overdone Dickens novel, for which Trollope intentionally mistakes it.

The sample of Dickensian invective that Bold reads in Chapter 15 is total fabrication, but it could pass as part of the condemnation of workhouses in *Oliver Twist* or of unqualified schoolmasters in *Nicholas Nickleby*. Popular Sentiment characterizes the typical warden of an almshouse as an unscrupulous minister inclined to drink up in port wine the money meant for his charges. This re-creation of a Dickensian clergyman is an amazing compilation from four novels: Trollope blends Stiggins (*Pickwick Papers*) with Chadband (*Bleak House*) and adds a touch of Bill Sikes (*Oliver Twist*); he also supplies two daughters who could have been Pecksniff's (*Martin Chuzzlewit*).

Besides a "huge red nose with a carbuncle, thick lips, and a great double flabby chin," the warden in *The Almshouse* has a "husky voice," a "hot, passionate, bloodshot eye" out of which he looks "cruelly," and an unseemly weakness for foul language (W, 148-49). Sentiment's opening chapter exaggerates not only in heaping upon one warden physical defects sufficient for several but in using multiple adjectives to make each defect additionally repulsive.

Trollope's warden is neither Bumble nor Squeers. Harding lacks the violent temperament, bunioned feet, and ill-fitting clothes that belong to "the demon" of Sentiment's almshouse (W, 148), but he does have affinities with Mr. Pickwick. Though slight of build where Pickwick is corpulent, Harding is "mild," with "grizzled" hair and "double glasses." His chief physical resemblance to Dickens's retired businessman is the "gaiters" indispensable to the raiment of both. The relationship emerges when Harding matures in old age during a crisis the way Pickwick grows up during his imprisonment in the Fleet.

Like Pickwick, Harding is initially one of the world's innocents who must acquire singular knowledge of the complex factors that ethical dilemmas present. To alleviate Mrs. Bardell's suffering, Pickwick compromises on a question of principle: although not guilty of breach of promise, he puts up the damages he swore never to pay. It is a case of personal triumph despite public defeat. Similarly, Harding discovers that it is more important to feel justified in one's mind than to be considered blameless by the world. Trollope suggests that from *Pickwick Papers* on, Boz took a wrong turning: he shifted from a memorable character, who did not like to be spoken ill of, to satirical novels of relentless social analysis that slander humanity's decision-making capacity and speak too harshly of society.

George Eliot pronounced Dickens false because unscientific; Trollope found him unreliable because unprofessional. To Eliot, Dickens appeared old-fashioned, a throwback to Matthew G. Lewis and Mrs. Radcliffe; to Trollope, he was hasty and slapdash, a manifestation of the modern. "In former times," Trollope reflects, "great objects were attained by great work"; reformers "set about their heavy task with grave decorum and laborious argument," publishing their ponderous "researches" in "folio pages" that took "an eternity to read." But Dickens is no improvement on the English preference for reform at a snail's pace; he is merely the other extreme. Thanks to Dickens's "lighter step," says Trollope, the work of setting the world right can now be done in manageable "shilling numbers," often after a single inspection of the problem area (W, 147-48).

Trollope wants readers to recall that Dickens solved the factory question by going to Preston, and improved British education after one look at

Yorkshire schools. As Tom Towers informs Bold: "It's very clear that Sentiment has been down to Barchester and got up the whole story there" (W, 144). A merciless enlarger, Sentiment will inflate the situation at Hiram's Hospital into the epitome of all creation, just as society becomes the universal prison in *Bleak House*, where Chancery makes everyone its ward. Barchester's almshouse, by contrast, illustrates Trollope's conservative idea of a microcosm as, literally, a little world,[14] one that reduces and clarifies the exterior universe by putting its solvable ills into less cluttered perspective.

The danger of running "down to Barchester" to drum up "the whole story" as quickly as possible is that, by investigating hurriedly, the topical novelist may actually state the case backwards. In the allegedly real Barchester that Trollope chronicles, the warden is unfairly persecuted by his aggrieved dependents. Popular Sentiment reports this the other way round: his *Almshouse* introduces a warden more devilish than Mephistopheles and eight angelic old men whom he defrauds.

Despite a starvation diet, Sentiment's beadsmen outdo Oliver and Nell in conversations so remarkable for "the beauty of the sentiment" (W, 149) that Bold thinks these men should be sent throughout the countryside as "moral missionaries" instead of wasting their lives in confinement as indigent pensioners. In truth, the inmates of Hiram's Hospital at first consider themselves fortunate; persuaded otherwise by outside interests— especially by Finney, the reformers' lawyer—they become gripers and ingrates, each resolved on having a "hundred pounds a year" (W, 16). The Manichean split between angels and devils in Sentiment's novel has no conceivable resolution except a struggle to the death, whereas misunderstanding in *The Warden* and the delusions that grow from it gradually evaporate.

The Warden is a sustained exercise in playing down a crisis that Dickens would have played up. Mock heroic martial metaphors abound. The idea of the clergy donning "good armour" and preparing "weapons for the coming war" in order to "defend . . . the citadel" of the church against "profane" reformers, "the most rampant of its enemies" (W, 45) invites comparison with events in Alexander Pope's *Rape of the Lock*. As always in the mock-heroic, deflation or diminution is done by inflation. The novel's David and Goliath story—Mr. Harding, a lowly precentor, triumphing over formidable Archdeacon Grantly—is made to seem a victory for smallness and modesty.[15] This victory has its analogue on the aesthetic level where a novel by the obscure Trollope defeats the world-famous Dickens. Trollope's fondness for the prosaic, so-called, is a technique he developed at least in part for the purpose of anti-Dickensian counterstatement.

As a social satirist, Dickens belongs to the school of Juvenal, Swift, and Rabelais, all enlargers. But Trollope, indebted to Pope, advises Dickens that one accomplishes more by belittling the target than by expanding it. Swiftian methods increase the size of the offense as well as its seriousness. The thrust of Trollope's conservative satire is to make men smaller than they think they are, which reduces the magnitude of their foibles and laughs things down to tractable proportions. In Chapter 11, for example, when Eleanor Harding renounces her lover for attacking her father's honesty, Trollope rechristens her "Iphegenia"; one realizes that the sacrifice she makes will not be permanent.

Trollope's enlargements are only facetious. Tom Towers, a minor political journalist, edits the *Jupiter* from "Mount Olympus" instead of Fleet Street and is said to speak from "the Vatican of England" (W, 130). The journalist's role and that of the *Times*, a model for the *Jupiter*, as shapers of public opinion shrink in relation to Trollope's insistence on their importance. Harding and his daughter are a redoing of the Lear-Cordelia relationships in Dickens's early novels, but Trollope tones down any suggestion of tragedy; this Lear is right to step aside. When Dickens and Carlyle—"Mr. Popular Sentiment" and "Dr. Pessimist Anticant"—are elevated to prominence as leading lights of the age, their exaltation is like being cited in *The Dunciad*. They are raised up only to have their oracular abilities, their clamorings for extensive reform, ridiculed as biased chatter.

Trollope's mock-heroic parallels, inflations transparently false, are an important part of his plan for simmering Dickens down. Sentiment's dishonest warden is of Brobdingnagian proportions, but Trollope minimizes Dickens by implying that Harding's alleged misappropriation of funds is no more earthshaking than Belinda's loss of a lock. Trollope implies that Dickens consistently writes in a mock-heroic vein without realizing it, which makes him an unpardonable exaggerator. Purportedly a realist, Dickens recruits his large audience by making "mighty contests rise from trivial things."[16] When *The Warden* reduces to trifles problems that *The Almshouse* exacerbates, the Victorian world picture steadily improves.

The warden's struggle with his conscience, taking center stage, contributes to the pervasive defeat of the large by the small and the private. Unlike Dickens, Trollope eschews irreclaimable villains in favor of ostensibly unexceptional human beings who are frequently in error or unsure for a time what course to take. Harding resolves the novel's crisis with a carefully considered intellectual decision. He need not be crushed like Dombey or turned inside out like Gradgrind.

Life, Trollope argues, boils down to decisions about conduct that only individuals can reach. The life process, realistically examined, is not biological (George Eliot's unfolding) or illogical (Dickens's interminable law case) but ethical. Unselfish personal choice, Trollope opines, is frequently synonymous with society's best interests.

The warden is one of Trollope's admirable eccentrics—possibly his finest—because he alone, in this novel, perceives that the essence of being human is arriving at difficult decisions to the best of one's ability, regardless of reformers, public commotion, the church's stand, or Sir Abraham Hazard's legal opinion. Social consciences, avid formulators of popular sentiments, and prophetic announcers like Dickens and Carlyle confuse public opinion with private conscience, as if the most significant matters in life were chiefly an occasion for group decisions made at the urging of a communal spokesman. As Harding makes up his own mind, he becomes the ideal. Ordinary yet heroic, Harding—not Bold or Popular Sentiment—personifies Trollope's conception of a saint for Victorian times.[17]

The resolution of Harding's case drastically revises the task novelists like Dickens and prophets like Carlyle assign themselves. A topical realist's job, Trollope decides, is not to indict entire systems but to present characters who seem to be real and to observe them making ethically demanding choices in particular circumstances convincingly rendered. This toning down of the novelist's function gains in complexity what it seeems to forfeit in scope.

In a cultural situation where the call for reform has gotten out of hand, one cannot always bring private behavior and public duty into perfect alignment, as the husband and wife reform team of Will and Dorothea Ladislaw (in *Middlemarch*) later do. Instead, notes Trollope, one must prevent public pressure, misapplied by factions and special interests, from dictating personal decisions. Harding withstands the conservative church, in the person of his son-in-law Grantly, which wants him to hold fast. He refuses to endorse the reform party in Parliament, represented locally by his prospective son-in-law Bold, which insists he be let go. The coincidence of Harding's having a son-in-law (actual or potential) on each side means that either way he could give the appearance of enlisting private support before making his decision public. Instead, maneuvering in London to ensure that the choice is his alone, he bows out quietly—indeed surreptitiously, as far as Grantly and Bold are concerned.

Trollope's modernity, David Skilton argues, lies in "his awareness" that "in the midst of a crowded world, the individual is, in the last analysis, alone."[18] But Trollope is only saying that decisions are inevitably personal—that is, made by individuals. This is not identical with the modern lament that man, deprived of communal standards, is unqualified to be his own oracle but must perform as such regardless. Although Harding must not yield to Grantly or Bold, he still has a distinctly Victorian obligation to behave in the general interest. Trollope does not question the existence of this interest or the individual's ability to discern it. Once Harding resigns, however, the problem around which *The Warden* is constructed disappears. Compared with the Chancery suit against Guilford or the disclosure that Jarndyce versus Jarndyce has consumed itself in costs, Trollope's ending is true anticlimax.

His ironies are quieter than Dickens's. As a result of the uproar at Hiram's Hospital, only Harding, ostensibly the guilty party, is better off: he has grown in conscience, a good man having become better. His life as precentor of Barchester and rector of St. Cuthbert's, "the smallest possible parish" within the cathedral close (W, 200), seems even more comfortable than the warden's job. The novel's politicians, such as Grantly (a parody of Charles Kingsley's "muscular Christian"), come up empty; its reformers, Bold and associates, have less impact on Barchester than Will and Dorothea will exert on Middlemarch. The inhabitants of the almshouse fare worse than Oliver Twist: by asking for more, they end up with less, for they must do without Harding's many kindnesses and the supplement he added to their daily allotment. The position of warden is simply abolished.

In short, Trollope goes contrary to Dickens's call for extensive change and George Eliot's subsequent faith in gradual, reformer-directed amelioration. His novel issues a reminder to overly severe journalists, expectant social evolutionists, and philosophical radicals that it is often best to leave well enough alone.

Part of Trollope's joke at Dickens's expense is that *The Almshouse* is both too quick and not quick enough: it begins before the topical novelist has gotten his facts straight; yet within the short time it takes Popular Sentiment to capitalize on Harding's plight, the warden has decided to relinquish his post, and would-be reformer John Bold has concluded that there was no intentional wrongdoing. In *Felix Holt* and *Middlemarch*, the reform process is not easily kept going, and it is exceedingly difficult even to get change started in *Bleak House*. But Bold finds that reforms begun too quickly are impossible to stop: they acquire momentum of their own. The status quo is so delicate a balance, Trollope warns, that it proves irrecoverable once disturbed.

To remain Eleanor Harding's suitor, Bold must drop his suit against her father; he has to ensure his personal happiness at the expense of the public role he first thought it his duty to play. Having read Sentiment's first number, Bold seems as anxious as Harding for a restoration of tranquility. He regrets aloud that "the case had become so notorious" (W, 144). Contrary to his name, he becomes a contrite reformer. When Felix Holt fills

Esther Lyon, another clergyman's daughter, with a reformer's zeal, George Eliot reverses Eleanor Harding's dampening impact on Bold. Just as Trollope redoes the warden of *The Almshouse* to correct Dickens's caricatures of the social servant, George Eliot amends Trollope's caricature of reformers so that men of Bold's stamp can become Victorian heroes, secular apostles whose prospective wives mature into efficient co-workers.

"I fear," Trollope editorializes, that John Bold "is too much imbued with the idea that he has a special mission for reforming"; Bold's "passion," Trollope continues,

> is the reform of all abuses: state abuses, church abuses, corporation abuses . . . abuses in medical practice, and general abuses in the world at large. . . . It would be well if one so young had a little more diffidence himself and more trust in the honest purposes of others—if he could be brought to believe that old customs need not necessarily be evil and that changes may possibly be dangerous; but no, Bold has all the ardour and all the self-assurance of a Danton, and hurls his anathemas against time-honoured practices with the violence of a French Jacobin. [W,18-19]

In this summation of Bold's character, Trollope's primary intention is not to rule out the idea of reform as the age's "special mission" but to debunk the kind of mistaken meddler he thinks the rantings of Dickens and Carlyle are likely to create. Nevertheless, once Trollope has spoken, George Eliot feels obliged to stress that her reformers, individuals like Felix and Esther, are primarily guardians and transmitters of the nation's cultural heritage, not automatic opponents of venerable procedure.

Trollope exaggerates as eagerly in the cause of moderation as Dickens does for the sake of accelerating reform. Anxiety about rapid social change seems excessive in *The Warden*. Grantly's fear that Bold is a "firebrand" is surely groundless. Bold is closer to what Mrs. Jellyby might have been like had she been masculine and able to concentrate on nearby problems. A surgeon with a reformer's enthusiasms, Bold may also embody Trollope's notion of the harm Woodcourt might have done had Dickens presented him in greater detail. Trollope wants to satirize Bold for posing a serious threat to orderly society and for being an irrelevant nuisance. The suggestion that "changes may possibly be dangerous"—more so, in fact, than resistance to them—and mock-heroic parallels between Bold and "Danton," Bold and "a French Jacobin," inflate and deflate his significance simultaneously.

The "Barchester Reformer" is compelled to moralize about the unforeseen perils of instigating social improvements: "To what a world of toil and trouble had he, Bold, given rise by his indiscreet attack upon the hospital" (W,144). Reformers, Trollope generalizes, frequently give rise not to a better society but to "a world of toil and trouble." Topical realists and overly eager reformers are alike in being doubly inconsiderate: insensitive to the feelings of involved parties and unable to predict consequences. Instead of controlling developments, Bold is astonished by them. Reformers of his ilk are seldom to be compared with providence. As the allusion to *Macbeth* implies, they resemble the witches whose intriguing utterances led Shakespeare's Thane of Cawdor astray. To escape censure, would-be menders of men should display Trollope's own low-key virtues as a novelist, such as discretion and "diffidence," not "ardour" and "self-assurance."

The caricature of Carlyle as "Dr. Pessimist Anticant" does not share the keystone fifteenth chapter merely because Trollope disapproves of the pessimistic salvos in *Sartor Resartus, Signs of the Times,* and especially the *Latter-Day Pamphlets;* Trollope also wants to dismiss the major supplier of Dickens's ammunition. He holds Carlyle responsible for much of the pervasive discontent underlying Dickens's dissatisfaction with specific facets of the status quo.[19] Without Carlyle, Trollope intimates, Boz would have continued to write comic novels or mishandle individual abuses, which are remediable, instead of regarding each abuse synecdochically, as a sick part revealing the diseased condition of the whole.

Not only is Anticant Scottish by birth, Bold recalls, but he "passed a great portion of his early days in Germany," where he learned "to look with German subtlety into the root of things" (W,139). His reformism, it follows, proceeds from an alien root and is inapplicable to the realities of England's situation. Like Peacock's caricature of Samuel Taylor Coleridge, Anticant is "vague, mysterious, and cloudy," a thinker whose entertaining notions become ridiculous when given "practical" extension by Dickens. Anticant and Sentiment constitute a perfect mismatch: one's far-fetched generalizations are used to corroborate, possibly incite, the other's misinterpretations of individual cases. By the time Chapter 15 concludes, *The Almshouse* has been made to seem the product of a Londoner looking at Barchester with the "German subtlety" he acquired from reading a Scotchman's prose.

Dr. Pessimist Anticant dislikes the self-congratulatory jargon spoken by England's well-to-do and the do-nothing members they send to Parliament, jargon designed to ignore existing abuses or gloss them over. But Trollope objects that Carlyle has given rise, in Dickens, to a new form of affected or inflated language: the cant of reform, which Trollope must now quiet down. The new cant is at least as bad as the old: it is the uninformed popular outcry for immediate, widespread change, which amounts to a shift from inaction to overreaction. It mistakes the speed at which society can assimilate improvements. Insisting that all things can and should be changed as quickly as possible, it fails to appreciate traditional processes and the proper means of repairing them when they cease to work smoothly. New cant is to old cant as Dickens's shilling numbers are to the folio volumes of previous reformers: simply the other extreme. Bureaucracies and the fallible men in charge of them do not deserve to be swept away or shaken up abruptly, Trollope insists, any more than they merit being called utopian. The cant of reform unfairly denigrates administrators and public servants—the cadre to which Trollope, in the Postal Service, proudly belonged.

The Warden subdues Dickens in order to stake out a middle ground, a practical social realism between old cant and new, just as the really useful topical novel occupies a space between yesterday's newspaper and the historian's judgment. The objurgations of social satire must be confined to "the occasional follies or shortcomings of mankind" (W, 140), which are neither as numerous nor as critical as pessimists like Dickens and Carlyle imagine. The novelist who would be topical and realistic must emphasize that the follies he exposes are "occasional," a virtual synonym for topical, not pervasive or indicative of the general state of things. Scandals, therefore, are logical subjects for topical realism, provided they are used to prove the soundness of the whole by furnishing interesting exceptions.

Trollope tries to make Carlyle as notorious as his implied opposite, Voltaire's Doctor Pangloss, spokesman for the old cant of optimism. New cant, as coined by Anticant, is fond of "reprobating everything and everybody": Carlyle takes for his only subject "the decay of the world" (W, 142), and Dickens follows suit in novels like *The Almshouse (Bleak House)*. Anticant's thesis sounds just as offensive to Victorian ears, Trollope claims, as Pangloss's perspective on the eighteenth century—his "best of all possible worlds"—was to Voltaire. Although he is misanthropic instead of euphoric, Dickens, Trollope implies, is as naive and misguided as Candide.

Like many Victorian novelists, Trollope states that he is thoroughly realistic because he has achieved greater verisimilitude than someone else. *The Warden* is two novels: one that Trollope is writing and one that he is refuting, one that is intelligible per se and simultaneously a parody of the other. Hence the necessity of double vision to see Trollope's novel and antinovel at the same time.

The Warden presents Trollope's world view. It is also a parodic critique of a rival writer's misconceptions about human nature, society's ills, politics, reform, clergymen, and the art and ethics of creating realistic novels. Trollope reinforces his claim always to be describing the real state of affairs by disallowing a hypothetical Dickensian version of one affair. Although

Trollope objects to stark contrasts between good and evil in Dickens's fiction, his counterstatement depends for its persuasiveness on equally sharp conflicts between his truth and Dickens's falsity.

In an age as secular and scientific as the Victorian era in the first decade past midcentury, legitimation of knowledge was already an issue. Would-be authorities had to establish their credentials in a society of many voices. Not surprisingly, the literary term *realism* was introduced in 1855: G.H. Lewes employed the word as a new empirical standard for measuring a novel's perspective against the actual world.[20] Such measuring went on in the Victorian novel constantly after 1850. Dickens's novels were soon found wanting, not "true, vivid, convincing—like life, in fact."[21] His competitors broadened—in effect, legitimized—their work by setting it off against his. Thus they began the practice of incorporating another novel within their own, parodying it in order to verify their claim to verisimilitude at the expense of a rival's.

Redoing another novel in the course of composing one's own often required a multiplot novel but was also a parody of multiplotting. Where the multiplotter tried to cultivate thematic variations in order to achieve a semblance of inclusiveness, the revaluator attempted to weed them out so as to assert exclusive rights to the truth. To neutralize Dickens's ardor and curtail his zeal, Trollope published a novel no thicker than Goldsmith's *Vicar of Wakefield*. *The Warden* became a reduction in magnitude for contemporary scandals by slenderizing Dickens. The compact size of Trollope's reply suggested that Dickens's list of social evils was as padded as his increasingly formidable multiplot novels. Trollope eschews multiplotting yet capitalizes on the technique by imagining Dickens's story running concurrently with a scaled-down revision of it.

Debunking a competitor's work enabled the revaluator to control temporarily the pluralistic society he was paradoxically helping to create. On one hand, he eliminated or modified a rival perspective in favor of his own, thereby simplifying the world's confusion; on the other, conflict between works like *The Warden* and *The Almshouse* signaled the arrival of a multifaceted, unfixable reality to which no one novelist's perspective could do justice. When the term *realism* came into use, in the same year that Trollope published *The Warden*, rival realisms were already competing for attention, Trollope subverting Dickens.

Literary wars between professed realists were manifestations of a new social situation: the multiplication of secular philosophies and individualized perspectives, none of which could be "like life, in fact" but only more so than another. The process of secularization that made the conventions of realism increasingly possible also made realism itself relative and multiple;

in the Victorian novel it quickly became as plural as the brand-new secular world it attempted to describe. In this sense, the Victorian novel is always realistic and, collectively, quite modern despite—indeed because of— pitched battles between the realists themselves.

With George Eliot and G.H. Lewes, Trollope dreaded that Dickens's indignant assessment of reality, his colorful explications of social problems, would become gospel.[22] Although nineteenth-century novelists were never a confederacy, many stood together against Dickens, striving to prevent his spirited delineation of an impersonal, irresponsible society in the throes of decomposition from becoming the popular conception and, as such, pass- ing into history. Hence Trollope's implication that his carefully weighed topical novel is closer to a historian's judgments than are Sentiment's hastier concoctions. Much of the flurry and incessant revaluation in the Victorian novel can be explained as an effort not just to deny Dickens his large contemporary audience but to block his appointment as special correspondent for posterity. Suspicion of Dickens's role as Juvenalian satirist, mistreating London as severely as Juvenal had assailed Rome, produced some of the best parody, all of it anti-Dickensian, written during the second half of the nineteenth century.

Trollope studiously avoided London settings, conceding Dickens this bailiwick. So did such other anti-Dickensians as George Eliot and Mrs. Gaskell, who campaigned against Dickens's dismal estimate of England's moral and social condition by looking beyond the metropolis upon which his analysis was mostly based. Pessimistic perspectives, they contended, become less credible if one examines Manchester, for instance, with a northerner's eye, or turns to provincial towns like Middlemarch, instead of dwelling on the nation's capital. Besides making Popular Sentiment a Londoner who misreads Barchester, Trollope suggests that *The Almshouse* is an exaggeration of conditions at Charterhouse (the London refuge vilified in *Household Words*) and therefore unreliable when compared with Trollope's retrospective on the three charitable institutions—metropolitan and provincial—that were his co-models.

Reviewers from the 1850s on rejected the idea of a comic novelist putting himself forward as a serious critic of society. They hoped to lessen the impact of Dickens's denunciations by stereotyping him as a comedian with pretensions. Evaluation of the later novels was "more and more affected," George Ford notes, "by the political and social predilections of [Dickens's] readers and critics."[23] But something more complicated was taking place in the novels themselves: writers like Trollope began a coun- teroffensive against Dickens's sweeping criticisms. When the critic for *Blackwood's* sat down in "the wilderness of *Little Dorrit*" to remember

Pickwick and weep, he was only echoing sentiments that Trollope had expressed two years earlier. Victorian novelists rarely published formal literary criticism because their creative works were frequently both literature and criticism, each a form of the other. In the 1850s, Dickens's rivals and reviewers began collaborating against him, with his competitors as the ostensible initiators of the conspiracy.

By revaluing Dickens, however, Trollope set himself up as an obligatory target for George Eliot. The nature of one hidden rivalry in Victorian fiction is to beget others. Dickens's wide-ranging critique of an inept judiciary and an incompetent civil service not only "alienated liberal and conservative alike"[24] but drove them further apart; quarreling with Dickens also brought home to the novelists in league against him the extent of their differences with one another. George Eliot recognized the anti-Dickensian parody in *The Warden* as a toning-down of the reform movement generally, not just a setback for radicalism. Dickens provided the principal target in *Felix Holt* and *Middlemarch*, but their author also took aim at Trollope by supporting progressive reform and carefully distinguishing it from Dickens's reprobation of the status quo.

Disagreements between major Victorian novelists, each professing faithfulness to the actual, were not ultimately political;[25] rather, they concealed philosophical disputes about the nature of things. Victorian novels are not, strictly speaking, thesis novels—which Trollope despised—or surveys of current attitudes toward life; but, largely thanks to Dickens, they do make complex statements about the life process. Although no Victorian novelist thought he or she lived in the best of all possible societies, Dickens seemed to be saying that it was, in fact, the worst. His statements and the counterviews they prompted were regularly disguised as ideological disputes over reform: whether there was need for change and, if so, its proper scope and pace. The reform question was a logical sparring ground for thinking novelists. They used it to ask, in the 1850s and thereafter, how good life was and how much could be expected from it as the second half of the century got underway.

Arguments over which novel was more faithful to reality were ultimately not about aesthetics, either; that was another guise that rivalry between philosophical perspectives eagerly assumed in a variable secular world. Revoking a rival's claim to be realistic was a shortcut to disproving his philosophy of life, which explains the prominence of revaluative parody in the Victorian novel. Once Popular Sentiment is exposed as a topical opportunist who gets his facts wrong about Barchester's almshouse, Dickens, not that charitable institution, needs to be reorganized. Victorian novelists were willing not only to disagree about the concept of realism, the nature of things, and the need for reform but to cloak discussion of their differences on any of these issues in terms of arguments about the others.

George Eliot's novels subvert the later, epical Dickens, but the target of Trollope's work is the earlier topical satirist. To dismantle masterworks in which severe measures seem called for because individual wrongs are shown to be interconnected, Trollope questions the handling of individual wrongs. If he could pick apart Dickens's approach to specific cases, the ability to synthesize society's failings into the sort of epical indictment that upset George Eliot would automatically become suspect.

The attack on *The Almshouse* is more insidious than George Eliot's subsequent parodies of *Bleak House* because Trollope could not purify Victorian realism in *The Warden* without endangering its vitality thereafter. Parodying Dickens as a topical novelist showed that writing realistic fiction is mostly a subjective affair. That Dickens borrows incidents from newspapers and periodicals does not guarantee devotion to the factual, as can be seen from the monstrosity *The Alsmhouse* is eager to create out of Harding's peccadillo. Thus there is no such thing as "an untouched transcript of real life as accurate and uncolored as history."[26] It is no more convincing, Trollope's parody of Dickens implies, for fiction to draw heavily on current events for its characters and incidents than to pretend that a novel is a biography or someone's private correspondence.

Taken proleptically, this makes George Eliot's stance as scientific sociologist just as preposterous as Dickens's assertion that the "nature" (personality) of the topical realist "is subdued / To what it works in, like the dyer's hand."[27] Trollope and Dickens are in proximity to events constituting a small chapter in the great drama of human improvement that the Victorian novel of social awareness records. Yet they disagree as markedly in their opinions of ecclesiastical scandals in the early 1850s as George Eliot later differs with Dickens about such larger matters as society's prospects for continued evolution. *The Warden* and *The Almshouse* refer to different worlds.

In Trollope one sees the form Victorian rivalries generally take: re-valuative parody is used as a means of contradiction or modification; the allegedly true supersedes the false. Realism—that is, the revaluing novelist's perspective—replaces or tones down mistakes and exaggeration. Trollope resorts to traditional parody in Chapter 15 with an outrageous burlesque of Dickens's style and technique, but this makes the new variety of parody he relies on throughout *The Warden* work even better. Giving excerpts from Popular Sentiment's opening number, Trollope purposely heightens Dickens's penchant for hyperbole; at the same time, he rewrites *The Almshouse* as *The Warden* to soften the melodramatic treatment that

Household Words accorded a recent scandal. In other words, the heightening makes the toning-down seem even more imperative. The strategy appears almost inevitable: since Dickens exaggerates, the way to discredit his excesses and upgrade the world his satires disparage cannot be simply to exaggerate further; that would be imitation.

Still, Trollope's experiment in revaluative parody seems ingeniously cautious. Although there is no mistaking his model for Mr. Popular Sentiment, Trollope refrained from attacking an actual Dickens novel. He therefore anticipated (and probably encouraged) George Eliot's subsequent parodies of an actual Dickens text. If *Felix Holt* is the classic instance of parodic rewriting in Victorian fiction, *The Warden* is the seminal.

Indirectly, *The Warden* intervened in the quarrel between Dickens and Mrs. Gaskell in *Hard Times* and *North and South*, which commented adversely on each other in 1854–55, just before Trollope published. Since Trollope's book incriminates the misuse of church funds yet exculpates one of the misusers, his double vision criticizes the one-pointed perspectives he disapproves of in less adroit topical realists. Mrs. Gaskell's apologia for Manchester and Dickens's denunciation of all such industrial centers enabled Trollope to register the same complaint about *Hard Times* and *North and South* that *The Warden* was written to lodge against *The Almshouse*. Moreover, by provoking Mrs. Gaskell, Dickens may have invited attacks from antisensationalists in sympathy with her, George Eliot and Trollope among them.

Whatever else prompted Trollope to compose *The Warden*, to ignore the stimulus of the article in *Household Words* is to keep hidden an important Victorian rivalry. It also obscures the idea of a multisided reality—modern life as competing realisms or discordant points of view—which Victorian literary battles of the sort Trollope fought against Dickens helped to initiate. Thanks to struggles between Victorian realists, life began to be portrayed in multiplicate from the 1850s onward. The idea of a common reality, one that an objective realism can portray for a secularized society, was always an imperiled ideal, even in the heyday of realism, long before postmodern critics decided that realism itself is a kind of cant or fiction.

Chapter Three

Mutual Recrimination

Hard Times
North and South

IN *Hard Times* (1854) and *North and South* (1854-55), Dickens and Mrs. Gaskell rewrite one another's characters, themes, and situations with unrelenting assiduity. Reading one novel in light of the other is like collating two texts on the same subject written in antithetical moods. Polite disavowals by both novelists aside, each book makes retaliation against the other a major concern. Of the many hidden rivalries in Victorian fiction, this is the most complicated: none reveals as clearly the advantages and drawbacks of writing revaluative parody.

Whether the subject is "Men and Masters" (Dickens) or "Masters and Men" (Mrs. Gaskell),[1] each novelist writes to question the other's mimetic skills; each accuses the other of lying. Mrs. Gaskell insists that events will never transpire at Milton-Northern the way they do in Coketown. Dickens believes that his anatomy of a grimy manufacturing town rules out Mrs. Gaskell's rosier view of industrial civilization. Although neither subscribes to the Gradgrindian dictum "Facts alone are wanted in life" (HT, 1), each pretends to offer nothing else but the facts of life. Animated competition between two confessed realists turns *Hard Times* and *North and South* into the only nineteenth-century novels to revalue each other simultaneously.

Not surprisingly, this competition has proved less noticeable than Trollope's revisions of Dickens in *The Warden* or George Eliot's attempt to replace *Bleak House* with *Felix Holt*. Neither Dickens nor Mrs. Gaskell had the other's entire text on hand, and each claimed to be staying out of the other's path. Nevertheless, although Mrs. Gaskell was under contract with *Household Words* and actually working for Dickens, she tried to bind back together everything he was putting asunder. Trollope and George Eliot entered the fray in defense of the Victorian era because of Mrs. Gaskell's failure to repair the oppositions in *Hard Times* as decisively as she had hoped.

Capitalizing on the same crisis in current affairs—a weavers' strike at Preston—and employing the identical model of a manufacturing city (Manchester), Dickens and Mrs. Gaskell used labor unrest in the 1850s to express divergent opinions on the future of human relations in a society whose new economic base would be its industries. Asking whether personal relationships would improve or degenerate was a way of examining life's larger outlines, a means of determining how livable, how progressive, the second half of the nineteenth century was likely to be. Each novelist tried to ascertain the moral and social consequences of continued technological advance. This double vision of a brand-new world, each version run according to its own internal logic, still disconcerts definers of realism.

Hard Times began its serial run in *Household Words* on 1 April 1854; *North and South* was scheduled to start in the same periodical in September. Mrs. Gaskell read early installments about Coketown with growing uneasiness and expressed to Dickens her dismay that his use of an industrial theme was stealing her thunder. To allay Mrs. Gaskell's anxieties about being pre-empted, Dickens replied: "I have no intention of striking. The monstrous claims at domination made by a certain class of manufacturers, and the extent to which the way is made easy for working men to slide down into discontent under such hands, are within my scheme; but I am not going to strike, so don't be afraid of me. But I wish you would look at the story yourself, and judge where and how near I seem to be approaching what you have in your mind. The first two months of it will show that."[2]

This missive, intended to be soothing, was sent on 21 April, by which time the first half of Book One of *Hard Times* had appeared. Dickens encouraged Mrs. Gaskell to follow his story closely as she worked on hers, to second-guess him and thus steer clear of unnecessary repetition. It sounds as if he was enclosing a portion of his manuscript for her perusal,[3] but all he probably meant was that she could deduce the remainder once the first eight numbers were out. Dickens received the first quarter of Mrs. Gaskell's novel in June, when half of his was already in print,[4] which would put him about one-third through Book Two. Then it was Dickens's turn to worry, for it must have been apparent that *North and South* was a parodic reply to *Hard Times*. A fight between the two for authenticity was under way.

Dickens's placating letter inspired Mrs. Gaskell to protect her integrity as a social realist by undermining his. The more she departed from Dickens's story to prevent it from overlapping hers, the greater the temptation to compose a rebuttal. Whether he had Slackbridge's men walk out or not, Dickens's opening chapters struck at the confidence Mrs. Gaskell intended to place in better understanding between classes as a panacea for new tensions generated within industrial communities. *Hard Times*, Mrs. Gaskell decided, was ignoring the romantic aspects of manufacturing, underrating the intelligence of the working man, and slandering the captains of industry whom cities like Manchester were beginning to spawn.

Having read *Mary Barton* (1848), Dickens was familiar with Mrs. Gaskell's hopeful response to a new era's social problems. He also knew her outline for *North and South*, having seen it "sometime in 1853."[5] One conjectures that he was writing all along to discredit what he considered a predilection for facile solutions. The more he tried to anticipate Mrs. Gaskell, the harder it became for her to keep on a separate track. In the summer of 1854, Dickens's position as Mrs. Gaskell's editor gave him a temporary edge. He seized upon it in hopes of forestalling writers from advancing their own interpretations of life by refuting his, an opportunity he sensed his anti-industrial novel was creating for his next contributor.

By 26 July, when Dickens had half of Mrs. Gaskell's manuscript,[6] all but the wrap-up chapters of *Hard Times* were already circulating. The ultimate advantage, therefore, belonged to Mrs. Gaskell: she could not be denied the last word, no matter how much of *Hard Times* is a reaction to what Dickens expected from *North and South* or knew of Mrs. Gaskell's fiction in general. Still, owing to proximity and the chances for give and take, Mrs. Gaskell never got Dickens in her sights as squarely as George Eliot would when she later took aim at *Bleak House*. Double vision requires ventilation of Dickens's case against Mrs. Gaskell along with hers against him. Dickens learned what he disliked about the industrial system as much from Mrs. Gaskell as at Preston; in reading him, she discovered which features of a new way of life she would have to explain and defend.

North and South seemed, in Dickens's judgment, false to the gravity of its situations. In Coketown, mill and schoolroom serve as coordinated parts of one large factory, the prototype for future urban settlements. The epoch of enlightened self-interest, dominated by Utilitarian theory and heartless entrepreneurs, shows signs of becoming a virtual dictatorship: Gradgrind and M'Choakumchild condition the public mind from childhood on, while Bounderby, a tyrant, bullies regimented workers. They pass "to and from their nests, like ants or beetles" (HT, 120). Conditions approximate the termitary society of Huxley's *Brave New World*, where the "swarming indistinguishable sameness" of "one hundred and sixty-two Deltas" on the menial staff at the Park Lane Hospital reminds the Savage of "maggots."[7]

Society in *Hard Times* is busily killing its spiritual and physical vitality.

In Mrs. Gaskell's seemingly perfectible world, rival powers—North and South, masters and men, middle and lower classes, business and culture—combine their strengths to form new alliances crackling with energy. The same economic source that pollutes rivers, stunts individual growth, and emits "killing airs and gasses" (HT, 48) to blacken Dickens's microcosm also fuels Milton-Northern; yet life, to Dickens's amazement, is not merely bearable in Mrs. Gaskell's scheme of things but vibrant and improving.

Hard Times is designed to be a barrier to the novels of reconciliation that Mrs. Gaskell wanted to continue writing. Troubles at Preston, says Dickens, are a lopsided struggle between ethically indifferent tyranny (capitalism in this case) and a long-suffering underdog (labor). He presents the criminal-victim relationship between owners and workers as an aggravation of existing enmities separating rich and poor, an imbalance of power that prohibits inclusion of a prolonged strike sequence in any industrial novel not misreading the facts. Deciding not to strike, Dickens tries to minimize *North and South*, if not subvert its message altogether, by excluding as implausible an event that Mrs. Gaskell considers privotal for her account of what could happen.

Armed with Dickens's letter of 21 April, Mrs. Gaskell turns foreknowledge of his intentions to her advantage. When Thornton the manufacturer, Margaret Hale, and her father the ex-parson explore the relative capabilities of labor and management, the industrialist carefully avoids "monstrous claims at domination made by a certain class of manufacturers," whose arrogance caused Dickens to start writing. In order to make strikes feasible and Dickens's promise not to include one a mistake, Mrs. Gaskell has Thornton tell Mr. Hale that "cotton-lords" are no longer as all-powerful as the term suggests. In Milton-Northern "the battle is pretty fairly waged" between bosses and men; neither side, Thornton maintains, wants "an umpire" or "meddler" (like Dickens) to mix in (NS, 124-25). By not striking, Dickens rules out Mrs. Gaskell's central episode; but a fair-minded Thornton, a laissez-faire industrialist who sees his men as worthy opponents, counters for Mrs. Gaskell by nullifying Dickens's pretext for taking up an industrial theme.

As Chapter 15 indicates, the Hales know of Dickens's April letter and seem to have been reading the specific charges Dickens levies against manufacturers in *Hard Times*. Thornton refrains from calling workers "hands" because Miss Hale disapproves. Her dislike has been formed by Dickens's observation that "the Hands" might find "more favour" with their masters "if Providence had seen fit to make them only hands" (HT, 49) instead of men with minds and stomachs. But Thornton insists one need not mistake "a technical term" for a reductive attitude. Mrs. Gaskell's manufacturer uses synecdoche as a convenience of speech, whereas Dickens is accused of making all masters diabolical behaviorists, like the genetic engineers in the Brave New World's Social Predestination Room.

Miss Hale tells Thornton she has heard that Milton's masters want their workers to be "large children—living in the present moment—with a blind unreasoning kind of obedience" (NS, 166). This sounds like the widespread "infantility" Bernard Marx decries in *Brave New World*; Deltas and Epsilons, retarded scientifically, do all menial tasks. But the Hales are simply conversant with Chapter 8 in Book One of *Hard Times*. In places like Coketown, Dickens claims, Utilitarians prevent "a considerable population" from acquiring "sentiments," "affections," and a capacity for "wonder." These stunted creatures resemble "babies"—whether twenty, thirty, forty, or fifty years of age (HT, 38). Thornton labels such reports a slander. "My theory," he explains, "is, that my interests are identical with those of my workpeople, and vice-versa." Thornton makes this humanistic principle clearer to the Hales by establishing its cogency on purely economic grounds.

In Chapter 17, Mrs. Gaskell calls further attention to Dickens's omissions: Margaret and Higgins try to answer the question "What Is a Strike?" Mrs. Gaskell inserts exposition before proceeding with the strike itself to prove that she comprehends, much better than Dickens, working-class situations and the working-class mind. Strikes substantiate her hypothesis that social evils result from breakdowns of communication and are remedied most efficiently by greater mutual understanding. Mrs. Gaskell's masterwork, due largely to the stimulus Dickens provided, is by turns a thesis novel, as is *Hard Times*, and a discussion novel promoting her ideas. Thus Thornton argues the thesis that parity exists between owners and men, and Margaret and Higgins analyze the nature of a walkout. In both instances, Mrs. Gaskell articulates her position while simultaneously refuting Dickens. *North and South* has been criticized for "clumsily" incorporating "stiff lecture-discussion" into a "fine and sensitive study of human relationships,"[8] but the discussions are a crucial factor in the anti-Dickens parody.

The coming age, Dickens and Mrs. Gaskell agree, belongs to groups. Owing to industrialization, a new chapter in the history of social relations is beginning. Dickens anticipates a group psychology hostile to individual needs; Mrs. Gaskell's rejoinder desires rival power blocs (and their members) to shape their behavior toward one another on existing units, such as the family. A logical outcome of Dickens's fears is the caste system of *Brave New World*, in which one is conditioned—whether Alpha, Beta, or Epsilon-Minus—to experience solidarity only with one's own kind.

Dickens's argument, implicit throughout *Hard Times*, is that assemblages prove inherently Utilitarian, having, like the cold-eyed, colorless Bitzer (HT, 3), no heart. In order to wield power, groups are compelled to dedicate themselves to the happiness of the greatest number. When Slackbridge delivers his speech on "Brotherhood" (Book Two, Chapter 4), the concept means solidarity, not concern for one's fellow man. It excludes owners automatically and ostracizes any union member reluctant to relegate personal principles to the collective will. In "the gospel according to Slackbridge" (HT, 189), as Stephen Blackpool sadly realizes, "private feeling must yield to the common cause" (HT, 110). Dickens disliked Slackbridge intensely because the unionist's unwelcome redefinition accurately forecasts what fraternity is likely to mean in the forthcoming world of competing power systems and consequent adversary relationships.

This is precisely the sort of world Mrs. Gaskell sets out to prevent by sending Milton-Northern the Hales instead of Slackbridge. To the as yet inchoate North of new manufactures, the Hales bring from the South a firm belief in the traditional Christian family unit. Unlike Higgins's household, the Hales' is held together by faith; unlike Thornton's, which is defensive, a self-enclosed citadel, the Hales' is a model of openness to new ideas. It is a cultural outpost, a missionary settlement reaching out to all around. Its effectiveness as leaven exceeds Sissy Jupe's limited and somewhat unbelievable impact on the Gradgrind household.

Although living in a suburb with the restrictive name of Crampton, the Hales think broadly in terms of the family of man. A victim of doubts, Mr. Hale has resigned the ministry, but the errand now is undoubtedly secular diplomacy: Milton-Northern needs mediators between the new, rough-hewn masters of the material universe and their awed but unruly subjects, not between God and His servants. The Hales accept both Thornton and Higgins into their circle, and Margaret eventually changes these long-time enemies, strangers to one another's virtues, into virtual partners if not actually brothers.

Mrs. Gaskell repairs the damage done to human relationships in *Hard Times* by using one of Dickens's ideals against him. She reinvokes the civilizing influences of home and hearth at a juncture when and in an environment where Dickens seems to have felt his secularized Christianity might be no match for new conditions. Rival factions in the industrial North will get along all right, Mrs. Gaskell suggests, if they model business dealings on the natural harmony of the Hales' home. As soon as Thornton notices the "graceful cares" (NS, 120) the Hales take of a new residence and their concern for each other, he compares his splendid domicile unfavorably with theirs. From the moment Thornton's aesthetic sense flowers, Mrs. Gaskell begins to "beautify" the life-style of Milton-Northern with "imaginative graces and delights" (HT, 226) and domesticate the machinery that is its livelihood.

Different attitudes toward groups determine rival strategies of presentation in *Hard Times* and *North and South*. Dickens thinks neither side in Coketown is right. It follows that he cannot appeal to Slackbridge or Bounderby, so he speaks past opposing parties to raise a universal outcry in favor of industrial reforms. He offers a foreglimpse of a new dispensation in which disputes will no longer be resolved solely by disputants themselves; Dickens counts on a third power group, the general public, to coerce feuding sides into agreement. Arousing popular sentiment, the tactic Trollope criticizes in *The Warden*, is not just financially lucrative; Dickens decides it gives the novelist his best chance of remaining useful in an economic system composed of vested interests.

Mrs. Gaskell deems reasonable the motives of both groups in contests like the one at Milton-Northern. She speaks to each side as if to estranged partners in a marital spat. Functioning as apologist, she defends management to labor, labor to management, and the good qualities of both to her audience. Instead of isolating guilty persons, she tries to pacify angry parties and close rifts in the social fabric. Except against Dickens, whose anxieties she continually resists, Mrs. Gaskell declines to be satirical. *North and South* illustrates the reconciliation process she thinks Dickens's severities only impede.

Individuals with integrity in Dickens's novels find themselves squeezed between opposing groups. Blackpool is spurned by his union and fired by his employer; neither labor nor capital understands or desires his principles. Louisa Gradgrind is trapped between her father and Bounderby, then between Bounderby and Harthouse; neither Utilitarianism nor big business appreciates a young woman's physical nature. In Mrs. Gaskell's redoing of Dickens's world, danger lies not in the new social formations an industrial economy makes mandatory but, as always, in the failure of selfish individuals to take the larger view. In *North and South*, the person who will not integrate correctly or wholeheartedly, a nonjoiner like Boucher, endangers reconciliatory interchange between competing groups that are merely quarreling individuals writ large.

John Boucher's plight parodies Blackpool's. Instead of showing a man let down by both sides, Mrs. Gaskell writes about a man who lets both sides down. Were masters and men to condemn the same individual, Mrs. Gaskell persists, he would have to be someone like Boucher. In the narrowly averted attack on Thornton's mill by hungry strikers, Boucher helps to transmute strike into riot, thereby driving the two parties further apart.

Weak and full of hate, Boucher cannot see beyond the effects of the strike on his own family. As he fights to get into the front rank, his facial expression, "forlornly desperate and livid with rage" (NS, 233), is also the mob's. Boucher's name, every bit as expressive as Blackpool's, comes from the French verb meaning *to stop, choke, shut up,* or *intercept,* practically a catalogue of the selfish individual's offenses against connection.

When Boucher first behaves insubordinately to Higgins, a scene Margaret witnesses, Mrs. Gaskell rewrites the confrontation between Blackpool and Slackbridge to put noncooperation in the wrong. Boucher is tempted to break ranks and return to work on the masters' terms. He complains that his family, especially "lile Jack," is starving. To Higgins's warning that strength comes only from unity, Boucher angrily replies that the union is "a worser tyrant than e'er th' masters were"; you must starve to death "ere yo' dare go again th' Union." The disgruntled laborer echoes Dickens's implied complaint about new power groups: "Yo' may be kind hearts, each separate," he rails, "but once banded together, you've no more pity for a man than a wild hunger-maddened wolf" (NS, 207). Instead of sending the would-be turncoat to Coventry, however, Higgins uses his own money to purchase food for Boucher's starving child. "An' th' Union— that's to say, I—will take care you've enough for th' childer and th' missus. So dunnot turn faint-heart," pleads Higgins, "and go to th' tyrants a-seeking work."

The switch from "th' Union" to "I" in Higgins's remarks emphasizes Mrs. Gaskell's conviction that negotiations between groups always boil down to an exchange between individuals. Against Dickens's tendency to show characters turned into abstractions by the depersonalizing forces at work in society, she converts abstractions into people: the union, ultimately, is Higgins, just as the North is Thornton and the South is Margaret.

In the siege of Thornton's mill, Mrs. Gaskell's finest sequence, Margaret places herself between its embattled owner and the angry rioters. Her action, like Higgins's pledge to Boucher, reduces public crisis to a personal level on which one can gauge infallibly the moral validity of concerted activity. Storming the factory no longer amounts to a confrontation between management and labor. When Margaret is felled by a stone meant for Thornton, the outbreak is redefined as the violation of one individual by another. To continue the assault would mean the virtual deflowering of the middle class, personified in Margaret, by the worst instincts of the lower, unleashed by Boucher.[9] But violent demonstration is wrong, all seem to realize instinctively, because, seen as potential rape, it specifically contradicts healthy marriage as the novel's paradigm for satisfactory industrial relationships.

After Boucher, having disgraced himself and his union, commits suicide—the ultimate act of disconnection—Higgins still treats the drowned man's family compassionately. Thornton reveals that at Higgins's urging he has "put one or two children," presumably Boucher's, "to school" (NS, 444), a kindness that surpasses Gradgrind's enrollment of Sissy at M'Choakumchild's institution. Both sides in the turmoil at Milton-Northern do all they can for, rather than to, the man who stood out against them both. Boucher's suicide is not martyrdom, like Stephen's accidental death, but a parody of it. The abandoned mine shaft that Blackpool tumbles into externalizes for Mrs. Gaskell the philosophical hole that Dickens's anti-industrial bias has trapped the power-loom weaver in from the beginning. Boucher dies more ignominiously than Stephen by lying face down in a shallow, dye-filled stream. Its pollution is surely the fault of the cotton mills, yet Boucher drowns himself—slides "down into discontent"—out of weakness and remorse, neither of which is useful to a forward-moving community.

"Loyalty and obedience to wisdom and justice are fine," Margaret tells her mother, "but it is still finer to defy arbitrary power, unjustly and cruelly used" (NS, 154). This speech occurs in "The Mutiny," a chapter that comes well before the strike episodes. Margaret staunchly defends her brother's conduct toward the tyrannical Captain Reid. The seemingly extraneous subplot involving Lieutenant Hale's insubordination deserves its place when one realizes that it spells out the rules for rebellion, which Dickens supposedly does not know and Boucher later violates.[10]

Like Nicholas Nickleby pummeling Squeers, Frederick has revolted against a bully, acted as a champion of the badly used. Captain Reid's authority, while at sea, could be checked by no other means; therefore, mutiny was justifiable. On shore, unless a bogus mutineer like Boucher interferes, the existence of groups like the union, Mrs. Gaskell maintains, makes acts of individual revolt unnecessary. Just as Frederick is not Boucher, Thornton is hardly Captain Reid. Bounderby, however, invites the kind of abuse that Frederick expends on his commander. Dickens, Mrs. Gaskell complains, presents the domination of Bounderby over Blackpool as if it were Squeers and Smike over again. Bounderby, accusing "that fellow Slackbridge" of "stirring up the people to mutiny" (HT, 112), may have confirmed Mrs. Gaskell's idea to do contrasting chapters on mutiny and strike. The implied joke is that Dickens, like Bounderby, cannot tell one from the other. Mrs. Gaskell utilizes both to dispute Dickens's estimate of the efficacy of strikes and to determine their ethical parameters.

A fugitive from English justice, Frederick appears in Milton-Northern only briefly to visit his dying mother. Margaret assists him to escape from Leonards at the Outwood station and then denies that she was involved. The incident drives a wedge between Thornton and Margaret. In *Hard Times*, by contrast, Louisa's brother drives her toward unhappy union with Bounderby. In *North and South*, Thornton, doing the job assigned to Sleary's circus in Dickens's novel, eventually makes good a brother's escape: he saves Margaret from an inquest into Leonards's death that would implicate Frederick and convict her of having told a falsehood.

The uprising of the strikers at Marlborough Mills gives Thornton the notion that Margaret cares for him, although she does not realize it and rejects his offer. Events at the station convince him that she cares about someone else when, actually, he is now uppermost in her regard. The riot and Frederick's close call intertwine the novel's love story with its economic themes. These scenes also enable Mrs. Gaskell to prolong endlessly the misunderstandings that keep Thornton and Miss Hale estranged. In a novel assiduously affirming conciliation, Mrs. Gaskell postpones by every conceivable means the most desirable association of all.

Thornton's glimpse of Margaret with Frederick, whom he mistakes for a lover, in Chapter 32 is not explained to everyone's satisfaction for twenty chapters. Immediate rapprochement could have occurred as early as Chapter 33, when Thornton inquires for Miss Hale upon hearing of her mother's death. But for "some reason or other," Dixon, the maid, never mentions Thornton's visit: "It might have been mere chance, but so it was that Margaret never heard that he [Thornton] had attended her poor mother's funeral" (NS, 340). Similarly lost opportunities to clear up the matter, including the separate deaths of Mr. Hale and Mr. Bell as each is about to intervene, occur one after the other. Finally, in Chapter 50, Higgins asks Thornton for news of Miss Hale and, quite by accident, tells his master that it was her brother Frederick he saw Miss·Hale with. In Chapter 52, the rapprochement of Chapter 51 turns into an engagement when Thornton repeats his proposal. Had Margaret not prompted an alliance between unionist and manufacturer, the confusion might never have ended.

The obstacles in the way of union between Margaret and Thornton are sufficiently credible when met singly but escalate to a parody of Dickens if reviewed and totaled. Mrs. Gaskell complained that the demands of serial publication constrained her to abbreviate the later portion of her novel, especially the love story, and speed toward resolution. Before releasing the hard-cover version early in 1855, she expanded the serial's twenty-first part into Chapters 44-48 to obtain the elbow room *Household Words* had denied her.[11] She also took the opportunity to get even with Dickens for his editorial interference by ridiculing the popular novelist's stock in trade: unrealistic delays that increase suspense. Interminable misapprehensions caused by events in the strike and mutiny chapters are a sort of mutiny on Mrs. Gaskell's part, a striking-back not at the domination of Manchester industrialists but against the tyranny of London-based journal editors. *North and South* tantalizes the reader expertly while parodying devices that Dickens used to boost sales of weekly serials like *The Old Curiosity Shop*.

In *Hard Times*, one is made to ponder Stephen's whereabouts for six installments after his departure from Coketown coincides with the robbery of Bounderby's bank; although innocent, he is already mortally injured when found and cannot be reunited with friends for long. Louisa begins to descend Mrs. Sparsit's staircase in the final chapter of the fifteenth installment, but readers must proceed to the last chapter of the sixteenth to learn her destination: to escape the temptation to commit adultery, she is fleeing from Bounderby, not toward Harthouse; her future is a kind of spinsterhood. Delay in *North and South*, by contrast, is always prelude to agreement; it offers the prospect of new and richer life once Margaret's blamelessness has been reestablished.

Behind the parody of Dickens's serial novels lie several serious points having to do with the primacy of good human relationships. Although Margaret lends Thornton money from Bell's legacy to her, his manufactury is saved by love, not capital; he and his lovely landlord will conduct their future business with the trust and respect husbands and wives have for each other. Nothing could illustrate more literally Mrs. Gaskell's premise that mercantile operations should pattern themselves after friendship and marriage. The eventual understanding the lovers reach validates Mrs. Gaskell's thesis that worthwhile connection is inevitable, no matter how painstakingly attained or long postponed.

Union for Margaret and Thornton is victory for the life force. This strong evolutionary drive goes deeper than sectional rivalries or bad feeling between classes; it cannot be deterred forever by such superficial barriers. Regulating economic problems that divide masters and men and alleviating distrust that regions of the country have for one another become similar: the process in either case is not much different from making friends or uniting lovers. Thanks to complications that take nearly two hundred pages to remove, cooperation between opposing groups seems no more monumental than breaking down misconceptions separating Thornton and Miss Hale.

Mrs. Gaskell's effort to demonstrate that better interpersonal relationships are the cure for modern problems, as well as the key to social progress, reverses Dickens's argument that human relationships are likely to be the foremost victims of modern ills. Divorce and separation, his dominant metaphors in *Hard Times*, clearly signify difficulties impending for the human spirit; they are also a desperate remedy, a means for wresting Louisa Gradgrind away from Bounderby, keeping Tom out of Bitzer's clutches, and rescuing Stephen Blackpool from Slackbridge, Bounderby, Coketown, and a drunken spouse. Having seen Preston and Manchester, the popular champion of home and hearth actually condones—in fact, encourages—disconnection. Showing the erosion of basic relationships and a consequent desire to sever them was Dickens's idea of effective anti-Benthamite satire. *Hard Times* foretells what happens when self-interest and devotion to progress through science and industry replace love as a cohesive and motivating force: husbands and wives relate to one another no better than masters and men. In depicting the deterioration of conjugal relationships, Dickens perfected a subversive tactic for heading off novelists like Mrs. Gaskell. When she responds to Coketown with a coalescing society, marriage—always her presiding metaphor—serves as the narrative's climax and goal.

Realistic novelists, Mrs. Gaskell contends, must teach the "great outer life" (in E.M. Forster's words)—the world of class struggles and disagreements between labor and management—to obey the same guidelines that apply to long-term friendships and happy marriage. Forster's epigraph for *Howard's End*, the exhortation "Only connect," sums up Mrs. Gaskell's pervasive theme. She wants to improve connections between individuals of different economic status, and between the arts and the world of "telegrams and anger."[12] On more than one occasion, Miss Hale sounds like Forster's Mrs. Moore. She instructs Thornton that "God has made us so that we must be mutually dependent" (NS, 169), just as Forster's idea of a modern saint insists that "God has put us on earth in order to be pleasant to each other."[13]

Mutual dependence is implicit in Mrs. Gaskell's title, and acts of connection abound in *North and South*. As opposed to Coketown, where laboring people regard churches (all "eighteen religious-persuasions") as an encroachment on the week's lone holiday rather than a source of comfort (HT, 17-18), in Mrs. Gaskell's novel an ex-minister and his daughter effect a remarkable communion: "Margaret the Churchwoman, her father the Dissenter, Higgins the Infidel, knelt down together" (NS, 297). Despite religious overtones, the prayer scene illustrates a Bloomsbury thesis, predominantly secular and humanistic, that Thornton and Higgins later jointly propound: in industrial Milton, just as in Wordsworth's Cumberland, differences of opinion are external and resolvable because "we have all of us one human heart" (NS, 511).[14]

Dickens anticipates the Lawrencian proposition that the bloodless philosophy of industrialism will devitalize interpersonal ties and weaken the overall social structure. His thesis can be deduced from chapters titled "Father and Daughter," "Husband and Wife," "Men and Brothers," and "Men and Masters," which show these essential relationships falling apart under new economic stress.

One result is likely to be an atrophy of body and soul, a catastrophe already in progress in Coketown and recognizable subsequently to modern readers in Lawrence's fictionalizations of Nottingham. As Fact continues to intrude upon Fancy, as business values seep deeper into imaginative and emotional life, "the heart of infancy," Dickens predicts, "will wither up, the sturdiest physical manhood will be morally stark death (HT, 226)—a Lawrencian forecast indeed. Dickens's advocacy of "a wisdom of the Heart" over a "Wisdom of the Head" does not make him anti-intellectual; it expresses reservations about the supremacy of scientific thinking and the splendors of evolution that look forward to Lawrence's murkier yet equally anti-Utilitarian support for older ways of knowing: a wisdom of the blood.

An industrial milieu—servitude to machines—has not dehumanized the "men of Milton," however; they display undiminished sexuality by indulging in "loud laughs and jests" (NS, 110). Millworkers whom Margaret passes in the streets express their good spirits by commenting on her looks in an "open, fearless manner," and Mrs. Gaskell accepts such improper conduct as a genuine tribute: admiration for a pretty girl exercises a resilient aesthetic sense, spontaneous even in a lowering environment. Margaret soon realizes that "outspokenness" in these men indicates "their innocence of any intention to hurt her delicacy." Her fateful encounter with Higgins takes place only because this perfect stranger compliments her on having "such a bonny face" (NS, 111). In *Lady Chatterley's Lover*, Connie drives past "weird, distorted" steelworkers and sees miners heading home from the pits "one shoulder higher than the other." These trolls, "creatures from another reality" than Mrs. Gaskell's, make Connie "absolutely afraid of the industrial masses." She recalls her dread, on a prior occasion, of "passing little gangs of colliers who stood and stared," vulgar and resentful, "without either salute or anything else."[15]

Dickens's workers yearn for "physical relief—some relaxation, encouraging good humour and good spirits, and giving them a vent" (HT, 19). Moderns interpret such "craving" as a need for stronger sexual self-expression. But Milton's work force has little in common either with Coketown's "stunted and crooked" laborers or with Lawrence's "unshapely colliers," in whom "the living intuitive faculty" (an elaboration on Dickens's concept of Fancy) has gone "dead as nails."[16] In Milton-Northern, the "physical manhood" Dickens is worried about survives sturdy and unimpaired.

Mrs. Gaskell's strong characters are admirable from the moment they appear. Nevertheless, Higgins, Margaret, and Thornton, with their propensity to interconnect, repair each other's deficiencies. They bring one another more fully alive, closer to excellence. In this regard, they parody Blackpool, Bounderby, and Louisa, none of whom alters either of the others for the better.

Each member of Mrs. Gaskell's trio adapts willingly to change and seems eager for life to press forward. Higgins and Thornton learn about labor and capital from each other. Thornton acquires the beginnings of an aesthetic sense from Margaret; Higgins reacquires a religious one; both men become better acquainted with civilization's past. Margaret and her father learn about the present and discover the importance of practical affairs. Miss Hale finds that fostering progress is one's sacred duty in life, and that the world of manufacturing and commerce possesses a beauty all its own.

Later, a firmer grasp of evolutionary theory enables George Eliot to develop further this beneficial exchanging of characteristics. When the Frenchified Esther Lyon marries the radical artisan and dedicated reformer Felix Holt, the marriage emphasizes cooperation on a scale broader than the economic. George Eliot amplifies Mrs. Gaskell's belief that progressive individuals, whose common interest is the evolution of mankind, must transcend dissimilar cultural backgrounds. *Middlemarch* celebrates a maturing social system energized by the interplay of diverse personalities whose different strengths and points of view gradually prove complementary.

The phenomenon George Eliot calls "the onward tendency in human things," the latent energy responsible for the evolution of personality through social interconnections, already permeates *North and South*, whereas Dickens's prophecy of bodily and spiritual atrophy for Coketown is skeptical of inherent upward exertion and can be said to discount it. So does the indictment of England's stagnant legal and political system in the novel before *Hard Times*. Although Dickens contributes to the secularization of Victorian life in numerous ways, his later novels prohibit any easy blending of humanism with evolutionary hypotheses. His social satire stands out against a scientific sociology that sees reform and evolution as mutually corroborative, virtually inevitable movements promising temporal salvation through continued social progress—a brand of Victorian realism that began to flourish in the 1850s (taking Dickens for its butt) and is often mistakenly equated with realism per se.

Mrs. Gaskell seizes upon evolution, a theory much discussed for at least a decade before *The Origin of Species*,[17] to justify her enthusiasm for places like Manchester. The industrial 1850s exhilarate her as a large step forward on behalf of civilization; innovations like the ones she prescribes for Marlborough Mills are presented as part of a virtual shift onto higher plateaus of existence. Mrs. Gaskell proceeds as if an implicit connection exists between enlightened self-interest, laissez-faire economics, and the emergence of the fittest—who, she optimistically assumes, are invariably best. "Domination . . . by . . . manufacturers," the prospect that outraged Dickens, does not alarm Mrs. Gaskell, who views it as another case of success for the able. That is how she presents her cotton magnate's rise, although, thanks to Margaret Hale, Thornton accepts greater responsibility for weaker specimens.

As Higgins, Thornton, and Miss Hale interconnect, they become variations in the Darwinian sense, positive modifications of the human type. They will help life to break out of old molds. Whereas the marriage of Bounderby and Louisa, without issue, is a dead end for both, the forthcoming union of Margaret and Thornton will transmit to future generations the favorable changes each produces in the other's temperament; this wedding of old and new pays tribute to natural selection for reaffirming the significance of traditional relationships.

Mrs. Gaskell's conception of evolution is martial as well as marital, but there is no contradiction. The real fighting in *North and South* begins after Margaret and Thornton make peace. Improved human relations bring different types together so that they can proceed with "the world's great battle" (NS, 348)—which is not animosity between Fact and Fancy or masters and men (trumped-up conflict, according to Mrs. Gaskell) but the scientific and economic contest that matches one man's inventive mind against another's in what is ultimately a joint attack upon the real enemy: a resistant material world.

Middlemarch and *Felix Holt* treat the momentum for reform, building since the 1830s, as a steady rhythm underlying modern secular life. George Eliot elevates her vision of social change into a binding natural law, a perfective principle within the nature of things. Her rendition of evolution as *organic* unfolding modifies the militarism in Mrs. Gaskell's prefiguration of social Darwinism. Eliot also links evolution with England's pastoral past, which an organic progression continues metaphorically despite new mines and industries, and thus accomplishes a second objective: cancellation of the ironic agronomy in *Hard Times*. "Sowing," "Reaping," and

"Garnering"—events Dickens announces in the book titles for *Hard Times*—apply the parable of the sower chiefly to Thomas Gradgrind. But the harvest George Eliot promises is a better life for all.

North and South comes to rest firmly on a traditional marriage, in which, however, the woman, as mediatrix, also organizes an acceptable *ménage à trois*. Mrs. Gaskell's secular trinity features Margaret (Culture) as the bond between her husband Thornton (Business) and her friend Higgins (Labor). This grouping serves as a healthy corrective for the unwholesome triangles that abound in *Hard Times*: Louisa, Bounderby, and Harthouse; Stephen, his wife, and Rachael; Bounderby, Louisa, and Mrs. Sparsit. Dixon regrets that "there are no longer any saints on earth" (NS, 520). Mrs. Hale's servant neglects the likelihood that Higgins, Thornton, and Miss Hale are slated to become secular patron saints of the industrial revolution. They eclipse the martyred Blackpool, the self-canonizing Josiah Bounderby, and the improbable Sissy Jupe.

Margaret Hale, Mrs. Gaskell's ideal Victorian woman, is a combination of Louisa Gradgrind and Sissy Jupe. More capable than the resourceless Louisa, she is also better equipped than Sissy, whose lack of formal training makes Dickens's idea of Fancy (the sympathetic imagination) seem synonymous with simplicity of mind. Thornton, not merely an alternative vision of Dickens's industrialist, studies classics under Mr. Hale so that he can unite the culture of the past with the scientific future. He will combine Bounderby's influence as the owner of a mill with the mind-broadening erudition that a shiftless Harthouse wastes on eloquent political speeches. Nearly as versatile, Higgins adds a highly developed moral sense (like Blackpool's) to the ability to mobilize one's fellows (like Slackbridge's).

A reunification of Dickens's counterpoints is therefore not apparent in only the pledging of Margaret Hale to Mr. Thornton, each standing for a different locale and its set of values. It is also evident in Mrs. Gaskell's formula for repairing Dickens's major characters. Each of her revisions of his *dramatis personae* joins two inadequate characters into a prototype of the more fully developed personality necessary in the scientific-industrial future. Like George Eliot's Esther Lyon, Mrs. Gaskell's characters are supposed to impress the reader as higher forms of life than Dickens's creations. In addition to correcting each other's shortcomings, Higgins, Margaret, and Thornton reconstruct the complementary strengths Dickens splits up among a hapless cast to illustrate how far he thinks the qualities Mrs. Gaskell wants to realign have been driven apart.

In Nicholas Higgins, Mrs. Gaskell imagines an effective organizer to place over against Slackbridge's demagoguery and Blackpool's helplessness. She fixes the split Dickens caused when he divided know-how, which Slackbridge possesses, from "perfect integrity" (HT, 49), Stephen's strongpoint. A competent, compassionate Higgins evens up the one-sided confrontation in Dickens's novel between powerful owners and powerless workers. Higgins adds mental stature to Dickens's characterization of the average workingman as a befuddled loom-weaver. Mrs. Gaskell's revaluation of *Hard Times* rekindles hopes for enlightened unionists, an articulate working class, and the revival of brotherhood.

Bounderby warns Stephen, at their first interview, not to call the institutions of his country "a muddle." In the second, Blackpool is fired by Bounderby for defending the class that has ostracized him. No wonder Stephen concludes, after just one talk with his boss, that "a black impassable world" (HT, 116) separates workers and owners, whether the latter oppress or neglect the former. "Who can look on't, Sir, and fairly tell a man 'tis not a muddle?" Stephen inquires of Bounderby (HT, 114). He is referring to the industrial system and, by extension, life in general.

Blackpool's famous speech and his frustrating encounters with Bounderby are rewritten in *North and South* to neutralize their negative import. After the strike collapses, Higgins, as ringleader, is denied a place by Hamper, his former employer. Having suffered deprivation along with his men, he is singled out for special punishment when they are permitted to return. "For sure," he laments, "th' world is in a confusion that passes me or any other man to understand" (NS, 382). At Margaret's insistence, however, Higgins petitions Thornton for work. Bounderby dismisses Blackpool, but Thornton hires Higgins; together they begin to cross the allegedly "impassable" gulf between master and man that Slackbridge, as his name implies, was incapable of spanning.

In *A Passage to India*, Fielding and Mrs. Moore wonder whether life is "mystery" or "muddle."[18] Blackpool's sentiments, which are clearly Dickens's also, favor "muddle," a contradiction of reason and form that goes all the way to life's core. But Higgins's "confusion" rephrases Blackpool's despair: the biblical-sounding phraseology suggests puzzlement over a "mystery." Life is a problem still to be solved, not a quandary in which proceedings are always marred by a fundamental perverseness.

Higgins waits five hours for a word with Thornton, and their first interview terminates disastrously when two strong personalities collide. Learning that the unionist had given an accurate account of his actions during the strike, however, the manufacturer precipitates a second conversation by going to Higgins's home, where the millowner's wealth and position are less apparent. Ensuing discussion resolves their differences and ends with "Making Friends" (Chapter 39). In contrast, Bounderby summons Stephen to their second meeting as a lord would a slave, and by the end of the "Men and Masters" chapter, they are not even related as employer to employee.

Instead of an alcoholic wife, Mrs. Gaskell burdens Higgins with a dying daughter. Bessy's lungs have been ruined by cotton fluff ingested on her job in the carding room. When Stephen attempts to rid himself of his unnamed spouse, "a disabled, drunken creature" (HT, 52) no longer employable, he discovers there is "No Way Out" (Part One, Chapter 11) either from his "misfortnet" marriage or from the power of life and death that negligent masters exercise over their dependents. Higgins and Bessy, by comparison, accept their bad luck without undue rancor.

Dickens considers it "doubtful" whether Coketown's "millers" are "quite justified in chopping people up with their machinery" (HT, 84). If, however, the struggle of technology against matter is a "battle," as Thornton insists, casualties are inevitable. In war, Mrs. Gaskell recognizes, statistics tell the true story: provided that losses are kept to a minimum and goals reached, one claims victory. People like Bessy must learn to view themselves as soldiers who fall in a good cause. Contrary to the hopelessness of the Sartrean title "No Way Out," direction in *North and South* is forward at all costs. "Exceptions" like Bessy, Mrs. Gaskell tells Dickens and the general public, must be "gently lifted aside out of the roadway of the conqueror"—Thornton as the Caesar of manufacturing—"whom they have no power to accompany on his march" (NS, 108) toward a better future.

The disease that kills Bessy resembles the consumption many nineteen-year-old Victorian girls contracted even without setting foot inside a cotton mill. On one hand, then, Bessy is an exception; on the other, her death is not all that extraordinary. Moreover, Higgins's daughter expires gracefully like Little Nell, of whom she is a slightly older version. The emotional release that Victorian readers enjoyed when weeping over Dickens's child-woman, rather than a reformer's indignation, is an appropriate response to factory-caused fatalities, which then become tolerable. "I shall have a spring where I'm boun to, and flowers, and amaranths, and shining robes besides," Bessy informs Margaret (NS, 112). Bessy is too frail to withstand the rigors of industrial progress, the argument goes, just as Nell was too good for this world. Both go to a better place, and Bessy's reward in the next world exonerates the mills in this. Just as Higgins is Blackpool plus Slackbridge, Bessy is Stephen's wife redone as Little Nell, but dying of specified ailments for a defensible cause.

Leaving Helstone for Milton-Northern, Margaret Hale also enters another world. She reenacts the crucial transition that Western society had just undergone from an agrarian to an industrial mode of life, reversing Bessy's fate and compensating for it. Miss Hale leaves "old worn grooves" (NS, 122) to take part in the dynamic future; the change, Mrs. Gaskell maintains, is the making of her. Consequent improvements in Margaret's character substantiate on a personal basis the new myth for Western civilization: technology and its servants—men like Thornton in cities like Milton-Northern—are bringing society closer to the threshold of perfection. A similar environment denies self-fulfillment to Dickens's females. Mrs. Gradgrind, Mrs. Pegler, Rachael, Sissy, and Louisa all find their womanly affections—as mother, sister, wife, daughter—frustrated and abused.

Although many of Margaret's actions in *North and South* deserve to be called heroic, her greatest triumphs occur in scenes that revise Dickens. Louisa Gradgrind never enters Blackpool's house until after he has been fired, but Margaret is familiar with Higgins's home long before he is out of work. She befriends and nurses his daughter more effectively than Rachael looks after Stephen's wife. During Stephen's second interview with Bounderby, he addresses himself instinctively to Louisa's kind nature, only to be dismissed anyway. Louisa yearns to be "serviceable" (HT, 121), but her assistance does not extend beyond the loan of two pounds that allows Stephen to leave Coketown on the journey that leads to his death. Margaret dissuades Nicholas from heading south and is instrumental in getting him hired by Thornton. No one can keep Stephen's wife sober, but Margaret blocks the doorway to prevent Higgins from resorting to drink after Bessy's death.

Margaret Hale successfully intercedes between Thornton and Higgins because she matures rapidly upon arriving in Milton-Northern. In the early going, she is a terrible prig: she looks down on "shoppy people" and refers to influential manufacturers as "tradesmen" (NS, 50, 102), considering Thornton a man beneath her family's "standard of cultivation" and "tainted by his position as a Milton manufacturer" (NS, 129). Thornton thinks she has the aloofness of an "empress," which is not entirely a compliment; she makes him feel like "a great rough fellow, with not a grace or a refinement about him" (NS, 99-100). In the context of Manchester, Margaret is like Jane Austen's heroines at Longbourn or Highbury: an admirable young woman whose perceptions need sharpening. She personifies the snobbishness that blinds southerners generally, southern artists especially, and Dickens in particular to the merits of the North.

Miss Hale's education assumes the un-Austen-like form of an introduction to the cotton industry. She is increasingly impressed, recognizing the progressiveness of the "cotton-lords" as a "kind of fine intoxication" (NS, 217). Unlike the drunkenness of Stephen's wife, the sensation Margaret experiences through contact with the industrial system elates her.

Margaret's growth in usefulness and awareness can be called, in reprimand to Dickens, a tribute to Fancy. The sympathetic imagination, seeing life through another's eyes, performs well in an industrial environment and seems nurtured by it. Dickens's imagination failed to notice Manchester's positive features, but Margaret responds warmly to Higgins, Bessy, and Thornton, three examples of humanity hitherto beyond her ken. As Higgins rightly observes, "North and South has both met and made kind o' friends in this big smoky place" (NS, 112).

By the time Margaret persuades Thornton and Higgins to "have a good talk" (NS, 293), she has eclipsed Emma Woodhouse. Uniting master and man, she becomes a new kind of matchmaker in Victorian fiction. With the real world of laboring Manchester as setting, Margaret adopts the superior medium that later belongs to percipient individuals like Virginia Woolf's Mrs. Ramsay, whose forte is dinner parties. Margaret's is a sensibility that modern industrial societies need more urgently than books or paintings: like Mrs. Ramsay, she is an artist who orchestrates interpersonal relations, doing in real life what Mrs. Gaskell can accomplish only in novels and Dickens not at all.

Louisa Gradgrind's "starved imagination," exposed exclusively to ugliness, is a "fire" with "nothing to burn" (HT, 10); she cannot get out of Coketown even in her mind. Margaret is not permitted to remain at Helstone, but Mrs. Gaskell presents her story as a parody of Louisa's dilemma. *Hard Times* begins in the prisonhouse of Gradgrindian educational theory; *North and South* starts in the palace of art, which it quickly forsakes for the workshops of the world. It commences with Margaret trying to rouse Edith, who looks like "Titania" and awakens "like the Sleeping Beauty" (NS, 35, 40). The storybook atmosphere increases when Henry Lennox refers to "Cinderella's godmother" as the ideal organizer for Edith's upcoming wedding. Helstone resembles "a village . . . in one of Tennyson's poems"; its trees sprout "crimson and amber foliage" (NS, 42, 60). In short, Margaret initially inhabits the kind of fairytale world— charming but pointless, in Mrs. Gaskell's estimation—that Dickens makes Louisa and her peers hunger for.

Summoned to play an active role in the affairs of men, Margaret will not waste her life assisting women like Mrs. Shaw to marry off their daughters, the stuff of countless Victorian novels. *North and South* opens in Jane Austen's world, which it rapidly dismisses as timid and uninteresting; moving to Dickens's, it finds his satire against places like Manchester so unfair that it must rewrite *Hard Times* extensively. Mrs. Gaskell parodies *Hard Times* and women novelists simultaneously when she reveals the romance to be found in industrialism by fashioning an industrial romance. Love between hero and heroine must overcome Margaret's southern prejudice against trade and Thornton's northern pride in wealth and power amassed through personal effort. These are palpable obstacles from contemporary life, formidable impediments to England's social progress. Reconciling them is more important than providing fuel for Louisa's mental life or a sensible husband for Elizabeth Bennett.

Mrs. Gaskell embarrasses Dickens further by rewriting the fairytales her rival admired and putting the revisions in the very contexts he maintained would destroy them. Margaret's involvement with Thornton, a "great rough fellow," retains subterranean allusions to Beauty and the Beast. Being poor initially, Margaret is Cinderella to this cotton-lord. She is also Sleeping Beauty, sexually and intellectually awakened to life's possibilities by a robust Prince Charming. Miss Hale, more than Sissy Jupe, deserves the latter's appelative: "a good fairy" (HT, 210). She is Thornton's fairy godmother, replacing his real mother, the possessive Mrs. Thornton, and staving off ruin with her marriage portion. *North and South* is both a bluebook on industrialism and a new fairytale for Victorian England. Romantic yet realistic, it answers Dickens's call for infusions of Fancy into the domain of Fact.

Under the influence of a Beatrice and Vergil (Margaret and Mr. Hale) and as a result of negotiating with Higgins man-to-man, Thornton also matures abundantly. He never renounces objections to government interference but acquires greater personal interest in his men. This leads to a reformer's concern for the entire manufacturing system, on which, he realizes, the country's welfare—not just his own—depends. At novel's end, Thornton is a wonderful composite: a laissez-faire industrialist and an extensive redoing of Bounderby, whom he excels from the start, he develops Owenite socialist tendencies; he also anticipates Henry Ford's glorification of the innovative factory owner as the best-qualified reorganizer for society at large.

Mrs. Gaskell revises Dickens's notion of the Victorian businessman (Mr. Dombey) as an unmarriageable icicle. Thornton is neither a sexual imbecile (Bounderby) nor an incapacitated lover (Clifford Chatterley); his vigor has not been reduced or perverted by his fondness for machinery. Although Thornton is never a tightwad, his generosity, once he falls in love with Margaret, outclasses Scrooge's after the miser has seen the light. The new dining room Thornton authorizes for Marlborough Mills hardly compares with Pickwick's successes at Dingley Dell or the Cratchit household on Christmas day; still, it is engineered to transcend both: Thornton's proposal will work year round, not just on special occasions. It is more practical, therefore more realistic than Dickens's jollifications.

When first confronted by Blackpool, a gourmanding Bounderby is "at lunch on chop and sherry." He accuses laborers of wanting "to be fed on turtle soup and venison, with a gold spoon" (HT, 54). The inequality of their respective positions—one man standing, the other seated and eating—could not be clearer: here truly are Dives and Lazarus. Bounderby's culinary fantasy of workers with epicurean tastes and Trimalchio's diet undermines his reputation as a man of facts. Mrs. Gaskell rewrites this incriminating scene by having Thornton inform Mr. Bell that he is "building a dining-room—for the men" (NS, 444). He and Higgins already sponsor a communal kitchen in the mill. They buy "a good quantity of provisions wholesale" and serve "hot dinners" that enhance the quality of the workmen's lives and improve their on-the-job performance. The new dining hall will institutionalize the existing communal kitchen.

As "club steward," Thornton does the purchasing and hires the cook; the men determine the menu and manage the operation. When a committee of laborers invites Thornton "to take a snack" with them, the "hot-pot" eaten is neither chop nor venison, but the millowner praises it as one of the best dinners he has ever tasted. Mr. Bell imagines there must be "rather a restraint" on conversation. But Thornton, speaking for Mrs. Gaskell's Bloomsbury thesis, insists that he is "getting really to know" his men and that "they talk pretty freely" to one another: "Nothing like the act of eating for equalizing men," Thornton concludes (NS, 446), as if replying not just to Bell but to Bounderby and Dickens as well.

The "experiment" with a communal kitchen and dining room introduces a family atmosphere at the cotton mill and turns Dickens's reverence for sacramental feasts against him. Mrs. Gaskell revitalizes the humanizing secular rituals that moderns dislike in Dickens's early novels but which his later books, agnostic in this regard, seem less eager to trust as religious surrogates.

Unlike Mrs. Sparsit, who claims to be "highly connected," Bounderby brags that he has "no connexions at all" (HT, 36). Connection as rapport, the concept behind Thornton's new dining room, holds little appeal for Dickens's millowner and aristocratic housekeeper. As a result, Blackpool's "dying prayer"—"that aw th' world may on'y coom together more, an' get a better unnerstan'in o' one another" (HT, 207)—will probably go unanswered.

In *North and South*, the weaver's last words are transferred to Thornton, who rephrases them as an article of the progressive industrialist's creed: he informs Colthurst that institutions fail unless they "bring the individuals of the different classes into actual personal contact. Such intercourse is the very breath of life" (NS, 525). More imaginatively than Henry Ford, Thornton envisions the factory as a perfect laboratory for experiments in reorganizing society; he is interested in exploring novel methods of fraternization between diverse social groups, methods the nation itself may subsequently imitate. The mill, Thornton maintains, is a place where masters and men can be "both unconsciously and consciously teaching each other" (NS, 524).

From the moment of introduction, Bounderby's fraudulence as both master and man is readily apparent. Dickens presents Bounderby's questionable masculinity as both proof and consequence of his incompetence as a master. Bounderby is

a rich man: banker, merchant, manufacturer, and what not. A big, loud man, with a stare, and a metallic laugh. A man made out of coarse material. . . . A man with a great puffed head and forehead, swelled veins in his temples, and such a strained skin to his face that it seemed to hold his eyes open, and lift his eyebrows up. A man with a pervading appearance on him of being inflated like a balloon. . . . A man who could never sufficiently vaunt himself a self-made man. A man who was always proclaiming, through that brassy speaking-trumpet of a voice of his, his old ignorance and his old poverty. A man who was the Bully of humility. [HT, 11]

Bounderby's domineering nature, his total disregard for refinement, turns the emergence of manufacturers into a cultural setback. The "puffed head," "swelled veins," "strained skin," and, above all, the appearance of "being inflated like a balloon" suggest misplaced erection. Although Bounderby inflates his ego incessantly, he has, perhaps as a consequence, a flaccid penis. His head swells and a torrent of masturbatory self-praise pours from his mouth, yet "the Bully" is no more able to reproduce than Clifford Chatterley; hence, he is a biological blind alley.

Mrs. Gaskell repairs Dickens's caricature of a northern manufacturer step by step. Margaret, suddenly looking up from her work, is struck by

the difference . . . between her father and Mr Thornton, as betokening such distinctly opposite natures. Her father was of slight figure, which made him appear taller than he really was, when not contrasted, as at this time, with the tall, massive frame of another. The lines in her father's face were soft and waving, with a frequent undulating kind of trembling movement passing over them, showing every fluctuating emotion; the eyelids were large and arched, giving to the eyes a peculiar languid beauty which was almost feminine. The brows were finely arched, but were, by the very size of the dreamy lids, raised to a considerable distance from the eyes. Now, in Mr Thornton's face the straight brows fell low over the clear, deep-set earnest eyes, which, without being unpleasantly sharp, seemed intent enough to penetrate into the very heart and core of what he was looking at. The lines in the face were few but firm, as if they were carved in marble, and lay principally about the lips, which were slightly compressed over a set of teeth so faultless and beautiful as to give the effect of sudden sunlight when the rare bright smile, coming in an instant and shining out of the eyes, changed the whole look from the severe and resolved expression of a man ready to do and dare everything, to the keen honest enjoyment of the moment, which is seldom shown so fearlessly and instantaneously except by children. Margaret liked this smile; it was the first thing she had admired in this new friend of her father's; and the opposition of character, shown in all these details of appearance she had just been noticing, seemed to explain the attraction they evidently felt towards each other. [NS, 121]

Thornton's "tall" and "massive" frame is not coarse or vulgar. His "deep-set" eyes and "straight" eyebrows suggest a capacity for penetration that not only connotes above-average intelligence but also comments upon Bounderby's sexual impotence. Lines in Thornton's face are "firm." His teeth, another masculine attribute, are "faultless," dazzling like "sudden sunlight" when he smiles. Bounderby always overshadows company, but a radiant Thornton emits heat and light.

Machinery, Mrs. Gaskell argues, does not make the laugh "metallic" and the sex organs limp. Margaret's beauty readily brings to life passionate elements in Thornton's previously businesslike demeanor. When she throws her arms around him as a shield against the rioters, each begins to summon the other in a fashion Lawrence uses to distinguish Connie and Mellors from inauthentic lovers. If Bounderby's tag name indicates the caddishness of industrialists, whether in bed or at work, Thornton's contains sexual implications of weight and sharpness that have nothing to do with his occasional prickliness of temperament.

Dickens makes Bounderby anti-life in the Lawrencian sense, virtually sexless himself and a threat to the potency of others. *Hard Times* posits a connection between Fancy, the ability to sympathize imaginatively, and sexual vitality. A person who cannot conceive what it would be like to be another cannot love. Thus Sissy Jupe, ineducable from the Utilitarian standpoint but sorry for the starving poor regardless of how great or how few their number, is the novel's only potential child-bearer. Like Lawrence, Dickens sees the industrial drive and the sex urge as deadly foes, but Mrs. Gaskell links manufacturing prowess with procreative energy.

Margaret recognizes Thornton's forcefulness early on and is physically attracted to him in spite of herself. After rejecting his first marriage proposal, she finds herself "under the fascination of some great power." Thornton's "deep intent passionate eyes" have the sort of "flames" (NS,

257) in them that Lawrence likes to reserve for the orbs and loins of Cipriano and Mellors, the first an Oxford-educated Mexican Indian (learned yet primitive and vital), the second a woodland gamekeeper uncorrupted by the collieries.

Besides serving as a revaluation of Bounderby, Thornton supplies Margaret with an example of manliness that is missing, by contrast, in her father. Using Hale as a foil for Thornton improves one's estimate of the North without demeaning the erstwhile clergyman; the juxtapositioning of Bounderby and Gradgrind in the first four chapters of *Hard Times* merely reveals detestable variations of unfortunate economic attitudes. An energizer physically as well as commercially, Thornton blends the resolution of Dickens's iron master, Mr. Rouncewell, with the virility of Charlotte Brontë's Rochester. He declares that he is "made of iron" (NS, 274), in contrast to Bounderby, who is full of air. Thornton is Mrs. Gaskell's reaction to Dickens's charge that manufacturers are a new class of parasite, vastly more harmful than con men (Jingle), hypocrites (Pecksniff), predatory lawyers (Vholes), or archconservatives (Sir Leicester).

Thornton and Hale are like Morlock and Eloi, but the contrast is not uncomplimentary to the former as it would be in H.G. Wells. Hale's delicate face and high forehead resemble a piece of china, pretty but fragile. Thornton, whose brows fall "low" over "deep-set" eyes, is a throwback to fundamental strengths the South has lost or outgrown. Thornton boasts that in his part of England the "Teutonic blood" is "little mingled" compared to the way it has thinned out further south (NS, 413-14). Such blood fits a man for life as Thornton insists it be redefined: "a time of action and exertion."

The atavismus in Thornton is also the harbinger. Like Lawrence's prescriptive heroes—none of whom, however, is an industrialist—Thornton possesses valuable reserves, or preserves abilities, that guarantee him the future. Simplicity and directness, the severe expression that easily becomes a smile of childlike enjoyment, make Thornton less refined, less specialized, thus more suited to grow rapidly in new directions. Mrs. Gaskell thinks that Thornton rightly proclaims himself and his fellow masters "the great pioneers of civilization" (NS, 171). Yet when Thornton commissions himself a captain of industry in the "war which compels, and shall compel, all material powers to yield to science" (NS, 123), he steps back into the novels of Sir Walter Scott. The domination of mind over matter will be both a triumph for evolution and the conclusion of a modern crusade. Calling for "all material powers" to yield to the new monarch called "science" makes Thornton sound like Ivanhoe.

Margaret's comparative analysis of her father and his new friend means that opposites attract in Milton-Northern, and "opposition of character" and "opposite natures" are raw materials for marvelously productive associations. As Thornton resumes his long-interrupted study of Homer, Mrs. Gaskell rewrites the scenes in which M'Choakumchild foists Utilitarianism on young academia. She presents the useful intervention of classical education in the mature life of an industrial town. Thanks to Margaret's father, Thornton (who is building an empire of his own) will never literalize the imagination as Bounderby does in telling Mrs. Sparsit that "Rome wasn't built in a day, ma'm" and then adding "Nor yet in a week" (HT, 154).

Although they are always tutor and pupil, Hale and Thornton take turns at each role. The former learns about the coming age from the man to whom he is restoring the past; Thornton's explanations of the factory system enlarge Hale's understanding as effectively as instruction in Homer expands the manufacturer's sensibility. The exchanges between Thornton and the Hales reverse Sissy's triumph over M'Choakumchild: Thornton restates without irony propositions that Gradgrind's favorite pedagogue uses to test Sissy. He defends Milton against Margaret's objections and clinches the argument by citing his own life. The multiple advantages of industrialization easily outweigh reservations expressed by the newly arrived Hales.

Thornton is made to seem conscientious and self-policing, unlike Bounderby, who is irresponsible and self-serving. Manufacturing corporations, Dickens complains, protest that they are "ruined" if they are "required to send labouring children to school" or "when it [is] hinted that perhaps they need not always make quite so much smoke" (HT, 84). Thornton, however, educates Boucher's children and has "altered" his chimneys so that they consume their own discharge, doing so even before Parliament "meddled with the affair" and required it by law (NS, 123). Milton-Northern is still a "dirty town" in which Margaret must wash her hands several times before noon, but Thornton remains aware of the pollution he creates and seeks remedies. To him, laissez-faire means being left alone to solve his own problems.

Pretending to be literally self-made, Bounderby is a telling caricature of laissez-faire. Dickens considers the idea that people should do as they choose, especially in commerce, a travesty of independence. He subverts this economic principle by restating it biologically, as Huxley does in *Brave New World* with Ford's theory of mass production. Laissez-faire becomes the determination to exist without interference or cooperation from anyone else. Bounderby's attempt at ontological self-sufficiency is part of his repudiation of all connections. He even conceals the existence of his doting mother in order to break all ties. Actually, he absorbs, exploits, and consumes, like a balloon that must be pumped up with the life's breath of others.

Having read Bounderby's boasts about his lack of antecedents, Mrs. Gaskell disarms Dickens's satire by making Thornton highly conscious of his. Although the cotton-lord is largely responsible for his own rise, he has a mother whom he acknowledges from the start with "tender respect": "I had such a mother as few are blest with; a woman of strong power and firm resolve" (NS, 125, 126). Mrs. Thornton is not the humble nonentity to which Bounderby has reduced Mrs. Pegler. With "strong power and firm resolve," she can be as formidable as Mrs. Sparsit; the pride Mrs. Thornton takes in her son's affluence rivals the social superiority Mrs. Sparsit exudes as a former Powler. Mrs. Thornton is a combination of Mrs. Pegler and Mrs. Sparsit. As a redoing of the former, she attests to the fact that industrialists enter the world in the conventional manner; as the equal of the latter, she shows that the mother of a Manchester manufacturer has the right to be pleased with her station.

Mrs. Gaskell argues that the self-made man should be appreciated as a triumph for human nature, not a monstrous rejection of it. *North and South* proposes Thornton as a more realistic example than Bounderby of self-generated success. The Milton manufacturer's sufferings on the road to preeminence rival Bounderby's catalogue of early hardships but are never exploded as fabrications. After Thornton's father speculated wildly and failed, he committed suicide, leaving his losses to his son. Thornton "lived upon water-porridge for years" until, his father's creditors having been paid, he could start his own mill (NS, 129). To Harthouse and Tom Gradgrind, Bounderby brags of eating "in his youth at least three horses under the guise of polonies and saveloys" (HT, 100). The two diets sound equally preposterous, but it is people who know Thornton, not the man himself, who tell Margaret this story of lean years.

Mrs. Gaskell delivers her finest stroke of revaluative parody when she shows Thornton reluctant to recite his life story. Bounderby, speaking about himself as always, declares that "you may force him to swallow boiling fat, but you shall never force him to suppress the facts of his life" (HT, 13). The Coketown manufacturer trumpets "his old poverty" until listeners know the tale of his rise by heart. Not so with Thornton. Realizing that he "could best have illustrated what he wanted to say" to the Hales about the glories of the industrial system "by telling them something of his own life," he hesitates: "Was it not too personal a subject to speak about to strangers?" (NS, 125). Thornton must overcome a "touch of shyness that brought a momentary flush of color into his dark cheek" (NS,

126). The account he then gives of himself marks the beginning of Margaret's understanding that industry is neither degrading nor hopelessly mundane.

To meet his father's debts, Thornton left Milton to accept employment in a draper's shop at fifteen shillings a week. Of this amount, besides feeding his mother and sister, he saved one-fifth. Such discipline, he reports, taught him "self-denial," an economic principle no true proponent of laissez-faire respects. Mrs. Gaskell thinks that Thornton's exile and voluntary enslavement merit comparison with the labors of Hercules and the wanderings of Ulysses. Mr. Hale suggests as much when he wonders if "the heroic simplicity of the Homeric life" that Thornton studied briefly as a boy gave him "nerve" to persevere (NS, 127). The suggestion is aimed at Dickens's audience. Mrs. Gaskell wants them to recognize economic hardship, staunchly endured, not as a blot upon the factory system but as the new form of true heroism for the Victorian industrial age and to see through Bounderby's propensity to mythologize himself without cause.

Bounderby's autobiographical impulse is central to *Hard Times* and an obligatory target for Mrs. Gaskell's revaluations because a success story of such magnitude would prove that the system works for anyone with the requisite stamina. Were this tall tale true, Dickens tacitly concedes, the impartial industrial-economic process might be beyond reproof. Utilitarians would be justified in lobbying to keep it free of restraint. Wretches—Blackpool's wife, for example—would be not victims but failures, their miseries as self-made as Bounderby's good fortune. But when the contents of the Bully's *vita* turn out to be identical with a balloon's, current economics cease to be a competition fair to all. Lies told to defend a system suggest the falseness of the system itself. Bounderby's philosophy is not supported by "the facts of his life"—but Thornton's is. Mrs. Gaskell rewrites Bounderby's lies with Thornton's truths, and the industrial system is repaired.

Gradgrind and Bounderby, "both eminently practical," can "furnish . . . tabular statements" showing that poor, disgruntled workers are "a bad lot altogether" (HT, 18), consequently chiefly responsible for their own plight. "Any capitalist" in Coketown, Dickens writes, "who had made sixty thousand pounds out of sixpence, always professed to wonder why the sixty thousand nearest Hands didn't each make sixty thousand pounds out of sixpence, and more or less reproached them every one for not accomplishing the little feat" (HT, 90).

Thornton's views on failure are remarkably similar to those of the typical Coketown capitalist, but Mrs. Gaskell eliminates Dickens's bitter sarcasm. Milton-Northern's cotton-lord dubs "all who are unsuccessful in raising themselves"—Margaret's euphemism for losers—"their own worst enemies": "It is one of the great beauties of our system, that a working-man may raise himself into the power and position of a master by his own exertions and behaviour; that, in fact, every one who rules himself to decency and sobriety of conduct, and attention to his duties, comes over to our ranks; it may not be always as a master, but as an overlooker, a cashier, a book-keeper, a clerk, one on the side of authority and order" (NS, 125).

Thornton's life story teaches that factory administration—if not ownership—is as open to hard workers with talent as any other profession with a strenuous apprenticeship. One need not turn sixpence into sixty thousand pounds to escape the rigors of a laborer's life; many raise themselves into management's ranks—"the side of authority and order"—by earning supervisory positions that require decency, sobriety, and attention but no outlay of capital.

Mrs. Gaskell regards herself as a progressive humanist, more honest than Dickens. Just as she accepts Bessy's death from fluff inhalation, she has Thornton refuse to let a few grim facts—the wasted lives of "unsuccessful" individuals—obscure the virtues of the nation's manufacturing operation; only sentimentalists like Dickens do that. The problem with emphasizing the country's strengths as its "great beauties," Dickens lets Sissy intuit, is that failures suffer just as much no matter what percentage of the population they constitute. Looking at society on such terms, Mrs. Gaskell replies, renders worthless any thriving community not absolutely perfect. A society with twenty-five failures out of a "million million" inhabitants, to borrow M'Choakumchild's figuring, has to be preferable to one with twenty-five per one million.

Since "the Bully of humility" erupts in Chapter 4 of *Hard Times*, Book One, a modest and dutiful Thornton can be introduced as early as Chapter 10 of *North and South*. When Mrs. Pegler punctures Bounderby's myth of self-generation in Chapter 5 of Book Three, Dickens, having seen portions of Mrs. Gaskell's manuscript, appears to be hitting back. Mrs. Gaskell sets out to depict the filial devotion she believes manufacturers display as naturally as other men. Aware of this impending reply, Dickens seems to concede Mrs. Gaskell's point but actually rephrases it in order to restate his own. He observes, first, that industrialists are so anxious to cast off all controls that they would deny the mothers who bore them if they could get away with it, and second, that hard-hearted manufacturers, even though born normally, are likely to discard a parent as callously as they turn away a disabled laborer whose services are no longer needed. If Dickens is reacting to a rejoinder from Mrs. Gaskell not yet in print, the chronology that places

North and South after *Hard Times* obscures, in this instance, the extent of the exchange.

From Mrs. Gaskell's point of view, Dickens could not fully recoup; he must come round to showing that the self-made man usually receives invaluable maternal encouragement. The gap between Thornton and Bounderby narrows in Mrs. Gaskell's direction, confirming her as the better realist. On the other side, exposing Bounderby as a phony was a stroke of genius too good for Dickens to pass up. Since he would be publishing first, he could emphasize the coldness of businessmen and cause Mrs. Gaskell's provision of a mother for Thornton—and his unembarrassed gratitude to her—to seem beside the point, the real issue being which seemed more credible in a large-scale manufacturer: Thornton's warmth or Bounderby's indifference.

Mrs. Gaskell's ambition is to deride Dickens repeatedly, extensively, and as soon as possible. But the hasty revaluator takes a chance analogous to the risk that popular dramatists had run, earlier in Dickens's career, by staging a novel before it completed its serial publication. Dickens could thwart imitators by disowning their endings with his; the death of Little Nell, for example, eviscerates Edward Sterling's play, which implied that the imperiled heroine would survive to marry Swiveller.[19] Similarly, Dickens could disarm revaluative parody of his satiric vision by lessening the discrepancy between his critique and a rival's premature retaliations.

"Parody" derives from the Greek *parōidia*, the counter-ode or satyr play put on by the same actors—now in grotesque costume—who had just appeared in a more serious drama. Dickens's rivals pretend that his satirical novels are no more realistic in their presentation of Victorian prospects than the counter-odes of classical theater; the problem is that works they see as lopsided have usurped the place that truer, more complex assessments of life should occupy. Thus Bounderby, a grotesque version of a Manchester manufacturer, misleads a public that has yet to see Thornton. Dickens's rivals reverse Athenian practice by concocting a new form of parody to supply the more ennobling works that once took precedence. These correctives—parodies or truthful redoings of Dickens's counter-odes—are to bring about renewed confidence in man and society.

But if the parodist fires before the target exists in final, printed form, later developments may accidentally if not consciously defuse revaluation. Using truth to undercut falsity means parodying a parody: negating a negative to return to something more constructive. This proves dangerous when works like *Hard Times* and *North and South* appear in quick succession and deal with similar locales. If the revaluing novelist revises too soon or too thoroughly (or both, in Mrs. Gaskell's case), the revaluation process automatically threatens to reverse itself. A kind of double vision results in which the novel being corrected also seems to be parodying its corrector.

Trollope and George Eliot learned from Mrs. Gaskell's close call. There was considerable delay between the exposé of Charterhouse in *Household Words* and the scrutiny of a provincial hospital in *The Warden*, and Trollope parodied an imaginary Dickens text that could not be misread as a counterstroke by the intended victim. Nor could *Bleak House*, which preceded *Felix Holt* and *Middlemarch* by fourteen and nineteen years respectively, be misapprehended as an attack on George Eliot's faith in society as a slowly evolving organism. Modifying Dickens's exaggerations or displacing him as an unrealistic irrelevance turned out to be both safer and more effective for Trollope and George Eliot than Mrs. Gaskell's heroic attempt at a point-by-point overhaul. In other words, if *The Warden* was the seminal and *Felix Holt* the classic instance of parodic revaluation, *North and South*, more exhaustive than either, was the most daring.

Coketown and Milton-Northern are the same place transformed into different worlds when drawn by rival social commentators. Mrs. Gaskell must contend with Dickens's disgust for the industrial landscape if she is to sustain her argument that civilization is taking a forward step.

Like D.H. Lawrence, Dickens shows an industrial center bringing a deathly visitation upon the countryside. The desolation they cause—"a blur of soot and smoke"—proves that new social processes, the rise of Fact and factory, are basically unnatural. "Seen from a distance," Dickens writes, "Coketown lay shrouded in a haze of its own, which appeared impervious to the sun's rays. You only knew the town was there, because you knew there could have been no such sulky blotch upon the prospect without a town. . . . Coketown in the distance [was] suggestive of itself, though not a brick of it could be seen" (HT, 84).

Coketown offends against nature because its pollution impedes the sun's rays. The impenetrability of the town's enveloping haze indicates that manufacturing and places where it is carried on are opposed to life itself. "Shrouded" like a corpse in the hellish grave of its own exhalations, Coketown dispenses with light and warmth. "Not a brick of it could be seen" because the town, ashamed of itself, prefers to remain invisible.

Mrs. Gaskell concedes the negative appearance of manufacturing towns but subtly repairs Dickens's satiric description as she does so. "For several miles before" Margaret and her father "reached Milton," their new home,

they saw a deep lead-coloured cloud hanging over the horizon in the direction in which it lay. It was all the darker from contrast with the pale gray-blue of the wintry sky. . . . Nearer the town, the air had a faint taste and smell of smoke; perhaps, after all, more a loss of the fragrance of grass and herbage than any positive taste or smell. Quick they were whirled over long, straight, hopeless streets of regularly-built houses, all small and of brick. Here and there a great oblong many-windowed factory stood up, like a hen among her chickens, puffing out black "unparliamentary" smoke, and sufficiently accounting for the cloud which Margaret had taken to foretell rain. [NS, 96]

Carefully, Mrs. Gaskell contrasts the "lead-coloured cloud" with "the pale gray-blue" winter sky. Far from obscuring the sun's rays entirely, Milton gives off a dark cloud that causes the sky to look brighter. The scene is almost pleasing, the product perhaps of an artist's skillful use of his palette. The "faint taste and smell of smoke" is hardly an actual presence but the absence of customary rural fragrances. "Straight hopeless" streets and uniform houses, cheerless though they seem, are harmless compared to samenesses in Coketown, where not only streets but people are "all very like one another"; where workers keep "the same hours," make "the same sound upon the same pavements," and "do the same work" (HT, 17).

Factories in Mrs. Gaskell's "Darkshire" town are not dark and dismal but "great oblong" structures, "many-windowed"; the Homeric epithet gives these buildings epic proportion. Agrarian imagery erases urban squalor: factories are "hens" around which the workers' houses cluster like "chickens"—in Mrs. Gaskell's industrial barnyard, towering edifices seem quite maternal. Black smoke emissions "sufficiently" account for the "lead-coloured cloud," as if explaining it away. Margaret mistakes the cloud for a sign of rain. Indeed, it is no more menacing or unnatural than a shower.

Dickens presents Coketown as a Gothic nightmare, a perverted fairy-land in which Gradgrind, an "Ogre" (HT, 7), and Bounderby, a self-inflating giant, distort normality. Coketown, Dickens writes, is colored an "unnatural red and black like the painted face of a savage" (HT, 17). "Serpents" of smoke uncoil from its chimneys. The town's "black canal" is outdone by its river, "purple with ill-smelling dye." As Dickens allows his imagination full rein, he preserves in the novel's prose the artistic sensibility that men of fact were allegedly attempting to extinguish.

Matthew Arnold's complaint that the modern age is "unpoetical"[20] can be explicated by the virtual précis of *Hard Times* that Wordsworth delivers in the 1845 edition of his poems: "Trade, commerce, and manufacturers have made our countrymen infinitely less sensible to movements of the imagination and fancy."[21] Dickens's surrealist Coketown is an attempt to be poetical in an anti-industrial novel that incorporates the disappointment of Arnold and Wordsworth. An abiding need for visual beauty readily acquires religious dimensions. Not only is Dickens's Fancy a faculty apparently located in heart and soul, but his call for "imaginative graces" (HT, 226) to suffuse a world of "machinery and reality" expresses a latent spirituality akin to Arnold's plea for more "sweetness and light." *Hard Times* speaks for those Victorian secular humanists who doubted that man's kingdom could ever be entirely of this world. Society cannot be getting better, Dickens surmises, if life grows uglier daily. His book challenges thinkers of Mrs. Gaskell's persuasion to show that truth and beauty have not become more dichotomous than ever.

Industrial towns, Mrs. Gaskell responds, improve upon better acquaintance, just as people do. She attempts to de-Gothicize Coketown: her Milton, with its red-blooded workmen, is down-to-earth, not at all terrifying. At the same time, she describes a Milton-Northern sublime enough to placate any poetic sensibility. After a dull life in a country parsonage, Mr. Hale soon discerns "something dazzling . . . in the energy which conquered immense difficulties with ease; the power of the machinery of Milton, the power of the men of Milton, impressed him with a sense of grandeur" (NS, 108). Energy and power impart to cotton mills a "grandeur" heretofore associated with storms, waterfalls, and mountains. The honest realist, Mrs. Gaskell contends, beholds in Milton-Northern an occasion for a new, more useful Romanticism based on appreciation of the human mind's inventiveness, its capacity to actualize its visions.

In *Hard Times*, the novelist is awestruck by a steam-engine's piston working up and down "like the head of an elephant" (HT, 17). Again Dickens permits his imagination full play but only to object that this weary machine resembles a mechanized animal; not surprisingly, it labors "in a state of melancholy madness." The mentality that devised it, Dickens suggests, might not hesitate to convert men into automatons. In *North and South*, Mrs. Gaskell corrects what she considers a paranoid misconception with a flight of fancy all her own: having heard Thornton explain "the magnificent power, yet delicate adjustment . . . of the steam-hammer," Mr. Hale recalls "wonderful stories of subservient genii in the Arabian Nights" (NS, 121-22).

The steam-hammer is an invention of man's brain, a product of his creativity; therefore, in Thornton's code of aesthetics, it ranks as one of the world's "marvels" (NS, 122); it can be appreciated just as fondly as a painting or poem. The elephant comparison suggests a natural world that is not so much evolving as being captured and enslaved, whereas the allusion to "subservient genii" posits the harnessing of hidden energy and invisible agencies. It shows science making real the spectacular achievements found hitherto mainly in fairy tales. Industrial technology, Mrs.

Gaskell maintains, will be a boon to poetry and culture; it will help man to realize his wildest dreams, not put an end to them. The golden age that poets dream about lies in the future, once the conquest of matter is completed. Mrs. Gaskell names her southern locale Helstone (hell/stone) to get even with Dickens for calling a northern city after an unpicturesque mineral; her representative industrial community bears the surname of England's greatest epic poet, further evidence that the coming state of affairs, a period of unparalleled dynamism, will not be "unpoetical."

The rivalry between *Hard Times* and *North and South* produces some of the finest ironies in the history of Victorian novel-writing. Mrs. Gaskell is certain she is redeeming social realism by parodying Dickens, yet she expends her ebullition in pointing out the Romantic side of factories and millowners. To let the air out of Bounderby, she pumps up Thornton. He would "rather be a man toiling, suffering—nay, failing and successless" in Milton "than lead a dull prosperous life . . . down in the South" (NS, 122). Such Faustian determination to keep on striving may be "rampant in its display, and savour of boasting," but unlike Bounderby's advertisements for himself, it seems "to defy the old limits of possibility" (NS, 217).

Dickens, on the other hand, maintains that he is rescuing Fancy—the creative imagination—from Fact but must argue that *Hard Times* is an instance of both. The novel that amounts to Dickens's defense of his craft also insists on being taken as a veritable blueprint for industrial reform. Dickens scours the creative imagination by exposing Utilitarians and laissez-faire economists as purveyors of fanciful aberrations; they are tellers of harmful fairytales about human nature and the constitution of societies. Dickens relishes the irony of being a prominent fictionist writing a satirical novel to explode "the fictions of Coketown" (HT, 90). These fictions, which include by extension all stories by a resident apologist praising an industrial metropolis, are not to be confused with unvarnished truths in his own disinterested novels.

Throughout *Hard Times*, the social critic enhances his veracity by charging that the "hard Fact fellows"—Utilitarians and capitalists—are self-promoters, propaganda artists who take greater liberties in perverting facts than novelists do. An accomplished liar, Bounderby is the best spinner of tall tales in Coketown. He tells Harthouse that smoke from the mills is "meat and drink," the "healthiest thing in the world in all respects, and particularly for the lungs" (HT, 96). In this regard, he prefigures the twisted imaginings of Clifford Chatterley, for whom "the very stale air of the colliery was better than oxygen."[22] Talking to Mrs. Gradgrind, Bounderby accelerates on cue from one lie to another, heaping detail upon detail like a dedicated realist. When he says he was "born in a ditch," she hopes it was a dry one; immediately, he fills it with "a foot of water." She hopes he did not catch cold; he replies that he "was born with inflammation of the lungs" (HT, 12).

The suppressed imagination, Dickens's point goes, is like the sexual drive: if frustrated, it manifests itself strangely, reshapes facts in odd ways. Bounderby and Gradgrind invent dangerous stories that disguise reality; they do not originate from the sympathetic imagination, the ability true artists encourage in a reader to fancy himself in another's place.

Mrs. Gradgrind's gullibility in quizzing Bounderby puts the injunction "never to fancy" (HT, 5) in a sinister light. The urge to fancy is conditioned out of Coketown's citizenry at an early age, just as Brave New Worlders are taught, in Neo-Pavlovian nurseries, to detest books and flowers. A population that never wonders never doubts. Like Mrs. Gradgrind, it cannot recognize embellishment and prevarication, which become useful weapons of the ruling elite. Until Dickens arrives, Gradgrind and Bounderby are the only licensed storytellers in town.

Bounderby and Gradgrind disguise fiction as fact. Dickens tries to save the day for art and fulfill his destiny by conveying fact through fiction. He writes *Hard Times* to show that creative writing will remain useful after the advent of places like Coketown. In the process, however, he discloses deep-seated anxieties that it may not. He foresees "hard times" for him personally as the need for his wares diminishes. Art plays a larger role in this novel than the novelist dares explicitly assign it. To halt the spread of dehumanizing industrial centers, the artist decries the philosophy behind technological developments, but oncoming circumstances constrain him to plead merely for the novelist's right to continued existence.

Dickens divorces art and industry, assigning Fancy and Fact to separate quarters lest the latter half of each pair overwhelm the former. Machines, Dickens concedes, are the new facts of life; art is, at best, an antidote or palliative that makes the new "reality" more bearable. In the Victorian England of 1854, Dickens was still a social prophet issuing dire warnings. But in the novel he published that year, the artist is in danger of being relegated to a reduced role, much like the marginal Sleary's, as a supplier of holiday divertissements.

The precariousness of "Sleary's Horse-riding"—art as an ideal already in shabby decline—is made clearer by Huxley's Brave New World. The hedonistic pleasures that its Controllers invent to keep the work force, when at leisure, mindless and debased easily sabotage Sleary's watchword: "People mutht be amuthed" (HT, 222). Obstacle Golf, Riemann-surface tennis, "the feelies," and, in particular, *soma* answer Dickens's call for an emotional outlet but exclude mind-broadening art. Ironically, when Mrs. Gaskell discovered a whole new province for art in celebrating the rise of manufacturing, which he intended to bemoan, the editor-in-chief found *Household Words* under contract to publish a sanguine view of a sensibility crisis he took so seriously he was writing *Hard Times* in self-defense.

But Mrs. Gaskell's reassurance tends to confirm his worst fears. In *North and South* she uses her artistry to assert that art is neither as imperiled nor as all-important as Dickens claims. One need not despair of art or man, Mrs. Gaskell consolingly explains: the latter's strengths are innate, and the former's benefits can be acquired at any of several stages, of which childhood, contrary to Wordsworth and Blake, is not necessarily the most desirable.

On the subject of liberal education, Mr. Hale often sounds like a disciple reciting Dickens's views, yet years of study have only served to turn him from a minister in the Anglican Church into a dissenter. When Hale suggests that Thornton overcame early hardship by imitating heroes he had read about, the reply puts proponents of literature as the prime nutrient for the sympathetic imagination (Dickens) and hero-worshippers (Carlyle) in proper perspective: Thornton states emphatically that the classics helped him "not one bit!"; he was "too busy to think about any dead people, with the living pressing alongside of me, neck to neck, in the struggle for bread" (NS, 127).

Life, Mrs. Gaskell chides Dickens, is essentially a Darwinian "struggle" for survival, a competitive horse race ("neck to neck"); "bread" or necessities come before the luxury of culture. It was the fight to subsist that formed Thornton's character, not Greek literature. The best schoolroom, it follows, is life itself, and the attributes one must have to be successful can be found not in books but within one's own breast. As Mr. Hale, reversing himself, later reminds Margaret, Thornton's "practical life" taught him early "to exercise good judgement and self-control," so that his intellect and personality are extraordinarily developed. Now that the successful manufacturer has earned for his mother and sister "the quiet peace" that accompanies financial security, he "can turn to all that old narration and thoroughly enjoy it" (NS, 127)—but as a reward for success, not a prerequisite.

Calling Homeric heroes "dead people" with nothing to tell us about the struggle for bread sounds rather unenlightened, as though Bentham were lecturing on the social value of poetry. But Mrs. Gaskell wants to remind Dickens's readers that the active, competitive life takes precedence over imaginative rumination: first there were Homeric heroes, then came Homer. In short, life goes before art; fact supersedes works of fancy. Thornton is not obliged to absorb the *Iliad* before behaving heroically. He performs his exploits in the commercial arena, and Mrs. Gaskell jubilantly records them. It is in this way that art and artists remain relevant in Victorian society. Mrs. Gaskell charges that Dickens unrealistically expects life to follow art, heroes to learn heroism by reading about heroes.

The primacy of life over art is the discussion topic in Chapter 40 of *North and South*. Thornton defends Milton-Northern against Mr. Bell's assertion that the industrial city is inferior to his beloved Oxford in affording leisure. Mrs. Gaskell's view is that life is principally for action, and Milton easily seems superior in this regard. Oxford and the pleasures of the mind become suspect: idle, selfish, perhaps even sterile—like Bell, a bachelor and hence childless. Milton-Northern represents real life for Mrs. Gaskell; Oxford, by comparison, is another palace of art, a monastic alternative to social involvement.

Dickens's position on Fancy in *Hard Times* designates him, in Mrs. Gaskell's opinion, an adherent to art over life. Ironically, the creator of *Oliver Twist* and *Bleak House*, whose education was closer to Sam Weller's than to an Oxford don's, is consigned to the overly aesthetic side in the crucial Victorian division that pitted the allure of the fine arts against the urgings of social consciousness. Thornton vanquishes Bell when he suggests that Oxford develop "something which can apply to the present more directly" (NS, 414). Bell's money is a case in point: left to Margaret, it belatedly finds use for itself in refinancing Thornton's mill. Bell has derived his income from Milton industries, but not until Margaret inherits do persons of wealth and breeding, as if taking Thornton's suggestion, become patrons of progress and manufacturing.

Admittedly, Milton-Northern is no threat to Oxford architecturally. But Mrs. Gaskell believes that a capacity for introspection and greater understanding of others develops through social intercourse, not from staring at fine buildings any more than from devouring books. Her characters thrash out their differences in discussion: frankness is preferable to Fancy. Too much emphasis on Oxonian pleasures during one's upbringing can reduce the attractions of one's real-life milieu, so Mrs. Gaskell substitutes Thornton's "inward strength" (NS, 414) for the sympathetic imagination Dickens said could be instilled only by artists.

In *North and South*, growth of the individual through social interrelations is supported by an analogy with the findings of modern biology. But the process also meets Matthew Arnold's requirements for the transmitting of culture. As Thornton, Higgins, and Margaret interrelate, they turn a fresh, free stream of thought upon each other's stock notions and habits.[23] Mrs. Gaskell thus reunites the science and humanities that Dickens virtually drives into separate camps.[24] Culture in Milton depends upon openness of mind; it means movement toward realization of one another's potential. Each treats the self and others as works of art in progress.

Mrs. Gaskell parodies the idea that Bounderby would behave nobly and display greater aptitude for marital bliss if he perused more fairytales. She laughs at the implication that Blackpool and his comrades would be more brotherly if they attended the circus frequently. No fairytales, no imagination, no talent for empathy, hence defects of the heart—thus runs one of Dickens's main complaints against Utilitarian Coketown. But Thornton's triumph over Mr. Bell and Milton's superiority to Oxford cause Dickens and his ilk to seem naive—Romantic rather than realistic—in their conceptions of how the quality of life is to be improved.

To Mrs. Gaskell's way of thinking, Dickens overemphasizes formative experiences in childhood. Against the Romantic premise that Sissy, Bitzer, Tom, and Louisa must remain forever the persons they become as adolescents at school, all the major characters in *North and South* undergo remarkable alteration later in life, as one might expect in a novel by a proponent of evolution. In a world of constant technological advance, reeducation is the keynote Mrs. Gaskell sounds. Just as Connie Chatterley and Mellors revitalize each other physically, Mrs. Gaskell's characters reorient one another toward social salvation. *North and South* revalues schoolroom sequences in *Hard Times* by making Milton-Northern a veritable institute for adult education.

Both novels assert the continuing relevance of art, but Mrs. Gaskell's does so by demonstrating the novelist's inferiority, as a shaping force in society, to men of practical ability who lead the active life. The irony of this upset Dickens but does not appear to have troubled his rival.

Paul Edward Gray's observation, apropos of *Hard Times*, that novels "do not ordinarily provoke . . . disagreements over literal truth" could not be wider from the mark.[25] Beginning with the rivalry between *North and South* and *Hard Times*, Victorian novels frequently did. Realism, from its inception, was a question of relative, competing realisms or rival subjective perspectives in a newly secularized world of innumerable possibilities. In depicting the fate of interpersonal relations in the imminent industrialized world, however, Dickens and Mrs. Gaskell ought to have conceded that they were talking as forecasters as well as reporters. Their novels express not only the way matters supposedly were in Preston and Manchester but also each novelist's opinion of the direction in which society seemed to be going. She foresees gratifying personal encounters leading to heretofore unheard-of socioeconomic prosperity; he predicts that such ends and means will prove incompatible. Each brand of realism became a blend of fidelity to actualities—subjective as that already was in a rapidly changing society—with a creative imagining of things to come.

Measured against *Living*, Henry Green's modern novel about factory life in Birmingham, neither *Hard Times* nor *North and South* appears interested in being completely factual. Green's book tries for ultrafidelity, a kind of recreation or reproduction of its subject. *Living* is designed to pass for life itself, the process painstakingly captured without comment in a novel shunning a thesis. Green's novels, says Elizabeth Bowen, "reproduce, as few English novels do, the actual sensations of living." Everything that happens does so, in Green's words, "to create 'life'" and is extremely important simply because it happens.[26] (Even so, one can argue, Green is sometimes far from being totally objective.) But Dickens and Mrs. Gaskell have cases to make for and against manufactures; they have theses to propound, axes to grind, controversial ideas to present.

Read in light of one another, *Hard Times* and *North and South* stand for the competition between utopian and dystopian elements that subsequently characterizes much so-called realistic Victorian fiction. The novels are a dispute between two conscientious social analysts, one of whom hopes for the best while the other anticipates the worst.

The ideal revaluator attends to the different truths each realistic novelist saw. By the late 1840s, England was on the verge of becoming an industrial kingdom, incredibly rich and energetic, in which, however, a million people were in danger of starving and half of the women could not read. In short, the country was, potentially, both utopia and dystopia. A believer in evolution, Mrs. Gaskell accentuates the good fortune of her Alphas—Margaret, Thornton, and Higgins—while worrying less about Boucher and Bessy. Like most dystopians, Dickens anguishes over misfits and malcontents. That honest drones of Blackpool's type and sensitive creatures like Sissy have been excluded from life's advance challenges the system that undervalues them, just as Winston Smith's presence is a sore point for the Party in George Orwell's *1984*.

Dickens writes ominously, drawing conditions not precisely as he found them at Preston and Manchester but as he imagines they will become if his misgivings are ignored. His propensity for effective exaggeration nicely complements the novel's ingrained anti-utopianism. Dickens positions Louisa before the fire in the final chapter and wonders, "How much of the future might arise before *her* vision?" (HT, 226), how far "into . . . futurity" can she see? Then he offers his own presentiments, claiming to see "the Writing on the Wall": Utilitarian economic policies that encourage scoundrels like Bounderby to construct purgatories like Coketown spell the beginning of the end for an unjust capitalist system that refuses to reform itself.

Dickens's dystopianism reveals itself further in the discrepancy between the harsh consequences envisioned and the feeble preventives prescribed. The novelist seems uncertain whether the catastrophes he warns of *should* be circumscribed; justice may require that they not be. The parallel with Babylon, intended to be foreboding, is fatalistic by implication. Dickens's World Controllers, the "Commissioners of Fact," must act to brighten the lives of Coketown's work force "while there is yet time": that is, before "romance is utterly driven out" of people's souls and England becomes a doomed civilization. Crushed spirits, Dickens realizes, will not bother to strike; they will revolt. "Reality," which Dickens claims to see more clearly than Mrs. Gaskell in both its extant and imminent forms, "will take a wolfish turn, and make an end" of all oppressors (HT, 125).

The futurist in Dickens is a dystopian who both fears and desires the purifying power that an uprising of unpacified workers might bring. His use of the phrase "wolfish turn" of events conveys mixed feelings: the expression connotes strength, ferocity, and a deserved retribution. Mrs. Gaskell must repair this unfortunate ambiguity and challenge the dystopian despair behind it by voicing her unadulterated disapproval of all animal behavior. When the rioting mob rushes Thornton's mill, she makes its chilling yell totally repulsive: "It was as the demoniac desire of some terrible wild beast for the food that is withheld from his ravening" (NS, 232). Instead of a wolf, one of Lawrence's symbols for manhood, Mrs. Gaskell presents an unspecified but "terrible" creature. She describes it in biblical language that implies an emanation from hell and stresses its carnivorousness, not its virility.

Mrs. Gaskell denies any need to play Daniel deciphering messages on Belshazzar's palace wall. Besides citing evidence for a positive prognosis, she exempts industrial centers from the kind of backward-looking judgment that the dystopian in Dickens attempts to pass. Manchester is a brand-new phenomenon, embryonic rather than apocalyptic, a promising arena for scientific invention and experiments in social interaction; uncomplimentary parallels with Babylonia are as inappropriate as old-fashioned notions of utopia drawn from More or Plato. Mrs. Gaskell dismisses Mr. Bell's charge that "Milton people" do not "reverence the past." Thornton contends that one should do so only "when the study of the past leads to a prophecy of the future" (NS, 414). But "to men groping in new circumstances," which is clearly the case in Milton-Northern, "the words of experience" as contained in the nation's literary and religious tradition do not automatically apply. It is time, Thornton continues, to move "out of the wisdom of the past" in favor of ideas that will "help us over the present."

Several times Thornton speaks disparagingly of "Utopia." He means the illusory classical ideal of an absolutely perfect, unchanging society that comes into existence all at once. Such a utopia Mrs. Gaskell considers the daydream of capitalism's critics, shortsighted individuals who reject the transitional because it is far from perfect. Surely Dickens is one of those who, says Thornton, "speak of Utopia much more easily than of the next day's duty": as a result, "that duty is all done by others," while shirkers look on critically, "ready to cry, 'Fie, for shame!' " whenever they disapprove (NS, 414). Utopia to Thornton is doing "the next day's duty," advancing on perfection a step at a time, which is the rate of acceleration that George Eliot's reformers subsequently adopt. Milton-Northern will never be the best of all possible worlds, but Milton men seem proud not only of accomplishments to date but of "what yet should be."

Before sending Higgins to Thornton in search of work, Margaret speculates aloud: "If he [Higgins] and Mr Thornton would speak out together as man to man—if Higgins would forget that Mr Thornton was a master, and speak to him as he does to us—and if Mr Thornton would be patient enough to listen to him with his human heart, not with his master's ears—" (NS, 384). One is struck, throughout this passage, by the hypothetical constructions. Like the dinner guests on Hamidullah's veranda in *A Passage to India*, who wonder if an Indian and an Englishman can be friends, Mrs. Gaskell wants to know whether men and masters can bridge the gap between their stations. She then presents events as she would like them to happen, so that *North and South* takes on aspects of a recipe or blueprint.

Historical criticism is wrong to suggest that one can resolve the issues separating Dickens and Mrs. Gaskell by taking a look at Preston to see what actually transpired. The "course of events Mrs. Gaskell described," K.J. Fielding concludes, "was very close to what actually happened." Both in fact and fiction, the masters were willing to import a large body of Irish "to break the strike."[27] Fielding's view, which speaks for the consensus, suggests that Dickens lost out to Mrs. Gaskell as a social realist the minute he disclosed his decision not to strike. More accurately, the weavers' walkout collapsed because laborers in neighboring manufacturing towns, with troubles of their own, were unable to continue contributing to the support of the Preston strikers. Neither Dickens nor Mrs. Gaskell could afford to emphasize this; doing so would have made the battle between Thornton and Higgins (who are evenly matched) and Bounderby and Blackpool (a one-sided contest) dependent upon a third party not on the scene.

But the principal cause of historical criticism's failure to satisfy is that it ignores the futuristic component of the debate between Dickens and Mrs. Gaskell. One is tempted to balance the consensus that Mrs. Gaskell was more faithful to developments at Preston (as well as to the spirit of the age) against the possibility that Dickens more clearly envisioned long-range consequences, especially for the environment. Despite subsequent industrial utopias, such as Bellamy's *Looking Backward*, Dickens, in retrospect, makes a better dystopian than Mrs. Gaskell a utopian. Yet she seems more farsighted than Dickens in at least one respect: she satirizes Margaret Hale's initial prejudice against Milton-Northern as an example of the ill-conceived hostility exhibited by England's upper crust toward industry and the practical men it brought to the fore. The attitude that owning, managing, and living near one's factories was vulgar helped to keep England technologically inferior to much of western Europe, as witness the country's general unpreparedness at the start of both world wars.

From one point of view, a Lawrencian Dickens, modern and heroic, protests the crimes that industry was preparing to perpetrate against the individual and the natural world. From another, Dickens the would-be gentleman assists in fostering an aristocratic disdain for ugly factories and the uncouth bounders who consider themselves industrial titans. By 1870, the year of Dickens's death, snobbish ideas of manufacture as a lower-class occupation had prevailed.[28] Mrs. Gaskell's decision to group Dickens with the aesthetes, supporters of art over life, seemed more credible when even children of men like Thornton believed it might be preferable to attend a university and adopt Mr. Bell's opinions.

That the quarrel between Dickens and Mrs. Gaskell over the fate of human relationships developed into a contest pitting Lawrence against Bloomsbury confirms the mixture of predictive elements with social realism in *Hard Times* and *North and South*. All four parties ponder the ideal combination of the resources their nation's different classes possess. They try to determine to whom the England of the future rightly belongs. Since Blackpool, Bounderby, and Louisa interrelate so poorly, Dickens can only cast a weak vote for Sissy's children. *North and South* contradicts *Hard Times* by marrying a Schlegel to a Wilcox, but later novelists—E.M. Forster included—have been reshuffling this revaluation ever since. When George Eliot marries a cultivated lady to the man of destiny, Felix Holt has Thornton's mental abilities and physical appeal while occupying Higgins's social position. In *Howard's End*, Margaret and Mr. Wilcox, culture and business, must invest with their respective virtues a child conceived out of wedlock by a middle-class woman (Margaret's sister) and a lower-class male. They raise this promising hybrid to be their heir. When Lady

Chatterley, wife of an industrialist, conceives the gamekeeper's child, she ensures the perpetuation of the imperiled life force in them both; Lawrence ridicules the resolution of *Howard's End* with a blow aimed simultaneously at Mrs. Gaskell's idealization of manufacturers and George Eliot's idea of the radical reformer as the natural man.

Hard Times, one reader argues, resembles a brightly colored oil painting, full of grotesques, whereas Mrs. Gaskell's realism is practically photographic.[29] Yet a millowner studying Greek with an ex-clergyman for a tutor is hardly more verifiable than an industrialist who preaches that inhaling factory smoke is healthy; it is doubtful that either could be found walking about in the Manchester or Preston of the 1850s. In the heat of argument, Dickens and Mrs. Gaskell present what each insists is a sketch from the life. Their opposing views of England's prospects drive Bounderby and Thornton away from the real at equal speed but in different directions. The caricature, since it came first, prompts a retaliatory excess: selflessness and the beginnings of social sanctity in lieu of greed and pomposity.

Confronted with an enormity like Bounderby, the New Criticism resolves to judge art separately whenever it disagrees with literal truth. An unlikelihood like Josiah Bounderby, Paul Edward Gray argues, fits neatly into the fictional world that Dickens builds around him.[30] The same holds true, one supposes, for an exemplary Thornton. Art, however, quickly begins to part company with reality and eventually to deconstruct if one elects this path. The revaluator must recognize the competition between rival Victorian realisms and the utopian or dystopian biases frequently involved. Otherwise, he is left with two different universes: not variations on reality by Dickens and Mrs. Gaskell but Dickens's world and literal truth, each independent of the other.

The only conflicts that remain in *Hard Times*, after Gray assumes his position, would have to be internal: within the novelist's mind and disclosed, even if unconsciously, through his work. The only question left for the critic to ask is whether the novel's themes and components mesh. If all things in *Hard Times* do not fit together as neatly as Gray claims or can be made to seem as disjointed as contemporary life has become, the novel proceeds to undercut itself. Deconstruction then becomes a postmodern extension of the New Criticism, a parodic sabotaging of its good intentions.

Judged strictly in light of the weavers' strike or as examples of literal truth, much of what Dickens and Mrs. Gaskell say in their mutually recriminative novels seems uncalled for. *Hard Times* and *North and South* cannot be confined to Preston or considered self-contained—hence prevented from looking ahead to us or askance at each other—without becoming less complicated: that is, less realistic, less referential, and less well wrought. Gray's paradox—that Bounderby is real primarily as a fiction—would not have carried weight with Dickens, Mrs. Gaskell, or their readers.

Tendencies toward idealization and caricature were widespread among Victorian realists. Ordinarily, this need not stop one from considering characters in Dickens or Mrs. Gaskell convincing enough for their creators' purposes. But when one tendency seems to call forth the other, idealization becomes a species of parody: like caricature, it overdoes representation by means of enlargement or exaggeration, even though it is virtues rather than vices that are being enlarged. Idealization and caricature in Victorian realistic fiction baffle historical criticism and leave the New Critic vulnerable to the deconstructionist. But they become more comprehensible if seen as manifestations respectively of the latent utopianism in novelists like Mrs. Gaskell and of anti-utopian satire in works like *Hard Times*.

Multireferential, *North and South* and *Hard Times* comment on each other as much as they do on the real world, while also looking to the future as well as at the present. Much of subsequent Victorian fiction, when written to discredit a rival (especially Dickens), contains an implicit utopian component.[31] Anti-utopian sentiments seem active in Dickens's social criticism from the moment when Mr. Pickwick, incarcerated in the Fleet, realizes that that institution magnifies rather than corrects the unfair ways of the world. But Dickens's dystopian satire did not begin offending rivals grievously until the 1850s, when the theory of evolution was starting to take hold.

George Eliot is being essentially utopian when she talks of the "growing good of the world" and presumes to illustrate it by putting society under her microscope in novels like *Middlemarch*.[32] Content too, though much less so, is Trollope throughout *The Warden*: he warns Popular Sentiment that social problems, not always as bad as they seem, will only be made worse by overzealous reformers. Dickens's anti-utopianism, no matter how modern an aspect it gives *Hard Times* today, appeared inexcusable to many of his contemporaries: it was too radical for someone like Trollope, yet antiprogressive and hence not radical and reformist enough (or only falsely so) to moderates like George Eliot and Mrs. Gaskell. *Hard Times* posited a darker world than either moderates or radicals wished to subscribe to and seemed not only to condemn the status quo but to question the possibility of peacefully accomplishing extensive change. The dystopian flavor of *Our Mutual Friend* prompted William Morris, in *News from Nowhere*, to imagine the other side of the coin, an ideal alternative to Dickens's dismayed vision. Unlike Dickens's earlier rivals, however, Morris believed he was completing his predecessor by supplying the missing ideal, which is different from parodying him out of fear and disrespect.[33]

Realism, writes George Levine, is "a self-conscious effort, usually in the name of some moral enterprise of truth telling and extending the limits of human sympathy, to make literature appear to be describing directly not some other language but reality itself."[34] For Levine, realism is best explained as a methodology. The discrepancies this shared approach produces between novels like *North and South* and *Hard Times* hardly matter. One objects to the implication of duplicity, no matter if well-intentioned: the realist is the purveyor of an illusion; he wants to "appear to be describing . . . reality itself." Levine's conception flirts with the structuralist's contention that all art longs to give itself away. A visibly "self-conscious effort," realism undermines its own premise: its pretense at dealing with "reality itself" is always uppermost in the author's mind and often transparent to all.

Levine notwithstanding, reality itself—not the appearance of it—is generally the Victorian realist's goal, but each sees it differently and has a different thesis to propose; each is embarked on a different "moral enterprise." Emphasizing common intentions or methods employed in common overlooks the debates, the competitions or rivalries, and the absence of a common reality to be realistic about. Even if the method were as uniform as Levine suggests, the nature of things had begun changing by the middle of the century from a shared reality to one that had to be fought over by social analysts with a variety of world views and temperaments, each convinced that his or her interpretation was the most reliable.

According to Deirdre David, Victorian realism is often an awkward blend of accurate representation and implausible transformation (her words for fictitious resolution). Using Mrs. Gaskell as a prime example, David argues that nineteenth-century novelists describe a rapidly changing society well enough but forfeit the modern reader's confidence because they seem less successful in settling the problems raised.[35] Here, too, Victorian realists seem ripe for deconstruction: good presenters but poor and possibly dissembling resolvers, they risk undermining their own analyses with inept conclusions.

Either *North and South* or *Hard Times*, however, has power to convince if read by itself; placed alongside its rival, each challenges the other's truthfulness. As a counterpoint quickly develops, each presentation begins to seem slanted, its realism not professedly fictional but clearly partial or relative—that is, neither completely objective nor whole but decidedly argumentative. Dickens and Mrs. Gaskell differ radically on solutions because they see the same things so differently from the start. The resolutions offered are influenced, in large part, by those she knows about in or he anticipates from a rival novel.

The solutions are also determined by the hopefulness or growing despair plainly evident in each novel's opening and middle sections. A sense of things to come shapes the novelist's opinion of current happenings as much as they, in turn, dictate the tone of coming events. Dickens visualizes Stone Lodge and M'Choakumchild's schoolroom from the bottom of "the Old Hell Shaft." Mrs. Gaskell sees her entire novel in light of the marriage upcoming at its conclusion.

Hard Times and *North and South* remain poised between transcription and prescription, depiction and advocacy. But the second half of each pair is inseparable from the first rather than a sudden change of mode. Neither self-enclosed nor a discursive argument, the Victorian multiplot novel adroitly melds thesis and counterthesis, often underscoring points by simultaneously challenging another novelist's philosophy. As a result, such novels were inherently controversial and continue to be so. In short, it was neither the epical nor the topical Dickens but the dystopian whom Mrs. Gaskell parodied. Unlike *The Warden*, which condensed cumbersome multiplot fiction, *North and South* was a reparative unfolding of a rival serial allegedly too cramped and crotchety to be right. Amazingly, when Dickens wrote to "congratulate" Mrs. Gaskell on the completion of her story, he hoped that she harbored no "disagreeable" feelings toward *Household Words* and invited her to contribute again.[36] In light of the intense conflicts between *Hard Times* and *North and South*, however, this letter must be read as a gentlemanly gesture, an effort to restore a superficial propriety after a prolonged bout of mutual recrimination.[37] In effect, Dickens and Mrs. Gaskell undermined simplistic ideas about realism virtually from its inception. She fashioned a parodic reply to the anti-utopian satiric novel he was already publishing to discredit the kind of optimistic industrial romance he expected her to write.

Chapter Four

An Ultra-Dickensian Novel

The Woman in White

WILKIE COLLINS once hinted that he could have done *A Tale of Two Cities* (1859) better than Dickens by revealing Manette's letter earlier. Dickens replied with a snub: if the story had been "done in your manner," he told Collins, it "would have been overdone," more ominously perhaps but "too elaborately trapped, baited and prepared." The "business of art," Dickens instructed Collins further, is to "lay the ground carefully, but with the care that conceals itself—to show by a backward light what everything has been working to—but only to *suggest*, until the fulfillment comes. These are the ways of Providence, of which all art is but a little imitation."[1]

As this letter makes clear, the intent of Dickens's historical novel was not just to create mystery or arouse suspense. Instead, Dickens wanted to give life a sense of direction, to "reveal," says K.J. Fielding, "a developing pattern" in men's affairs.[2] Collins's hint, Dickens's snub, and the former's subsequent efforts to prove himself an outdoer of Dickens (rather than an overdoer) led to a decade of intense rivalry that ended only with Dickens's death.

In the final chapter of the eighteenth number of *Bleak House*, Dickens achieved apotheosis as a serial novelist with the climactic revelation to which the preceding forty-eight chapters had built. Expecting Jenny, "mother of the dead child," Esther Summerson turns over a body at the entrance to the burial ground; she finds Lady Dedlock, her own mother, "cold and dead" (BH,763). The twenty-sixth installment of Collins's finest novel takes aim at the eighteenth number of *Bleak House*. Collins ends "The Second Epoch" of *The Woman in White* (1860) with Hartright reading the inscription on Laura's tomb, only to discover his beloved still alive and standing beside him. The scene revives the argument Collins had with Dickens the previous year about providence's ways and art's obligation to mimic them.

Throughout *The Woman in White*, Collins purposely disregards the advice about patience and restraint tendered in Dickens's letter. In the twenty-sixth installment, a novelist Dickens thought of as his protégé obtains extra mileage from an episode reminiscent of the most melodramatic disclosure in *Bleak House*. Lady Dedlock's demise, Collins implies, exhausts the repertoire of the country's leading sensational realist; but when Laura Fairlie surprises Hartright, the final third of Collins's novel is still to come. From mistaken identity and mysterious death—two Dickensian ingredients—Collins goes on to extract additional revelations, each more unexpected than the last. Dickens's follower claims to be the leader, better at sustaining suspense than the author of *Bleak House* and better at resurrecting characters (recalling them to life) than the creator of *A Tale of Two Cities*.

In the latter novel, which preceded *The Woman in White* in *All the Year Round*, the successor to *Household Words*, Dickens does not spring his major surprise until Darnay stands trial a third time for crimes against the state.[3] The unexpected announcement that Manette has unwittingly become his son-in-law's accuser causes a sensation during Darnay's second appearance before the Paris Tribunal. In Chapter 10 of Book Three, the twenty-seventh of thirty-one parts, the recitation of Manette's letter parallels in excitement, although it cannot match for pathos, Esther's discovery of Lady Dedlock's body. Thus when Collins introduces additional pyrotechnics after the deceptively climactic revelation at Laura's grave, he contradicts the methodology of two Dickens novels simultaneously. Collins implies that he knows more about patterns and their development because his novels continue to unravel them long after the point at which his rival's stop.

The competitive regard Collins had for Dickens manifests itself as a kind of creativity contest. To construct more arresting fiction out of essentially the same components, to rework Dickens's characters, plots, and technical devices more dramatically—that is always one of Collins's main objectives.

Dickens depended on multiplotting to capture a new multiplicity virtually synonymous with the rise of secular modernism. Two narrators and multiple plots were mandatory in *Bleak House* because life had become increasingly difficult to encompass, harder to explain, with one set of eyes and a single story. In *The Woman in White*, Collins triples the number of narrators and allows one plot to become many in the sense that each narrator is able to recount only a fragment of it. Using a convoluted story line pieced together from numerous narrations, Collins contends that he derives a stronger impression of multifariousness and relativity than Dickens attains through a plurality of separate plots that gradually interconnect.

Collins did not aspire to discredit the sensational brand of realism in which Dickens specialized; on the contrary, he wanted to wrest control of it from him. It was not the epical, topical, or dystopian Dickens but the sensational realist whom Collins hoped to eclipse. Throughout *The Woman in White* he professes to do better than Dickens the kind of novel Dickens thought he did best.

Like Trollope and Mrs. Gaskell, Collins wrote his own novel by simultaneously rewriting Dickens. But for him, refutation meant going further in the same direction or finding better means to the same ends, rather than quieting Dickens down or contradicting his satirical outlook. If Dickens creates a story that turns upon look-alikes in *A Tale of Two Cities*, Collins will do the same, in his opinion more plausibly, in *The Woman in White*. If *Bleak House* anatomizes the ills caused by the irresponsibility of individuals, groups, and institutions, Collins will enunciate in greater detail the evils of propriety, which he finds more extensive.[4]

The Woman in White parodies as it imitates, imitates as it parodies, one exercise repeatedly fading into the other. Collins's stellar performance, his breakthrough novel, demands to be read twice at the same time: as a tribute to Dickens and also a challenge to his supremacy. Homage persistently turns into rivalry because Dickens becomes an impediment while remaining an example. Being compared to the Inimitable helps a novelist on the rise; after that, it can only pin him down in second place. To supersede Dickens as a melodramatic realist and corrosive social critic, Collins realized that he would have to replace him as the era's most popular entertainer.

Being more realistic, Collins decides, means driving home one's moral vision—one's precepts for better living—more resoundingly than one's competition. Where Dickens and Collins overlap, both assume that the more startling one's use of the sort of characters and scenes the other also favors, the stronger one's didactic prowess because a rival's statements are rephrased in capital letters, with significant detail more sharply portrayed. Collins aspired to be Dickens writ large, bigger and better. He developed undoing by outdoing into a surprisingly successful strategy: in another peculiarly Victorian form of parody, another instance of hidden rivalry, one melodramatic realist enlarged upon another to show that he was willing to go to greater lengths in the pursuit of truths that novelists who took fewer risks inevitably miss.

In the twenty-sixth number of *The Woman in White*, Collins launches his bid to supplant Dickens as the Victorian novel's foremost authority on the workings of providence. Reflecting upon his reencounter with Laura, Walter credits "the Hand that leads men on the dark road to the future" (WW,435) with arranging their reunion. Until that moment, neither suspected that the other was still above ground. Collins maintains that his version of providence is more realistic than Dickens's—that is, more vivid and affecting, consequently more useful didactically—because it makes what happens seem more unmistakably providential. Once one realizes that Collins is laboring to outshine Dickens as a philosopher by outdistancing him as a master of mystery and suspense, providence emerges as the logical subject, agreed upon by both parties, to decide the issue.

Talent for manipulating delays and a capacity to perceive hitherto undetected designs within the nature of things go together; each is to the other as means to an end. The more protracted a novel's resolution and the firmer its settlements when they finally arrive, the more convincingly the sensational realist teaches that life—even at the dawning of a secular, materialistic age—still responds to extratemporal pressures. That confidence in providence was never simply a Victorian convention becomes manifest when one comprehends how seriously Dickens and Collins took each other's efforts to be its architect.[5] Each wanted to be its spokesman in the struggle against more optimistic renditions of the life process in the novels of their mutual opponents who minimized providence's authority.

The Dickens letter quoted above, one of his most important, outlines melodramatic realism's primary responsibilities. At a time when many intellectuals considered it unfashionable if not ridiculous to speak of supernatural direction, Dickens endows the mystery novelist with a special mission: detecting providence's carefulness, despite its increasingly hidden or obscured designs. In large, complicated novels the melodramatic realist can uncover programs which the general reader may then perceive in real life, amid the welter of a modern, scientific, industrial society. The artist's goal is to demonstrate, in Carlyle's words, that "there *is* justice here below," that the "great soul of the world *is* just" even if the corporate body of society seldom is.[6]

The sensational realist, Dickens asserts, knows best how to illustrate the contention—or deliver the warning—that justice eventually wins out. No matter how bleak and counterproductive the human situation periodically becomes or how belated the redressing, the novelist of mystery and suspense encourages readers to reaffirm life's basic rhythms. Dickens mollifies his own pessimism and negativity, thereby vindicating life itself, whenever he depicts days of reckoning as the faroff events toward which all his satirical creations move. The incidents that sensation novelists utilize often deserve to be called extraordinary; the lessons taught, however, are meant to register on the secularized Victorian consciousness as eternal truths.

Compared to the reader's daily round, the complex but unwinding plots of novels like *Bleak House* and *A Tale of Two Cities* may seem contrived, even spectacular. They become less so if accepted as condensations of global or planetary activity, marvelous rumblings going on all the time but subterranean or imperceptible until they emerge to become history. The melodramatic realist unveils the "fulfillment" that all the rumblings have "been working to." He supplies the "backward light" that links effects to their causes. All artists automatically imitate providence, but in Dickens's opinion the suspenseful realist does so consciously, hence more than other novelists do. His artistry, although vastly humbler than Milton's, nevertheless illuminates God's ways and stands as their explanatory justification.

Dickens's letter to Collins about providence is strongly Carlylean in flavor. "Towards an eternal centre of right and nobleness, and of that only, is all this confusion tending," wrote the Scottish-born philosopher.[7] This goal of peace after turmoil and upheaval, an essentially Christian pattern of salvation following travail, describes the destination of *Bleak House*, *A Tale of Two Cities*, and *The Woman in White*, even if Dickens and Collins compete to see who can reach it by the most roundabout path. To the extent that one feels Carlyle to be correct, such melodramatic fictions cease to be escapism or sheer entertainments and become imitations of life—or, if not of life, then of a particular philosophy about how the life process works.

The argument Dickens opened with Collins in 1859 underlined the resolve of both novelists to stress the paramountcy of providence as an abiding supernatural superintendence in an era daily becoming more profane. But they differ sharply over the amount of fateful intervention to unveil at one time. Dickens prefers a single climactic revelation; volleys of surprises weaken the sense of "fulfillment"; they compromise one's impression of an inexorable purposiveness, a principle of retribution biding its time at the heart of things.

Collins favors a larger, longer series of revelations that coalesce to form a system he considers tighter and fairer; otherwise, providence seems to be absent for lengthy periods, as if concealed to the point of neglectfulness and unconcern. Collins charges that Dickens, like Carlyle, must eventually resort to cataclysms, during which providence becomes blind force, an engulfing chaos. No wonder it is often unwilling, perhaps unable, to distinguish an individual's innocence—Charles Darnay's, for example—from the guilt of his class. Collins expresses fewer reservations about the continuing visibility of God's plans and less dread of their enactment.

Constant and steady even when not immediately in evidence, Collins's providence reminds one of its attentiveness with periodic interventions. These increase in size and frequency so that the result is crescendo instead of cataclysm. The incineration of Sir Percival Glyde rivals Krook's combustion for spontaneousness and is arguably even more terrifying, but this disaster is also made to seem part of a sequence of reprisals: it leads to further dispensings of justice that could not happen before it or without it.

Collins's providence is always on the job at life's darkest moments, patiently drawing long-range good out of present suffering. As the highly moral nature of providential interference begins to become clearer in *The Woman in White*, it provides the believer with sustenance not unlike grace. The instant Hartright realizes he is to be unfairly separated from Laura, he suspects the existence of a larger plan, a "chain of events" linking them that not even his "approaching departure" will "snap asunder" (WW,101). The many months between his retreat from Cumberland and the fortuitous reunion at Laura's grave turn out, in retrospect, to be part of a comprehensive settling of accounts. Not only is Laura restored to her proper place, but the life process rids itself of a treacherous Italian spy and a fraudulent English baronet whose crimes have gone unpunished for years. Collins insists that this outcome is a matter of Dickens being outdone, not overdone.

"Unembodied Justice," writes Carlyle, "is of Heaven," therefore "*in*visible to all but the noble and pure of soul." Only men "who *can* withal see Heaven's invisible Justice, and know it to be on Earth also omnipotent" stand "between a Nation and perdition."[8] Novelists who unscramble providential designs keep the idea of justice in society alive. But Collins's embodiment of justice's energies in protagonists like Hartright refashion those lieutenants of providence in Dickens whose nobility of soul is much in doubt. The Defarges, for example, pervert true disinterestedness when discussing life's manner of meting out justice: "Vengeance and retribution require a long time," says Madame Defarge. "It is the rule" (TTC, 229). Her husband laments that they will "not see the triumph" of the Jacquerie. "We shall have helped it," his wife steadfastly replies (TTC, 231). To make providence more palatable as a regulatory force, Collins revalues Dickens's unappealing personifications of its judicatory power. Walter Hartright is much more attractive as a penetrator of guilty secrets than Tulkinghorn (in *Bleak House*). Together, Walter and Marian Halcombe constitute a drastic overhaul of the malignancy in figures like the Defarges. These agents of providence retain a positive valence akin to the aura of holiness surrounding Felix Holt and Esther Lyon. Hartright and Marian become Collins's version of modern, secular saints. Dedicated redressers, they retain their popular appeal and yet pursue justice as ruthlessly as did the Defarges.

Walter and Marian acquire judicial authority by increments as the result of personal effort. Once they resolve to cooperate with providence in procuring rightful heirs for Limmeridge House and Blackwater Park, they are assigned the additional tasks of bringing to light Philip Fairlie's sexual misconduct and punishing Count Fosco for betraying the Brotherhood. When George Eliot later sets out to replace providence with evolution—its thoroughly secular, allegedly more scientific substitute—her agents of progress through gradual reform, figures such as Felix Holt and Dorothea Brooke, must challenge Collins's smartest improvement upon Dickens: the evolution of providence's lieutenants from despicable creatures like the Defarges into social servants as admirable as Hartright and Miss Halcombe. They seem as far above the Defarges biologically as George Eliot will insist her Esther Lyon is above Esther Summerson.

Dickens creates grotesques like Tulkinghorn in *Bleak House* or "The Vengeance" in *A Tale of Two Cities* deliberately. He wants to frighten a society that hides its sins or perpetuates past offenses. Having aroused the ire of providence, one cannot tell, Dickens warns, what fiends may be let loose. One cannot be sure what new injustices—persecution of a guiltless Darnay, for example—will spring from society's unrequited wrongs. Collins believes that the novelist should never let such total confusion develop. To personify a "care that conceals itself" but never sleeps, the sensational realist must never surrender control by waxing quite so apocalyptic; Dickens's severities give providence a bad reputation.

Agents of providence are unprepossessing in Dickens, Collins surmises, because the powers they profess to serve are inflexibly punitive, impossible to identify with. Madame Defarge foresees the approaching revolution as "an earthquake" (TTC, 230), an irrational, uncontrollable outbreak. "Tell the wind and the fire where to stop," she declaims, "not me!" (TTC, 435). "When the right time comes," she advises, "let loose a tiger and a devil; but wait for the time with the tiger and the devil chained" (TTC, 231). Collins objects to the defamation of providence as mindless natural force, less obedient than wind or fire. Providence in Collins is not just something feral to be unleashed. Collins's providence is also a containing, restrictive agency, often as anxious to hold things together as to tear them apart, disciplinary but not heedlessly destructive, and therefore a more intelligible factor than its counterpart in Dickens.

Images of providential activity in *The Woman in White* improve greatly when examined not just per se but, through double vision, as reconsiderations of Dickens's imagery as well. Walter's comment about being "linked" to a "chain of events" does not make him a demon or tiger to be let loose at the right moment; instead, the metaphor sets limits and establishes rules. A "chain" of events connotes fixed progression, deducible rather than visible and less diabolical than Madame Defarge's temporary restraint of the devil. When Marian senses that a "long series of complications . . . had . . . fastened round" her (WW, 305), one should picture a protective girdle where formerly, without reference to Dickens, the diction suggested only a cage.

To outscore Dickens, Collins anthropomorphizes the animalistic attributes with which Madame Defarge invests retaliation: his providence is a "Hand" that both cradles the just and crushes their enemies. Dickens's attempt to be anthropomorphic, Collins complains, actually dehumanizes. Stampeding feet, responsible for the "Echoing Footsteps" (TTC, 268) audible throughout *A Tale of Two Cites*, misrepresents Fate as a faceless mob, a many-legged monster rushing from afar for the pleasure of trampling Lucy and her daughter, who are even less culpable than Darnay.

Collins dislikes the Carlyle who talks of Fate exclusively as "the writing on the 'Adamant Tablet' " or predicts that society is careening toward the "Tarpeian Rock" at the "*road's end*," where "the abyss yawns sheer!"[9]—the aspect of Carlyle that prompted Dickens's wrathful metaphor of "the great grindstone, Earth" (TTC, 339). Yet Collins's rendition of providence is not like the attempts of Trollope or Mrs. Gaskell to discredit Dickens as an exaggerator. Collins only *appears* to be playing Dickens down; from another viewpoint, he is consistently extending him, going further in praise of providence by lengthening its foresight and increasing its powers of discernment. Providence unwinds to a greater degree in *The Woman in White*, says Collins, because its machinations stretch beyond scenes in which *Bleak House* and *A Tale of Two Cities* reach a climax or come to a halt; it also functions more accurately—that is, more selectively—in settling scores.

Dickens explodes a country's corrupt legal system in one novel and overthrows the irresponsible nobility of an unregenerate foreign nation in another. By contrast, Collins merely straightens out several injustices in Cumberland that are caused by a stifling sense of propriety. He unravels secrets where Dickens prefers to detonate them, thus presenting a more competitive and hence more formidable alternative to George Eliot's evolutionary unfolding of character and community. Collins's more sophisticated providence displays greater cognizance of individual merit and needs. Lady Glyde struggles as desperately as Darnay, because the sins of the fathers fall upon their offspring as regularly in Collins as they do throughout Dickens, but her fate is ultimately kinder than Lady Dedlock's or Dr. Manette's, even though her sufferings prove at least as instrumental as theirs (and more effective than Darnay's) in bringing well-kept secrets to light and unmasking long-standing villainy.

Collins's unique brand of discipleship, particularly his efforts both to amplify and fine-tune Dickensian providence, should be added to the list of reasons behind George Eliot's decision to parody Dickens in *Felix Holt* and *Middlemarch*. Revaluing the popularizer of Carlyle, a philosopher whom she considered a prophet of doom, seemed even more imperative when that philosopher's pupil grew influential enough to inspire a disciple of his own.

Criminals who deserve to be chastised by providence look more like victims when hunted down in Dickens by agents with whom the reader has little sympathy. The French aristocracy seems less detestable as *A Tale of Two Cities* wears on. One decides against the denizens of Saint Antoine as fervently at novel's end as Dickens pities them at the outset. But a more disastrous confusion of moral focus, in Collins's opinion, occurs in *Bleak House* when Sir Leicester's attorney-at-law, "An Oyster of the old school, whom nobody can open" (BH, 129), sets out to uncover Lady Dedlock's secret past.

An emblem of society's propensity to conceal its sins, to deny its obligations, Lady Dedlock is undeniably reprehensible. To Collins's consternation, however, Dickens cannot avoid making Tulkinghorn, the agent of providence who stalks Esther's mother, a virtual ally of propriety. Even in a secular, relative world, says Collins, providence becomes a clearer sign of God's law the more it is used to show that propriety is only man's. Throughout *The Woman in White*, Collins works to improve upon Dickens by keeping providence separate from propriety: he depends upon the former to overrule the latter.

Lady Dedlock, thanks to Tulkinghorn's probings, evokes too much pity. Collins's illegitimate baronet, Sir Percival Glyde, is a victim of propriety who then changes steadily for the worse; Esther Summerson's mother, far more passive, seems almost totally at the mercy of unfeeling convention. The dismay her sorrows awaken in the reader inevitably lessens the blame she should earn as a personification of neglectful community. Since Miss Barbary tells her that her illegitimate daughter died "in the first hours" of life (BH, 388), Lady Dedlock is guilty of transgressing society's sexual code but less so of avoiding her duties as a parent. Her anxiety to conceal the consequences of her one passion in a world that holds her to a loveless marriage, Collins argues, ought not to earn her a fate as unpleasant as Krook's—freezing to death instead of burning. In Collins's opinion, the evils of propriety are already monumental. They need not be confusingly equated by Dickens with the country's failure to recognize Jo's plight or clean up the squalor of Tom-all-alone's. Through repeated attacks upon the proprieties, Collins labors to distinguish the desirability of a sexual revolution from Victorian fears of a political one.

Collins was convinced that by 1860 the worship of propriety had become one of the besetting evils of Victorian life. Not Pride, not Self-ishness, not even Irresponsibility—capital offenses to which Dickens de-voted a major novel apiece—did as much harm. *The Woman in White* is an ultra-Dickensian novel in which Collins advances an idea that was not just important to him personally but of greater consequence nationally he said, than some of Dickens's.[10]

The Woman in White profits from reassessment as a virtual thesis novel: its complex critique of the Victorian obsession with propriety is part and parcel of its revaluation of the supposedly insufficient theories about the workings of providence in *Bleak House*.[11] One's estimate of the intel-lectuality of Victorian fiction, Dickens's in particular but that of mel-odramatic realists and the period generally, improves proportionately when a masterpiece by a disciple of the age's leading sensationalist is up-graded.

Historians account for the strict regulation of acceptable behavior within Victorian society as a middle-class reaction to eighteenth-century laxity.[12] What began as moral earnestness produced an age of "observance" rather than "assurance."[13] Thackeray complained that enforced reticence confined the artist to a small portion of the real world, but he knew better than to make an innocent reader blush. The Dickens who satirized the limited mentality of Mr. Podsnap and other self-appointed standard-set-ters, in *Our Mutual Friend* (1864-65) also wrote *Oliver Twist* without men-tioning Nancy's occupation. By comparison, Collins mounts a thorough, systematic attack. Concealed behind a multiplicity of narrators, he expres-ses contempt for a society that was giving up on faith but demanded that "the proprieties be observed,"[14] whatever the cost.

Collins agrees with Dickens that civilization seems to be deteriorat-ing—natural ties are loosening, community becoming a thing of the past—but he wants to show how vigorously unnatural, artificial bonds—the proprieties—are being tightened in their place. Society's wickedest sys-tems, Collins instructs Dickens's readers, are its *invisible* man-made laws rather than the written ones his mentor had assailed. Collins attempts to prove himself as adept as Dickens in using shortcomings in the legal system as a lever for criticizing society in general: he attacks England's inheritance laws, especially where the rights of the illegitimate are concerned, and condemns the inadequate protection of women who become victims of one-sided marriage contracts.[15] But Victorian England, he argues, is held more firmly in bondage by intangible restraints than by Chancery, the Marshalsea, and other malfunctioning institutions. Consequently, providence's ability to countermand the sense of imprisonment produced by an unreasonable moral code, not just to admonish irresponsibility, attests to the periodically self-correcting propensities of the life process.

As Collins doubtless realized, Lady Dedlock is a terminal victim of unkind social mores. Inspired by Dickens's creation of a symbolic female whose conduct allegedly underscores society's most serious failing—neglect of its responsibilities—Collins resolves to do the same thing, only better: in Anne Catherick, the pupil invents a satiric symbol for the pressures of propriety which he claims his teacher used unfairly to destroy Esther's negligent mother. In sum, writes Collins, propriety is a collective madness whose strictures grow stronger after the rationale behind their inception has faded, just as corrupt institutions behave more tyrannically as they become less serviceable. Collins's generalization is neatly embodied in the white-clad Anne Catherick, who haunts *The Woman in White* as effectively as fog permeates *Bleak House*.

Anne's ghostly figure disproves the judgment that powerful symbolic images, Dickens's forte, were beyond Collins's ability.[16] In the simple-mindedness of Anne's resolve to wear nothing but white, Collins parodies the preoccupation of his age with observing the proprieties. By novel's end, everyone's excessive concern for decorum begins to seem more quixotic than Anne's spotless costume. She continues to wear white long after the death of Mrs. Fairlie, whom she hoped to please by doing so. Anne's limited comprehension and restrictive wardrobe make her fixation with an unsullied appearance a reflection of the British public's stubborn adherence to narrow moral codes, its moral retardation. Her "unusual slowness in acquiring ideas," Mrs. Fairlie once noted, "implies an unusual tenacity in keeping them, when they are once received into her mind" (WW, 84).

Like *Bleak House*, *The Woman in White* can be read as a parable for society: an exciting mystery expressing a moral truth. Lady Dedlock's struggle to conceal her past parallels society's determination to ignore its sins: tolerating slums and failing to rehabilitate their inhabitants, Dickens implies, is as reprehensible as forsaking a child. Similarly, Lady Glyde's loss of position and identity and Walter Hartright's fight to recover them for her stand for the threats to individual liberty that Collins detected throughout Europe in the 1850s: the suppression of an individual's freedom can be accomplished by rigid societal conventions in one country as easily as by government decree in another.

One must remember that Laura Fairlie, an heiress who dresses "unpretendingly" in "plain white muslin" (WW, 80), is also a woman in white. Just as an illiterate, secretive Krook underlines the Lord Chancellor's incompetence and procrastination, Anne Catherick's simple-minded resolve to wear nothing but white ridicules England's preference for comforting rituals of respectability. But Laura is equally significant as Collins's imperiled symbol for what should be the inviolability of the individual. Dickens constructs his parable about neglectful society and the consequences of concealing vital relationships around providence's efforts to expose the guilt of one emblematic woman. Collins aspires to outdo this: he builds his satire against overmuch concern for propriety around providence's endeavors to protect the innocence of *two* symbolic women.

Through the sufferings Anne and Laura endure, Collins symbolizes different aspects of the torment that too much regard for appearances can cause. The half-sister symbolizing pressures from propriety, Collins proceeds to prove, can be substituted for the half-sister representing the right to individual freedom, with no one much the wiser. This not only illustrates the illegitimate, "sickly likeness" between the two; it also discloses the detrimental relationship between appearance and reality, verisimilitude in place of rectitude, that a hypocritical Victorian society has succumbed to.

Actually, Collins resorts to *three* symbolic women. Anne's mother is the woman in black, with "black silk gown," "black net cap," "iron-grey hair . . . in heavy bands," and "slate-coloured mittens" (WW, 504). Of all the prisoners of propriety in Collins's novel, Mrs. Catherick serves the stiffest sentence: psychological confinement as well as geographical restraint. Next to her, Dickens's Mrs. Clennam, the instance of self-incarceration that Collins wants to surpass, fairly sparkles. If Anne symbolizes the foolishness of a society trying always to appear spotless, Mrs. Catherick stands for the kind of death-in-life one can be reduced to by the struggle to live down one's past and regain respectability. Whenever Mrs. Catherick runs to the window so that the passing clergyman will bow to her, she constitutes a chilling reminder that respectability is a matter of perseverance plus artifice; it can even be extorted. In steady pursuit of propriety, Mrs. Catherick behaves as if she were superior to providence. Her determination to "claim . . . back" her character even if "years and years" are required (WW, 507) amounts to a design imposed upon life. Having subdued the clergyman, she prepares to coerce a bow from his wife.

Walter Hartright has a prospectus, too, the tripartite plan for retribution announced to Mr. Kyrle. He will restore Laura to Limmeridge House, have her name removed from what should be Anne's tomb, and make Fosco and Glyde "answer for their crime" (WW, 465-66). Such a design enjoys Collins's support because it ties in with the program of a judicial providence. Hartright's work as a detective in Laura's service designates him a cooperative agent or avenging angel employed by higher powers.[17] Mrs. Catherick, who works exclusively for herself, is a grotesque: her behavior enables Collins to embellish Walter, thereby separating him further from Tulkinghorn and the Defarges.

Mrs. Catherick is thought to have been guilty with Sir Percival of a sexual indiscretion similar to Lady Dedlock's with Captain Hawdon. But Mrs. Catherick's conception of Philip Fairlie's child, before wedding Catherick, is the well-kept secret from which the novel's intrigues develop, just as the mystery of Esther's parentage lies close to the heart of *Bleak House*. Mrs. Catherick's real crime was being an accomplice to forgery. Her offense, assisting Glyde to insert a fraudulent notice of his parents' marriage in the register at Old Welmingham, is thus neither the sexual act she committed nor the one she does penance for.

Nevertheless, Collins believes that Mrs. Catherick's case better serves to typify providence's inherent sense of poetic justice than Lady Dedlock's does. Esther's mother, having chosen riches and position over poverty and motherhood, perishes in Jenny's clothes. Once told that her child had died at birth, she herself dies in garments borrowed from the mother of a dead child (BH, 763). Providence in *his* novels, replies Collins, arranges penalties more cleverly suited to the crime. Mrs. Catherick is permitted to recover her social standing over a lifetime of exaggeratedly proper behavior. But society's image of her as a fallen woman reinstated by the community is a forgery she is compelled to continue perfecting indefinitely; thus it is forgery she is condemned to after all. Lady Dedlock, by contrast, is said to have sinned against responsibility but, Collins objects, what she is called to account for is violating the proprieties.

Dickens presents Jarndyce versus Jarndyce as a capital illustration of societal irresponsibility: as the suit runs its seemingly interminable course, those who sought redress from Chancery are instead ruined by that court. The case consumes in costs all the money not only the original suers but their children, too, expected from it. In *The Woman in White*, Collins contrives to demonstrate that society's unrecorded laws can be made to militate even more disastrously against the security they were supposed to provide. Jarndyce versus Jarndyce and the doubling of Laura in Anne are extraordinary occurrences. Collins competes with Dickens to see who can extract the more pertinent warning from the more remarkable incident.

When Fosco and Glyde substitute Anne Catherick and Laura Fairlie for each other, they install appearances in place of reality. This, says Collins, is the process Victorian morality is founded on, so society detects nothing amiss; despite the cruelty of the deed, everything still seems to be in proper place: a disturbed Anne (really Lady Glyde) is restored to the asylum after a more easily intimidated Laura (actually Anne) suffers a fatal heart attack. Polite society, hesitant to challenge appearances, remains thoroughly deceived. As Walter bitterly complains: "In the eye of reason and of law, in the estimation of relatives and friends, according to every received formality of civilized society," Laura is dead and buried; the real Laura, having escaped from confinement, is supposedly Anne Catherick, a deluded imposter (WW, 434). Fosco's brilliant plot obtains Lady Glyde's money and incapacitates Lady Glyde herself because it secures the cooperation of society, which resolutely endorses the crime.

The night Laura must spend on the road after leaving Sir Percival to return to her uncle is used to effect the plot against her. Mr. Fairlie permits Fosco to house Lady Glyde overnight in the latter's house in St. John's Wood, where the switch is to be made, when the count observes of this arrangement: "Here is comfort consulted—here are the interests of propriety consulted" (WW, 630). "Every received formality of civilized society" becomes Walter's enemy in that, having been Fosco's instrument, it remains his protection; taken in by the count, all persist in condoning Anne's death and Laura's expulsion. In the guise of a mystery novelist, Collins the social critic satirizes his contemporaries for using poor judgment and ruining their instincts with an unnatural set of rules that make goodness vulnerable to villainy whenever the latter cloaks itself in respectability.

The evils of propriety in *The Woman in White* seem meant to outnumber those brought about by irresponsibility in *Bleak House* or by the heartlessness and neglect of the French aristocracy in *A Tale of Two Cities*. Propriety prevents Walter Hartright, a drawing-master, from marrying Laura Fairlie, an heiress; then it compels her to wed Sir Percival Glyde out of respect for her late father's wishes. Her "secret misery," says Marian

Halcombe, is that she remains trapped between love for Walter, which is natural and good, and her official betrothal to Sir Percival, which symbolizes propriety as artificial and cruel "restraint" (WW, 97). Propriety prohibits Marian, as a woman, from interfering strongly in Laura's unhappy marriage. She remains helpless even after Glyde no longer dissembles with the "perfect delicacy and discretion" he exercised prior to the wedding (WW, 194). Finally, acting always with an eye to the preservation of proper appearances, Glyde, tutored by Fosco, gains control of his wife's money when Anne Catherick and Laura Fairlie, look-alike half-sisters, are made to change places.

Collins examines propriety in *The Woman in White* with the subtle intensity Dickens reserved for such aberrations in *Bleak House* as litigiousness, model deportment, and skewed philanthropy. Everyone in Collins's novel is tainted by an unjustifiable concern for propriety, marked by it, he insists, to a greater degree than Dickens's characters are prisoners of Chancery. Thoroughly admirable individuals sometimes cater to propriety automatically: when Marian reaches London to verify Laura's death, she repairs "to a respectable boarding-house . . . recommended by Mrs. Vesey's married sister" (WW, 440). The house's reputation increases in Marian's eyes because the endorsement comes from a married woman. Villains prove no less deferential to decorum. Although Fosco is the self-professed opponent of the proprieties, he knows what the English will (and will not) tolerate: laying hands on a woman's income or identity is all right, but not her clothes. Finally cornered by Walter, he emphasizes that Lady Glyde's "own clothes were taken away from her at night" in his London house "and Anne Catherick's were put on her in the morning, with the strictest regard to propriety, by the matronly hands of the good Rubelle" (WW, 630). Insisting on the nurse's matronliness, Fosco tries to be as discreet as Marian is when referring to Mrs. Vesey's "married" sister.

Even lesser personages are satirized for allowing themselves to become the victims of propriety. Eliza Michelson, Sir Percival's housekeeper, is so blinded by her preoccupation with it that she misses the callous conspiracy unfolding around her. She sees "no impropriety" when the countess allows the count into the fever-stricken Miss Halcombe's bedchamber, for Fosco is a married man. As the self-righteous clergyman's widow contributes her account of events at Blackwater Park, she unwittingly convicts Sir Percival and the count of grossest fraud yet carefully exonerates Fosco "of any impropriety" (WW, 390); that is, she absolves him of overt impoliteness, the only kind of offense many characters in the novel seem conditioned to recognize and resent.

The good-natured Mrs. Clements, too, allows reverence for propriety to obscure more important concerns. Throughout a painful interview with Walter Hartright, she seems more anxious about Anne's funeral than the questionable circumstances surrounding her death:

"Did you say, sir," said the poor woman, removing the handkerchief from her face, and looking up at me for the first time, "did you say that she had been nicely buried? Was it the sort of funeral she might have had if she had really been my own child?"

I assured her that it was. She seemed to take an inexplicable pride in my answer—to find a comfort in it which no other and higher considerations could afford. "It would have broken my heart," she said simply, "if Anne had not been nicely buried—" [WW, 497]

Assurances of Anne's proper burial keep Mrs. Clements's heart intact, even though her unfortunate girl was hurried into the grave by persecutors and entombed as someone else.

The specious comfort that correct observances bring, the satisfaction of doing things properly, outstrips the solace that "higher considerations" should afford. Propriety, it seems, has become a surrogate religion in *The Woman in White*. For Collins, as he proposes to extend Dickens, preserving appearances is the ultimate form of irresponsibility: a kind of wilful moral blindness, a way not just of failing to confront evil but of glossing it over. Not surprisingly, he treats insistence upon the proprieties as an impediment to sight much worse than Mrs. Jellyby's "Telescopic Philanthropy," which permits her (in Richard Carstone's words) to see "nothing nearer than Africa" (BH, 37). She can envision projects for "cultivating coffee and educating the natives of Borriobola-Gha" (BH, 38) but remains oblivious to her family's needs and the chaotic household she mismanages. Similarly, Mrs. Michelson sees intentional breaches of etiquette but not heinous crime; Mrs. Clements takes pride in a fine funeral without suspecting the abduction and intimidation that made one necessary.

In Collins's opinion, Dickens is the lesser satirical realist because he fails to acknowledge Victorian society's obsession with the proprieties, rather than its shunning of proffered responsibilities, as the main cause of secrets, secret lives, and the conspiracies mandatory to protect or expose them. To prove this contention, Collins increases the quantity and, in his estimation, the gravity of a secrecy already epidemic in *Bleak House;* indeed, there are more secrets to be kept in *The Woman in White* than in *Bleak House* and *A Tale of Two Cities* combined. Lady Dedlock's secret motivates the many detectives in *Bleak House*, both amateur and professional; it turns out to be Esther's secret as well. By contrast, although Glyde's "Secret" (the fact of his illegitimacy) is the only one Collins capitalizes, Philip Fairlie's turns out to be at least as important. Furthermore, Mrs. Catherick, although supposedly unfaithful to her husband, has not only kept Philip Fairlie's secret but is obliged to guard Sir Percival Glyde's as diligently as he does. Many of the English in *The Woman in White*, as well as the foreigner Fosco,[18] depend for present happiness, indeed for survival, on suppressing compromising events in the past.

Collins seconds Dickens to the extent that providential exposure overtakes the nefarious secrets of Fosco and Glyde. But the erstwhile protégé lays greater stress on the proliferation of secrets, new ones constantly being fashioned to protect old even among the sympathetic characters. Walter confesses his "secret" love for Laura, whom propriety dictates he regard only as his pupil (WW, 88). Once Laura returns his affection, artist and student become a secret society, an emotional conspiracy. When Marian learns Walter's secret, her regard for propriety forces her to separate the lovers so that Laura can keep her promise to her father. This action earns Marian a place in a new conspiracy: the sisters have "a secret between them" that they must endeavor to keep from Laura's future husband. Proliferation of secrets and secret societies, Collins tells Dickens, is another price England will continue to pay as long as the country puts too much emphasis on maintaining an outwardly proper social order.

In *A Tale of Two Cities* Dickens had just argued that Victorian England was unwise to consider itself more progressive, hence less vulnerable to internal social upheaval, than eighteenth-century France. Collins's opinion is that a propriety-ridden society has even less right to feel superior to undemocratic countries. Throughout *The Woman in White*, he consistently parallels political repression in Italy with the restrictions that propriety imposes upon freedom in England. It is as if Victorian society, thanks to illiberal notions, were as oppressed morally as the nineteenth-century Italy Professor Pesca has fled from is stifled politically.

On the surface in *The Woman in White* rules are followed, amenities observed. But the society Collins presents is a hotbed of frustrated desires, including Walter's for Laura, Sir Percival's for legitimacy, and Mrs. Catherick's for greater community acceptance. In *Bleak House*, obligations are ignored and denial of associations is the rule, yet connections become evident as patterns emerge. Similarly, beneath the veneer of sociability the characters strive to maintain in *The Woman in White*, complex schemes develop, miniature versions of Italy's secret societies form, bitter struggles take place: Sir Percival persecutes Anne Catherick; Walter tracks down Fosco and Glyde. From preoccupation with polite appearances, Collins implies, stem the Gothic realities that repression produces. Thus Fosco sips England's social beverage while his wife engages in household espionage. Cruelly polite, the count obliges Marian to serve tea while the countess is recovering Marian's letter for help by drugging the unsuspecting Fanny—using tea, of course (WW, 336).

To the radical moralist in Collins, subsurface turmoil makes Victorian society, which only appears highly civilized, worse than Dickens portrayed it. The Victorian insistence on regulated behavior, society's false sense of what constitutes uprightness, has produced the ultimate inversion: hell instead of heaven—which explains Collins's numerous allusions to *The Divine Comedy*. As the Dante of this daylight underworld, the novelist charts an inferno of his characters' own devising.

The opening chapter of *Bleak House* unveils a civilization slipping backwards instead of evolving. Everywhere Dickens finds "mud," "fog," and "mire": Londoners have forsaken all semblance of community and the city is reverting to primal slime. Victorians, Collins goes on, are not merely "losing their foot-hold" (BH, 3) on the evolutionary ladder, as foot-passengers in Dickens's dreadful city seem to be doing. Rather, like inhabitants of Dante's seventh circle, the point Pesca and the "young misses" he is tutoring have reached (WW, 40), they are also creating a hellish environment by denying the natural and condoning the replacement of art with artifice.[19] This nonsalutary process enfranchises monsters like Fosco and Glyde, the former a magnificent reincarnation of Satan.

As the epitome of subterfuge and repression, Fosco's duplicity exceeds that of the Lord Chancellor who "sits . . . at the heart of the fog" in Temple Bar (BH, 4). Also, Dantesque landscapes, especially at Blackwater Park, do more than give added plausibility to the Gothic machinery of Collins's plot; they are part of an attempt to outstrip Dickens's use of such machinery. Dickens sets providence the task of halting, occasionally, society's downward slides; Collins assigns providence the harder job of thwarting man's recurrent tendency to create hell on earth.

The Woman in White contains two major characters who are illegitimate, not just one as in *Bleak House*. Anne Catherick and Sir Percival Glyde are variant forms of the harmful distortions to which too stringent an application of society's moral rules can lead. In *Bleak House*, disdain for irregularities of birth furnishes an index to the community's neglect of unfortunates. Collins suggests that mistreatment of the illegitimate also shows society's hatred for exceptions to its rules and its hidebound resistance to change: that is, to reforms that would broaden tolerance or extend privilege. Laws discriminating against bastards, Collins explains to Dickens, are the outgrowth of unwritten codes and attitudes, which are the real culprits.

Esther Summerson professes to have little wit and less narrative skill; she claims no special gift for observation, yet the reader's interest in her story never flags. She is not only coauthor of one of the century's best novels but improves as a writer-commentator the more the Esther her tale is about learns and matures. Like Jane Eyre, she sets down her own life story, thereby signaling that she has assumed control of her destiny. Anne Catherick, by contrast, in a novel teeming with narrators, is incapable of reciting her history—indeed does not know it correctly. Glyde's sole act of authorship conceals the past: he forges himself into existence in what amounts to revision downward of Esther's self-realization through autobiography.

The further *Bleak House* proceeds, the better adjusted its illegitimate heroine becomes. Anne Catherick, in Collins's ammendment, remains an undisputed case of arrested development, and Sir Percival virtually personifies insecurity. Apart from the baronetcy he is not entitled to, he has no place in society, no reason for existing. Dickens allows Miss Summerson's innate worth to come out, and her circle continually widens. Without a patent of nobility, Collins counters, only penury and friendlessness await Glyde.

Contrary to modern critics who find Esther's personality too good to be true, Collins protests that her good fortune is. Having pointed out that providence in Dickens presses too hard on Lady Dedlock, Collins appends that, realistically, the unfairness of Victorian society in both its legal and moral systems would ensure equally unkind treatment of her daughter. Yet Esther, rescued by a fairy godfather, marries her Prince Charming despite having slept away much of her beauty thanks to fever from smallpox.

Esther is illegitimacy born of irresponsibility, the result of passion put before duty. Anne Catherick and Sir Percival are both instances of illegitimacy caused and perpetuated by a parent's fear of being discovered to have disregarded propriety. Propriety thus emerges as a greater social evil than irresponsibility because Anne Catherick's sufferings and Glyde's, taken together or separately, exceed Esther's.

Glyde is a victim before he becomes a criminal. He commits a forgery in the marriage register for the same reason he subsequently mistreats Anne Catherick and abuses his wife: he wants to suppress the impropriety his father committed by neglecting to marry his mother. Although cruelty and foul temper tell against him, he is arguably more of a martyr to propriety than either Laura Fairlie or Esther Summerson. Dickens's heroine does not arrive at the entrance to the graveyard in time to rescue her mother. Collins hoped to outdo Dickens by making Glyde's efforts on behalf of his mother even less successful. Collins's scorn for the criminal does not conceal a criticism of society for having produced, in this tormented soul, so futile a sense of propriety: Glyde, the novelist exclaims, dies for committing a forgery that "made an honest woman of his mother after she was dead in her grave!" (WW, 552).

If offenders regularly turn into victims (Lady Dedlock) and victims into criminals (Madame Defarge), right and wrong, Collins charges, grow blurry; wrongdoing never ends. Yet Glyde is a victim who becomes a criminal. *Bleak House* and *A Tale of Two Cities*, Collins complains, unwisely try to frighten readers twice over: Dickens's retributive agency overtakes those responsible for social wrongs without being able to halt the spread of injustice. This inspires mistrust in the proficiency of the providential order that one is being encouraged to look to for recompense. In *The Woman in White*, however, Collins is not averse to showing secrets multiplying from secrets faster than providence can disclose them.

Collins dwells upon the aptness, not to mention the greater sense of finality, with which his providence eventually acts. Once Hartright restores Laura's proper identity, she is freed from further responsibility to atone for her father's sins, whereas it proves impossible for Lady Dedlock to live down her past. When Glyde, driven to desperation by Hartright's investigations, burns to death trying to cover up his original felony in the same vestry where he perpetrated it, an offended moral order exacts a hellish but definitive revenge. The fire that consumes Sir Percival punishes the Glyde family once and for all. Throughout *The Woman in White*, boasts Collins, a stricter economy prevails: the same startling incidents are utilized to demote propriety and elevate providential superintendence. Collins astonishes the reader with a sensational conflagration that is more realistically presented and more directly deserved than the disaster Dickens can only impose obliquely upon the untouchable Lord Chancellor through the more combustible Krook.

Collins strives to outdo Dickens at describing the vindictiveness with which the nature of things requires the next generation to pay for its parents' sins. Such dire inheritance disproves the twin notions that Victorian society is proper and progressive. Hartright quotes Exodus 34:7 to sum up *The Woman in White*: "The sins of the fathers shall be visited on the children" (WW, 575). Had the proprieties been less binding at Varneck Hall and Blackwater Park, the liaison between Philip Fairlie and the eventual Mrs. Catherick and the unsanctified union of Glyde's parents might not have spawned more serious crime.

When Dickens quoted the same biblical passage, he meant that each generation takes the consequences for its predecessor's sins of omission: that is, for the reforms they failed to introduce. Collins intends to outdo

Dickens on the subject of inherited penalties in that children in *The Woman in White* have to bear consequences graver than the parent's crime, as the half-sisters do, or else go even deeper into wrongdoing trying to avoid those consequences, which is the course Glyde chooses. Since the half-sisters and Glyde all suffer, Collins validates his contention that the era's overbearing sense of appropriate behavior harms those who observe the rules as well as those who follow rules hypocritically or hide their crimes behind them.

Radical social critics, Dickens and Collins nevertheless remain conservatively Victorian because of their reluctance to forgo larger, nonsecular frames of reference. They are progressive mainly to the extent that they trust in a moral force, based in the nature of things, whose job it is to safeguard against the permanent triumph of evil or error. Collins is anxious to appear both the more unorthodox and more traditional of the two. He needs providence in *The Woman in White* to frustrate villainy; life opens out for Hartright and Laura only to the extent that it closes in upon Fosco and Glyde. Openness is Collins's modern-sounding corrective for overmuch propriety, but providence is his hedge against anarchy. In his view, turmoil from unexpected combustion in *Bleak House* or from revolution in *A Tale of Two Cities* is virtually self-defeating: it makes chaos, which providence is supposed to prevent, serve as the punishment for irresponsibility. Contrary to what deconstructionists might say, Collins is not at odds with himself; he merely sounds more convincing and more modern on one of his subjects than on the other. Most twentieth-century readers can applaud his attack on propriety even if they remain skeptical about his confidence in providence, compared with which Dickens's apocalyptic thunderings seem more believable in a nuclear age. By discrediting propriety without being equally persuasive in salute to providence, Collins both impedes the secularization process and intensifies it, for he hastens the arrival of a world without rules.

At the conclusion of *The Woman in White*, Collins's original point about Dickens's mishandling of the ways of providence in *A Tale of Two Cities* has become several. Beginning with a revision of Dickens's timetable for providential intervention, Collins proceeds to reconstruct the master's system of providential rewards and punishments. Collins objects that wrongdoing in *A Tale of Two Cities* never ends, yet he turns a victimized Glyde into a criminal because he believes he understands when to be firmer than Dickens, when fairer. He decides that he knows when to have providence move faster than it does in Dickens, when to appear more deliberate, when to underscore the permeation of a social evil such as propriety and yet make subtler distinctions regarding individual degrees of guilt. Proximity to one's target, a drawback for undoers like Mrs. Gaskell, is a plus for the outdoer. *The Woman in White* follows closely upon *A Tale of Two Cities* so that Collins can show how quickly he can cap his rival.

Hartright's problems with propriety begin simultaneously with Collins's novel. On the road to London, in the middle of the night, he encounters "a solitary Woman, dressed from head to foot in white garments" (WW, 47). Walter must overcome the suspicion that he is being solicited by a prostitute. Fortunately, his instincts as a man of integrity are impeccable; he is not misled by "the perplexingly strange circumstances." Since he does not know "what sort of woman she was," it is to his credit not to have "misconstrued her motive in speaking even at that suspiciously late hour and in that suspiciously lonely place" (WW, 48).

Regardless of what propriety might dictate, Walter becomes involved when the woman in white asks for trust as well as help. "The loneliness and helplessness of the woman," he says, "touched me. The *natural impulse* to assist her and to spare her got the better of the judgement, the caution, the worldly tact, which an older, wiser, and colder man might have summoned to help him in this strange emergency" (WW, 49; italics added).

This is how Collins tries to improve upon the melodramatic realism he learned from Dickens. An extraordinary incident drives home a highly charged ethical or social observation that is also suited for use in more mundane circumstances. Through a "strange emergency," the sensation novelist underlines his moral point. Collins's lesson is that inclination should sometimes get the better of conditioning. He submits his thesis that "natural impulse," which society squelches in its "older, wiser, and colder" members, is often superior to "judgement," "caution," and "wordly tact," all of which are propriety's accoutrements.

Collins springs the escapee from the asylum on Walter and the reader within the novel's first fifty pages. He attempts to do this as quickly and effectively as Dickens had Defarge lead Mr. Lorry and Miss Manette to her father: in a garret, they discover "a white-haired man," recently released from the North Tower, seated "on a low bench . . . very busy, making shoes" (TTC, 55). Of the two commencements involving released captives, it is difficult to decide which manifestation causes the greater stir or leaves more questions to be answered later. Nevertheless, Collins tries to make good on his complaint about Dickens's tardy revelation of Manette's letter. To challenge the master's dictum only to "*suggest*" early on, rather than underline, he does both. Anne's significance for Walter, like Manette's for Darnay, must wait, no matter how ominous the implications. But although the apparition in Dickens's novel carries no immediate comment on the irresponsibility of the French aristocracy, Collins's devaluation of England's oppressive sense of propriety has already begun.

The first *two* chapters of *Bleak House*, "In Chancery" and "In Fashion," transport the reader from one locus of irresponsibility to another. The first *three* women Hartright encounters seduce him away from propriety. Marian Halcombe, an admirably outspoken violator of "female propriety" in her conversation (WW, 61), is the second improper woman Walter succumbs to in as many days;[20] then he commits still another offense by falling in love with Laura. As a mere drawing-master, Walter is only "admitted among beautiful and captivating women much as a harmless domestic animal is admitted among them" (WW, 89). Eventually, by marrying Laura and redressing the wrongs society has done her, Walter also reasserts his individuality and recovers his masculinity. He has as much need as Esther Summerson to prove himself socially acceptable and worthy of love.

Walter's campaign against propriety, ironically an effort to set matters right, retaliates against everything that drove him from Laura's side and then permitted her to be refused her proper place. At a tremendous cost in time and energy, Walter turns back the clock to the day on which Anne Catherick was buried as Laura Fairlie. At Laura's ceremonial reinstatement as herself, when Walter opens "the proceedings" (WW, 637), he is exacting legal satisfaction unavailable to him or her in a court of law. Fosco and Glyde—the first a fugitive on the Continent, the second already dead—are convicted *in absentia* by a jury of Mr. Fairlie's tenants. Propriety itself, society's set of unwritten laws, is put on trial for poor judgment. Having been, with providence's aid, as good a detective as Bucket, Walter proves a better lawyer than any of that tribe in *Bleak House*.

Collins takes over and enlarges upon the satirical metaphor for life that Dickens invented in *Bleak House*, the idea that living in Victorian England is like becoming enmeshed in an interminable law case, engaged in a perpetual call for justice. *The Woman in White* can be described as a novel not only written about a long call for justice but actually designed to resemble an extended case. The many narrators whose depositions Walter collects testify in the ongoing suit he brings against the proprieties. Inasmuch as Laura's troubles began with her father's indiscretions, Collins prolongs matters over more than one generation, long enough to rival Jarndyce versus Jarndyce. Then he adjudicates his law case to the reader's satisfaction, thinking to outdo Dickens twice over.

Himself a lawyer, Collins goes contrary to Dickens when he presents Gilmore and Kyrle as disinterested friends of the Fairlie family, not as parasites or vultures. Similarly, George Eliot's reformers redo Dickens's portrait of Mrs. Jellyby and Trollope's of Mr. Bold. But Collins's principal goal is to reveal providence as virtually an alternative legal system that works with greater "care" in *The Woman in White* than in *Bleak House*. With Walter as both solicitor and barrister, providence achieves due process.

The final step in the resurrection ritual is the procession to the church-yard, where a "throng" of Mr. Fairlie's tenants and villagers "see the false inscription struck off" Anne's tombstone "with their own eyes" (WW, 639). For society's sight impediment, its ability to recognize impropriety but not crime, Collins's agent of providence effects a cure.

First as doer, then as author, Walter outshines his counterparts in *Bleak House*. He assembles the narratives for *The Woman in White* virtually as a religious act, a votive tribute to providence for aid received. His collection of the many testimonies that make up the novel, including his own, is meant to surpass the feat of interweaving Esther's autobiography and the third-person narrator's satire into a coherent novel about the condition of England.

Walter gradually recognizes in providence a fearful but just admin-istrator of mankind's affairs. He has more reason to do so than anyone in *Bleak House* or *A Tale of Two Cities*. Providence brings Walter out on the London road when Anne needs help, leads him to Cumberland and Laura, keeps him safe during the semisuicidal expedition to Central America, reunites him with Laura at the grave in which she is supposedly buried, helps him to unmask Glyde and Fosco, and bestows Limmeridge House upon his son.

These incidents are not sops that Collins tosses his readers.[21] Instead, they are the work of a novelist who, like Dickens, thinks detective stories highly civilized; the successful investigation of a crime indicates that, despite the enormous amount of evil in the world, there is sometimes enough good to offset its persistent activity. More convincingly than Dickens did, Collins wants to demonstrate that detective stories imitate the rhythms of life; they are expressions of respect for life's long-range ability to redeem the deserving and rid itself of malefactors.

The indignities heaped upon Count Fosco at novel's end are intended to offset the rewards showered on Hartright. Although Collins invests the count with wit and charm, he commissions Walter the true foe of excessive propriety and rejects the calculated perversion of such enmity, which is Fosco. Collins never depicts his corpulent villain as a sincere opponent of social constraints; on the contrary, he portrays him as a criminal master-mind whose conspiracy against Laura and Anne succeeds for a time because no crime appears to have been committed.

Doubtless, Fosco is deputized to express Collins's contempt for the stolidity of Victorian England. "I say what other people only think," the outspoken Fosco boasts. "When all the rest of the world is in a conspiracy to accept the mask for the true face, mine is the rash hand that tears off the plump pasteboard, and shows the bare bones beneath" (WW, 259). But when Fosco's actions are measured against his own manifesto, they expose his falseness. Tearing off pasteboards is never among Fosco's accomplishments. His plan to improve his own fortunes along with Sir Percival's requires the substitution of Anne Catherick for Laura Fairlie in a conspiracy tailored to install a mask for the true face. Ironically, Fosco misreads a "fatal resemblance" as a heaven-sent opportunity; thus the novel's arch-exploiter of the proprieties speeds up the retribution process for crimes he and Glyde committed separately years before.

Liberty and self-determination are ideals that Fosco, Collins's expert at counterrevolutionary espionage, always labors against. Whether infiltrating the Brotherhood in Italy or dipping into the mail bag to intercept Marian's letters at Blackwater Park, Fosco is more than an agent of suppression: he is the enemy of its enemies. Consequently, the harshest judgment in *The Woman in White* descends upon the count. Collins takes pains to prove that he is no more an "amoralist"[22] than Dickens is. Exalting Walter, Collins hopes to appear more munificent than his competitor; bringing down Fosco, he insists on being seen as the sterner judge, allowing the moral order to demand from his finest creation the severest penalty.

Not only does the Brotherhood have the count assassinated, but his corpse is treated disrespectfully as a public spectacle in "the terrible dead-house of Paris" (WW, 642). Secretive, conspiratorial, Fosco is subjected to complete exposure, a dagger wound over the heart and the letter "T" for traitor carved into his arm. His enormous naked body, an improper sight for English eyes, is a carnival attraction to the French. The alleged foe of England's moral humbuggery would not strip Lady Glyde of her costume but readily took away her name. Now, unclaimed, he is deprived of clothing *and* identity. He is revealed as a foe of brotherhood, a false friend of the freedom and openness he pretended to favor when styling himself the opponent of "moral clap-traps." Hartright's final glimpse of the count recalls Dante's view of Satan at the nethermost point in hell, reserved for traitors.[23]

In the closing pages of *The Woman in White*, Collins puts the finishing touches to the announcement of rivalry with Dickens that he issued with the twenty-sixth number. He replays Esther's discovery of Lady Dedlock's body yet again by redoing the incident as Walter's discovery of Fosco's ironic fate, thus attempting a double revaluation of the most sensational disclosure scene in Dickens's masterwork. This time, instead of approaching a country burial ground, Walter enters the Paris morgue. Suspense builds as "slowly, inch by inch," he presses through the crowd, "moving nearer and nearer" to Collins's final revelation. Not knowing what to expect from the place or the multitude, Hartright is astounded to behold the duplicitous count's "massive" corpse "exposed" to the public's "flippant curiosity" (WW, 642-43).

The "care that conceals itself," Collins is replying to Dickens, ought always to be looked at in two ways: it should be just as paternal as it is judicial. Collins contends that his novel more skillfully captures this dual aspect. Sparing Lady Glyde by reuniting her with Walter, who thus obtains his heart's desire, Collins stresses providential benevolence; fate looks out for Laura more assiduously than her father did or her uncle seems willing to do. At the same time, the "dreadful end" reserved for Fosco, every bit as ironically fitting as Lady Dedlock's, supplies a better sense than Dickens allegedly has of providential governance as comeuppance, the more commonly emphasized aspect of "fulfillment."

The close of *The Woman in White* becomes for Collins a clearer instance than anything in Dickens of the delight providence takes in poetic justice. Like Lady Dedlock, Fosco is never what he pretends to be. But his deceptions, shielded by manipulation of the proprieties, do far more harm. The conspiratorial count lying naked to the world is a blow not just to propriety but to all concealment of villainy behind its facade. Fosco's fate strikes the author of *The Woman in White* as a truer, more powerful illustration than Lady Dedlock's cruel demise of the inescapable justice that "everything" in life is always "working to."

In the Dickens-Collins play *The Frozen Deep* (1857), Dickens eagerly assumed the role of Richard Wardour, the Arctic explorer who perishes from the strain of saving his rival, Frank Aldersley, portrayed by Collins. Both men admire the same woman, Lucy Crayford, who can be made to stand for the general public that artists strive to please. Looking back at this drama in light of events from 1860 until Dickens's death, the modern revaluator suspects that both novelists came to interpret the play's central arrangement symbolically with reference to their own relationship; they came to see it as a work about outdoing and undoing, if indeed the thought of viewing its rivalries that way had not already occurred to them in 1857. Wardour's actions impressed Collins as the concession one novelist owes his designated successor. In *The Woman in White*, Anne Catherick, who meets her fate in Laura's place, is not the stronger of the two, as Wardour was, but a paler version, a weaker forerunner, of her more attractive half-sister.

The expedition that Wardour and Aldersley undertake resembles Sir

John Franklin's search for a Northwest Passage, which culminated with the explorer's disappearance in 1845. Charges of cannibalism had been brought against the Franklin expedition as recently as 1854, when a rescue operation returned with grizzly stories of the party's last days but no actual evidence. One learns that Dickens "contributed heavily to Collins's original draft" of *The Frozen Deep* because the play afforded the troubled novelist "relief from the marital unhappiness . . . that agitated him during 1856-1857."[24] But the melodrama's obsession with self-sacrifice and its flirtation with the theme of cannibalism suggest a second anxiety: Dickens's mounting fear of being consumed by his rivals and his distress at the ignoble sentiments their reworkings of his novels aroused within him. Mrs. Gaskell had revised *Hard Times* extensively in 1854-55, and Trollope revalued Dickens in *The Warden* less than a year before.

A mediocre vehicle at best, *The Frozen Deep* excited Dickens as a chance to explore pressing artistic uncertainties that his rivalry with Collins would soon bring to a head. Where Collins underlines the idea of substitution or self-sacrifice as succession, Dickens suggests that the individual who promotes another's welfare at his own expense is always shown thereby to be the superior creator. He is the progenitor without whom a rival like Aldersley could not draw breath.

Instead of victimizing Aldersley to save himself, Wardour expends his strength to preserve the other man. Dickens insisted that the play raise the "terrible suspicion" that Wardour has murdered Aldersley, then dispel it in order to reaffirm one's faith in human nature.[25] Wardour is sorely tempted when he holds the upper hand, but he behaves nobly. Just as when Carton resolves to do a "far, far better thing" (TTC, 480) than he has ever before attempted, the inference is that he has the better part, that he outdoes Darnay as Wardour triumphs over Aldersley. Such inference would not have been lost on Collins. Whatever Darnay and Aldersley subsequently achieve, Dickens implies, including the happiness they enjoy, redounds to the persons who made it possible and elevates them further.

Compared with Collins's explanation of the resemblance between Anne Catherick and Laura Fairlie, however, Carton's likeness to Darnay seems unaccountable. The discovery that Philip Fairlie fathered both girls clarifies the genetic phenomenon at the core of *The Woman in White*. When Collins borrows from *A Tale of Two Cities* the idea of employing look-alikes, he changes more than gender. Discrediting Dickens's fortuitousness is the means by which he makes his own reliance on a *doppelgänger*, essentially a Gothic rather than a realistic device, seem more plausible. Collins revises Dickens's use of doubles to show that providence is more provident than his rival imagines: even in the case of the unfortunate Anne Catherick, who enters Walter's life "like a fatality" (WW, 97), it never wastes human suffering.

Anne's involuntary martyrdom leads to the overthrow of Fosco and Glyde. Carton's voluntary death, a minor consequence of violent revolution, is mostly a by-product of revenge long overdue; it fails to slake the Jacobin thirst for aristocratic blood. Similarly, Lady Dedlock's death in *Bleak House* does not ventilate a prisonlike social system. But when Anne Catherick perishes from the villains' misuse of her in the scheme to obtain Laura's money, she dies too soon; therefore, the brilliant plan Fosco and Glyde must proceed with anyway has a fatal flaw in its timetable for Walter to discover: the woman said to have been Lady Glyde is shown to have succumbed in London before Laura was lured from Blackwater Park into Fosco's trap. Providence, Collins maintains, sees to it that Anne eventually helps to release Laura from the marriage that her earlier attempted interference failed to prevent.

In *A Tale of Two Cities*, providence supplies Carton for Darnay and Darnay for Carton: each extricates the other from an untenable situation. Carton rescues Darnay and is thereby recalled from a dissolute existence. Collins does not object to this simply because he considers it too convenient dramatically, hence overdone; rather, Dickens's attitude toward propriety, much too conservative for Collins, is again the issue. As Darnay's "double of coarse deportment" (TTC, 111), Carton regains a sense of moral purpose through an ennobling act of self-sacrifice. Substituting himself for Darnay means placing his higher nature above his coarser self. In Collins's estimation, Dickens unrealistically equates resurrection, which is secularized as the recovery of one's true being, with a return to conventional notions of rectitude. It is as if self-realization were merely a matter of being recalled from a bohemian life-style to the codes and standards of one's community, standards which Dickens often questions but which are suddenly assumed to be salvationary.

Throughout *The Woman in White*, the value of sacrificing oneself for a presumably superior person or kowtowing to one's allegedly higher self remains suspect. Wardour's behavior, revalued by Collins, is no more meritorious than Carton's seems probable. It follows that the idea of Dickens making way for a successor is a euphemism for having to give way. Anne Catherick shapes her life, particularly her resolve always to wear white, in memory of Mrs. Fairlie. Laura sacrifices herself in marriage according to her father's wishes. Collins uses his look-alikes to suggest that too great a concern for propriety (defined as the duty one thinks one owes to another) can only mean forfeiture of one's real self, which is then excruciatingly difficult to recover, as Anne and Laura both learn.

In 1859-60, Dickens and Collins both wrote novels in which characters replace characters they resemble. This flurry of activity came at a time when Collins was trying to take Dickens's place as the Victorian period's foremost sensational realist, and Dickens was preparing to fight back in order to retain the top spot. Using doubles who step into one another's shoes reveals how deeply the idea of undoing a competitor by outdoing him at his own game preoccupied both novelists.

Chapter Five

Undoing by Outdoing Continued

Great Expectations

The Moonstone

MOST OF THE prior reconsiderations of the Dickens-Collins exchange minimize its complexity: either Collins is said to have exerted a "stultifying influence on Dickens,"[1] or his alleged impact is dismissed as a myth.[2] The motive in both cases seems to be a desire to protect Dickens's integrity as an artist, to ensure his unassailable preeminence. This goal becomes ludicrous in view of Dickens's difficulties with George Eliot, Trollope, and Mrs. Gaskell. Recent attempts to acknowledge a prolonged Dickens-Collins interaction but confine it to a personal relationship, a matter of only biographical importance, conceal even further one of the nineteenth century's fiercest rivalries.[3]

It proves more rewarding to recognize a Dickens understandably wary of Collins's success, not bitter or envious[4] but goaded to reassert his supremacy. Dickens quickly realized that he had to outdo, whenever possible, the man by whom he felt he was in danger of being outdone. Collins's uncanny ability to make Dickens's obsessions his own drove the older novelist even more firmly in directions he had previously chosen. Collins, for example, came out strongly, in *The Woman in White*, against subservience to the proprieties. So Dickens created the Podsnaps in *Our Mutual Friend* to satirize again the Victorian concern with preserving respectable appearances. Dickens thought he had settled the issue in *Bleak House* and *Little Dorrit*, along with a related matter: the harmfulness of secrecy. In *Little Dorrit* (1855-57) he had castigated, in the person of Mrs. General, society's preoccupation with surfaces and had invalided Mrs. Clennam to illustrate the damage that electing to be secretive about one's sins can do.

Nevertheless, with publication of *The Woman in White* in 1860, Dickens found himself being assimilated, amended, and on occasion outclassed by a younger novelist he had mistaken for his apprentice. In self-defense he resolved to revalue Collins as speedily as Collins was reworking him. Tensions between *The Woman in White* and the Dickens novels that bracketed it in *All the Year Round*—*A Tale of Two Cities* and *Great Expectations*—reveal two novelists eager to imitate and surpass one another simultaneously. Far from having "stultifying" effects, this rivalry—more than the earlier contest between Dickens and Mrs. Gaskell—was one in which each participant pushed the other to new heights.

Throughout the first phase of Dickens's response to Collins, revaluation generally means reassertion. So basic a strategy proves highly efficient but keeps Dickens mostly on the defensive. In *Great Expectations* (1860-61) Dickens has no choice except to restate his preference for a single climactic disclosure toward which the entire novel accelerates. The overwhelming question becomes the identity of Pip's benefactor, which Dickens withholds as long as possible, although clues abound. *Great Expectations* is not only Dickens's comment on the mid-Victorian optimism of his less sensational rivals; it is also an effort to quell a sort of palace revolution by a subordinate trying to assume command of the melodramatic novel.

In reply to Collins, providence in *Great Expectations* combines an educative with a punitive role: it schools Pip even as it chastens him. When the older and wiser Mr. Pirrip reflects upon his inaugural visit to Satis House, he identifies it as the "memorable day" in his life. He was then under the illusion that Miss Havisham would eventually declare herself his secret benefactor; he later accepts Magwitch's claim to the role. In retrospect, only providence seems to deserve the title. Mrs. Joe, Miss Havisham, and Magwitch become, by comparison, inadequate prototypes, each of whom illustrates in a different way the folly of total dependence on earthly guides. Dickens writes an inverted fairytale in which the frustration of false hopes, in particular the idea that money makes the man, is a difficult lesson for a prospering nation to digest when it is on the brink of global supremacy. But the tale is also paradoxically a sign of the superintendence each reader is encouraged to believe is looking out for him personally.

Speaking for Dickens, Pip observes that what has transpired in his case "is the same with any life. Imagine one selected day struck out of it, and think how different its course would have been. Pause you who read this, and think for a moment of the long chain of iron or gold, of thorns or flowers, that would never have bound you, but for the formation of the first link on one memorable day."5 Is the "long chain" that binds Pip "of iron or gold"? Is it covered with "thorns or flowers"? The point of Dickens's moral fable is that the answer is both. Despite repeated references to leg chains, convicts, prisoner's clothes, and prisons, *Great Expectations* is ultimately the story of Pip's deliverance, his ascent from false and demeaning attitudes to true gentility. Dickens wants to offset Collins, whose providential chain of events in *The Woman in White* made providence's activities in *A Tale of Two Cities* seem unmindful of individual needs. Dickens lays claim to a supernatural agency at least as paternal as the forces that assist Walter Hartright. In *Great Expectations*, even more than in *The Woman in White*, providence builds character.

At the same time, however, Dickens parodies the weakest point in Collins's novel: Pip's history redoes Walter's astronomical rise from drawing-master to master of Limmeridge House. *The Woman in White*, despite effective satire on Victorian obsessions with propriety, contains a success story to rival Dick Whittington's. Hartright's rise is just as essential to Collins's attack on social convention as it is to the celebration of providential direction behind the life process. Having fallen in love with Laura, Walter aspires to marry above himself; in spite of numerous obstacles, not least of which is society's opposition to such a match, he eventually has his way. Pip's sufferings in pursuit of Estella, the coarseness she alerts him to in his person and station, the years of separation during her unhappy marriage, and the uncertainty of an enduring relationship even when they meet again all revise downward what Dickens considered Walter's unrealistic success with Laura Fairlie.

Hidden rivalries and the double vision they necessitate supply a hitherto unsuspected reason for Dickens's willingness to alter his novel's original conclusion at Bulwer-Lytton's behest. Dickens gave in not just as a concession to popular taste but because he realized he had passed up an opportunity to enlarge upon his parody of the success story so crucial to *The Woman in White*. The reunion of Walter and Laura, one recalls, was Collins's reconsideration of Esther's discovery of Lady Dedlock's corpse. That discovery and Collins's parody of it were also on Dickens's mind as he revamped the final lines of his thirteenth novel.

The original ending, which took place on a London street, needed only two short paragraphs. Estella, now remarried, misjudges Pip's condition because she assumes that "little Pip," Biddy's son by Joe, is Pip's child. Estella and Pip look on each other "sadly"; the morally improved hero concludes that his former tormentor has learned, through sorrow, the pain his heart once had to bear (GE, 521).

In the new ending, several pages long, Pip pushes open a gate in the fence around the remains of Satis House. He might as well be in a graveyard, as Walter was in the twenty-sixth installment of *The Woman in*

White: where the old house and brewery once stood, ivy grows "green on low quiet mounds of ruin" (GE, 518). Gazing down the "desolate garden-walk," Pip beholds a "solitary figure" (GE, 519), whose identity, even the fact that it is a woman, is revealed almost as slowly as Lady Dedlock's to Esther. Unintimidated by Collins's revaluative parodies, Dickens repeats with variations a former triumph that he reasserts is beyond Collins's powers.

Collins's goal in the cemetery scene, only two-thirds of the way through *The Woman in White*, was to outdo the climactic discovery that Dickens built up to until the next to last number of *Bleak House*. The ending of *Great Expectations* designates Walter's reunion with Laura a mandatory *terminus ad quem*. Dickens's rejoinder reinstates this stopping point and discounts as fairytale Collins's continuation of his novel toward additional surprises. If Pip correctly foresees "no shadow of another parting" from Estella (GE, 521), it will not be because exciting adventures await them. Unlike Hartright, who tracks down Glyde and Fosco, Pip slays no dragons to release his princess. Estella's captors, internal and invisible, are the psychological damages that have brought her to a greater understanding of Pip. Acting as physician to Estella's crushed spirits is the unspectacular future Dickens assigns Pip.

Dickens has been accused of reversing himself with a more promising conclusion; actually, he is intent on criticizing a rival novelist's even happier resolution. He replies to Collins's charges against *A Tale of Two Cities* by making providence more responsive to the individual's requirements. But he still demands that his supervisory agency be more rigorous, hence less generous, in educating Pip than Collins's was in rewarding Walter. Ahead of Pip lies the arduous task of bringing a "bent and broken" Estella (her own words) back to life (GE, 520). Having been remade through greater disappointment than Hartright experienced, Pip is meant to seem more qualified than his rival as a resurrection man. Laura's recovery of her true self was also on Hartright's agenda, but once he had destroyed Sir Percival, she became his wife, and then regained inner strength in direct proportion to his successes against her remaining enemies.

Rekindling Estella's spirit will ultimately benefit a lonely Pip. Nevertheless, determination to perform this service has little to do with having great expectations. Laura's restoration to her real identity culminates with Walter's son being named heir to Limmeridge House. The restorative process for Estella's emotional life will call for charity and self-sacrifice not unlike Joe's kindnesses earlier when he nursed Pip back to health. Pip sees his chance to become Estella's benefactor and takes it eagerly.

That Pip's sadder lot amounts to a cooler, more realistic reflection on

Walter's accomplishments is not without ironies that Dickens may not have fully perceived. For the first time in several rivalries, he must occasionally fight on the side of restraint. Although Hartright was supposedly an improvement upon the savage Defarges, it is Pip who is mellowed by providence: he forgoes revenge upon all who abused him while seeking it themselves. He even rescues Miss Havisham when she accidentally sets herself on fire, a favor Hartright is powerless to perform for his and Laura's tormentor, a trapped and burning Sir Percival Glyde. The modern revaluator can argue that Dickens's hyperbolic satires were always pro-restraint. Previous tilts with Trollope and Mrs. Gaskell may have been brought about by Dickens's failure to share their more optimistic expectations for the nation's progress and well-being, but a novel about the perils of being overly expectant that ends on a note of forgiveness has to seem like a departure for Dickens, a satire against excess. Whenever Dickens declines to outdo Collins in *Great Expectations*, he implies that his rival has already overextended himself.

The revaluation of Collins throughout *Great Expectations* is one of several indications of a profound change underway in Dickens's last fictions. Compelled to exceed Collins in some areas, Dickens pulls back from his rival's sensationalism in others. He evinces a desire to infuse melodramatic realism with the kind of added attention to psychological veracity that one expects from Trollope and even more from George Eliot. Collins helped alert Dickens to the limits and limitations of melodramatic realism, and in *The Mystery of Edwin Drood*, Dickens finally got around to revaluing his allegedly more psychological rivals on their own grounds. But there he examined the darker side of the self, just as novels like *Bleak House* and *A Tale of Two Cities* shed light on grimmer aspects of the social process. In both cases Dickens was illuminating subjects he felt his more sanguine competitors had unrealistically ignored. While revising Trollope and George Eliot, Dickens hoped to underscore his supremacy on all sides by developing a greater sense of interiority than a fellow melodramatic realist like Collins allegedly possessed, yet not restricting himself to the blander mirrorings of life in anti-sensational novelists, so-called.

As a satire on mistaken ambitions, *Great Expectations* is Dickens's adverse comment on his own upward drive. It counterbalances the defense of the novelist's calling in *Hard Times*, an indirect *ars poetica*. The older novelist felt he knew more than Collins about the ambiguous rewards of struggling to rise by the arts in Victorian England; he made his inverse fairytale do extra work as a warning to the aspiring outdoer that life at the top of the tree may not be worth the climb. Parodying Collins as he himself had been parodied was a way of communicating this unhappy message.

As does *The Woman in White*, *Great Expectations* begins with a prisoner escaping to freedom with the hero's help. Dressed like a ghost "from head to foot in white garments,"Anne Catherick accosts Hartright at midnight in summer on the London road (WW, 47). It is "towards evening" on Christmas eve when Magwitch starts up "from among the graves" and threatens to cut Pip's throat (GE, 9-10). Magwitch's eruption, which seems to be a resurrection but is not, is designed to outstrip both Anne's sudden manifestation in the guise of a spirit from another world and Laura's apparent return from the dead: Dickens shows that he can use one scene to surpass a couple from Collins. When Laura confounds Walter, only a third of Collins's novel remains to unfold; but Magwitch's rise would reestablish Dickens's superior inventiveness in that an entire novel would follow from it.

Asylum escapee and convict in flight from "the Hulks" are rival symbolic personages, each of whom fatefully—that is, providentially—interrupts the life of a novel's protagonist. Anne's spotless costume commissions her to stand for the absurdity of propriety, a societal force Collins debunks as a self-denying obsession with outward signs or semblance. The unsavory Magwitch becomes yet another subversion of the era's ridiculous confidence in appearances: the consensus that wealth, no matter how dubious in origin, guarantees the individual his importance and gentility.

But Dickens is not content simply to pit his symbol against Collins's; he appropriates Collins's woman in white for his own purposes by adroitly refashioning Anne Catherick into Miss Havisham. Her self-imprisonment, the opposite of the escape that triggers Collins's novel, augments satiric statements about the distorting effects of money and ambition that Dickens also stresses dynamically through Magwitch. Given the extent to which Collins cannibalizes *A Tale of Two Cities*, especially for the idea of using doubles,[6] Dickens's reuse of a woman in white hardly seems unfair.

Harry Stone indexes a plethora of plausible sources for Miss Havisham,[7] but the modern revaluator need look no further than the two novels that preceded *Great Expectations* in *All the Year Round*. Both *A Tale of Two Cities* and *The Woman in White* are crammed with characters whose lives were brought to a sudden halt by injustice. The "white-haired" Dr. Manette, for example, never loses the appearance of a man "whose life always seemed to him to have been stopped like a clock, for so many years, and then set going again" (TTC, 348-49). Hints for Miss Havisham can also be found in Madame Defarge and three of Collins's characters besides Anne Catherick: Mrs. Catherick (Anne's mother), Mr. Fairlie (recluse and hypochondriac), and Walter Hartright.

Madame Defarge's normal life can be said to have come to a halt years previously when her sister was fatally wronged by the brothers St. Evrémonde. Having taken the aristocracy in general as object for her revenge, she has "knitted on with the steadfastness of Fate" (TTC, 148), her work being a "register" in code (TTC, 222) of the names of candidates for the guillotine. Mrs. Catherick stops her life like a clock for years while she labors to retrieve her reputation. When he exposes the conspiracy Fosco and Glyde mounted against Laura, Walter successfully turns life back to the day he was unfairly parted from her.

Dickens does more than get even with Collins for using doubles: he combines Mr. Fairlie's reclusion, Anne's white costume, and Mrs. Catherick's time-reversing life-style with the revenge against an entire species sought by Madame Defarge and the stoppage of time Dr. Manette experiences. The revaluating novelist reshapes all of this material into the "corpse-like" Miss Havisham (GE, 70), whom no one can resurrect as Walter restores Laura. Dickens's perpetual bride, the new woman in white, overshadows Collins's rendition to become the more unforgettable symbol, the starker instance of arrested development. But Miss Havisham stands for the frustration of unrealistic expectations—indeed, by extension and with Magwitch, for the inevitable collapse of all mercenary or vengeful attitudes of mind. Dickens thought such attitudes more detrimental in Victorian society in the second half of the nineteenth century, hence more of a setback, than the inordinate devotion to propriety that his rival had just used a retarded woman in white to decry.

The Woman in White sold more copies of *All the Year Round* than did *A Tale of Two Cities*. This situation left Dickens, who was both Collins's rival and his editor, with mixed feelings: he shared in Collins's success, but that success came at Dickens's artistic expense. When *No Name* followed *Great Expectations* in Dickens's periodical, however, the dilemma of the editor-competitor resolved itself temporarily, for in 1862 Collins's efforts to usurp his master's preeminence hit a snag.

Part of the problem stemmed from Collins's failure in this book to select a specific target. He appears to be roaming the Dickens canon, plundering at will. Captain Wragge is a second-rate reincarnation of Micawber's loquacity and Jingle's unscrupulousness; Michael Vanstone becomes Magwitch in reverse, a cruel withdrawer of gentility from Magdalen and Norah rather than its bestower; Captain Kirke can be dismissed as a grown-up version of Walter Gay in *Dombey and Son;* and George Bartram seems no better than a pale rendition of such early Dickens heroes as Nicholas Nickleby and Frank Cheeryble. Having just created a complex personality like Pip's, Dickens had reason to breathe easier, to feel both superior and safe.

Nevertheless, *No Name* replies to *Great Expectations* that the problem in Victorian society is not entertaining false hopes but having legitimate ones taken away by mankind's improvidential laws. The Vanstone sisters must be treated as "nobody's children" because their father's will turns out to have been made before he was legally free to marry their mother. Although clearly an injustice, dispossession of the Vanstone sisters remains too isolated a misfortune to count as a national disgrace. It constitutes no more of a brake upon the country's well-being than the minor scandal Trollope uncovered at Hiram's Hospital. It is no permanent barrier to social progress and certainly not a serious, philosophical critique of shortcomings traceable to the very nature of things.

Being nobody's progeny—having no rightful family name—hardly compares with getting caught up in the venality and bureaucracy Dickens satirized as the condition of England in *Little Dorrit*. Yet Dickens's original title, the ironically apologetic *Nobody's Fault*, probably inspired Collins to outdo irony with indignation; hence the imperative stress on unfair deprivation in his title. Having Norah and Magdalen declared "nobody's children" is like being able to find no one at fault for society's ills: both amount to disclaimers of responsibility, examples of Catch-22. With no one to blame, said Dickens, defects in the system become effects without causes and thus cannot be remedied. Similarly but less alarmingly, Magdalen and Norah are no one's progeny because they cannot be heirs; they cannot inherit because, as illegitimate offspring, they are nobody's progeny—which brings them full circle.

The anguish the Vanstone sisters suffer is as much due to the loss of financial security as to forfeiture of name, as if Collins, not so much disputing the moral of *Great Expectations* as simply ignoring it, is reequating money with status. Satire on England's inheritance laws, especially an instance both singular and single, cannot compete with the deadly aim Dickens took at the British legal system in general by using Chancery to incriminate society's uncaring institutions.

The biggest mistake in *No Name*, however, is procedural: Collins follows a "new course"[8] devised to vindicate more conclusively the strategy Dickens criticized in the letter he wrote Collins about the way providence works. True to a prefatory promise, Collins reveals "midway in the first volume" the "only Secret" *No Name* contains, just as he advised Dickens to introduce Manette's curse upon the St. Evrémonde family earlier in *A Tale of Two Cities*. Once Collins's sole secret is out, namely that Mr. Vanstone has only recently married the mother of his children (upon having learned of his first wife's death in Canada), the "main events" have all been "purposely foreshadowed."[9]

Collins tries to sustain expectation and suspense by "following the train of circumstances" through which "foreseen events are brought about." But actually having exposed the skeleton in the Vanstone family closet and blamed society for forcing them to keep it there, the novelist says nothing more. He sadly misjudges his own strengths by forgoing the series of increasingly surprising surprises that made *The Woman in White* so absorbing an attempt to improve on Dickens's conception of providence.

Mainstays of the Gothic abound in *The Woman in White* as they do throughout Dickens. Unlike Walpole and Mrs. Radcliffe, Collins never creates a melodramatic plot principally for its own sake; he does so to make melodrama a vehicle for social criticism. He wants to speak out against propriety and illustrate his confidence in providence as a superior court of justice. But *No Name* offers nothing on a par with Hartright's late-night encounter with a ghostly Anne Catherick. The railway accident that removes Mr. Vanstone "mid-way in the first volume" deprives Collins of an arresting overture and a shocking climax simultaneously. It occurs offstage and is remarkable mainly for the financial disasters it causes.

Collins creates the impression that he is backing down, retrenching on several fronts. Compared to Lady Dedlock and Captain Hawdon, for example, or Philip Fairlie and the eventual Mrs. Catherick, Magdalen's parents are easily absolved for passing as Mr. and Mrs. Vanstone. The first two pairs are beset by an immovable social framework, a moral code of questionable value, whereas a simple act of Parliament—never a Dickensian panacea—could have exonerated the third pair or at least protected their children.

Along with Hartright, Marian Halcombe matures into an agent of providence, a female lieutenant; Magdalen is arguably as much a ward of providence at novel's end as its confederate, and she achieves less understanding of its ways. Hartright steps outside the proprieties to aid Anne and then Laura because, as his name states, he learns to follow the directives of a good heart, the superior guide Collins recommends. Magdalen's given name has unfortunate biblical associations, suggesting that Collins is ambivalent about her conduct; her surname seems to curtail her activities in the van of social progress. Like Carstone's, it removes any implication of speed or suppleness.

Nevertheless, Magdalen Vanstone is morally superior to Mrs. Catherick and far more resourceful than Laura Fairlie, to compare her with two previous women in Collins who struggle to be reinstated where they claim to belong. Whether disguised as Harriet Garth, or plotting to induce the son of her father's legitimate heir into marriage, or masquerading as a parlor maid, Magdalen exhibits commendable courage even when troubled by conscience. Dickens evidently considered her pluck in questionable circumstances unconvincing, if not actually morally repugnant. Throughout *Our Mutual Friend* (1864-65) he tried to outdo and still discredit Magdalen's resort to disguise and impersonation: these devices are reused and upgraded as the means Rokesmith and Boffin employ to improve Bella.

Magdalen becomes Miss Bygrave to entrap the sickly Noel Vanstone into marrying her. She will ruin this usurper of her father's fortune, provided he dies once she is automatically his heir. The plan Boffin and Rokesmith jointly implement traps Bella into realizing that she is mistaken to yearn for wealth. Their undertaking, although devious, is as praiseworthy as Pip's resolve to restore Estella's power to love.

In both *No Name* and *Our Mutual Friend*, inheritances—a metaphor for the impact of money on character and social standing—are of prime importance. The argument that pitted Dickens's Pip against Collins's Hartright continues. Having undercut Walter's success with Pip's disappointments, Dickens now amplifies and curtails Collins's situations simultaneously. Where Magdalen is left to her own cunning, Bella has not one but two benefactors, a sure sign that providence—for which benefactors are deputies—remains active. Revaluation turns the tables on Collins to the extent that Boffin and Rokesmith, who play providence for Bella's benefit, are never as open to censure as Wragge and Magdalen sometimes seem in their efforts to right her wrongs. Miss Vanstone and the Captain always remain closer to Hartright and Marian Halcombe than to the Defarges, but they cannot even approximate Collins's earlier pair, who continue to rise in the reader's estimation the more they overstep prescribed bounds. Dickens restates in *Our Mutual Friend* the same lessons Magdalen learns in *No Name*: the splendor of being in love and the danger of associating this condition with having money. He strives, however, to convey his message more realistically than Collins by reusing the same melodramatic devices less improbably and more engagingly.

No Name remains of interest to the modern revaluator of hidden rivalries primarily because of its deficiencies. It stands alone as the major instance of Victorian revaluation directed against Dickens that one can point to as a failure. Dickens's pupil-turned-competitor was unable to reclaim the figure of a woman in white once Dickens took it over for his own purposes in *Great Expectations;* unfortunately, *No Name* contains no central symbol of equivalent force or range. Its thesis is of limited consequence, the story seldom as exciting as *The Woman in White*.

Collins concentrates on one injustice in *No Name*, as opposed to his previous catalogue of the evils of propriety, and the impact of the sins of the fathers on their children is less convincing. Vanstone's mistake in not making his daughters legitimate is actually more of an oversight than a sin; it seems a pale imitation of Glyde's father's sin of omission or Philip Fairlie's failure to acknowledge Anne as well as Laura.

The paleness is doubly regrettable. It weakens *No Name* in that the hardship Magdalen and Norah endure is not only greater than the parental oversight it descends from but far too harsh by *any* standard. Yet Magdalen, no matter how driven, cannot be allowed to plunge deeper into objectionable schemes to avoid her punishment than Glyde did by institutionalizing his wife and hastening Anne's death. Thus Collins compromises the success of his earlier efforts to outdo the consequences of parental malefaction that Dickens examined in *Bleak House* and *A Tale of Two Cities*.

Applied to *No Name*, double vision works adversely for Collins. The more persistently the novel calls attention to its kinship with Dickens's work, the more it suffers by comparison. What Collins insufficiently realized in 1862 was the high price that undoing by outdoing extorts from the aspiring outdoer: in such a rivalry as he dared to initiate, one must keep raising the stakes. The outdoer cannot follow one revaluation of the novelist he hopes to overshadow with another novel that is merely as good as the first or, like *No Name*, a less effective parody. For Collins to substantiate his boast to be Dickens writ large, he had to be Dickens writ larger each time than the last; otherwise, it would appear that the challenger was wearing down or had been repulsed. Ironically, Collins's failure to improve upon himself negated his second effort to improve upon Dickens.

As the second decade of the realism wars was about to commence, Dickens had little doubt where he stood with Trollope and Mrs. Gaskell, but *No Name* must have assuaged his anxieties concerning Collins. It offered the prospect of a talented revaluator subsiding into the less threatening role of imitator-disciple; it indicated that perhaps Collins was only better-than-average after all. Having replied to Collins once in *Great Expectations* and again, with greater ease, in *Our Mutual Friend*, Dickens doubtless thought he was winning, perhaps had actually won, the contest between them.

No Name, however, proved to be an exception, a hiatus for Collins and a false respite for Dickens. With *The Moonstone*, more so than in *Armadale* (1866), Collins resumed reinterpreting the Inimitable—surely an ironic sobriquet by 1868, if not before—with renewed vigor and greater success. Having devised ways to carry outdoing forward, he reached a peak in his revaluative efforts to succeed Dickens as the era's premier sensational realist, even if, by a slim margin, one still designates *The Woman in White* his masterpiece.

Collins's ambition was not only to outdo the social satire on middle- and upper-class irresponsibility in *Bleak House* but to overshadow the psychological complexity of Dickens's attack on perverse attitudes toward wealth in *Great Expectations*. In *The Moonstone*, Collins ventures beyond Dickens's anti-evolutionary theory about the way ill-fated societies, such as the England of *Bleak House*, become corrupt from within; he expands Dickens's idea into a study of the deepening interiority of evil. Wisely, he returns to satirical investigation of life's intangible restraints, not the proprieties this time but those hidden factors or flaws within human nature itself that endanger, possibly even rule out, happiness for the individual and progress for society. The increasingly respectable exteriors that maleficence and hypocrisy have learned to assume in the second half of the nineteenth century become the developments Collins examines to the detriment of *A Tale of Two Cities*. He refashions the device of characters who have doubles into one where many have a double, twofold self.

The moonstone itself is a multifaceted symbol, standing for, among other things, financial respectability, the wealth of nations. Even more than do Pip's inflated monetary expectations, however, this treasure has a dark side. The Hindoos guarding it realize that they assume sacred responsibilities; it brings hardship, even the curse of destruction, on all who abuse its trust—which, unfortunately, all the British do. Having plundered the precious diamond from India, the outwardly respectable English—first Herncastle, then Miss Verinder, then Godfrey Ablewhite—diligently secrete it. They do so not just to prevent the Indians from recapturing this prize but to stop one another from stealing it. The theft of the moonstone in Collins's second-best novel resembles the evils caused by propriety in *The Woman in White;* both show that, with increasing frequency, modern society's problems originate at the top, among the socially respectable.

Regardless of the supposedly progressive nature of the times, a capacity for wrongdoing, fostered by feelings of anxiety and discontent, clearly persists in *The Moonstone*. This capacity, Collins implies, is concomitant with society's propensity to unfold: the more a nation advances—through colonial expansion into India, for example—the more intricate kinds of crimes and criminals it spawns. Crime serves as a persistent dystopian metaphor for the societal pressures that prompt it. Commission of a theft in Lady Verinder's secluded house in Yorkshire suggests that man's darker self remains a permanent part of the human condition, an aspect of the nature of things that polite societies ignorantly activate and then unwisely overlook.

Since criminal activity can be found well up the social scale in *The Moonstone* and on the international level also, it cannot be regarded as the

monopoly of unregenerate felons. Nor can it be dismissed as the soon-to-
be-eliminated consequence of ill-designed, outmoded, or mismanaged
institutions. Dickens had been maintaining as much since *Dombey and Son*.
Some of life's ills, his later novels surmise, are seemingly intrinsic and
ineradicable, a case of perennial deficiencies within human nature that
continually take on new shapes. Throughout *The Moonstone*, Collins labors
to make these satiric observations his own, to phrase them more vividly
than Dickens did.

Sergeant Cuff is not simply an endeavor to surpass the sagacity of
Inspector Bucket. Collins proposes to take over, in fact, to vastly improve
upon, the Dickensian method of decoding an imperfect reality. Collins's
detective boasts an expertise for solving white-collar crimes; Bucket, like
Inspector Field, his real-life model,[10] knows the underworld better than
Lady Dedlock's drawing room. Counting on Cuff's specialty, Collins
claims that his novel outstrips Dickens's later fictions: it uses middle- and
upper-class crime more convincingly to challenge the epoch's cultural
myth of accelerating social progress, its romantic belief in continuous
evolutionary development.

Twice in his 1868 novel Collins redoes the scene from *Bleak House* that
can be called the touchstone sequence for nineteenth-century sensational
realism: Esther's unexpected discovery of her mother's body at the gate to
the burial ground. On the paint-smeared nightgown worn by the person
who took the moonstone from Rachel Verinder's cabinet, Franklin Blake
reports seeing "My Own Name!": "I had discovered Myself as the
Thief."[11] More dramatically than the eminently respectable Lady Dedlock
reveals a secret past, Blake uncovers a secret self, hitherto as invisible to
himself as it has been to the rest of society.

More than one hundred pages later, Collins revalues the climax of *Bleak
House* yet again. Blake is unable to bear the sight of the dead sailor who, it
turns out, is the real thief in disguise, the person who removed the
moonstone from Mrs. Verinder's premises and thus actually stole the
precious gem. Sergeant Cuff and his juvenile assistant, Gooseberry, a law-
abiding reincarnation of the Artful Dodger, entreat Blake to "come . . . and
look." The hero approaches as warily as Hartright crept towards Fosco's
corpse in the Paris morgue. Stripped of wig and false beard, the body on
the bed at the Wheel of Fortune is discovered to be not a foreigner, not even
a stranger, but an intimate of the Verinder household: Rachel's cousin and
former fiancé, Godfrey Ablewhite (MS, 441).

Collins carries two steps further Dickens's depiction of an outwardly
respectable community with much to answer for. Having been given
opium, Blake removes the moonstone from Miss Rachel's room without

realizing he has done so. Ablewhite then smuggles the diamond out of the house and maintains possession for a year, with no one at first suspecting him except the indefatigable Hindoos. Collins's version of English society is even blinder than Lady Dedlock to the extent of its duplicities (Blake); when acutely aware, this society struggles harder and more hypocritically than she did to conceal its faults (Ablewhite). Both times in *The Moonstone*, unexpected discovery turns out to incriminate someone apparently more unassailably respectable than Lady Dedlock. The reader is well acquainted with her past long before the final revelation, but neither Blake nor Ablewhite allows his other self to become known before it is suddenly unmasked. Until the end of the "Fourth Narrative," Blake is not even sure his other self exists, although he has been alerted to the possibility. In Blake's case as well as Ablewhite's, Collins stresses the internal nature of evil.

The three "mahogany-colored Indians" (MS, 18), a trio of Hindoo priests dedicated to retrieving their holy relic, cannot have stolen the diamond from Lady Verinder's house because it is sealed tight—all doors and windows locked the night of the robbery. Collins's readers are free to distrust the mysterious Hindoos—in short, to display prejudice; but foreignness, the novelist cautions, has little to do with genuine darkness, which is internal and inherent. Doubly an inside job, crime in *The Moonstone* takes place inside a secured house—virtually a microcosm for England—and the thief is eventually discovered within the family.

The Indians finally smother Ablewhite to revenge themselves on the English, although Herncastle, the original culprit, is already dead. They punish the man who stole the moonstone from Herncastle's heir and steal back their heritage. Collins concludes *The Moonstone*, as he did *The Woman in White*, with a sensational disclosure of providential retribution that tries to cap its predecessors both within the text and in his chief rival's major work.

The moonstone becomes the novel's pervasive symbol for other things besides a nation's wealth. This "Yellow Diamond," which Collins describes "growing and lessening in luster with the waxing and waning of the moon" (MS, 4), also stands for the irrational, darker side of man's nature. It symbolizes duality, hidden darknesses beneath respectable exteriors. Just as men do, the moonstone harbors "a defect, in the shape of a flaw," in the "very heart" of its composition (MS, 38), a veritable heart of darkness. Meant to adorn the forehead of the "Regent of the Night" (MS, 283), as the Indians call their god, the gem shines "awfully out of the depths of its own brightness, with a moony gleam, in the dark" (MS, 63). Bright yet awful, gleaming in darkness, it conjures up all that is foreign not to Victorian

Britain as a nation, but to man's daylight, social self in all climes and countries.[12]

On the other hand, *Robinson Crusoe*, the favorite reading of Betteredge (the Verinders' steward), represents a less complicated, far less realistic world, readily governed by middle-class Protestant virtues. Although he is shipwrecked, Crusoe's training saves him: the thrifty habits and moral principles learned over a lifetime work handily even in exotic situations. But happenings in Lady Verinder's house are invariably stranger than events on Crusoe's island. A theft in *The Moonstone* both is a theft and yet technically is not one, depending on whether or not one can be said to rob a thief. The Hindoos steal from Ablewhite the gem he took from Franklin Blake, who had no right to take it from Miss Verinder; she was bequeathed the moonstone by her uncle, who took it from the Indians. The inadequacy of Betteredge's quotations from Defoe to cope with human nature and household crises in *The Moonstone* is Collins's slap at less melodramatic realists who denigrate his so-called sensationalism.

"A famous gem in the native annals of India," the moonstone transforms first Herncastle and then Ablewhite into thieves. The former, although officer and gentleman, steals the diamond while supposedly restraining British troops from plundering Seringapatam. The latter snatches it while still enjoying a reputation as a selfless fund-raiser for such charitable causes as the Mother's-Small-Clothes-Conversion-Society. The origin of this group appears to lie in Dickens's sketch of "The Ladies' Societies."[13] At first glance, this is an unlikely group of associations for anything except foolishness to come from. But the phenomenon of respectable sources for antisocial behavior is what Collins wishes to make more familiar. Even a sleepwalking Franklin Blake, who removes Rachel's most prized possession from her room to his for safekeeping, manifests man's darker self. Removal suggests "symbolic defloration"[14] and is thus a nighttime disclosure of subconscious carnal desires that Blake's proper daytime self would have found appalling.

In *The Moonstone*, Collins advances beyond the interest Dickens began to take—by fashioning Carton after Darnay—in the use of look-alikes or alternative selves as a metaphor for dual personalities. Collins is convinced he is extending Dickens by converting the latter's use of doubles into the double selves for which they were the prototypes. Double selves in Ablewhite and Blake are crucial to Collins's parody of Dickens; they are central to his exercise of double vision. Ablewhite's dark side advances the plot while simultaneously correcting *A Tale of Two Cities*: the darker self, Collins instructs Dickens, invariably subverts the good, particularly if it is ignored or repressed. One can own up to this underside to one's character, as Blake does heroically but belatedly; still, it cannot be neutralized by having it come to the rescue the way Carton ascends the guillotine for Darnay.

To parody Carton's death in Darnay's place, Collins presses beyond a depiction of the thief's ascendancy over the philanthropist in Ablewhite: for Carton's adoration of Lucy, one witnesses a nighttime self actually within Blake coveting the Miss Verinder he courts respectfully by day. Unlike Darnay, who is set free by Carton, Blake must liberate his darker side in order to enjoy life in the future with Rachel. Courageously, he does so, eventually displaying a perturbing interiority that polite society would have preferred him to keep hidden.

Collins emphasizes hidden selves in place of Krook's smoldering stomach or Lady Dedlock's secret past as analogues for society's concealment of internal problems. Krook explodes in *Bleak House* as a warning to corrupt communities about revolution, if not collapse, from within. But Dickens gives the Lord Chancellor's double an ignitible inside, virtually a hidden self within a character already a secret self for another character. Collins shuns this kind of doubling, which is, he suggests, overdone. He tries to outdo Dickens with two interrelated instances in which characters face ruin when overcome by an interior personality. In the opinion of Dickens's former pupil, Blake and Ablewhite make telling points about internal corruption in society and human nature more realistically than Krook did, not to mention twice as insistently.

In *Great Expectations*, Dickens suggests that a graspingly ambitious creature lurks behind many a gentleman and his fortune. Similarly, the heirs to the moonstone owe their increased wealth to Herncastle's heinous acts. But within Ablewhite and Blake, Collins proceeds to disclose even less pleasant realities than those behind Pip, realities more problematic for allegedly progressive societies to accommodate than a goblin like Magwitch. Ablewhite's secret self, Collins maintains, is a greater challenge to society than Pip's secret benefactor. The bogus philanthropist brings disaster not only upon his ward, from whom he embezzles, but does more harm than Magwitch can to society's self-confidence, to its belief in the validity of the appearances it puts forth. Society knows it does not want Magwitch but thinks it requires men of Ablewhite's stamp.

Pip is corrupted by the reigning system of values, not by a darkness within him looking for its vehicle, seeking a way out. Thus Magwitch merely presides over Pip's social rise from afar, not from within. Pip's unsavory guardian angel is always an outsider struggling to get inside and doing so only vicariously, by proxy. The real danger to modern society,

Collins tells Dickens, hardly comes from desperadoes who want to acquire a veneer of respectability; such renegades are generally easy to recognize as permanent outcasts, no more likely to prove assimulative than Sikes or Fagin. The main danger originates, instead, within supposedly cultured personages who already display a respectable veneer but can manipulate it to hide deceitful hearts.

Mr. Pirrip signals his self-realization by accepting responsibility for Magwitch as his "secret sharer." He overcomes his aversion and conceals the convict in his rooms almost as willingly as Conrad's sea captain, the unnamed narrator of *The Secret Sharer,* hides the murderer, Leggatt, aboard his ship. When Collins puts a secret sharer within Blake and Ablewhite, however, he charges Dickens with misjudging his own inventiveness. It is Dickens's ex-pupil, not Dickens, who sounds more modern if revisions of *Great Expectations* in *The Moonstone* are reexamined in light of Conrad.

Pip acknowledges that Magwitch is the uncouth basis for his own more seemly exterior. He informs Herbert Pocket that Magwitch is "strongly attached" to him (GE, 367); he repeats the phrase until it sounds biological as well as emotional. Dickens rewrites *Frankenstein* effectively and yet his success, in Collins's opinion, obscures the unprecedented horror implicit in Pip's recognition of Magwitch as another self he has been harboring all along: "The imaginary student," recalls Pip, "pursued by the misshapen creature he had impiously made was not more wretched than I, pursued by the creature who had made me" (GE, 363). Pip recognizes the irony that this time the monster has made the gentleman. Collins asserts that Dickens should have gone on to show that the two, monster and man, have actually become inseparable, each within the other.

The unnamed sea captain in *The Secret Sharer* remembers his impressions upon first seeing his double: "It was . . . as though I had been faced by my own reflection in the depths of a somber and immense mirror."[15] Conrad seems merely to be duplicating the resemblance Carton bears to Darnay or Anne Catherick to Laura Fairlie. But the captain is not talking about look-alikes or about Frankenstein and his monster, for other is really inner; reflection is actually projection of a hitherto unsuspected internal self. Just as Blake searches for a thief but sees, instead, his "Own Name," the captain beholds an externalized version of his antisocial self. More than Darnay and Carton, or Pip eyeing Magwitch, Blake seems entitled to pronounce words similar to the captain's.

Collins replies further that one cannot expel the secret self by sending Magwitch abroad, as England's magistrates did, or by smuggling him back out of the country when he dares to return, which is Pip's contingency plan.[16] It is unrealistic, Collins insists, to think one can ever banish a part of oneself; Pip's actions hardly surpass Ablewhite's attempted flight to Amsterdam.

Pip's secret benefactor, the figure who makes the young man's innermost desires possible, is a transported convict illegally returned from Australia. In *The Moonstone*, however, foreignness works more ironically as a metaphor for evil. There is nothing un-English, Collins repeatedly insists, about duplicity and duality, nor about sexual desires which the Victorian sense of propriety suppresses to the point of denial. Collins uses Ezra Jennings, along with the Hindoo priests, as part of a satiric distinction between two types of foreignness: one is internal, dangerous, and unrecognized in most cases; the other is external, easily seen, and too hastily condemned.

Jennings cuts an eccentric figure in Yorkshire largely because the unprepossessing appearance of Mr. Candy's medical assistant—his "piebald hair" and "gypsy complexion" (MS, 318)—indicates a "mixture of some foreign race in his English blood" (MS, 364). Jennings is one of several characters in *The Moonstone* whose outward self, unpleasant in this case, one must revaluate thoroughly.

Actually, Jennings externalizes the opposite of the truly malignant moral darkness the English seem ignorant of within themselves. In Thomas Candy's opinion, Jennings deserves respect as a great man: he is a martyr to the disease that kills him as well as an expert on subliminal states, delirium, and the subconscious. He has been alienated from residents of Frizinghall because of society's suspicion that extraordinary appearances are automatically wrong and improper, certainly not respectable. Jennings is a victim of an uncalled-for mistrust of strangeness. Collins hints that being an outsider—having an admixture of Eastern blood—enables Jennings to become a genuine benefactor to Franklin Blake. Only he can decide how to summon the nighttime self from within Blake, just as Indians, who venerate the moonstone, have better understanding than the English of duality in human nature, which the gem symbolizes.

To exonerate Franklin Blake from charges of having stolen the moonstone and pawned it, Jennings conceives "a bold experiment." His idea is to recreate the circumstances under which Blake supposedly pilfered the diamond. In particular, he recommends repeating the unaccustomed draught of opium the sleepless hero was given unawares. Jennings is virtually as responsible as Sergeant Cuff for bringing to the surface the secret selves within Blake and Ablewhite. Only after Blake has been cleared does Cuff settle on Ablewhite as his prime suspect. The novel's strongest believer in revaluation, Jennings trusts that reenactment or replaying will show what really happened. Collins places similar faith in himself whenever he redoes a scene from Dickens.

When Collins presents Miss Clack as Ablewhite's staunchest admirer, he is not just attempting to surpass Dickens's satiric treatment of misguided do-gooders (Mrs. Pardiggle, Mrs. Jellyby). She unwittingly reveals herself to be a poor judge of character and a nuisance besides, enabling Collins to rival Browning along with Dickens.[17] A remark by Collins's talkative female works more impressively than Jennings's gypsy blood or England's prejudice against Hindoos to underscore the indigenousness of evil, whether personal or societal. Inadvertently, Miss Clack incriminates man's unexplored dark heart as the principal threat to a modern society's well-being. Man's interiority, Collins emphasizes, is as mysterious as the moonstone's. "How soon," Miss Clack moralizes, "may our own evil passions prove to be Oriental noblemen who pounce on us unawares!" (MS, 197).

Miss Clack refers to an early incident in which the Hindoos seize Ablewhite in search of the gem he has already deposited with Mr. Luker. If "the Christian hero" (MS, 195) can be overcome physically, surely by mistake for someone else, then lesser mortals, says Miss Clack, must be even more vigilant lest they succumb to temptations. These, she presumes, bombard us from without. Her pious observation, no more badly skewed than the rest of the moralizing in her narrative, makes sense when correctly applied to Ablewhite and respectable society as a whole. Collins underlines the unreliability of Drusilla's other comments in order to imply the real meaning of this one: "Oriental noblemen," removable external factors that overly optimistic reformers might like to blame for life's imperfections, regularly turn out to be inherent in human nature, in short, "our own evil passions."

Like Jennings's non-English blood, Miss Clack's views on Hindoos clarify the main argument of *The Moonstone*. The novel's twofold proposition is that foreign is not evil, evil is not foreign. Despite the world's ability to right itself periodically, there is no steady, foolproof drive toward perfection. Faults are intrinsic to all temporal, secular order; they seem foreign in England chiefly because the country's worst failings are often allowed to persist unacknowledged, just as darker selves within Ablewhite and Blake go undetected for a long period.

Godfrey Ablewhite, unlike Ezra Jennings, has the name and appearance of a modern-day matinee idol.[18] Unfortunately, his hypocrisy exceeds that of Stiggins and Chadband combined. If Jennings champions revaluation, Ablewhite suffers from it most: first Rachel and then a second lady with a fortune reverse a decision to marry him. On second attempt, Sergeant Cuff, another believer in reconsideration, correctly predicts the identity of the novel's villain by naming Ablewhite. To the tract-dispensing Miss Clack, a relentless Evangelical, Ablewhite personifies "the Christian hero"; actually, he incarnates fallacious popular notions of such a figure. An ostracized Jennings, shunned and disliked, is compelled to regard himself as a failure, while Ablewhite becomes "the most accomplished philanthropist (on a small independence) that England ever produced" (MS, 56).

Ablewhite and Jennings are opposites, not doubles, yet each has a double or second self to contradict the personality implicit in his outward form. Taken individually or in counterpoint, Jennings and Ablewhite confound the simplicity in depicting a bohemian Carton as the squalid version of Darnay or an alcoholic, disgruntled Orlick as Pip's violent self unleashed. Inside the dark-complexioned Jennings, despite a fatal intestinal disease, one encounters nothing but kindness and light. From the whited sepulcher that is Ablewhite, a contemptible second self emerges; eventually, it seems more outlandish to the philanthropist's friends than "the man with the piebald hair" at first does to Franklin Blake. *The Moonstone* extensively revises presumed affinities between a seemly exterior and authentic goodness, a stereotype Collins thinks Dickens does not challenge forcibly enough. Appearing thoroughly English and outwardly respectable is no guarantee against being deeply divided inside.

Pip learns about deficiencies in his outlook and internal makeup from Orlick's violence, Wopsle's debacle on stage, and the revelation of Magwitch as his patron. Franklin Blake has *four* examples to shed light on his predicament: Cuff, Jennings, Ablewhite, and Rosanna Spearman. If the creativity contest demands variations on a theme, instances of self-division in *The Moonstone* outnumber cases of inflated hopes in *Great Expectations*. Jennings and Cuff prove more ingratiating than their external appearance, whereas Ablewhite's fair exterior is grievously fraudulent. Rosanna Spearman illustrates most poignantly the harm one does to one's own person and to others if not on good terms with all facets of the self.

A "grizzled, elderly," and "miserably lean" detective "dressed all in decent black" (MS, 96), Sergeant Cuff looks at first like a constabular Tulkinghorn. Unexpectedly, he also brightens considerably whenever the subject is roses. When Cuff comes out of retirement for a second chance at solving the theft, he has undergone "metamorphosis" to become a countrified rose gardener. In a "broad-brimmed white hat, a light shooting-jacket, white trowsers, and drab gaiters" (MS, 430), he has "changed," in Franklin Blake's opinion, "beyond all recognition," yet clearly for the better.

Even the exemplary sergeant is thus two-sided but in a fashion that permits him to outdo Wemmick in *Great Expectations*. Wemmick leaves business behind in Little Britain for the more natural self he exhibits at Walworth. Cuff finally discards totally the professional persona beneath which he suppresses his more colorful self while unmasking respectable criminals like the two-faced Ablewhite. An attractive but formerly repressed alternative self issues from Cuff to accentuate Ablewhite's nefarious transformation. Restyled as a country squire, Cuff alters from dark to light. Ablewhite does the reverse: when he redeems the moonstone from Mr. Luker, he tries to conceal the thief and defrauder within by entering the bank in Lombard Street disguised as a "dark man, dressed like a sailor" (MS, 438).

The artificial coloring Ablewhite imparts to his skin is not a contradiction to the argument thus far. Collins is not suddenly saying that society's ills are alien to the self or independent of it. He does not think that the criminal impulse to cheat and deceive can realistically be depicted as a foreigner, a person of a different race. On the contrary, Ablewhite's disguise is yet another way for Collins to discredit the notion that behaving dishonestly and hypocritically is foreign to the English character. Ablewhite, not Collins, believes that looking dark and foreign best cloaks his true identity.

To consummate a crooked design, Ablewhite causes his internal, criminal self to take on the outward appearance that popular prejudice expects of a thief. The fair-haired Englishman wishes to look as Eastern as possible, no doubt to increase suspicion of the Hindoos once it becomes known that a dark-skinned man received the moonstone from Mr. Luker. Ablewhite's disguise supplies fresh evidence of his duality while confirming the hypocrisy he shares with the rest of British society.

Godfrey's assumed complexion, it follows, is paradoxical: put on to conceal and mislead but ultimately to capitalize on the public's bias, it nevertheless reveals and incriminates. Unlike Jennings's displeasing exterior, Ablewhite's darkened skin, his false outside, is truer to the core than the handsome facade he usually maintains. It is actually Ablewhite's sinister self reaching the surface; as it takes over, the result is an involuntary disclosure of the inner darkness his philanthropical outside has learned to hide. The only time foreignness actually connotes evil in *The Moonstone* is when it is being used calculatingly in an effort to conceal it.

Unlike sprightly changes in Cuff, Ablewhite's disguise is ultimately unsuccessful: Godfrey easily eludes Blake and Mr. Bruff at the bank, but the "mahogany-colored Indians," whom respectable society judges unfairly as thieving murderers,[19] detect the good-looking but deceitful Ablewhite beneath the unsavory appearance of a foreign sailor.

Unlike Defoe's resourceful mariner, always sensibly British, the much-traveled Franklin Blake distresses Betteredge by displaying "many different sides to his character"; educated abroad, he has "his French side, and his German side, and his Italian side," with the "original English foundation" able to show through only "every now and then" (MS, 44). Betteredge's insular prejudices are soon put to rout by Ablewhite's behavior: both of the philanthropist's sides or selves are thoroughly English. But the reprehensible, dominant underside stays concealed until the end; it does not become visible at intervals, as Blake's fundamental English side is said to do.

Conceivably, multiple elements in Blake's character are products of Betteredge's imagination. If not, they are still unlike the two sides to Ablewhite: none of Blake's foreign traits bears responsibility for the disappearance of the moonstone; nor do his European characteristics impede its recovery. It is the darker, nighttime self within Blake that makes his life a "perpetual contradiction" (MS, 44) once the moonstone has disappeared, his outer self trying to determine what the inner self has done. This subterranean self, foreign to no man, transfers Rachel's priceless possession from her room to his and then recedes into the subconscious as the opium trance that released it wears off. Following Jennings's instructions, Blake later repeats the dosage in hopes of exculpating himself. His resolve not to deny or cuddle his subconscious self is a display of moral superiority over Pip as well as Ablewhite. Instead of Pip working to get Magwitch out of England, Collins shows Blake daring to confront the stranger inside himself before the assembled community. The theft of the moonstone is restaged in front of most of the same guests who had been scandalized by the diamond's disappearance exactly one year before.

Blake publicizes the darker aspects of his human nature, facts of life polite society fails to recognize. He does not differ from the novel's other jewel thieves merely in that his misconduct is drug-induced; unlike the others, Blake moves toward greater self-knowledge. Herncastle's villainousness was always uppermost, permitting polite society to ostracize him as an exceptional case. Ablewhite, one realizes, has been fully cognizant of his baser self all along; he has schemed successfully for years to indulge and protect it.

The quest to recover the moonstone proves just as critical for Franklin Blake, whom Rachel accuses of the theft, as it is to the three Hindoos. All four regard their efforts as an exercise in reintegration and self-recovery. The common goal is regaining self-esteem, not just public respect. Only with the sacred gem can the Hindoo priests, descendants of those responsible for guarding it, return home and attempt to resume their "high caste" as

"Brahmans" (MS, 72). Blake cannot marry Miss Verinder until they both understand that in taking the diamond, his desire for its better protection was inseparable from sexual desire for her. Society, represented by the Verinder residence, can then continue on a sounder basis. In *Great Expectations*, Satis House, where the personalities of Pip and Estella incur severe damage, is destroyed forever, a sign that neither of Dickens's pair can ever recover completely. But Blake and Miss Verinder plan to reopen her mother's home and face the world again.

In Collins's opinion, Franklin Blake is ultimately as heroic in *The Moonstone* as Walter Hartright in *The Woman in White*. Walter allows the dictates of propriety to drive him away from Laura but later restores her to her rightful place in order to take his alongside. Blake's darker self is permitted to assume its place as part of his personality; he regains his position as Rachel's intended because he brings to light a darker self whose surreptitious activity threatened to cause a permanent separation not only between himself and Rachel but from his own physical nature. Within Blake this nature has been forced to subsist in so repressed a state that Collins feels entitled to present it as his hero's double, virtually an alternative, criminal self.

Parodic revaluation throughout *The Moonstone* focuses on Pip and Estella, who were Dickens's revision of Walter and Laura. Blake comes to terms with his secret self in a regeneration process that Collins hopes will eclipse Pip's. Neither Franklin Blake nor Rachel Verinder regains the innocence each possessed at the start of Collins's novel, but together, as the book concludes, they seem about to win through to a higher form of it. They are certain, Collins suggests, to progress toward a mutual understanding well beyond the reconciliation Pip expects to achieve with Estella.

Collins's couple stand to gain in intimacy because Blake bridges the gap between his daylight and nighttime conceptions of both himself and Miss Verinder. If it was premature for Blake to remove from Rachel's cabinet a precious gem symbolizing virginal femininity, she was overly proper in treating sexuality as a prize to be locked away, an aspect of the self to be kept hidden.

Even in Dickens's second ending to *Great Expectations*, Pip and Estella appear crestfallen, beaten down by life. Blake and Miss Verinder (especially the former) do not emerge from their psychological ordeal in a reduced state, purged yet scarified; on the contrary, implies Collins, they become more self-aware and are fully alive and intact for the first time. Whether or not Pip and Estella are reunited, the title of Dickens's novel remains ironic. Although Blake and Miss Rachel never have the moonstone back in their possession, they learn the lessons it symbolizes. Collins wants

Blake and Rachel to seem entitled to greater expectations, with regard to each other, than either could anticipate from additional riches. Dickens's chief rival contends that he knows more about great expectations than Dickens does.

It is not Rosanna Spearman's past, her former career as a thief, that drives this servant of Lady Verinder's to suicide. Inability to cope with her inner self—an unrequited love for Franklin Blake—proves the fatal cause, not suspicion of theft. Although hardened by a reformatory, Rosanna is yet another of Collins's prisoners of propriety: she takes her own life because it would be "disgraceful" to reveal her hopeless passion while "a living woman" (MS, 308). Rosanna finally declares herself in a letter she makes certain Blake will not read until after her death.

Ironically, Rosanna perishes because Collins's protagonist fails to know himself in time to forestall her despair with a kind gesture. Yet her fate is destined to illuminate his condition. Hiding Blake's paint-smeared gown, ostensibly an act of love on Rosanna's part, postpones the solution of the crime. The servant impedes Blake's recognition of his interior self and drowns her own. When Blake finds the gown Rosanna hid for him and sees his name thereon, he is primed to fathom the real nature of an inside job. With the telltale garment in hand and the example of Rosanna's sad fate in mind, he is prepared to confront the phenomenon she fled from through death: the existence of an internal self that one dreads to let others see.

Rosanna's drowning is tragic in a sense quite different from Ablewhite's suffocation. His tumble from a respectable position as supporter of ladies' charitable organizations occurs in an upstairs room at the Wheel of Fortune, a place aptly named. Rosanna, by contrast, is an Ophelia figure who deserves pity rather than contempt. Betteredge, her Polonius, misunderstands her; her idol, Blake, is indecisive or puzzled for much of the novel. Ignorance of self, Collins lectures his former mentor, not delusions of grandeur as seen in Mr. Wopsle and Pip, is the danger Shakespeare's famous tragedy warns against; it is the graver danger for Victorian England.

Rosanna's station in life and a less than captivating appearance—she knows she is hardly the world's "most beautiful creature" (MS, 309)—bring on terminal despondency. A servant's secret yearning for the master is Collins's idea of a more intense study of sexual frustration than Pip's hunger for Estella. It also shows that self-division is not exclusively a male prerogative. Women have secret selves too, Collins demonstrates, not just secret pasts. Dickens portrays several self-tormenting females (Harriet Beadle, Miss Wade, Mrs. Clennam, Miss Havisham), but members of the fairer sex in his novels generally suffer less than men from having to present to the world the expurgated self that society demands.

The "Shivering Sand" claims Rosanna as surely as Tom-all-alone's infects the rest of London and Jarndyce versus Jarndyce ensnares Richard Carstone. An image for the repressed self, quicksand is another of Collins's answers to the success of Dickens's major symbols. Collins tries to invent memorable symbols that have greater internal or psychological reference. Problems deep within individuals, Collins argues, not just corruptions internal to the social system, determine the unsatisfactory conditions under which men live. The moonstone and the Sand are like the woman dressed always in white who personifies the absurdity of obeying the proprieties instead of one's inclinations: all three point inward to invisible causes, not just at such visible consequences of society's aberrations as the Circumlocution Office, Satis House, Krook's rag-and-bottle shop, or the Harmon dust mounds.[20] Collins's symbols in *The Moonstone*—a precious gem, a treacherous stretch of quicksand—disclose respectively a duality in human nature, which British society insufficiently acknowledges, and an inward seething of repressed emotion, which the individual ignores at his peril.

In *Our Mutual Friend*, the Harmon dust mounds represent the filthiness of lucre more concretely than Pip's abhorrence for Magwitch can do in *Great Expectations*. Throughout both novels, Dickens blames society's problems mainly on money. The worship of wealth and the pursuit of status are identified as predominant social failings, not the obsession with propriety that Collins satirized in *The Woman in White*. To disagree, Collins reemphasizes misunderstanding of the self as one of the primary causes of society's ills. A community's capacity for greater self-awareness, Collins maintains in *The Moonstone*, is a more important consideration than its attitude toward money or gentility; not selfishness but unawareness of the self is ruining Victorian life. Collins's response to *Great Expectations* is to reiterate his view that obeisance to the proprieties accurately illustrates society's preoccupation with surfaces, showing its preference for appearance and illusion, its willful ignorance of darker internalities.

More ambitious than Trollope and Mrs. Gaskell, Collins extensively parodies several Dickens novels at a time, but *The Moonstone* does not repeat the strategical errors in *No Name*, where Collins prowled through the Dickens canon for themes and situations to outdo. Although one can maintain that the attack on Dickens widens in *The Moonstone* to include the corpus from 1852 on, three redeeming factors provide concentration in the midst of breadth: *Great Expectations* is an object of steady reconsideration; *Bleak House* and *A Tale of Two Cities*, principal targets in *The Woman in White*, receive another drubbing as Collins resumes where he left off in 1860; and, most important, *The Moonstone* extends a theme that *Bleak House, A Tale of Two Cities*, and *Great Expectations* pursue in common. Society's problems, Collins tries to stipulate more emphatically than Dickens did in all three, emanate from within, as do the individual's failings.

Collins wants the flawed individual and imperfect society, illustrations of the internality of corruption, to become interchangeable metaphors, each capable of standing for the other more effectively than happens in Dickens. Ablewhite and Blake are society in microcosm, just as Joseph Conrad will show Marlow's Kurtz to be. Conversely, societies to Collins are the problems within Blake and Ablewhite on a larger, less manageable scale. One finds the dark heart Marlow watches Kurtz discovering inside himself more comprehensible in view of the European rapacity it epitomizes. British society is said to be as ignorant of itself as Blake or as dedicated to dissembling its real nature as Ablewhite.

Mrs. Gaskell hoped to minimize a community's difficulties by treating them as an enlargement of disagreements between individuals or within families, an idea that George Eliot also favored but Collins parodies. Taking a cue from Dickens, he shows that analogies between flawed individuals and unsatisfactory social conditions do not make either easier to perfect; on the contrary, each seems to explain the other's deterioration, as if each were both cause and effect.

The title of *A Tale of Two Cities* implied that convulsions in the Paris of 1789 furnish a paradigm for potential disturbances one can expect in London and throughout England if society's upper divisions continued to ignore the lower. Dickens's insubordinate pupil amplifies these charges in *The Moonstone*: he warns that crime and deception will flourish as long as the uppermost part of men's human nature, the rational, propriety-worshiping self, insists on ignoring and alienating the lower. Collins insinuates that Dickens misunderstands the full analogy one must construct between blindness to political and economic injustice in society and individual unawareness of deeper, darker aspects within the self.

What Herncastle and the soldiers did to India, Ablewhite and Blake seem willing to perpetrate against Miss Verinder: if taking her most valuable possession is a virtual deflowering, plundering the moonstone from the Hindoos in the first place was akin to raping a continent. It was as reprehensible as ravaging Africa for ivory will seem in Conrad's *Heart of Darkness*, except that Collins insists one need not travel so far to uncover the darkness within.

In *The Moonstone*, providence graduates from supplying unlikely alternative selves (Carton for Darnay) to uncovering secret sharers. This it accomplishes as patiently as it exposed secrets and secret pasts in *The*

Woman in White. The "care that conceals itself," Dickens's definition of providence, is more than a match for the divided personality that wants to conceal part of itself out of deference to propriety. To surpass Dickens as a psychological as well as a sensational realist, Collins attempts to chart patterns within human nature, not just in the more visible arena of national affairs. Inner deterioration, the very opposite of "fulfillment"—that, Collins contends, is what everything in Victorian life "has been working to," outward indications of progress to the contrary. Hidden selves within Blake and his contemporaries provide the key to explaining mysterious events in *The Moonstone.* How best to deal with such modern phenomena is a more profound question, in Collins's opinion, than asking what events culminate in an "Appointed Time," whether for an explosion inside Krook as a warning to the country's archaic legal system or for the storming of the Bastille in the previous century by France's own citizens.

The detective who would be providence's lieutenant in *The Moonstone* must be a psychologist as well as a social scientist and historian. Neither Darwin nor Carlyle—neither evolution nor retribution—provides a sufficient first principle, Collins implies, to decipher the life process. In addition to shining a "backward light" on all that has gone before, the melodramatic realist must learn to shine a light inward. He must examine hidden recesses within his characters, recesses as Gothic in their way as the secret passages and forbidding cellars once favored by less realistic sensationalists.

As agent of providence, Blake, not Ablewhite, becomes the novel's true philanthropist. He stands up for integrity by helping to expose the hypocrite in another and by embracing all aspects of human nature within himself. Like Marlow in *Heart of Darkness* and the unnamed captain in *The Secret Sharer,* Blake is not only interested in his darker side but loyal to it in a manner Collins can condone. Not exactly a prototype for either Marlow or Kurtz, Blake seems, in retrospect, a bit of both. His presence in *The Moonstone* makes Collins more modern than most realize and Conrad less unheralded.[21]

That Ablewhite plans to destroy the moonstone is hardly surprising; with gems cut from the larger diamond, he hopes to raise money to replace sums stolen from his ward. The total value of the gems would exceed the worth of the single diamond, as if division were more commendable than unification. The success of such a plan would have allowed the representative of duplicity and duality to destroy the novel's symbol for the flaw in human nature that he personifies but wishes to conceal. When Carton substitutes for Darnay, double-dealing is not remedied but simply put to good use. Collins contends that he outshines Dickens as a promoter of "fulfillment": the novelist supports reintegration of the self by making it a common goal for providential design and the novel's plot. Blake enlists Jennings and later works with Cuff to thwart Ablewhite, thus abetting the Hindoo effort to preserve the moonstone undivided.

As did *A Tale of Two Cities*, *The Moonstone* tells a story about two countries and their respective cultures. Parisian scenes serve as a warning in Dickens of calamities to be avoided if the English are to prove wiser than the French. But Indian spectacle in Collins is used to put the British in an inferior light, as did comparisons with Italy in *The Woman in White*.

Early in the novel, Blake's father, reluctant to serve as Herncastle's executor, justifies having accepted this commission when he learns that a jewel worth "twenty thousand pounds" would otherwise have been "lost to the family" (MS, 38). By contrast, the Hindoos finish the story with a celebration for the return of a religious artifact meant to enlighten, not enrich. Although the moonstone darkens the understanding of the English, most of whom visualize it in monetary terms, it serves as a beacon drawing Indians by the thousands to an open-air ritual. This public ceremony, at which the symbolic gem is displayed to multitudes, discredits Blake's father's sense of family loyalty as a constricting ideal, on a par with the proprieties and easily perverted to society's detriment. The religious observances that conclude *The Moonstone* denigrate even further Herncastle's reprehensible actions in the opening sequence.

The Hindoos hold their "great religious ceremony . . . in honor of the god of the Moon . . . at night" (MS, 460). The "calm of the night" combines with the "moonlight of the East" and the "wild red flames of cressets and torches" held by "tens of thousands of human creatures, all dressed in white" (MS, 461), to bring the opposition of light and dark that pervades the novel into aesthetic harmony. In England, such opposition was often ironic: evil within Able*white* versus the kindness of the dark-skinned Ezra Jennings. As a culture, India demonstrates better comprehension of human nature's positive and negative characteristics, disowning neither. Collins's Hindoos are attired all in white only for a special occasion. When Anne Catherick dressed that way constantly, she symbolized unnaturalness, the tyranny of Victorian England's sense of propriety.

The goings-on at Kattiawar are reported in a letter to Mr. Bruff from Mr. Murthwaite, who refers to himself as the "semi-savage person" the lawyer met in England during the disturbances at Lady Verinder's. A stand-in for Blake at the Indian rituals, Murthwaite reveals a Hindoo-Buddhist side to his character and thus becomes the final example of doubling for Collins's protagonist to learn from. To the extent that Murthwaite ceases to be English and begins to seem and sound Indian, he is able to formulate the novel's concluding observations. Through Murthwaite's reporting, Blake's personality acquires an Indian side useful in his ongoing development as a student of the life process, a synonym in both Dickens and Collins for the ways of providence.

Given the orderliness of the Hindoo devotees and their clearer perception of life's dualities, one wonders which half of himself, the true Englishman or his outward disguise as a Hindoo-Buddhist pilgrim, Murthwaite should consider uncivilized. The well-orchestrated ceremony is in sharp contradiction to the shameful preparations of the Parisian rioters whom Dr. Manette observes sharpening their blood-stained weapons in the courtyard of Tellson's Paris branch (TTC, 336-40). Collins's Indian scene comments satirically on the way crowd behavior, thanks to unsatisfactory social conditions, has been represented in the Victorian novel generally (in *Felix Holt* and *North and South*, for instance, as well as *A Tale of Two Cities*).

Having frequently ventured into parts of Central Asia closed to Europeans, Murthwaite is "lean enough and brown enough" to watch a Hindoo religious gathering by adopting Eastern dress. Unlike Ablewhite's resort to darkness as a shield, Murthwaite's duplicity—like Blake's recognition of man's darker side—facilitates exploration into territory that the majority of his peers lack the courage to penetrate. A seeker not a taker, Murthwaite cannot add to his knowledge or round off the moral for the story Blake is reassembling unless he commits this intrusion. In the last scene of the epilogue, it is nevertheless an Englishman who is foreign and would be unwelcome if his nationality were not concealed. As the explorer watches happenings no stranger than those he saw at Lady Verinder's, Collins does comparative sociology: he gives readers a final reminder that the evils in *The Moonstone* were never Oriental—that is, foreign or external—in origin.

After a "lapse of eight centuries," Murthwaite writes, "the Moonstone looks forth once more over the walls of the sacred city in which its story first began" (MS, 462). The invasion of a Mohammedan conqueror in the eleventh century first caused the moonstone to be removed from Kattiawar and hidden at Benares. In the eighteenth century it was stolen and restolen, just as Herncastle steals it from the Sultan of Seringapatam. Without Herncastle, who turns out to have been an unwitting instrument of providence, the long-suffering Hindoos might never have regained their relic. Their unshakable faith in providence is finally rewarded. The setting-to-rights has been as slow-moving and invisible to the unschooled eye as geological changes; it is meant to appear just as wonderful, just as relentless. The gem is restored to its rightful place just as Lady Glyde regained hers at Limmeridge House.

During eight centuries, the moonstone has gone from being a diamond "in the forehead" of "the god of the Moon" to an "ornament in the handle of a dagger" (MS, 5), associating it successively with wisdom and death. Murthwaite recalls that its "splendor" had "last shone" upon him "in England, from the bosom of a woman's dress," where it is a thing of beauty but suggests sexual pleasures, which it seems both to beckon toward and to prohibit. The moonstone always has a double impact in Victorian Britain: its appearance at Lady Verinder's brings about the destruction of Ablewhite, who has long been a fraud, and triggers greater self-awareness in Rachel's future husband.

The moonstone's travels do not carry it farther than Collins takes Dickens's fascination with doubling by the end of the diamond's story. Collins's epilogue suggests an unfolding that is also temporal process doubling back upon itself in corrective measure. "So the years pass, and repeat each other; so the same events revolve in the cycles of time," Murthwaite's letter concludes (MS, 462). Blake must repeat the opium dosage and reenact the taking of the moonstone in order to go forward to greater self-awareness. His actions are a miniature version of the larger turn of events that corroborates them, events that result in a precious gem being replaced in the god's forehead where it originated and belongs. The symbol of duality in human nature is restored through a doubling back of time.

Doubtless, immersion in Hindoo customs accounts for the explorer's final remarks. But life is often a matter of "cycles," the novelist lectures his more progressive rivals; it is not simply an upward curve of steady, ameliorative ascent. Patterns of rise and fall, repetition and readjustment, can always be discerned co-existing with, if not in counterpoint to, movement forward. A brief excursion into Hindoo culture shows this more clearly than did Dickens's preoccupation with revolutionary France. Besides "what everything has been working to," Collins demonstrates what events have been working back to—another method of imitating the ways of providence and shining a "backward light" on its regulatory procedures.

The adventures of "the Yellow Diamond" are tied to the advent in India of successive conquerors—Mohammedan, Mongolian, and now English. These invasions typify the sudden upheavals through which life periodically alters course. The moonstone, as a symbol of the rise and fall of its possessors, carries a stern message about the waxing and waning of empire that seems to contradict the idea, biological in origin, of life and society as slowly maturing systems. Often-conquered Hindoos would dismiss as utopian Felix Holt's confidence in peaceful transition of a nation's cultural heritage from one era to the next. Still, in *The Moonstone*, only the Indians exhibit a cultural awareness similar to what Holt recommends. The English merely pass on material possessions in their wills.

The three Brahmans who bring the gem back home, however, are separated from it and one another forever. These agents of providence make reparation for their ancestors' failure to protect a religious relic but are "doomed" to be sent off in "three different directions" before the moonstone, reset in their god's forehead, is publicly displayed (MS, 462). The banishing of the three Brahmans reminds readers that society has scant prospect of perfection or total integration as its denouement. This is the unvarnished truth about life in Victorian England, India, and elsewhere throughout history, Collins insists; his story's points apply to all, despite the unusually mysterious incidents it employs and the exotic foreign setting at the close. Indeed, both are necessary to obtain a more informed angle on the nature of things than could have been supplied by familiar events closer to home.

Evidently, Collins thought that he had won more than a fight with Dickens to speak for providence. He considered his former teacher and model played out. Nine years earlier, he and Dickens had started writing competing fictions, each offering his explanation for the unsatisfactoriness of Victorian life while simultaneously disputing not so much the pertinency but more often the intensity of the other's satire. Each contended he had penned the more damning critique. In 1868, over three and a half years had elapsed since the last Dickens novel had begun to appear. With *The Moonstone*, Collins anticipated a confirmation of Dickens's retirement. The younger novelist expected to certify himself Victorian society's ablest practicing melodramatic realist, pursuing the complexities of human nature and the problem of persisting evil in society in ways beyond Dickens's ken.

He was wrong. By the time Dickens died on 9 June 1870, he had completed enough of *The Mystery of Edwin Drood* to convince the modern revaluator of hidden rivalries that significant reprisals lay in store for Collins.

Chapter Six

Inimitability Regained

The Mystery of Edwin Drood

INSTANCES OF wrongdoing or wrong thinking at society's upper levels abound in Dickens's novels. Besides Dombey and Gradgrind, the list of white-collar villains includes Casby, Merdle, Podsnap and Veneering. The respectable exteriors of Casby and Merdle conceal slum lord and swindler. Prior to 1870, Dickens also painted comic portraits of split men in Wemmick and Mr. Lorry, good-natured souls who conscientiously separate a better self from a business persona. In *The Moonstone*, with successful creations like Ablewhite and Blake, Collins advances beyond Dickens: he perceives more acutely that the themes of self-division and of criminality among the respectable should overlap. Once again, Collins worries Dickens into restating his case, and reiteration quickly leads to revaluation.

John Jasper, Dickens's ultimate malefactor, seems designed to overshadow Blake and Ablewhite so thoroughly that he will seem unprecedented. *The Mystery of Edwin Drood* (1870) shows signs of culminating in a reenactment sequence that would prolong and expand the restaging of the moonstone's disappearance. This sequence, unlike the one in Collins's novel, would take place less than a year after the actual crime but would determine the fate of a missing person, not just the whereabouts of a diamond.

Insofar as hidden rivalries are concerned, *The Mystery of Edwin Drood* deserves elevation in the Dickens canon as the work that could have been the aging novelist's supreme effort with the multipurpose novel. It would have vindicated much of Dickens's previous fiction, especially *Bleak House* and his novels of the 1860s, while simultaneously attempting to outdistance

Collins conclusively. In addition, Dickens wanted to begin settling accounts long pending against Trollope and George Eliot.

Dickens and Collins agreed that the divided personality was civilization's newest species of discontent, the product of unexampled pressure
from an oppressive, uncharitable society. Both satirists contended that the
respectability of this society was of dubious merit, as was its capacity for
self-reform. The split man could also be seen as an antiprogressive development, a psychological setback fraught with anti-evolutionary implications.
Dickens decided that Collins must not be allowed to take full credit for
analyzing this phenomenon, and that novelists like George Eliot and Mrs.
Gaskell deserved to be sharply criticized for overlooking the problem of
duality when they offered, in Felix Holt and Mr. Thornton, positive
versions of the man of the future.

One finds more characters with some type of double or second self in
The Mystery of Edwin Drood than varieties of secret sharer in *The Moonstone*.
Before focusing on the competing personalities within Jasper, one should
notice the telepathy that allows the Landless twins to share each other's
emotional life, Crisparkle and Honeythunder as the positive and negative
faces of philanthropy, Mr. Sapsea's unintentionally parodic imitation of the
Dean, and Miss Twinkleton's "two distinct and separate phases of being."[1]

Miss Twinkleton is a prim schoolmistress by day and a "sprightly"
gossip after dark. Every night she transforms her "scholastic" self into a
bright-eyed lover of the latest scandal, a side of herself that her young
charges at the Nuns' House "have never seen" (ED, 53); indeed, each of her
two selves or "phases" can exist only by remaining (in this case pretending
to remain) "as ignorant" of the other "as a granite pillar." This comic
variation on Jasper, along with the other examples, shows that Dickens
intended to leave no doubt which melodramatic realist understood duality
and self-division more profoundly and depicted it more extensively.

The final chapters, Dickens told his biographer, would take place "in
the condemned cell."[2] Impressed by the novel's high point, the reason for
all that went before, readers would hardly fail to notice that the deserving
occupant of society's most undesirable cubicle was now a respectable
choirmaster from Cloisterham, not a denizen of London's underworld.
Instead of "Fagin's Last Night Alive,"[3] Dickens would do Jasper's. He
would reassert his superiority in a manner closed to a less experienced rival:
by rewriting one of the most renowned scenes from his own work.

Substituting Jasper for Fagin would emphasize the striking changes
that had taken place since 1839 in the threat to polite society's survival.
Looking back over three decades, Dickens could claim to be more knowl-

edgeable about the evolution of the criminal mentality, no longer the possession mainly of outcasts but now ensconced within a reputable member of a society allegedly improving faster than any on earth. If Dickens could outdo Collins at underlining this irony, he would regain undisputedly the position he had held prior to publication of *The Moonstone*. He would again become the popular expert on the internality of corruption and the increasingly acceptable disguises adopted by late Victorian criminality.

Jasper's turbulent interiority, central to Dickens's conception of the psychology of modern man, can be accounted for as a recrudescence of the persistent Manichee. Dickens explains that man is always, in part, antisocial, hence never completely vulnerable to bills of reform. Having moved back and forth between Cloisterham and an East End opium den, Jasper combines in his experience, and internalizes within his dual personality, Fagin's den and the Brownlow-Maylie world. Originally, doubleness through self-division in Dickens was a potentially curable sociological matter, which the opposing tugs Fagin and Brownlow exert on Oliver's pliant nature crudely externalized. When Jasper replaces Fagin in the death cell, he also subs for Oliver as a representative of all earthbound pilgrims. Unlike Oliver, however, Jasper cannot choose one place over another because the murderer-choirmaster carries heaven and hell inside himself.[4]

Jasper, more than Pip, is a gentleman-monster or monster-gentleman. He appears to be split into a daytime and nighttime self, just as Dracula subsequently is.[5] Rosa Bud tells Helena Landless that Jasper terrifies her because she feels "as if he could pass in through the wall when he is spoken of" (ED, 95); likewise, closed doors and locked windows pose no barrier for the bloodthirsty count. Like Dracula, Jasper readily asserts a hypnotic power over women. Rosa complains that he seems to haunt her: he is always "whispering that he pursues me as a lover, and commanding me to keep his secret."

Jasper's eyes compel compliance most strongly, Rosa continues, "when a glaze comes over them": that is, when the lusting murderer within him becomes the uppermost of his twin personalities. Suffering under Jasper's gaze in Chapter 7, Rosa grows too "frightened" to go on playing the piano. "It was," she confesses to Helena, "as if he kissed me, and I couldn't bear it, but cried out" (ED, 96). Edwin informs Rosa that his uncle "didn't like to be charged with being the Monster who had frightened you" (ED, 93).

Dickens has not surrendered the image of Frankenstein's monster, which he used in describing Pip's relationship to Magwitch in *Great Expectations*. In 1870, he adapts Mary Shelley's story more skillfully to his argument that men and societies continually generate new evils from within. The monster fashions the gentleman in *Great Expectations* and then returns to stalk his fairer creation as its secret sharer or frightful other self. In *The Mystery of Edwin Drood*, the monster that society has made is interpreted as a projection of its deviant self, an expression through Jasper of thwarted or repressed energies.

The murderer bottled up inside the choirmaster, Dickens implies, has been created collectively by polite society: that is, formed in revolt against its strictures. Jasper has been programmed to prey upon Cloisterham as cruelly as his secret inner self abuses and contaminates the outer. Stoker's *Dracula* is an age-old curse upon community. But Jasper is both timeless and a contemporary burden: the eternal Manichee revisited upon society and a counter-evolutionary brake which the life force applies to the Victorian era's overconfidence in progress, not to mention its naive belief in the restraining authority of the proprieties.

Unlike Pip and Magwitch, or Frankenstein and his creature, Dickens's monster shares a bodily home with a representative of the respectable world that spawned him. Choirmaster and murderer exist more symbiotically in *The Mystery of Edwin Drood* than daytime and nighttime selves in Blake or defrauder and philanthropist in Ablewhite. Dickens insists that neither Blake nor Ablewhite but John Jasper is the true monster of respectability.

The nocturnal "expedition" the choirmaster goes on with Durdles, a prowl "among the tombs, vaults . . . and ruins" of Cloisterham Cathedral (ED, 149), conveys further the suggestion that Jasper, "a dark man" (ED, 43), is as vampirelike as Fagin was devilish. The choirmaster's room could pass for a coffin: "It is mostly in shadow. Even when the sun shines brilliantly, it seldom touches" Jasper or his possessions—not "the grand piano in the recess, or the folio music-books on the stand, or the bookshelves on the wall." In short, although Jasper casts a shadow, he shuns daylight; both he and his world seem averse to it.

Had Dickens lived to complete *The Mystery of Edwin Drood*, the murderer within Jasper would have been hunted down more dramatically than Cuff and Blake track Ablewhite to the Wheel of Fortune. Tartar, Neville and Helena Landless, and probably Datchery would have joined Crisparkle to lead the pursuit. One assumes that Dickens would have confined the chase sequence to Cloisterham. But some idea of the potential for excitement in this episode can be obtained from the last fifty pages of Stoker's novel, where the pursuit of Dracula stretches from London back to the Carpathians. Once at bay, the murderer inside the choirmaster would have drawn upon all of the defiant, antisocial energy at large throughout the community, the mass of unsatisfied hunger and desire which he personifies and brings to a head.

It would not be necessary to drive a stake through Jasper's heart, as was reportedly done to Quilp.[6] Nevertheless, outside help would be required to purge Cloisterham, to expunge Jasper from the community whose failings, having produced him, have come back to haunt it. As purifiers, agents of justice, the quintet that subdues Jasper would be more attractive than the Defarges or Tulkinghorn, grotesques whom Collins considered unsavory personifiers of retribution. Datchery demonstrates none of Van Helsing's knowledge of philosophy, medicine, and the occult, but the description Stoker's vampire-hunter gives of those he rallies by "solemn compact" against Dracula applies to Datchery and the group that would trap Jasper: both contingents are "chosen instruments" of God's "good pleasure" (D, 314).

One need not explain Jasper's chaotic inner state by referring to Dickens's private life, though the actress Ellen Ternan, disenchantment with the artistic temperament, and a dual tendency to be artist and rebel may have played some part.[7] Primarily, however, Dickens hoped to invent a horror that would magnify, for didactic purposes, the underside of civilization, fundamental failings within human nature and drawbacks in the human condition—not just in Dickens's own. His suggestion of a vampire in Jasper's makeup accomplishes this without overtaxing credibility to the extent that Stoker's singular monster subsequently does.

Lucy Westenra, whom Dracula's bite transforms into one of the Un-Dead, retains the outward features of a beautiful young woman from sunrise to sunset. At other times, whenever the creature in her is opposed or aroused, her sense of propriety vanishes, her expression becomes heartlessly cruel or "voluptuous" and wanton (D, 168). Like Dracula, Lucy exemplifies life working against its own best interests, the negative aspects destroying the good points. Dracula's favorite meals are young children and the wives of his enemies: "Your girls that you all love are mine already," he taunts his pursuers (D, 324). There is a hint of the vampire as repressed energy in Franklin Blake: inside a house sealed against intruders, the darker side of his double self comes to life and walks by night to remove Miss Verinder's most valuable treasure from her room, a crime symbolic of rape. But a choirmaster who seems outwardly respectable yet kills his own nephew and lusts after his victim's fiancée outdoes all of Collins's sensational disclosures at once; he eclipses not just Ablewhite, the embezzling philanthropist with a mistress, but also Blake, the young gentleman who subconsciously desires to violate the woman whom his daylight self envisions as his future bride.

Drood's homicidal uncle is a more dangerous perversion of an authority figure than the irresponsible fathers in Dickens's earlier fiction;[8] he portends for his victims a fate worse than abuse or chilling neglect. The manslayer within this apparently responsible citizen is the vigor of Victorian life gone sour, its prowess constricted and misapplied. Having been frustrated, Jasper seems bent on sapping the vitality of others.

Rachel's thieving uncle in *The Moonstone* behaves like an errant fairy godfather; Herncastle's legacy, a fabulous diamond not only stolen but symbolically flawed at its core, amounts to a tainted and troublesome inheritance. Receiving it is worse, perhaps, than having to recognize an actual convict as the source of one's gentility and wealth. Magwitch, one recalls, enjoys being called "Uncle Provis": "That's it, dear boy!" he instructs Pip. "Call me uncle" (GE, 354). Both uncles make disreputable sources for economic prosperity and the social status it confers. But Dickens conceives of Jasper as the ultimate avuncular villain.

Instead of conferring wealth and future prospects, no matter how problematic, Jasper schemes to take them away. Edwin Drood's guardian and trustee aims to undo his nephew more thoroughly than Ablewhite defrauds his ward. Jasper covets the diamond ring Drood is to give Rosa upon their engagement more heinously than Ablewhite wants the moonstone. The dark side of Jasper yearns to possess Rosa herself more desperately than Blake's nighttime self desires Rachel. In Jasper, Dickens joins the malignity of Fagin to the sexuality in figures like Sikes and Quilp. The respectable choirmaster's lust is treated uncompromisingly as an antisocial element, impossible to defuse. Dickens rewrites Collins on this score to contend that his competitor solved a critical situation unrealistically by subdividing split personalities into two different varieties of transgressor: one is predominantly a financial offender and inexcusable; the other poses chiefly a sexual threat but, owing to the defrauder's death in his stead, is more retrievable than Darnay.

Sergeant Cuff writes that Mr. Godfrey Ablewhite's life had "two sides" to it: "The side turned up to the public view presented the spectacle of a gentleman, possessed of considerable reputation as a speaker at charitable meetings. . . . The side kept hidden from the general notice exhibited this same gentleman in the totally different character of a man of pleasure, with a villa in the suburbs which was not taken in his own name, and with a lady in the villa who was not taken in his own name either" (MS, 445).

Dickens finds this explanation of Godfrey's behavior, including Cuff's attempt at levity, contrived—that is, shallow, belated, and psychologically implausible. The older novelist resolved to outshine the younger by showing him what a "gentleman" harboring a "totally different character" inside himself would actually be like.

Contrary to villains like Ablewhite and Sir Percival Glyde, in Collins's novels, Jasper's violent-erotic self has little to do with a shortage of funds. In Jasper's case, sexual torment predominates; it aggravates the contempt the homicidal personality within the choirmaster feels for "oppressive respectability" (ED, 51). An insurgent physical nature and the "cramped monotony" (ED, 48) of a "daily drudging round" are combined furies that drive Jasper's darker side to murder, not just to fraud or theft (even if the theft in Collins is shorthand for the urge to deflower). Desire to retain position and reputation becomes the focal point of Ablewhite's struggles, as it was for Glyde. The same desire compels Blake to submit to Jennings's experiment with opium and then, having acquitted himself of a crime, to continue searching for the real thief. The repressed self within Jasper lusts after the unattainable at the *expense* of reputation and position; it has developed a sharper sense of the insufficiency of social prominence and professional success as guarantors of happiness.

Pip acquired this sense late in life but was eventually better able to resign himself. Collins, Dickens argues, was unfair to criticize *Great Expectations* in *The Moonstone* on grounds that it ignored oppressive proprieties and attributed society's problems mainly to a pervasive craving after status and wealth. The inadequacy of reputation and success to compensate for life's inevitable emotional letdowns, not just simple greed, was the larger problem Dickens insists that *Great Expectations* ultimately addressed. Jasper's story clarifies this issue. Dickens defends his earlier novel in *The Mystery of Edwin Drood* the way Collins spoke up for *The Woman in White* in *The Moonstone*.

Dickens charges that Collins has Ablewhite, the man supposedly with an extensive secret life, commit a crime for money rather than passion. The revelation that Ablewhite stole the moonstone for gain after Blake tried to take it in lieu of Rachel herself allows one action to palliate the other; either Ablewhite should have operated from Blake's sexual motivations, or Blake should have led Ablewhite's secret life. Consequently, Dickens's study of Jasper's duplicity, his leading of a secret life governed by violent-erotic drives, is not only a triumph for the would-be psychological novelist but a major instance of revaluative parody.

Jasper is two villains in one: he is Edwin's guardian and probably his killer, Rosa's tutor and her would-be deflowerer, just as Ablewhite is his ward's unscrupulous trustee and Blake symbolically takes Miss Verinder's virginity. To outdo Collins, Dickens planned to put Blake and Ablewhite back together. He would reunite, in one much more complicated individual, two interrelated self-divisions which he believed Collins unrealistically split into separate cases, the more difficult of which was then pronounced curable. In *The Mystery of Edwin Drood*, Dickens reexamines *The Moonstone's* ray of hope: he disagrees that sexual frustration in modern society, and the hypocrisy it leads to, can be separated from other causes of duplicity and overcome simply through greater frankness.

Because Jasper combines the opium-released secret sharer within Blake and the extensive double life Ablewhite is said to have led, he is allegedly a more credible double personality. Dickens shifts to his villain the darker carnal desires Collins explored obliquely in his hero but for which he only directly punished the thief and defrauder in Ablewhite. Collins is accused of having deputized one of the novel's divided personalities (the false philanthropist) to take the blame both for his own misdeeds and those of another (Rachel's successful suitor). This resolution, it follows, is scarcely less convenient than allowing Carton to stand in for Darnay. Dickens uses Jasper's double self to retaliate for the manner in which Collins reused the idea of doubles in *The Woman in White* to imply that Carton's physical resemblance to Darnay was biologically improbable.

Collins's hypocritical philanthropist steals in order to preserve his pleasures: the suburban villa, a mistress. The side Ablewhite diligently shows the public labors to keep the other side—the "man of pleasure"— alive and well. Dickens finds ridiculous a split personality in which one half so eagerly abets the other. Jasper's other side is never so cooperative. It seems to take over unbidden. The choirmaster experiences a seizure when- ever the personality shift from uncle to murderous rival occurs. In his astonished nephew's words, Jasper suddenly looks "frightfully ill": "There's a strange film come over your eyes," Edwin exclaims (ED, 47). Similarly, Oliver underwent some sort of symbolic death—the bullet wound received on the housebreaking caper with Sikes, for example[9]— before passing out of Fagin's domain into Brownlow's.

In the garden of the Nuns' House, Rosa finds the intensity of Jasper's declaration of love intimidating. Similarly, despite speaking as host to guest, the choirmaster cautions his nephew to beware of the "restlessness" and "dissatisfaction" of a "poor monotonous chorister and grinder of music" (ED, 49). In both scenes the lustful, murderous Jasper has taken control of the respectable musician, and all through the novel Jasper's darker self periodically overthrows the choirmaster's personality without the latter's knowledge or consent. But this would not have been revealed definitely until the death-cell sequence that was to end the novel. Still, once it became evident, Dickens would clearly have parodied Ablewhite's unrealistically congenial coexistence with his meaner side and, in the same stroke, announced that he had been outdoing Blake's opium-induced secret sharer all along; its emergence would have seemed harmless compared to Jasper's subtler and more malevolent personality shifts.

In Dickens's opinion, Albewhite has two daylight selves, one of which is specious and both ultimately detestable. Presenting Jasper's more intricate character is the shortest and surest way to assert that Collins's conniving philanthropist is not a very sophisticated example of the duality of the human spirit. Ablewhite is never uncertain about who or what he is— only the misdirected reader is confused on this point—nor does he epitomize a new development; instead, he recalls Pecksniff and Tartuffe. The older novelist would show the younger the difference between leading a double life (Ablewhite) and having a double self (Jasper).

Blake's nocturnal self, too, would be made to appear insufficiently other and not enough like a hunted criminal when measured against the murderer inside Jasper. It is Jasper, not Blake, who, to apply Betteredge's words, would "pass his life in a state of perpetual contradiction with himself" (MS, 44). The repressed sensualist in Blake, Dickens's redoing of Collins would suggest, actually yearns to be domesticated, to be reconciled with the daytime world at Lady Verinder's. The lustful element only demands a fairer share; it longs for recognition and inclusion rather than dominance. Contrary to Jasper's furtive secret sharer, Blake's nighttime self capitalizes on any opportunity to call attention to itself. An unexpected opium dose, which weakens the hero's inhibitions, enables his darker side to apply for reintegration. Dickens would object, through Jasper, that self-division is a more grievous antisocial catastrophe than Collins realizes.

Blake uncovers his secret sharer and makes peace with it publicly after voluntarily reenacting his part in the disappearance of the moonstone. In the closing pages of *The Mystery of Edwin Drood*, Dickens could have rewritten this scene to reveal the unreality of Collins's reenactment episode. Jasper would not so easily regain self-control merely by introducing the manslayer within him to polite society. Instead, one imagines that Jasper would resist to the final moments the painful, possibly self-destructive confrontation between the polar twins inside himself.

With the two sides to Blake and the mix of philanthropist and philanderer in Ablewhite, Collins believed he had taken doubling a critical step forward; Dickens would respond that his rival had hardly completed the process they both began studying with Carton/Darnay and Laura Fairlie/Anne Catherick. Admittedly, Collins clumsily internalized an intensely symbolic psychological condition that Dickens at first only groped after by spatializing it in look-alikes who are opposites temperamentally. In 1870, however, Dickens would combine aspects of Blake's case with details from

Ablewhite's and delve deeper than he thought Collins could into the compound that results.

When an importunate Jasper persecutes Rosa, the possibility of violation, the suggestion of impending rape, seems more sinister than it ever becomes in *The Moonstone*. Although end of term has arrived at the Nuns' House, Rosa, being without parents, is left there practically alone. When Jasper comes to profess his love, she "shudders at the thought of being shut up with him in the house" (ED, 226). In desperation, she interviews her music tutor outdoors because "many of its windows command the garden, and she can be seen as well as heard there, and can shriek in the free air and run away" if necessary. Jasper, too, is aware that "many windows command a view" of their conversation. Having touched Rosa once, he prevents her from retiring by saying "I will not touch you again, I will come no nearer to you than I am" (ED, 228).

Nevertheless, Jasper accosts Rosa more ghoulishly than an outwardly grotesque Quilp besieged Little Nell. As the potential violator speaks in the respectable choirmaster's voice, Blake's nocturnal advance upon Rachel Verinder seems benevolent by comparison. In Chapter 19 of *The Mystery of Edwin Drood*, one witnesses the "dark secret love" of "the invisible worm" trying to find out the "bed" of the rose (Rosa Bud) to destroy its life. William Blake's lyric strikes Dickens as a better study than Collins's Franklin Blake of evil inhering within good.[10]

It is possible to see the impulse to deflower, first in *The Moonstone* and then more dramatically in *The Mystery of Edwin Drood*, as symbolic repetitions of man's fall. The recurrent urge attests to factors within human nature that always prove injurious. They do not just impede the Hindoos' plans for recovering their relic or the arrangement between Bud and the elder Drood to marry Rosa to Edwin; such factors interfere with the working out of any grand or utopian design. If there exists a perennial flaw in human nature that polite Victorian society brings out in new and virulent form, Dickens resolves to depict it more disturbingly than Collins did. He contends that Jasper's behavior in the garden with Rosa shatters perfectibilitarian illusions about human nature more decisively than Ablewhite's secret life or Blake's nighttime opium trance.

Due to the revolt of a violent-erotic inner self, Jasper plays not only the part of a fallen Adam but the serpent's role as well. As the choirmaster presses his suit unsuccessfully, the personality of Rosa's music tutor and Edwin's uncle is displaced by the lusting murderer's. Jasper then tempts Rosa to favor him lest he frame Neville Landless for a crime his darker side knows he has committed himself. Even being dressed in black as a sign of "deep mourning" for a beloved nephew takes on added significance when

Jasper's tone and personality start to shift. His attire is not unlike Dracula's; it also seems Mephistophelean, hence doubly appropriate to a "poor" (that is, humble) chorister who begins to exhibit "working features" and "convulsive hands" that are "absolutely diabolical" (ED, 229).

Jasper's face looks "wicked and menacing, as he stands leaning against the sun-dial—setting, as it were, his black mark upon the very face of day" (ED, 228). Blake's nighttime or carnal self, despite the intent to soil Miss Verinder, is never made to appear this repulsive. Jasper's lustful inner self, more indicative than Blake's of man's deep-set deficiencies, leaves a stain upon life. Although Jasper casts a "Shadow on the Sun-Dial," one has a premonition of Dracula courting a reluctant maiden, and the impression is joined to a reprise of the devil seducing Eve.

Dickens would have been hard pressed to secure for such a villain the satisfying breakthrough to higher innocence that a kinder Collins allows Franklin Blake. Putting a bad end to Jasper would reveal that unifying the divided self and then realigning it with society-at-large are steps in a more delicate operation than Collins realized. To be more convincing than Collins's pair, Jasper would have to reenact his misdeeds, as Blake does, and then perish, as does Ablewhite. Dickens's contention would be not that society fails to survive full disclosure of its ills, but that it should not expect to approach perfection; it will never have goodness without concomitant evil to struggle against. Having tried to make similar statements throughout *The Moonstone*, Collins must surely have agreed. Yet that is precisely the luxury Collins is accused of granting himself when he redeems Blake but lets the Brahmans smother Ablewhite.

Dickens would revise but not repudiate the ending of *A Tale of Two Cities*, which Collins criticized for allowing bad to rescue good. Once flushed into the open, the murderer within Jasper would enlighten (but not exonerate) the seemingly innocent half of this dual personality. He would thereby release the choirmaster from perplexity as efficiently as Carton set Darnay free from prison.

Although Jasper was intended to cause a greater sensation than Blake and Ablewhite together, Dickens's investigation of man's dual nature would never have become as theatrical as Robert Louis Stevenson's. Masao Miyoshi wrongly conjectures that *The Mystery of Edwin Drood* "foreshadows the dual personality novel of the nineties."[11] Actually, it might have rendered such a novel superfluous. One must uphold Charles Forsyte's contention that had Dickens "lived a few months longer, the world would never have heard of Dr. Jekyll or Mr. Hyde."[12] Yet even this compliment underrates Dickens both as an outdoer of Collins and as a novelist so percipient on occasion that he could preempt writers even profounder on the subject of duality than Bram Stoker or Stevenson (e.g., Joseph Conrad).

Indeed an oddity, *The Strange Case of Dr. Jekyll and Mr. Hyde* is not one in which the more recent author enhances the modernity of a predecessor while revealing Victorian traits that abide within his own constitution. By comparison with Stevenson, Dickens and Collins emerge as superior psychologists and social critics. The later writer's reuse of their themes furnishes an additional way of looking back at their rivalry, for Stevenson fares better when measured against Collins than against Dickens.

Dr. Jekyll and John Jasper are both highly respected individuals, each with a sinister side that projects itself as a separate personality. Both make painful transitions from one self to the other, although Jasper's are subtler. Both are killers, but Hyde's unpremeditated clubbing of Sir Danvers Carew seems extraneous to the plot, whereas Jasper's well-laid design against Drood is central. Hyde poisons himself when Utterson and Poole break into Jekyll's study in search of the doctor, leaving the outcome of both stories to hinge upon a missing body: the absent Jekyll, having succumbed permanently to his usurping baser self, is thought to have been done in by Hyde; Landless is accused of murdering Drood. Jekyll swallows powders of his own concocting to switch back and forth between his proper self and Hyde; the murderer within Jasper appears to be an opium-addict. At no point, however, does Stevenson's story complete or outclass the work that would have precluded it.

Dickens's tale was to terminate with Jasper's confession. The ending in Stevenson cannot equal the commotion such a disclosure, climaxing in self-awareness or self-detection, would have set off: Jekyll's letter of confession is merely read aloud by his lawyer. It captures the reader's attention but seems no more innovative technically than the written admission of guilt Walter wrings from Fosco in the closing pages of *The Woman in White*. Nor is it much deeper psychologically than Cuff's letter to Blake explaining Ablewhite's behavior.

The shock of watching Hyde retract into Jekyll sends Dr. Lanyon to his deathbed. Jekyll's account of the event, although chilling, is simply a precursor of the obligatory transformation scene in modern horror movies. Jasper's death-cell discovery of his murderous second self would have been less stagy yet more traumatic for him, his auditors, and the reader. A Jasper whose personality is regularly taken over by an unpleasant interloper whom he is unaware of but cannot help camouflaging more skillfully than Jekyll conceals Hyde—that is Dickens's superior idea. It explains how Jasper can cherish Drood in one breath and threaten him the next, how he can persecute Rosa in the presence of her friends without attracting the general notice. Inward alteration that leaves Jasper virtually unchanged outwardly is not nearly as eye-catching as Jekyll compressing himself into a simian Hyde—more "like a monkey" than a man[13]—but it strikes the modern revaluator as the graver anti-evolutionary possibility.

A sedate Jekyll transmogrifies himself into a "hardly human," "troglodytic" "fiend" with "Satan's signature" on his face (RLS, 13, 7). Although voluntary at first, the change eventually seems closer to Gregor Samsa's nightmarish metamorphosis in Kafka's story than to Jasper's deep-seated duplicity. Jekyll realizes that he is losing control when he goes to bed as the good doctor and awakens as Hyde (RLS, 59). This "pale and dwarfish" second self, so cretinous that it gives onlookers "a strong feeling of deformity" (RLS, 6), presupposes an "evil side" to man's nature that is, to use Jekyll's words, "less robust and less developed than the good" (RLS, 55). Logically, this less formidable baser self should be powerless to release itself or to deceive as to its intentions should it get free. Dickens's villainous protagonist, by contrast, illustrates equality in duality, the murderous Jasper being as imposing, perhaps more so, than his cohabitant.

Jekyll reports that passersby shrink from Hyde as if from the evil within themselves "because all human beings, as we meet them, are commingled out of good and evil" (RLS, 55). In shunning Hyde, his fellow men avoid any increase in self-knowledge. But the horrified reader of *The Mystery of Edwin Drood* would not be able to shrink from Jasper; along with those who extract the final confession, he would reluctantly sympathize with the choirmaster's predicament. Dickens's reader would accept it (Jasper would also) not as a "Strange Case" but as human nature's situation generally. Identification with Jasper as an alter ego for everyman would be stronger than any bond between the reader and Jekyll; it would parallel the choirmaster's recognition of his darker other self and thereby prove the commingling of good and evil in man more effectively. That "man is not truly one, but truly two" (RLS, 52), the deconstructive thesis of Jekyll's seventeen-page confession, thus seems a step backward—not a parodic revaluation of Dickens's final fiction but an instance of redoing as retrogression.

In Stevenson's story, certainty that Hyde is Jekyll and vice versa is kept from other participants in the action as long as possible. This imitation of the emphasis Dickens and Collins placed on suspenseful delay is less original and of less consequence for one's grasp of modern man's interiority than Dickens's apparent intention: since the choirmaster does not seem to realize the extent of his duplicity, Dickens would withhold until last the solution to mysteries in his novel from the one character whose divided personality contains the answers.

Unlike Jasper, Jekyll and Hyde are not "truly two." Incredibly, they have "memory in common" (RLS, 60): each is fully aware of their mutual past and thoroughly hostile to the other. Dickens's conception of doubleness seems keener and is more satirical in that Jasper has repressed all knowledge of the murderer within. He remains ignorant about the darkness of his inner being, Dickens implies, just as the Victorian period wishes to be nescient not only of impropriety but of less optimistic philosophies regarding the unfolding of the life process. In shallower creations such as Ablewhite and Dr. Jekyll, doubleness is mostly self-engendered. The secret sharer or second self is always cleverly manipulated, indeed exploited, by the public personality.

Like Ablewhite, Jekyll has always cunningly "concealed" his "pleasures." Despite being "the very pink of the proprieties," he secretly indulges an "impatient gaiety of disposition" (RLS, 5, 51). In short, he behaves deceitfully long before an accidental research discovery enables him to satisfy his grosser appetites as Edward Hyde. If Jekyll's concealed pleasures were always comparable to Hyde's brazen misdeeds, they go further toward perdition than Blake's suppressed lust, but a "vicarious depravity" (RLS, 57) courtesy of Hyde, stops far short of Jasper.

On the loose as Hyde, Jekyll is not really an expression of modern man's psychological disorder. He is not much more of a revelation of interior turmoil than Ablewhite was when disguised as a foreign sailor. The powders that allow Jekyll to become "polar twins" (RLS, 53) initially impress him as a stroke of good fortune, a greater boon than the opium Jennings instructs Blake to swallow in order to invite his nocturnal self into the open again. Jasper's plight discredits more than the idea that Collins's Blake can easily reintegrate his darker side with his daytime self; it also rules out, in advance, Jekyll's utopian hopes of segregating man's vicious aspects in a separate being. When Stevenson crushes these hopes, he merely echoes the import of Dickens's unfinished story.

Jekyll's attempts to capitalize on man's inherent duality make him the victim of his own failed designs, not just of a polite society that disallows his pleasures. Having determined to profit from "the strange immunities" of his new position as two personalities in one person (RLS, 56), Jekyll little suspects that his "second and worse" self (RLS, 60), if nurtured, will eventually seize control. At the outset, Stevenson's experimenter is not unlike H.G. Wells's misguided utopians such as Dr. Moreau, Cavor the lunar explorer, and even the well-meaning Time Traveller. They either expect too much from the future or believe that one can interfere with evolution in positive ways.

If "housed in separate identities," Jekyll postulates (RLS, 52), the good and evil within man will each experience total gratification. Dr. Jekyll can continue smoothly on an upward path because Edward Hyde's antics relieve his violent-erotic tendencies. Dickens, one can argue, anticipated Stevenson when he invented Jasper to ridicule as pseudoscientific the notion that any individual or society will evolve to the point where enjoyment of good without the burden of evil becomes possible.

Casting off evil as a separate self, an alien being domiciled in a different identity, is no more sophisticated than having Carton beheaded as a scapegoat for Darnay. Jekyll believes in "provinces of good and ill which divide and compound man's dual nature" (RLS, 51-52). His naiveté, in speaking of good and evil as different places, reintroduces Fagin's den and the Brownlow/Maylie world. Stevenson criticizes the kind of simplistic moral and metaphysical scheme that Jasper was meant to supersede. As both avuncular murderer and lustful choirmaster, Jasper is divided and compounded, yet his two selves remain inseparable.

The case of the Cloisterham chorister, then, is quite extraordinary: more pronounced than most, but more indicative than Jekyll's of the universal situation. One concludes that Jasper and his victims are victimized by social pressures that aggravate ineradicable flaws in human nature. Jasper's ability to escape punishment for so long results from an intrinsic duplicity (more serious than Blake's) that was neither consciously sought nor willingly exploited (unlike Jekyll's and Ablewhite's). *The Mystery of Edwin Drood*, had Dickens completed it, would have dealt severer blows to the evolutionary optimism of Victorian novelists like George Eliot and Mrs. Gaskell than *The Moonstone* or Stevenson's story could.

Jasper might have been closer in kind to Kurtz in *Heart of Darkness*, whom Forsyte and Miyoshi never discuss, than to Jekyll, Blake, or Ablewhite. In Conrad's novel, Kurtz enters the Congo as "an emissary of light," an "apostle" of civilization.[14] Yet he later appends to his report to the International Society for the Suppression of Savage Customs a note on methodology: "Exterminate all the brutes!" (HD, 51) The jealous murderer in Jasper, unlike Hyde, resembles the potential exterminator in Kurtz: each knows all about his better self, whose corporeal reality he can take over, but is not known in return. The choirmaster-murderer, part of whom sincerely loves his nephew, anticipates the emissary-exterminator in that he, too, seems to have an excruciatingly negative moment of self-awareness in store.

Had Dickens been able to continue, Kurtz would have suffered through his deathbed epiphany, on the subject of internal darkness, over a quarter of a century after Jasper's disillusioning meditations in "the condemned cell" on the same topic. Jasper would experience his arresting shock at the precise moment the reader's worst suspicions about Drood's uncle are confirmed. The reader would learn for certain that Jasper the choirmaster is also Jasper the murderer when Jasper finally does. The conviction that evil is neither foreign nor external in nature would strike the reader through Jasper's sudden self-perception of his duplicity; it would do so almost as compellingly as when Kurtz finally connects the rapacity of the European colonial enterprise with a hitherto unexamined darkness in his own heart.

In Marlow's hearing, Kurtz utters one climactic self-condemnation, from which his sudden awareness of the activities of man's darker side throughout the centuries can be inferred. Jasper, concluding an account of the murder of Drood with some similar exclamation, would not spare listeners—including his astonished respectable self—the grim details Conrad considers "unspeakable." With the choirmaster overhearing his murderous other self reliving crimes, Jasper would be both Marlow and Kurtz. In "the condemned cell" prior to suicide or execution, the respectable choirmaster, discovering a murderer within himself, would be like Kurtz having his horrible epiphany as well as like Marlow watching Kurtz have it.

A temporary ascendancy for the choirmaster over his homicidal double would mean a moment compounded of acceptance of guilt, repudiation of all sins committed, and reconciliation with the baser self. Had Dickens granted such a moment to Jasper—an outcome which the existing text does not put beyond his options, *The Mystery of Edwin Drood* would upstage *Heart of Darkness* even further. Jasper would attain an insight equivalent to Kurtz's recognition of "The horror! The horror!" within himself (HD, 71). As Marlow does with Kurtz, Dickens would give Jasper credit for a "supreme moment of complete knowledge" previously denied to any character in Victorian fiction. Jasper would comprehend more about the innermost recesses of human nature in a second or two of intense introspection than Copperfield and Pip learn in a lifetime. For Jasper as for Kurtz, there would be a "summing-up," a passing of judgment, an "affirmation" of man's capacity to recognize his failures, hence "a moral victory" (HD, 72). Collins's rehabilitation of Franklin Blake would seem trivial by comparison, however plausible. Dr. Jekyll also claims that he has realized "the horror" of his "other self" (RLS, 66)—unfortunately, not until the powders that transform the increasingly arrogant Hyde back into Jekyll are about to run out.

The radical reformer in Dickens still contends that society's problems can be overcome, even if the battle has to be fought again and again. But the conservative or dystopian, confirmed and equally influential in his personality well before 1870, would add that society should not base its hopes for progress on the philosophy that life is fundamentally all right, that a community's failings do not reach to the core and thus can be eliminated with greater ease as evolution accelerates. Rosier outlooks, the implication goes, must be combatted as sociological aberrations brought on by the new emphasis on growth and mutations in biological science. Dickens satirizes these aberrations for being unrealistic: they are as fanciful and self-defeating—ultimately as anti-humanistic—as Frankenstein's experiment, whether it recurs in Magwitch's creation of Pip as the perfect gentleman or (had Dickens lived to read about it) as Jekyll's attempt to remain the perfect gentleman by concentrating his depravities in Hyde.

Despite its being only half finished, Dickens gives indications in *The Mystery of Edwin Drood* that he would have been able to outdo *The Moonstone* as a semimodern artifact—a forerunner, in effect, of Conrad's explorations of the evils beneath modern society's civilized veneer. Ironically, Dickens's final revaluation of Collins, a would-be usurper, went far toward filling slots fate had reserved for *Heart of Darkness* (1902) and *The Strange Case of Dr. Jekyll and Mr. Hyde* (1886).

It should be evident by now that Collins's novels are one of the finest sources for clues to possible developments that Dickens could have used to complete *The Mystery of Edwin Drood*. Double vision requires that one read existing chapters of Dickens's last novel both for themselves and as an attempt to outdo Collins; it also means leafing through *The Moonstone* and *The Woman in White* to discover which of this competitor's melodramatic successes Dickens might have felt pressured to redo had he lived. The modern revaluator should scrutinize Collins's novels for targets to be parodied in *The Mystery of Edwin Drood* as intensely as readers must search for clues to Little Nell's fate by observing what befalls her parallels or stand-ins when she is offstage. *The Mystery of Edwin Drood* is an unusual instance, but one must keep the importance and extent of hidden rivalries in Victorian fiction more than ever in mind. Collins's novels join the explanatory letter Dickens wrote to John Forster on "Friday the 6th of August 1869" and one's knowledge of incident and technique in Dickens's previous fictions: together, the three serve as interdependent informants.[15]

There can be no definitive resolution to *The Mystery of Edwin Drood* because its author so effectively withheld his. This realization testifies to the success of the twenty-two chapters extant. Revaluing Collins's work with Dickens's half-novel in mind is not another attempt to do the artist's work for him.[16] Nor will it account for all the loose ends Dickens left untied. Instead, one draws upon the rivalries studied in previous chapters to imagine how Collins's best scenes might look if rewritten by Dickens, who had ample provocation to outdo them.

Is Drood dead? This is a question much like an earlier one: will Nellie die? It seems to demand the affirmative. But one sees Dickens leaving his options open as long as possible, just as he once prolonged anxiety for news of Little Nell's declining health for nine consecutive numbers. The range of possibilities available to Dickens on 9 July 1870 was still quite broad. No wonder "rumours subsequently abounded" that Dickens experienced "trouble with the novel, and could not even see a way to solve the mystery himself."[17] An embarrassment of riches for the satirical social critic engaged in revaluative parody, a reluctance to sacrifice too soon one practicability in favor of another, may have been a major problem.

Throughout *The Moonstone*, the central mystery is the identity of the jewel thief. Collins expects readers to be doubly surprised when, having exposed Blake's nocturnal self, he finally divulges a hidden side to Ablewhite as well. When Dickens explores Jasper's deeply divided nature right from the start, it seems as if he were finally taking Collins's advice to present earlier such telltale items as Manette's letter against the St. Evrémondes. Only in retrospect, however, from the scenes in "the condemned cell," would shifts taking place all along in Jasper's dual personality become absolutely clear. Although Dickens seemingly forfeits all chance for delay by having only one plausible murder suspect, he actually increases it. The question of whether a crime has even been committed heightens suspense in *The Mystery of Edwin Drood* and prolongs detection. Even the probable murderer would not be able to answer this question until the final pages.

As long as possible—longer, in fact, than the place he had reached by the last day of his life—Dickens conceals absolute certainty that Drood has been slain. Jasper's comprehension of himself as the murderer can thus be held off much longer, at least until after a corpse has been found. At that juncture, the painful fusing of two awarenesses, the avuncular choirmaster's and the murderer's, would become an obligatory scene. As a climax, it would triumphantly outdo two of Collins's best scenes simultaneously: the unmasking of Ablewhite and Franklin Blake's misleading discovery of his own name on the nightgown of the alleged jewel thief.

Whether Drood turned out to be dead or alive, Dickens could at last repay Collins in full for repeatedly aspiring to outdo Esther's finding of Lady Dedlock's body at the conclusion of *Bleak House*. If Drood is indeed dead, as appears likely, Dickens would improve upon Collins by accomplishing some of his best work in his final novel after the point at which *The Moonstone*, having used up all its surprises, stopped: that is, after the discovery of a corpse. One assumes that Jasper would be tricked into reenacting the crime or at least into satisfying himself that Drood perished when attacked; either way, Edwin's body or what remains of it would be unearthed.

Exposure, pursuit, and capture would merely be prelude to an even greater apprehension at the conclusion of the choirmaster-murderer's verbal reconstruction of the actual crime: traumatic self-awareness. This mental process—internal, psychological, yet thoroughly sensational—would be recorded in scenes that Angus Wilson believes could have been "tremendous."[18] Peeling away the choirmaster to isolate the murderer inside would make removal of Ablewhite's false beard seem hackneyed.

Once Blake is shown not to have pawned the moonstone, Collins has another ten chapters at his disposal to spring one last surprise: Ablewhite's duplicity. To compete with Collins on this account, Dickens need not allow Drood to escape or someone other than Jasper to do him in. Assuming Drood dead and Jasper his murderer, Dickens still has abundant opportunities to rival Collins as a master of suspenseful delays: he must uncover not just the identity of the criminal and the whereabouts of his victim's body but the real name of Jasper's mysterious and dedicated pursuer, Dick Datchery.

Revelation of the person disguised as the "single buffer" (ED, 217), Dickens felt, would excel the unmasking of Ablewhite because Datchery's identity is the best-kept secret in either novel. Four candidates—Bazzard, Grewgious, Helena Landless, and even Drood himself—are theoretically still viable by Chapter 22—although Bazzard's claims seem strongest—if indeed Datchery is someone in disguise and not a new character. In the twenty-second installment of *The Moonstone*, by comparison, possibilities are less numerous. The thief cannot be Rosanna Spearman, Miss Verinder herself, or the much maligned Indians. Once the culprit turns out not to be Blake, Ablewhite can be implicated by a simple process of elimination. Consequently, Collins moves Ablewhite offstage following completion of Miss Clack's narrative, and he is kept out of the reader's mind as much as possible prior to the novel's climax.

Jasper's act of self-discovery was supposed to trigger more despair over human nature than Cuff's detection of Ablewhite did but not more than the reading public could stand or Dickens himself desired. The real person hidden beneath Datchery's white wig and "tightish blue surtout" (ED, 216) would emerge as a form of compensation, a pleasant surprise. Dickens would conclude by exposing Jasper as a greater threat to society than Ablewhite and Blake combined while also furnishing a commendable instance of duplicity and disguise. Unlike Jasper, Ablewhite, or Magdalen Vanstone in *No Name*, the individual pretending to be Datchery would cultivate a second appearance and an alternative personality for entirely admirable ends.

On the other hand, let us suppose Drood has escaped but without learning the identity of his attacker. Ned's eventual reappearance before his murderous guardian would be the ultimate in unexpected manifestation. It would not only be more surprising than Esther's discovery of Lady Dedlock's body but superior to a ghostly Anne Catherick's accosting Walter Hartright on the London road or Laura Fairlie's apparent rise from the dead beside her own grave. Drood would be the resurrection man *par excellence*, eclipsing the grave-robber, Jerry Cruncher, and making Manette's recall to life seem rudimentary in comparison.

Should Datchery turn out to be Drood, Dickens's victim would suddenly become better at disguise than Ablewhite in his sailor's outfit and more talented as an amateur detective than either Hartright or Blake. Surpassing John Harmon in *Our Mutual Friend*, Drood would solve his own apparent murder, thus saving his uncle from execution but nonetheless incriminating the violent-erotic self within Jasper and ridding the community of a dangerous assailant, an antisocial force.

Edmund Wilson contends that *The Moonstone*, "in which a band of Hindu devotees commit a secret murder in England seems to have inspired Dickens with the idea of outdoing his friend the next year with a story of a similar kind."[19] But the murder of Ablewhite at the Wheel of Fortune causes an uproar. It is no more "secret" than Drood's disappearance and the resultant split of Cloisterham into two camps: one of the opinion he has fled, the other believing him dead. In *The Woman in White*, however, when Fosco and Glyde switch Anne Catherick and Laura Fairlie, their crime is not apparent to anyone but its victims. This embarrassing situation for polite society is what Dickens could have tried to outdo. Just as Collins regularly did, Dickens would parody more than one of his rival's novels at the same time.

If Drood is alive, Dickens would present a crime evident to everyone except the victim, thus enlarging upon Collins's mistrust of society's ability to evaluate appearances. This mistrust, one must remember, forms the corollary to Collins's dislike of the proprieties.

All three novels—*The Woman in White*, *The Moonstone*, and *The Mystery of Edwin Drood*—challenge society's belief in the value of preserving proper appearances: they show how easily guilt can look like innocence, innocence like guilt. Felix Aylmer claims that Jasper is actually trying to shield Drood from a vendetta: Islamic Egyptians allegedly have a grudge against the Drood family on account of Edwin's father, who violated Muslim taboos when he married an Islamic woman. If so, Muslims are to be imagined stalking Drood the way the Brahmans shadow Herncastle's heirs. If Jasper is indeed a "hero" who has killed an Islamic avenger, not Drood, but must "pass for a villain"[20] until the denouement, Dickens, by exonerating him, could outdo Collins dramatically on the subject of misleading circumstances. In *The Moonstone*, these point first to the Hindoos, then to Blake, never to Ablewhite before the ending. Similarly, in Dickens's novel, the murderer is clearly not Landless but then would not be Jasper either, even if the vendetta should prove successful and Drood be dead.

If Aylmer's solution is correct, Jasper's innocence would be more surprising than Franklin Blake's, and more unexpected than Ablewhite's guilt.[21] But for Jasper to turn out blameless and commendable, Dickens would have to forgo altogether his investigation of duality as a symbolic proof that evil is as much an internal aspect of man as goodness is. Nor could he build toward a grand confessional in which the respectable choirmaster, assuming Fagin's place, has a negative epiphany and meets his murderous other self. Should Jasper be anything else than a double personality, half of which is a murderer, then the re-enactment of the crime, the unmasking of the killer inside the choirmaster, and the climactic self-realization of a horrendous duplicity—all scenes to outdo the most exciting sequences in *The Moonstone*—would be prohibited.

One can hardly blame Dickens for postponing decisions as long as he could or for giving tantalizing hints about the outcome—trial balloons, so to speak—to Forster, Luke Fildes (his illustrator), and his own children. The modern revaluator pities Dickens for the richness of his dilemma: he could attempt to excell Collins in whichever of several mutually exclusive directions he decided to take. To bring Drood back, perhaps to allow him to spy on Jasper as Datchery, would enable the novelist to supersede several of Collins's finer melodramatic episodes involving resurrection and reinstatement. But Dickens could not have passed up the reenactment and confession sequences. Not only are they more exciting as alternatives but more psychological, more experimental. The first option would give Dickens several chances to redo and outdo Collins at the same time, but the second would transport the older novelist well beyond his estimate of the younger writer's capabilities.

Jasper's psychic reintegration, his two halves or selves becoming fully aware of each other for a moment at least, could be considered the maximum in recovery or self-possession. It would stand as the supreme rehabilitation, a resurrection or reunification superior to Blake's comeback and even to Drood's, had the latter been permitted to return to Cloisterham unscathed. Dickens could not save Jasper's life and restore him to society as forgivingly as Collins let Blake return; nevertheless, having illustrated the imperfectibility of man more impressively than Collins's double-dealers, Jasper, unlike Ablewhite, would still be able to "save his soul alive."[22]

The "originality" in the story "of a murder of a nephew by his uncle," Dickens told Forster, "was to consist in the review of the murderer's career by himself at the close, when its temptations were to be dwelt upon as if, not he the culprit, but some other man, were the tempted. The last chapters were to be written in the condemned cell, to which his wickedness, all elaborately elicited from him as if told of another, had brought him."[23] Major attributes of the concluding episodes, as outlined in this letter, were to include a "condemned cell" and a murderer from whom a recapitulation of the crime would be "elaborately elicited," "elaborately" being the key word. An experimental sequence that might have been proto-Joycean, the recountal would be conducted by the murderer "as if" the fatal assault on Drood had been committed by "some other man." Dickens expected this "review" to make him one of the leading exponents of psychological realism while reconfirming him as the era's premier sensationalist.

Just getting Jasper into "the condemned cell," where the "last chapters were to be written"—that is, one assumes, taken down from dictation—affords Dickens excellent opportunities for parodic revaluation. Overshadowing *The Moonstone*, Dickens could feature not one but two reenactments in *The Mystery of Edwin Drood*, the first mainly physical and thoroughly sensational, the second equally dramatic but entirely internal or psychological.

In the first redoing, the murderer in Jasper would lead Drood's friends to the missing body by retracing his steps the night of the crime. This time, Neville Landless, not Drood, would perish, possibly in the scuffle to seize Jasper, while Tartar and Crisparkle would make the actual capture. A jewel *not* stolen, the "ring belonging to Miss Rosa's mother" (ED, 144), would identify Drood despite "the corrosive effects of the lime" into which Jasper threw the body after removing from it all other jewelry Drood was known to be wearing.[24]

Jasper could be tricked into this costly replay if, when again under the influence of opium, he is reliving the crime and spies Helena disguised as Drood. "Each time" they fled from their cruel stepfather, Neville tells Crisparkle, Helena "dressed as a boy, and showed the daring of a man" (ED, 90). She is apparently an even better master of impersonation and disguise than Miss Vanstone, who makes her living for a time on the provincial stage in *No Name* as a female version of Charles Mathews. Unlike most females in Stoker's subsequent novel, Helena is neither attracted to nor terrified by vampirelike traits: "Not under any circumstances," she tells Rosa, would she "be afraid" of Jasper (ED, 93).

A replay of Drood's murder would eclipse, in numerous respects, the reenactment at Lady Verinder's. Apprehending Jasper would give Dickens an opportunity for a stupendous scene that Collins must omit by not being present in Ablewhite's room or inside his mind when the Hindoos creep in to smother him. In a hoax designed to provoke Jasper into trying to redo the murder, Dickens could use Helena to interpret Drood without letting readers know, until the last second, that it is not the supposed victim come back. The reader could be made to share Jasper's perplexity. There would be double uncertainty: whether Drood is really alive and, therefore, whether Jasper is his assailant rather than his murderer or even completely innocent. Were Helena and Neville both to impersonate Drood at different points along the way to the cathedral crypt or the Sapsea monument, wherever Drood is buried, Dickens could multiply confusion and suspense indefinitely. He could reuse Ablewhite's forte, disguise, to expose hypocrisy rather than conceal it.

Dickens's answer to the question posed by the title for Chapter Fourteen—"When Shall These Three Meet Again?"—could run as follows: at a restaging of the crime beginning from the fatal dinner to which Jasper invited Neville and Edwin on the previous Christmas Eve. Dickens could use the redoing, with Jasper drugged and Helena as Drood, to fill readers in by retracing the movements of uncle and nephew after the party disbanded. A second dinner would not be indispensable, since merely catching sight of someone dressed as Drood would be enough to set Jasper off if the murderer within him were in control and under the influence of opium. But a repeat of the dinner party would not only be more elaborate but more prolonged and thus more exciting than Blake's reenactment of his actions the night the moonstone disappeared.

The idea for repeating the crime would have to come from Datchery, perhaps with assistance from the Princess Puffer. If Datchery is Bazzard, his career as a failed playwright would come in handy as he devises a scenario for removing from Cloisterham its "thorn of anxiety" (ED, 140-41). Even more than Jennings, Bazzard, performing as Datchery, would be the underrated man, the neglected genius, coming to the fore. At Datchery's instigation, the Princess would finally concoct the right mixture of opium to make her customer do more than hint at his recent commission of some enormity. The opium woman's hatred for Jasper could stem from involvement long before, perhaps in another country, with either Rosa or the Landless twins,[25] but this would not be necessary. Mr. Sapsea and Mr. Honeythunder, reviling Neville to the last, could participate reluctantly in Jasper's arraignment. Were Deputy to summon them after helping to capture Jasper, he would play a part in the trackdown similar to Gooseberry's in *The Moonstone*. Should Drood's body turn up in the Sapsea monument, the murder would be as embarrassing to the mayor's reputation for sagacity as the revelation of Ablewhite's duplicity must have been to Miss Clack and other extollers of his charitable endeavors.

That two reenactments were a distinct probability in *The Mystery of Edwin Drood*, the second more astounding than the first, can be deduced from Dickens's comments on Miss Twinkleton, a comic parallel for Jasper: "As, in some cases of drunkenness, and in others of animal magnetism, there are two states of consciousness which never clash, but each of which pursues its separate course as though it were continuous instead of broken (thus, if I hide my watch when I am drunk, I must be drunk again before I can remember where), so Miss Twinkleton has two distinct and separate phases of being."[26] She is a proper schoolmistress during the day and a gossipy romantic after nightfall, neither phase ever intruding upon the other. Similarly, Jasper would have "two states of consciousness which never clash," the choirmaster's and a murderer's. To depict how each state "pursues its separate course as though it were continuous instead of broken" would be the unique challenge facing Dickens throughout *The Mystery of Edwin Drood*.

If for "drunkenness," in the passage above, one reads opium-taking, one has the basis for the first purely physical reenactment. Jasper would seek to murder Drood again, either under the delusion that the first attempt failed or that he was now doing it for the first time (probably the former). The murderous choirmaster would operate in a trance but seem more alert, more menacing, than Blake in *The Moonstone*.[27]

To make Jasper's "two states" finally collide, however, mesmerism ("animal magnetism") sounds like the correct prescription. To underline Collins's limitations as a psychologist, Dickens would not just show Jasper before and after a personality shift as was done with Ablewhite and Blake, or rapidly passing through one, the process Stevenson sensationalizes unduly with Jekyll and Hyde. Once Jasper is taken, Dickens would attempt to bring both selves within the prisoner before the reader virtually at the same time. He would try to make both the respectable choirmaster and his darker self articulate. Toward the climax of the confession sequence, Jasper's "two distinct and separate phases of being" would begin to intrude upon each other; at some point, they would speak so closely to each other, by turns, that they would seem to be present jointly. The murderer would talk from within the choirmaster, and the latter, recognizing the former's presence for the first time, would struggle against it. Apparent decomposition would reveal the true state of affairs, the dual reality that lay behind appearances all along. Collins, by contrast, could not present Blake as suitor and would-be violator simultaneously or have Ablewhite behaving at once like both thief and philanthropist.

Looking back over Dickens's novel from "the condemned cell," the reader would understand, whenever Jasper did, how each of the two "states" or "phases" had seemed to itself "continuous." But he would also realize that each had seemed unbroken in a different way. On several occasions, after his violent-erotic self subsided, Jasper resumed his daily grind as though no personality change had taken place. His puzzlement over these experiences would be used to make him more amenable to hypnosis as a means of explaining what happened during those times he can only remember as absences from himself. When the choirmaster's respectable self was uppermost, his antisocial side, hating this facade, simmered until it could reemerge. Having done so, it pursued its goals again just as though its grip on Jasper's outward form and speaking voice had never been interrupted. During the mesmeric proceedings a kind of exorcism from the murderer's point of view—the violent-erotic self would resist being ferreted out as vigorously as the choirmaster at first would refuse to acknowledge it.

With both "states" in Jasper finally incarcerated, Dickens would have sensational options at his disposal that were unavailable to Collins once Blake and his nocturnal self became acquainted. Having been subdued as the murderer, Jasper could recover consciousness as the choirmaster. If he already knew about his other self at this juncture, he could narrate the deeds of that secret sharer with a most original objectivity; on the other hand, if Jasper did not as yet possess full self-awareness, he would find his imprisonment inexplicable. This, obviously, is the richer alternative, a more baffling situation for Jasper than Blake seeing his own name on the thief's gown. Jasper could then agree to a suggestion, from Datchery or the Minor Canon, that he recreate his past actions verbally while under hypnosis, just as Blake accedes to Jennings's opium experiment.

A comprehensive verbal reconstruction of the murder would not be less sensational because of the initial physical reenactment. On the contrary, the first reenactment would delay this mandatory final accounting and increase the suspense associated with it. If a tricked Jasper, wishing to reassure himself, simply led Drood's friends to the body or went through the crime again to the point where his murderous intent became dangerous, possibly fatal, to the person disguised as Drood,[28] the physical replay would still need three supplements from the psychological one: it would terminate without a complete description of the murder itself and without having divulged not just the inception and growth of Jasper's murderous feelings but his emotional state during the crime and immediately afterward.

Whether Jasper is hypnotized without prior knowledge of his other self or to squeeze that knowledge from him, the recounting could at first resemble the broken, stream-of-consciousness narration with which *The Mystery of Edwin Drood* opens. Jasper would relive the murderer's opium dreams. Such a stretch of narrative, more experimental than anything of its kind prior to Joyce, might look, on the printed page, like the brief sample Jennings shows Blake of "disconnected words and fragments of sentences which had dropped from Mr. Candy in delerium" (MS, 378). But Dickens would venture far beyond the short paragraph of reconstructed babbling that Collins attempts (MS, 379). Unscrambled, Candy's words explain Blake's behavior on the night that the moonstone disappeared; Jasper's narrative would provide the only access the rest of Cloisterham can ever have to developments the night of Drood's mysterious disappearance.

Were Helena to hypnotize Jasper, Crisparkle and Datchery (or Grewgious perhaps) could supply missing connectives in Jasper's narration just as Jennings did with Candy's. Gradually growing more coherent, Jasper would put his "scattered consciousness" (ED, 37) and his divided self horrifyingly together. The conflicting sides of his character would draw closer with each word of his increasingly lucid narrative; both would converse with his interlocutors and suspense would become unbearable, the reader—along with Jasper and his hearers—inching toward the awful realization.

Just as Franklin Blake fulfills his resolution to solve the disappearance of the moonstone even if it means self-incrimination, Jasper would be able to keep his promise: "I will fasten the crime of the murder of my dear dead boy upon the murderer . . . I devote myself to his destruction" (ED, 201). The outcome would be bitterly ironic, recalling Oedipus's tragic inquiries but establishing the Jasper Complex (duality, self-division) as the modern sickness. Such a supreme act of self-detection would be the ultimate example of painful discovery in the annals of sensational realism. Anticipating the clearing up of a mistake, Jasper would condemn himself as a murderer. Dickens would surpass his own melodramatic masterpiece, the scene in which Esther unexpectedly turns over her own mother's body in the snow. Since Collins initiated a rivalry by trying to outdo that scene, the older novelist would have the last word by proving that only Dickens can outdo Dickens.

The letter to Forster emphasizes that the "originality" of *The Mystery of*

Edwin Drood—that is, Dickens's triumph over Collins—was to be a matter of both content and technique. Jasper's unprecedented perception of human duality would entail a man talking about himself as if about a total stranger. He would demonstrate a unique instance of double vision: two vantage points, different yet interdependent and eventually connected, on the same events.

Dickens would outdo, for a brief space, the twin perspectives he used throughout *Bleak House*. He would also compete with Collins's use of multiple subjective narrators, each of whom tells only those incidents he or she participated in or observed. Jasper would be subjective and objective simultaneously; he would be both participant and observer in regard to all he relates but never, until the final sentences, fully present as either. To outdo Collins once and for all, Dickens would join Blake's sudden self-awareness to Cuff's unmasking of Ablewhite and take the combination an experimental and psychological step further, which Collins had over-looked.

In both reenactments in *The Mystery of Edwin Drood*, Dickens would surpass Collins when it comes to giving Eastern or foreign trappings to an English crime. Opium, a substance oriental in origin, would be utilized to entrap Jasper. Jennings could use it only to clear Blake, not to catch Ablewhite. Taking opium does not split Jasper's personality the way it brings Blake's inner self to the surface. Rather, the choirmaster's second self is an opium addict who can be got at by means of this addiction. The foreign drug Jasper's violent-erotic self relies on in order to engage in wish-fulfilling fantasies would ironically prove instrumental for his undoing after one fantasy, the killing of the choirmaster's nephew, has been carried out.[29]

Jasper may also be adept at animal magnetism. Some mysterious force, conceivably emanating from Jasper, directs Crisparkle to the Weir so that he can discover Drood's shirt-pin and gold watch.[30] Helena Landless, whose psychic powers include telepathic communication with her brother, could hypnotize the choirmaster into confessing what his opium-eating second self has done. In short, opium would work contrary to its function in *The Moonstone*: it would help to keep the dual personalities in Jasper separate. But Dickens would introduce an additional marvel, mesmerism, to make the choirmaster gradually aware of his secret self. Instead of being the origin of a murderer (had Neville killed Drood), Ceylon would produce a mentality powerful enough to thwart him.

Jasper, it follows, cannot be "a dark man" (ED, 43) in the racial sense. If he were, Dickens would not be as emphatic as Collins in stressing the

Englishness of society's ills. Instead, evil in *The Mystery of Edwin Drood* would acquire a genuinely foreign complexion, and one of Collins's satirical successes in *The Moonstone*—his quashing of the Victorians' sense of social (indeed national) superiority—would go uncontested. If, on the other hand, Dickens entirely domesticates Jasper, if society's problems remain internal, homegrown, the novel forfeits the sense of foreign intrigue that Collins exploited with the Hindoos in *The Moonstone* and the Brotherhood in *The Woman in White*.

Correcting several of Aylmer's suggestions and embroidering on others, Forsyte errs by proposing a disgruntled Jasper who is Drood's elder stepbrother by a Muslim woman, their common father's first wife. In Aylmer's version, Jasper appears malicious but has been protecting Edwin from a curse brought upon the Drood family by their father during his stay in Egypt. The Muslim woman, says Aylmer, has been put to death as an apostate from Islam, and the elder Drood has taken revenge against her relatives and thus incurred, for himself and all Droods, the unending enmity of an entire family. If Jasper has killed anyone, Aylmer maintains, the victim must have been an agent of this family. Forsyte's Jasper is a man "profoundly divided by background and by blood."[31] The murderer is the foreign half of a transplanted, English-educated Jasper, the true elder son seeking revenge against the half-brother who has unknowingly replaced him.

Although Aylmer and Forsyte differ radically on Jasper's guilt, their continuations are otherwise similar and thus suffer from the same weakness. The latter's makes evil foreign rather than British and inherent, while the former's explanation cancels Dickens's preoccupation with the internality of evil altogether. An Egyptian Jasper, whether guilty or heroic, goes contrary to the hidden rivalries between Dickens and Collins. The climax to their revaluative parodies of each other's work during the 1860s would be nullified. An Egyptian Jasper would not be a rewrite of Blake and Ablewhite. This would do worse than weaken Dickens's chances, in 1870, of regaining control of the argument that society's failings are too deeply internal ever to go away; it would also compromise the claim that tedious respectability, England's excessive regard for propriety, is a major cause for the emergence of Jasper's second or antisocial self. Dickens's desire to outstrip Collins indicates that a thoroughly English murderer is called for.[32]

Jasper's secret sharer kills chiefly from frustration and envy but without reference to injustices committed previously in some other culture. The choirmaster's violent-erotic self, unhappily circumstanced in Cloisterham, would inevitably become jealous of Drood's prospects: remunerative employment in Egypt and a beautiful bride, both of which are virtually given to him. Thus Jasper gives himself away when he sets Landless and Drood against each other. He contrasts the former's condition and his own, two have-nots, with his nephew's diffidence in the face of so much good fortune: "It is hardly worth his while," Jasper observes, "to pluck the golden fruit that hangs ripe on the tree for him" (ED, 101).

Unfortunately, minimizing the past would negate a theme nearly as important to Dickens as the internality of evil. It would downplay the interest he and Collins express, starting with *Bleak House* and *The Woman in White*, in visiting parental sins upon a subsequent generation. Continuations by Forsyte and Aylmer ingeniously preserve this interest. That one pays for the mistakes of one's predecessors is a dystopian *caveat* that contradicts the purely forward-looking idea, in George Eliot's novels, of each generation building upon the last. In 1870, Dickens wants to outdo *The Moonstone* without losing sight of *Felix Holt* as a supplementary target. He needs a conclusion denying alienage to evil without refusing sins from the past their impact on current events or excluding the involvement of a foreign culture, preferably oriental, in young Drood's disappearance.

Conceivably, a parentage plot would have figured prominently in the second half of *The Mystery of Edwin Drood*, concerning Jasper's relationship either to Edwin or, less likely, to the Landless twins. Should Jasper turn out to be Drood's half-brother, Dickens could bring to bear upon Edwin a vendetta for which his father would be responsible. If the offense committed was to break taboo, either by seducing an Egyptian woman or marrying her in a non-Islamic ceremony or both, Dickens could remind Collins that an overly stringent sense of propriety can be the villain in more cultures than one. The pungency of Dickens's satire against British propriety as a particularly egregious example of undue restraint would be lessened, but linking Jasper to Drood through a mutual father guilty of sexual misconduct would make up some of the loss. Dickens would outdo the similar explanation Collins offered for Anne Catherick's resemblance to Laura Fairlie by exceeding its tragic consequences.

Even without an Islamic blood feud, a troublesome legacy from the past could prove more of a burden in *The Mystery of Edwin Drood* than Herncastle's bequest of the moonstone to Rachel Verinder. The legacy would at first seem comparatively harmless. In *The Woman in White*, Laura Fairlie obeys the will of her father and unwisely marries Sir Percival Glyde against her inclinations. Rosa and Edwin, whose marriage was preordained by their respective fathers, dare to shrug off this sort of binding arrangement. Dickens could show that they pay a terrible price just the same.

Breaking with bonds from the past, Dickens would maintain, is never the simple matter Esther Lyon finds it when George Eliot presents her version of his Esther Summerson. Eliot uses the ability of her characters to cast off the consequences of prior events, to adopt brand new directions at will, as a fictionalized form of natural selection. It implies a kind of conscious mutation of one's fate and personality. Misfortunes befalling Edwin and Rosa would discredit George Eliot's tendency, in Dickens's opinion, to make change look easier than it is.

When Jasper observes Rosa and Edwin conversing intimately in Chapter 13, he does not know of their having just resolved never to become man and wife. The point is not only that Jasper eliminates a nonexistent rival, but that Rosa and Drood have been victimized all their lives by a decision made decades before. Neither can repudiate it in time to prevent it from leading to a greater wrong. Sir Percival commits forgery to cover up his father's failure to make him legitimate. Dickens would not need a vendetta to expand upon Collins: he would demonstrate that misery from errors in the past proliferates into the present even if Rosa and Edwin, unlike Glyde, choose not to perpetuate it: that is, whether one refuses to be governed by the past and its mistakes or not.

Giving Jasper an Egyptian mother as well as a dual personality could make him a combination not just of Blake and Ablewhite but of that pair plus Ezra Jennings. The choirmaster would join the repressed sexuality of the first to the double life of the second and be discovered to have foreign blood in him like the third. Through Jasper, Dickens would parody the unrealistic inversion of moral connotations in *The Moonstone*. Evil is never a question of black and white, he would inform Collins, even if, for sensation's sake and to upset conventional minds, the whiteness is made suspect and darkness (or foreignness) is treated positively. It is overly schematic and false to life, Dickens would object, to show Ablewhite depraved despite his name, Jennings laudable regardless of his foreign look, and the dark-skinned Hindoos dressed in white robes the most honorable of all. Dickens could use a partially Egyptian Jasper to argue that Collins's satire in *The Moonstone* was nearly as naive as the notion of evil it attacked.

The danger in this option, which Forsyte's extension of the half-novel illustrates, would lie in not preventing the radical division in Jasper from coinciding with recurring personality shifts from choirmaster to murderer. If the former were to appear to be thoroughly English and the latter oriental, the assumptions of the Hindoos' guilt that Collins uses to satirize English prejudice would simply be reinstated in another form. Dickens would have to be certain that the more homicidal Jasper becomes, the less automatically dark or Egyptian he would seem; that could explain why Grewgious describes Jasper's face, following a transition from choirmaster to murderer, as "lead-colored," "ghostly," and "white" (ED, 191). But this strategy would only bring the revaluing parodist back again to the inverted connotations for light and dark that he would be trying to ridicule in Collins.

In view of Dickens's insistence that society's evils arise from deep within itself, the choirmaster's darkness is best defined as chiefly spiritual and sociological. Outward signs and a character's immediate environment are never used in Dickens to convey another external characteristic, such as a distinctively foreign appearance. The darkness that carries over into Jasper's "sombre" manner and determines the umbrageousness of his room must come from within him. Jasper's "thick, lustrous, well-arranged black hair and whisker" are not automatically indicators of an Eastern origin (ED, 43). They make him seem older than twenty-six but are primarily signs of a violent nature firmly self-repressed. They suggest an erotic internal self, unhappily confined within the narrow boundaries of a cathedral town's mores.

Readers should be reminded of the "black-haired" Mr. Murdstone and his "dark," "gloomy-looking" sister with her "very heavy eyebrows"; both, says Dickens, have a "gloomy taint" in their blood.[33] Jasper is not only a revision of Fagin, the antisocial self now ensconced among the upper classes; he is also a more interesting reincarnation of the restrained vigor, the blend of maleficence and respectability, in Murdstone.[34] Despite regular attendance at services, the choirmaster does not possess the wine merchant's capacity to sublimate. Jasper's inner self derives no solace from the cathedral and, presumably, lacks all belief. Paradoxically, Murdstone has an "austere and wrathful" religion to keep him in check, yet through it he gives full vent to his cruel energies.

Instead of contrasting Ablewhite, the alleged "Christian hero," with Jennings, a dark-complexioned outcast, Dickens presents two studies of blackness. He sets Jasper, who is probably thoroughly English, against Neville Landless. Neville and his sister are "both very dark . . . almost the gypsy type," and impress Dickens as "beautiful barbaric captives brought from some wild tropical dominion" (ED, 84-85). Discriminating one kind of darkness from another, says Dickens, is harder than separating a whited sepulchre like Ablewhite from a dark-skinned ministering angel like Jennings. Dickens would assert that evil in *The Mystery of Edwin Drood* does not come from Ceylon along with the Landless twins; it is not an import the English must guard against as their empire expands. Instead, evil brews within a context unmistakably British and inimical to foreigners like Landless. To make the indigenousness of evil within Western man and society clearer than Collins could, Dickens contrasts two dark men: the volatile but innocent Neville Landless, a "gypsy" from Ceylon; and John

Jasper, who is "sombre"—grave, reserved, and melancholy, English traits all—but seethingly murderous.

Remembering Ablewhite's masquerade as a dark-skinned sailor, Dickens has the murderer within Jasper hit upon a better idea: from the start he will conceal beneath a foreign coloring a heinous deed that is strictly familial. Fears the Hindoos arouse throughout *The Moonstone* inspire Ablewhite's choice of a disguise. It affords him every chance of deflecting blame from himself to foreign parties if he succeeds in smuggling the moonstone out of England. Just as a respectable philanthropist cannot be mistaken for a dark-skinned sailor, the Lay Precentor of Cloisterham Cathedral would never be thought guilty of a murder performed in accord with Thug ritual.

The moment the Landless twins arrive, Jasper becomes Dickens's attempt to go Collins's use of a "dark man, dressed like a sailor" (MS, 438) one better. Important features of Thug ritual include meticulous preparation and some means of laying the blame on another. Jasper the murderer, who is already within a man "dark" by nature, hides his internal blackness by shifting suspicion for Drood's disappearance more elaborately to the East than Ablewhite thought possible. The presence of Neville Landless provides Jasper's secret sharer with an immediate occasion for a methodical murder that has evidently been planned out in detail for some time.

As the Hindu word *thugna* (to deceive) suggests, India's Thugs were masterful hypocrites, virtually walking metaphors for dual personality, although they were always conscious of their duplicities. Good citizens and model husbands at home, they became ruthless brigands on expeditions in the service of the goddess Kali. Thugs relied on their good standing in the community to camouflage secret activities. Operating in imitation of a Thug, the murderer in Jasper would demote Ablewhite's impersonation of a foreign sailor to harmlessness.

Before murdering a victim for his money, Thugs went to great lengths to win his trust. Jasper continues to insist upon his devotion to Edwin long after the murder. The "large black scarf of strong close-woven silk" (ED, 180) that Jasper takes to wearing, ostensibly to protect a tender throat, is too conspicuous an addition to his costume to be incidental. When he winds it around his throat or loops it over his arm, murder seems imminent—and Jasper begins sporting the scarf shortly before Drood's disappearance. Indeed, Dickens told his illustrator, Luke Fildes, "a secret": namely, that "Jasper strangles Drood with it,"[35] presumably in Thug fashion, even though these assassins seldom worked alone.

The "inventory" the uncle has taken "in his mind" of the jewelry his nephew normally wears (ED, 176-77) is also part of the ritual preparation

Thugs made before strangling their victims. Dickens would use this part of the ritual ironically: Jasper's care in counting the potential spoils would do him in. A gem not removed when it should have been, the diamond ring Jasper thought Edwin had given Rosa, would incriminate the murderer during the physical reenactment of his crime. Ablewhite's corpse is discovered but not the moonstone. Drood's body, when found, would be too badly decomposed for identification were it not for the diamond ring, which would be recovered.

Like a Thug, Jasper may have drugged the wine at the Christmas Eve dinner. He seems to have done so in the "Daggers Drawn" chapter: Dickens writes that "Edwin Drood's face has become quickly and remarkably flushed by the wine; so has the face of Neville Landless" (ED, 101). Drugging was standard practice to weaken a potential victim's resistance. Jasper's "expedition" (ED, 151) with Durdles through the cathedral crypt is even more Thuglike. It includes a close look at some quick-lime likely to prove useful for disposing of Drood's corpse. This little journey with Durdles is a rehearsal, much as Thugs would practice a crime; or else it amounts to a search for a burial spot no one will later be able to find, for the body of a Thug's victim was seldom discovered.

That Durdles should be "always prowling among old graves and ruins, like a Ghoule" is "nothing extraordinary," Dickens remarks. Then he confides that the choirmaster's eagerness to accompany Durdles seems "unaccountable" (ED, 151). The word is employed archly to aggravate the reader's curiosity. Showing Jasper imitating Durdles's ghoulishness and following Thug ritual preparations for a murder are complementary strategies. Dickens realized that giving Jasper the characteristics of a Thug, without being so absurd as literally to make him one, would work even better to emphasize duplicity in human nature than simply having the choirmaster-murderer resemble a vampire.

Taken in by Howard Duffield's essay, Edmund Wilson gives credence to the ludicrous view of Jasper as Lay Precentor in an Anglican cathedral by day and worshipper of Kali at night.[36] Subsequent attempts to dissociate Jasper from Thugee point out discrepancies between some of the murderer's actions and those expected of a bona fide Thug. But the objectors never explain everything away; on the contrary, they repeat those aspects of Thug ritual that Jasper performs correctly until it becomes difficult to overlook them.[37] Revaluative parody, the product of hidden rivalries in Victorian fiction, supplies a solution. If the murderer within Jasper is to be considered a Thug, he acts from conscientious imitation of an Indian strangler and does so, in large part, as a result of Dickens's resolve to outdo Collins's success with the Hindoos in *The Moonstone*.

In a more uncanny manner than Miss Clack could ever have envisioned, an oriental gentleman would "pounce on" (MS, 197) Cloisterham—the choirmaster's dark side adopting an Eastern demeanor for more villainous purposes than Ablewhite's. It would not be surprising if Jasper's well-stocked bookshelves were found to contain Philip Meadows Taylor's *Confessions of a Thug*, a fictionalized autobiography of Ameer Ali, which Dickens had read. It was just one among dozens of books and articles that kept the infamous Indian cult continuously in the news during the Victorian period and thus available for use by sensation novelists.[38]

Ultimately, the "large black scarf" is probably intended for Jasper himself, if not as the instrument of his release from "the condemned cell" by suicide, then as a sign of his date with the hangman. Oriental factors— opium from China, a Ceylonese Helena's mesmerizing talents—would prove crucial in capturing Jasper. Strangulation in imitation of the style practiced by Thugs could be used to dispatch him. *The Moonstone* ends with Mr. Murthwaite, an Englishman disguised to look oriental, witnessing an Indian ritual that comments unfavorably on Western cupidity. *The Mystery of Edwin Drood* could have concluded with an English choirmaster triumphing over the murderous darkness inside himself by Eastern means: through a strangulation self-inflicted yet more sensational than Ablewhite's death at the hands of the Brahmans.

Dickens would capitalize on Jasper's taking of his own life to outdo the earlier strangling of Drood. The murdering uncle who threw his nephew's strangled body from the cathedral tower would pass judgment on himself in an attempt to rise above his inequities. A second strangling would confirm Dickens as the master of doubling; it would also make Collins doubly regret his mistake in letting Ablewhite be smothered offstage.

At the conclusion of *The Woman in White*, an Italian-based secret society overtakes the traitorous Fosco. Representatives of a Hindoo cult roam the countryside in *The Moonstone* and scheme in London. Dickens would try to accomplish equally startling feats of intrigue more subtly in one novel, not two. He would show the murderous second self inside a respected choirmaster emulating the cool-headed treachery of an exotic Indian brotherhood in order to conceal, even from the respectable half of his own personality, the nativeness of his passionate crime. Drood's death would be made to look like retribution come from afar. But the foreignness would be a greater illusion than it turned out to be in *The Moonstone*. The oriental whom the gentlemanly Jasper becomes would be a disguise for the suppressed, violent-erotic self that Dickens held responsible for the Manichean split in modern, Western man.

In addition to being less readily assimilable by society than Ablewhite or Blake, Jasper would be Dickens's means of discrediting characterizations of the ideal man that were offered for public approval by his rivals among less sensational realists.

As a new breed of malcontent, Jasper would prove more problematic for the community to come to terms with than Trollope's old-fashioned Septimus Harding, whose unworldliness baffles Dr. Grantly in *The Warden*. As an insider, Jasper would upset polite society's confidence in its superiority more than an outsider like Felix Holt does. George Eliot's man for the future, an articulate artisan, marries above his class but prefers to remain a working man and to challenge stereotypical conceptions of the group he belongs to; he believes it holds the key to a better future for humanity. The murderous choirmaster poses a greater threat to accepted methods of thinking about man in relation to groups than Mr. Thornton's theories do in *North and South*, even though this innovative industrial planner is Mrs. Gaskell's idealization of the new sort of practical thinker modern technological society supposedly needs.

Dickens's villain subverts the merits in all of these presentations when part of him behaves diabolically. His violent-erotic self works contrary to an outwardly respectable appearance. The split parodies the uninhibited forwardness Holt displays as an agitator for life's revolutionary drive, a helper for its alleged tendency toward steady, nonviolent improvement. When Margaret Hale suspects Thornton loves her, Mrs. Gaskell notes that she "shrank and shuddered as under the fascination of some great power" (NS, 257). Jasper's ability to disconcert Rosa—"He has made a slave of me with his looks" (ED, 95)—deflates Mrs. Gaskell's romantic view of Eros.

In *North and South*, potency and a capacity to run new factories appear complementary. They guarantee not just progress but an exhilarating future partnership, after marriage, between Thornton's private life and public self. Progress and personal sexual fulfillment will be accomplished simultaneously because, by implication, they are virtually synonymous in a civilization that has no demonic underside, no drawbacks or reverse currents. The industrialist's "faultless and beautiful" teeth, his "deep-set" eyes, "intent enough to penetrate into the very heart and core of what he was looking at" (NS, 121), bear little resemblance to Dracula's facial features.[39] For the lustful murderer within Jasper to be vampirelike works effectively as a rebuttal of Thornton, in whom is epitomized the thesis that "power" (erotic, industrial, evolutionary) is mostly positive, ultimately productive, and almost invariably expended for society's furtherance.

Unlike Septimus Harding, Jasper cannot leave the limelight for a sinecure. Despite being technically innocent, Trollope's warden resigns from Hiram's Hospital to avoid further scandal. But he remains part of his community as "precentor of Barchester" and is said to "chant the litany as no other man in England can do" (W, 210). At the conclusion of *The Warden*, Harding occupies a celebrant's position not that dissimilar from the one Jasper, although a layman, is in from the start. The difference is that the secret sharer within the choirmaster of Cloisterham Cathedral finds the drudgery of his daily round unbearable. In the final chapters, had they been written, Jasper's fate would be a parody of Harding's commendable yet comfortable retreat: he would retire from cathedral to prison.

Fittingly, Dickens's story about dual personality is a double-purpose novel. *The Mystery of Edwin Drood* can stand on its own as an independent effort, Dickens's indictment of the hypocrisies fostered by Victorian social pressures. At the same time, besides trying to outdo Collins on this controversial subject, Dickens hoped to settle scores with some of his less sensational rivals for their revaluative parodies of his work. Settling up goes further than using Jasper's duplicity to debunk a saintly Septimus Harding or question the utopian social activism of Felix Holt. Trollope and George Eliot argued that the human condition, including social conditions in England, was better than Dickens reported. To confound such opposition, Dickens would show that problems in the real world had been accurately described in his novels for nearly three decades; that world consistently fell short, he would prove, of presentations that were unduly promising in George Eliot, undeservedly commiserative in Trollope. *The Mystery of Edwin Drood* signals a rekindling of Dickens's creative flame. He would demonstrate his vitality by opening up new directions for himself as an artist. He would also reassert the validity of his highly critical attitude toward society, increasingly strident in his work since *Bleak House* but especially so after competition with Collins began.

Jasper would serve as chief witness for the prosecution in the case Dickens starts to build against George Eliot in 1870. The choirmaster-murderer's reconstruction of his crime must be imagined with Felix Holt's "Address to Working Men" for comparison. This speech, currently in print as an appendix to George Eliot's anti-Dickensian novel, first appeared in *Blackwood's Magazine* for January 1868. Jasper's confession about the dark side to his personality would challenge George Eliot's confidence, expressed through Holt, that the "human nature we have got to work with" in order to bring about "great changes" is sufficiently malleable (FH, 616, 620).

Holt stresses man's sanity, his rational faculties. He refers to civilization as if the word itself had magical properties making it interchangeable with the idea of progress. Throughout Holt's speech, George Eliot celebrates a hidden energy, a benevolent underside to life, a timeless principle of ordering, natural and organic, that operates stealthily beneath all the wrongs in society. Jasper's testimony in "the condemned cell," a disjointed soliloquy in place of Holt's well-made oration, would convict George Eliot—and Trollope as well—of having misjudged the depth of perversity in human nature. Dickens would disclose in modern man an irrational, unregenerate element. Remembering the parodic revaluations of *Bleak House* in *Felix Holt* and exacerbated further by Holt's "Address," Dickens could permit Jasper to damn civilization for its ignorance of man's makeup. The murderer within the choirmaster could accuse polite society of having driven him beyond the point of despair.

Jasper versus Holt would not just be a debate between one of civilization's discontents and one of its champions. The former's remarks would be bolstered by a negative epiphany in which he confronts his interior self. This would reveal a sinister undercurrent, a festering heart of darkness, as opposed to Holt's concept of regular growth from sound roots. George Eliot's protagonist cannot bring to life the organic principle of order he praises, but Jasper would amaze listeners by becoming, under hypnosis, the secret sharer who allegedly lies beneath the respectable surface in all men. Dickens's new novel was to serve as a battering ram to knock down the constructs George Eliot thought she had set up permanently when writing *Felix Holt* to replace *Bleak House*. *The Mystery of Edwin Drood* was intended to be as impressive psychologically as anything George Eliot could manage and yet more suspenseful than Collins. It would achieve thereby a forced blending of the dominant warring brands of Victorian realism, with Dickens crowning himself master of both.

Described in Dickens's opening sentence as "an ancient Cathedral town," Cloisterham has none of the quaint timelessness Trollope bestows on "the cathedral town of . . . Barchester," his microcosm for the human situation. "The unrestored Church and the city around it," Andrew Sanders observes about Cloisterham, "seem neither picturesque nor possessed of the latent strength of a Barchester."[40] Nor does its provinciality show signs of being disturbed by the progressive stirrings so evident in the Treby Magna George Eliot had just surveyed in *Felix Holt*. Dickens questions the realism of both settings and the optimistic argument each makes concerning the life process. Cloisterham is neither proudly standing still, an advertisement for the moral worth inherent in the status quo, nor moving forward as a beneficiary of society's internal evolutionary momentum.

Like the year itself as the novel opens, Cloisterham is entering its autumnal phase: "fallen leaves lie strewn thickly about" (ED, 40) and, thanks to the ruins of a monastery and a "Cathedral crypt," the town is "abounding in vestiges of monastic graves"; it has "an earthy flavour throughout" (ED, 51). Although the seasons change for the better by the novel's midpoint, this "flavour" never varies—making the resurrection of Drood, his return from being thought dead, most unlikely. Dickens suggests that Cloisterham is not a prison like the London of *Bleak House* and *Little Dorrit*, but, even worse, a mausoleum. The town's unawareness of its true state is nicely symbolized by the Sapsea monument with its ludicrous inscription, which its author considers a tourist attraction and a message to posterity.

In Cloisterham, the government (Mayor Sapsea), the Church (the dean), and private philanthropy (the visiting Mr. Honeythunder) form an unholy trinity from which genuine interest in the betterment of society is conspicuously absent. Each member seems heartless personally, and the agency he represents is either misguided or moribund. Each competes with the other two at misconceiving the human condition. That such a society should harbor a dual personality like Jasper's is only natural in that he magnifies the discrepancy between declared purpose and actual performance in Sapsea, dean, and Honeythunder.

Dickens leaves London behind in *The Mystery of Edwin Drood* to tackle two of his rivals on their own ground. In *North and South*, Mrs. Gaskell could imply that Dickens, a southerner, knew little about the Manchester she dwelt in. But Cloisterham is obviously the Rochester familiar to Dickens since childhood. Its resident saint would not be the passive Septimus Harding but a muscular, athletic Minor Canon with the same first name.[41] Crisparkle's fitness would doubtless prove of use in subduing Jasper at some crucial moment during the reenacting of Drood's murder. Taking an active hand in vindicating Neville Landless, Crisparkle would triumph over Honeythunder more resoundingly than Septimus Harding's resignation had discomforted the reform-minded Mr. Bold, and his eventual union with Helena Landless, which Dickens predicted in his letter to Forster,[42] would bode better for the future than the wedding George Eliot arranges between Felix Holt and Esther Lyon. Dickens would turn utopian planner not to predict better times in earnest but to illustrate the shallowness of George Eliot's hopes. The Minor Canon and Miss Landless represent a potential fusion of different strengths, races, and cultures. They easily make the marriage of a French lady to an English artisan, which George Eliot thinks radical, seem less remarkable. Dickens offers a more interesting genetic combination. If civilization is to surge forward toward perfection through a highly selective mingling of society's best, says Dickens, why not be really imaginative?

Although evil is not foreign in *The Mystery of Edwin Drood*, some of the characteristics needed to supplement the English temperament apparently are. Children with Crisparkle's honesty and good-natured vigor plus Helena's strong will and extraordinary mental powers should be more durable and possess higher IQs than the educated workers Holt and Esther plan to raise. The offspring of Mr. Thornton and Margaret Hale will be only the North and South of England, not the East and West of orient and occident. Dickens would taunt both Mrs. Gaskell and George Eliot with the suggestion that Helena and Crisparkle might be parents of the coming race.

Otherwise, however, Cloisterham is not a place in which one can watch human nature correcting and improving itself. Reciprocal modification of character, the process whereby Esther breaks down Felix's foolish resolve never to marry while his social concerns endow her life with a sense of purpose, is missing from *The Mystery of Edwin Drood* more noticeably than from Dickens's previous fiction. This time it appears to have been flatly contradicted, deliberately ruled out.

Jasper's failure at self-integration interrupts the search, in the nineteenth-century British novel, for secular saints whose existence would make the secularization of the temporal order seem justified. It also accentuates the refusal of less melodramatic novelists to examine realistically the darker side of human nature.[43] It does both of these things because Dickens parodies George Eliot's belief in the efficacy of social intercourse. The power of meaningful community to improve and perfect one's character would not be seen to work in Neville Landless's case and seems to have worked in reverse for Jasper.

Landless hopes to become less hotheaded in England, a place where Holt, addressing the workers, downplays the danger of revolution by extolling man's rationality. Yet according to Dickens's letter to Forster, the young man from Ceylon would not have survived to the conclusion of the novel. He may have been fated to perish through impetuosity, perhaps by confronting the murderer in Jasper without waiting for assistance.[44]

Jasper engages in no therapeutic interchanges. On the contrary, he attempts to manipulate Sapsea and Crisparkle whenever he converses with either, not to mention his instigation of the quarrel between Drood and Landless. The secret sharer in Jasper capitalizes on deficiencies in the personalities of others, while the choirmaster remains at the mercy of the split in Jasper's own character. Whenever Jasper goes from uncle and choirmaster to murderer and tormented lover, Dickens subverts the beneficial exchange of strengths during social interaction that functions so kindly in George Eliot's novels. The major exchange that occurs in *The Mystery of Edwin Drood* is between the two personalities within Jasper. This, unfortunately, is a total exchange of one personality for another without any ameliorative interchange of traits that might reclaim the darker. Until the closing pages, neither of Jasper's personalities has the inclination or capacity to behave with the other's betterment in mind.

For Jasper to be the devil-at-large in Cloisterham, he must be an established presence, not an outsider like Popular Sentiment in Barchester, or else Dickens's revaluation of *The Warden* could not succeed. Trollope's caricature of Dickens invades Barchester to support Bold's call for ecclesiastical reforms. The community's problems, Trollope argues, would be more easily resolved if outsiders did not meddle. In Cloisterham, Jasper, one supposes, might have gone undetected had it not been for the intervention of nonresidents and foreigners: the Landless twins, Tartar, Mr. Grewgious, and, presumably, Datchery.

Jasper's passion threatens Rosa more than Harold Transome's marriage proposal sets a trap (of luxurious ease) for Esther Lyon. But the choirmaster does not return from foreign parts as did Harold, the novel's false radical, who arrives from Smyrna. Dickens's threat to communal stability is parodically different from its counterparts in *The Warden* and *Felix Holt* because it is internal. The modern revaluator of hidden rivalries in Victorian fiction considers this another reason for vetoing the suggestion that Jasper is an actual Thug, trained in India, or Drood's older half-brother by an Egyptian mother. Similarly, if Jasper reminds one of a vampire, he is surely Cloisterham's own, not an import from Transylvania, just as the predatory Vholes, in *Bleak House*, is a bloodsucker brought into existence by a corrupt legal system. Fosco and Rigaud (*Little Dorrit*) notwithstanding, Dickens's insistence that there are no foreign devils—that is, his emphasis on the interiority of evil in man and its consequent inherence within society at all stages of its unfolding—is not just stronger than Collins's; it is also a calculated affront to Trollope and George Eliot because it parodies the rosier moral and political philosophies of status-quo-ite and evolutionary optimist about equally.

Jasper's double self is the product of a hypocritical and deteriorating social system for which decaying Cloisterham is symbolic. But looked at in yet another way, the widening split between Jasper's contradictory personalities is not just a breakdown signifying the separation of society's declared purposes from underlying realities. It can be added to other systems of slow but steadily pernicious growth that proliferate throughout the novels of Dickens and Collins. The list includes the interminable suit of Jarndyce versus Jarndyce (*Bleak House*), Madame Defarge's knitted register of deserving candidates for the guillotine (*A Tale of Two Cities*), the repressive accumulation of social restrictions known as propriety (*The Woman in White*), and the several generations of sacrifice and exile it takes for the Brahmans to repossess a stolen religious relic (*The Moonstone*). As long as the moonstone remains unrecovered and Jasper at large, it would be unrealistic, Dickens and Collins maintain, to express the enthusiasm Felix Holt voices for civilization as a "wonderful slow-growing system" (FH, 616) or that George Eliot herself subsequently feels for "the growing good of the world" (MM, 613).

Periodic eruptions of Jasper's darker side at first do not seem to amount to as effective a comeuppance for society as the collapse of Mrs. Clennam's house in *Little Dorrit* or the symbolic combustion in *Bleak House* of the Lord Chancellor in the person of Krook. But this resurgence of the perennial Manichee, says Dickens, is a psychological catastrophe lying in wait for human nature if hypocritical civilizations, heedless of man's darker side, continue to breed more advanced varieties of frustration and discontent. Jasper's dual personality restates what now appears to have been an anti-utopian thesis put forth in the opening lines of *A Tale of Two Cities*. The mix Jasper becomes of Drood's guardian and nemesis shows the "best" and "worst" not only coexisting in time, as they always do, but cohabiting as twin states within one man.

Compared with Krook, Jasper is the more dangerous time bomb. Human nature, as symbolized by the murderer-choirmaster, seems more vulnerable than Krook to destruction from within. Jasper is no surrogate for villainy among the respectable but the thing itself, the man of the future, not a stand-in for the administrator of an archaic, self-consuming institution. The idea of a society containing a number of men like Jasper—indeed, the implication that all men will be more and more like him to some extent—outdoes the consternation that Krook appearing in multiple would cause. The second, darker personality in modern man, Dickens warns, can seize control at any time. Jasper's double self, therefore, is a more disturbing phenomenon than Krook's explosion as a double for the Lord Chancellor.

In 1870, Dickens finally attempts to settle the score with G.H. Lewes for that critic's reservations about spontaneous combustion. The defenses Dickens offered in Chapter 33 of *Bleak House* and again in the preface to the completed serial were feeble expedients. They made George Eliot's subsequent depictions of society's unfoldings seem more realistic than any threat of internal detonation. But Jasper's case marks a return to the offensive; Dickens uses it to issue a sterner admonition about the way societies can disintegrate. In *Bleak House*, Dickens says that destruction is "inborn, inbred, engendered in the corrupted humours of the body itself" (BH, 431). Nothing could be clearer, more anti-utopian, or more skeptical about the evolution of communities. In *The Mystery of Edwin Drood*, Dickens advances his case by showing that "corrupted humours of the body itself" can refer equally to the body politic or the darkness inside Jasper's outwardly respectable corporeal frame. Indeed, these are mutually reinforcing. The choirmaster's recognition of a darkness within himself, not any rival sequence in Collins, would outdo Krook's combustion and so come to stand as the classic case in Victorian fiction for the thesis that evil is primarily an inside job.

Guppy and Weevle merely find the greasy residue, "like black fat" (BH, 426), that was once the rag and bone man. But Jasper's interlocutors would witness the actual consumption of the choirmaster's avuncular personality by its rival, darker self and then an even more traumatic reversal of this disaster as the choirmaster retook control and Jasper came face-to-face, as it were, with his duality. Krook dies "the same death eternally" (BH, 431) that all unjust authorities and institutions must suffer. Nevertheless, he can burst into flames only once and does so both without witnesses and before achieving much insight into his symbolic role. The choirmaster's murderous secret self trades places with his avuncular personality at key points all through the novel. The final eruption would make these points comprehensible and prominent; the reader would recognize that dual personality is a better symbol than a double of the Lord Chancellor for the proposition that society's good qualities are forever endangered by recurrent emanations from within.

At the end of Chapter 15, Grewgious witnesses a preliminary to the climactic transition that would take place in "the condemned cell." After Jasper learns that he need not have murdered Drood to covet Rosa, he is constantly referred to not as "John Jasper" but only as "it" or "the ghastly figure" (ED, 191). As Grewgious breaks the news, the murderer within the choirmaster comes forward: "dreadful starting drops or bubbles, as if of steel" cover his face. The "ghastly figure" emits "a terrible shriek" before collapsing into "a heap . . . of clothes upon the floor," a mere "it" (ED, 192) for Grewgious to look down at just as Guppy and Weevle gaze at "the cinder" that was Krook.

But it is "John Jasper" who is revived from his "fit or swoon" by Mr. and Mrs. Tope as Chapter 16 opens. Himself again, Jasper seems to have no recollection of his collapse. Eating and drinking normally, he assumes that Edwin's decision not to marry Rosa is good news: it seems to rule out jealousy as a motive for murder, thus improving chances of Drood's being alive. But the murderer inside Jasper is likely to burst forth again on short notice. This could happen at least three more times, although Dickens lived to transcribe only one of them: the interview with Rosa in the garden of the Nuns' House. Other instances would be during Jasper's physical reenactment of the crime and in the course of the verbal reconstruction under hypnosis—this being the severest outburst, possibly fatal.

Sudden flare-ups of the murderer from within the choirmaster result from the steady breaking-down of an initially unified personality under detrimental social pressures. Suddenness and steadiness, however, are both negative factors in Jasper's case. They enable Dickens to fire what turned out to be a parting shot against George Eliot's supposedly more scientific idea of realism. Her application of the theory of gradualism to the historical process struck Dickens as the promotion of a half-truth into a generalization. More convincingly than Krook's combustion and with greater immediacy than the political uprising that imperils Darnay, Jasper's story challenges the assumption that life moves forward, for the most part smoothly, along an indiscernible upward curve.

The idea for *The Mystery of Edwin Drood* lodged itself in Dickens's imagination by late summer of 1868, the year *The Moonstone* pushed circulation of *All the Year Round* beyond the sales *Great Expectations* had achieved. In short, Collins's reply to *Great Expectations* had just outsold Dickens's response to *The Woman in White*.

Dickens showed the first three chapters of his new novel to the visiting James T. Fields in October.[45] Less than a month later, in writing and polishing a reading from *Oliver Twist*, Dickens introduced the murder of Nancy with stupendous results.[46] Thus *Oliver Twist* was freshly in mind in the final months of 1868 and throughout the following year. Dickens's hostile feelings toward the wife from whom he had separated and the friend who was now a major rival also acted as similar creative stimulants on the new dramatic reading and the new novel. It is no wonder that Dickens is supposed to have identified with Jasper. Nor is it surprising that Jasper is a middle-class replacement for Fagin and Sikes, within whom the criminal instinct was formerly located.

Clearly, the period from 1868 to 1870 was Dickens's time for reprisals. He tried to settle old scores, if only through violent fantasies cleverly worked out within the confines of his art. If a dramatic reading of the scene in which Sikes clubs Nancy to death served as a vehicle for revenge upon his wife for a failed marriage, *The Mystery of Edwin Drood* was even more double-barreled: Rosa's would-be lover kills his younger rival in the very novel a melodramatic realist writes to vanquish his main competition.

When Ablewhite steals the moonstone, he does not just deprive Franklin Blake—his wealthier, more secure rival—of a precious gem; temporarily, he also takes Rachel Verinder's love and respect away from Blake. It would not have been difficult for Dickens to perceive in this situation from *The Moonstone* the threat that Collins might similarly damage the senior novelist's popularity and earning power. *The Moonstone* and *The Mystery of Edwin Drood* demand double vision from the modern revaluator because Dickens and Collins tended to discuss their rivalry figuratively in these novels while also pursuing supremacy through ingenious modifications of each other's key themes and characters.

The Mystery of Edwin Drood, one must reiterate, revolves around the elimination of a younger rival. Ten years earlier, Dickens's revisions of Collins's work on *The Frozen Deep* toyed with this possibility, but Wardour and Aldersley were not blood relatives. The tie between Drood and Jasper indicates how much stronger the connection between older novelist and protegé-competitor had become in the former's mind. "Of all the characters in *The Mystery of Edwin Drood*," Sue Lonoff astutely observes, "Drood himself bears the closest resemblance to Collins."[47] If Nancy receives belatedly the fatal blows a disappointed Dickens meant for Kate, Ned dies for Wilkie. It is as if Dickens were redoing *The Frozen Deep*, after a decade of rivalry with Collins, in order to have Aldersley perish at Wardour's hands. These two cases of substitution—Nancy for Kate, Drood for Collins— have little in common with Carton's doubling for Darnay. But they are not unlike Anne Catherick's involuntary death by proxy for Lady Glyde or the latter's imprisonment in place of the former, two scenes that the general public would not know were targets but that Dickens could take intense personal pleasure in trying to outdo.

By the late 1860s, Dickens felt that he could retain most of the audience George Eliot hoped to divert towards her own allegedly more scientific brand of realistic fiction, even though he had to compete much harder for its attention. Those who read *Felix Holt*, for example, also read *Our Mutual Friend* and continued to reread *Bleak House*. It was less clear, however, whether Dickens could afford to divide his readership with Collins indefinitely. That his one-time disciple had become the premier attraction in *All the Year Round* was especially upsetting: Collins was producing the kind of melodramatic excitement Dickens specialized in and doing so in the master's own periodical.

Dickens had no lack of precedent for newcomers supplanting older pros. He needed only to recall how arrogantly he himself had secured the upper hand over Robert Seymour thirty years before, when control of *Pickwick Papers* was at stake, or the ease with which *Sketches by Boz* eclipsed

Pierce Egan and Robert Surtees. Now he could revaluate those early triumphs in his career from the displaced artist's perspective, perhaps even regard Collins as a sort of long-delayed comeuppance.

When one reconsiders the embattled Dickens's situation from the mid-1850s on, it no longer seems amazing that he drove himself so hard. On one side, he was beset by less sensational novelists who claimed to be more scientific as social critics, more reliable reporters of recent events, and on the other by a disciple turned competitor. Given this two-pronged assault on Dickens's preeminence, becoming obsolete and taking a consequent plunge back into poverty were hardly imaginary terrors.

Hidden rivalries in Victorian fiction show the modern revaluator another reason Dickens turned so eagerly to readings from his own work. The idea for the readings occurred to Dickens while he was writing *Dombey and Son* (1846-48) but he acted upon it only after Trollope parodied him in *The Warden* and Mrs. Gaskell in *North and South*.[48] Personal appearances gained Dickens an access to his audience that neither George Eliot nor Collins had sufficient talent or inclination to dispute. Dickens exploited a twofold advantage, the authority of his presence and the power of the spoken word as firsthand testimony. He could outshine a rival like Collins by bringing his novels alive in front of his readers. Testifying in person, Dickens could asseverate that he was not used up, not about to let himself be outdone, canceled, or replaced. His presence would imply that he was a more active, more visible witness to recent events than any of his detractors, hence the superior, more truthful social commentator.

Having noted several of the many similarities between *The Moonstone* and *The Mystery of Edwin Drood* (opium use, a missing jewel, a mystery with an Indian motif), Sue Lonoff maintains that Dickens's later novels "appear to owe little to the fiction or advice of Wilkie Collins" because Dickens "radically transformed whatever he borrowed or paralleled."[49] One cannot recognize spirited competition, steady rivalry over a ten-year span, only to disregard parodic revaluation on grounds that it does not resemble more obvious forms of disagreement or more conventional transmissions of influence. Dickens's transformations of Collins, like those Collins visits upon Dickens, are never so radical that they cannot be coaxed out of hiding. Moreover, they alert the reader to intellectual disagreements between ostensible allies in the counterattack that sensationalists mounted against scientific realists, so-called. As Dickens and Collins transform each other's characters and themes, they appropriate and revise each other's ideas; the revaluation process shapes and reshapes the novels involved.

That "there is probably no intense social, philosophical, or moral purpose" behind Dickens's unfinished novel is a gross misreading.[50] A better grasp of the network of hidden rivalries in Victorian fiction would have prevented this undervaluation. Even if Dickens were not insisting on the inherence of evil in man and society as a way of discrediting the world views of Trollope and George Eliot, it would still be unfair to deny the presence of serious "purpose." Dickens's determination to repell Collins's challenge to his superiority as a creator of alarm and suspense supplies *The Mystery of Edwin Drood* with mission enough.

If revalued as a critique of Trollope and George Eliot as well as of Collins, *Edwin Drood* is still technically not a multiplot novel. But it is surely a variation on the format by being so multipurpose, one purpose being to withhold the plot, an account of what actually happened to Drood, so that a multiplicity of solutions or plots arise. These provide another illustration of how relative everything was becoming. Several answers to the mystery seem plausible, yet there would finally be only one—except that, as ironic proof of the new indeterminateness, it would accompany Dickens to the grave.

The Mystery of Edwin Drood versus *The Moonstone* is not the classic case of revaluative parody—George Eliot's world, not Collins's, is antipodal to Dickens's, hence a much more thoroughgoing revaluation—nor the seminal instance nor the most recriminatory. But Collins's rivalry with Dickens, from novel to novel over an entire decade, is the longest-running; it is also the most cannibalistic, an attempt to ingest not just one or two books but virtually all of the later Dickens.

Undoing by outdoing remains unique among hidden rivalries in nineteenth-century British fiction because it must be seen, in retrospect, as both a pitched battle and a thriving partnership. It can be called an intramural competition in which both parties honed skills and developed new ones. In 1870, the honing and developing Dickens did in order to reassert his inimitability was also part of a final extramural contest with the less melodramatic realists among his opposition.

Even when they disagreed, Dickens and Collins gave scant comfort to their mutual adversaries. In this regard, it does not matter which one considers worse, a pervasive irresponsibility that obscures basic human relationships or an excessive sense of propriety that holds things together artificially by helping to conceal the true nature of man. Either way, the idea of life as a progressive communalization suffers. To put it another way, Dickens and Collins could not help conspiring as they competed. They disagreed as to who better understood interiority but combined against George Eliot to mean by this term man's inner darknesses. They extended themselves to see who could place stronger emphasis on society's habitual need for some form of providential supervision but contended that the somewhat pessimistic attitudes they shared toward the human situation and prospects for its improvement were truer to life than any other novelist's. That such attitudes were purveyed in the most attention-getting manner possible they considered primarily a question of strategy or poetic emphasis, no indication of a lack of veracity.

Collins's disregard for *The Mystery of Edwin Drood*—he called it "the last laboured effort, the melancholy work of a worn-out brain"—must be reconsidered as a last-ditch attempt at self-defense.[51] In 1868, Collins wrongly supposed that Dickens was ready to be supplanted by his former pupil; he found himself, in 1870, the primary target of Dickens's unfinished novel. Collins tried to pretend that he would not have been outdone (perhaps conclusively) even if Boz had lived to resolve the story.

Not having a completed product to deal with, Collins was effectively prevented from continuing the competition beyond his rival's death.[52] Modern revaluators are entitled to guess which scenes from Collins might have been parodied in the final chapters of *The Mystery of Edwin Drood*, but doing so was impractical for Collins. He would have been responding in print to parodies never actually written, an act of anticipation akin to paranoia. For parodic revaluation to work, if only subconsciously, readers need to have perused the original that is being redone.

Instead of constituting a falling-off, *The Mystery of Edwin Drood* bristles with its author's unabated confidence. Dickens grows so certain of his ability to vanquish his closest rival that he finds time and space to reprimand Trollope and George Eliot too. He tries to outstrip Collins's efforts to psychologize a melodramatic realism that was first seen in a new light as early as *Great Expectations*.

Revaluing Collins was the crucial step in Dickens's overdue response to the supposedly more psychological realists among their mutual rivals. Had Dickens survived into the 1870s, subsequent novels—prompted by George Eliot's return to the attack in *Middlemarch*—might have expanded the counteroffensive that commences as a concomitant to revaluation of *The Moonstone*.

Concentration in both *The Mystery of Edwin Drood* and *The Moonstone* upon the increasing internalization of evil and the greater respectability with which it cloaks itself did not mean that Dickens and Collins came to believe that providence was no longer a mark of divine intervention in men's lives.[53] Instead, the new preoccupation was the second stage of an ongoing argument central to the melodramatic or sensational branch of Victorian realism; attempts to ascertain the continuing importance of providence were merely the first step.

Providence is not defunct in *The Mystery of Edwin Drood*. Datchery was intended to be its agent. His services seem called for because guardians from the social order, who abound in Cloisterham, fail to prevent tragedy: not just the dean and Mayor Sapsea but, more specifically, Jasper as Drood's guardian, Grewgious as Rosa's, and Crisparkle as Neville's. Melodramatic realists employ the divided personality along with long-awaited days of reckoning as complementary metaphors, adjoining ways of insisting that man and his world are inescapably fallen; neither is a self-perfecting organism.

That evil is not a foreign substance; that it abides deep within man; that he is best depicted as a mix of light and dark; that the society for which he is a microcosm needs the threat of periodic shake-ups to jolt it forward or at least temporarily arrest its backsliding; that the temporal order will never unfold into the perfect place because, although its soul is disposed toward justice, it still gives indications of being wrong "somewhere at the root"[54]— these are not unrelated tenets thrown together haphazardly. On the contrary, if one employs double vision, they emerge from the competing novels of Dickens and Collins and coalesce to form a credible moral stance, a coherent world view.

Chapter Seven

"That Arduous Invention"

Middlemarch

GEORGE ELIOT was well established by 1872. She did not need to write against Dickens, as Trollope did in the 1850s, to make room for herself; nor, unlike Mrs. Gaskell, did she have to avoid being preempted. In *Felix Holt*, she had already produced what has been called the masterwork of parodic revaluation, an unflinching, total revision of Dickens's finest satirical novel. *Middlemarch*, consequently, turns out to be a unique testament, in the annals of hidden rivalries, to Dickens's authority. During the first two years after his demise, an eminently successful rival novelist felt compelled to cancel his reply to her parody of him by updating and enlarging her original attack.

As a modern emanation of unsavory energies repressed within the self and by the community, the murderous choirmaster in *The Mystery of Edwin Drood*, was the age-old vampire and perennial Manichee in new and more disconcerting form. John Jasper exhibited more psychological complexity than any of Dickens's previous villains. Yet he was less attractive morally than Fagin or Quilp, despite a presentable exterior—indeed because of it. George Eliot decided it was necessary to articulate again her earlier objections to Dickens's realism while inventing Bulstrode to revise Jasper, thereby removing this recently installed obstacle to her evolutionary philosophy of social change. She discovered that she could graft her rejoinder onto a reworking of prior parody. Debunking *Bleak House* over again, along with selected scenes from other Dickens novels, provided a fuller context, a broader foundation; it bolstered the guesswork in her revision of Dickens's half-novel. In George Eliot's opinion, her extension of her revaluation of him easily neutralizes his extension of the negative outlook she had already

sufficiently refuted (or so she thought) six years before. *Middlemarch* reiter-
ates George Eliot's own point of view in the course of a reprise of the parody
of *Bleak House* in *Felix Holt*. For the modern revaluator of hidden rivalries
between Victorian novels, this constitutes a double dose of double vision.

The favors that Will Ladislaw and Dorothea Brooke or Dorothea and
Lydgate do for each other's personality reconfirm the beneficial exchanges
between Felix Holt and Esther Lyon. Exchanges of personality traits,
refinements of mind and soul through social interaction, are both more
numerous and of greater intricacy in *Middlemarch* than in *Felix Holt*, where
they occurred mainly between prospective husband and wife. Social intercourse continues to ensure the evolution of personality and a community's
coalescence. So the process whereby character develops or is put together
overshadows threats of self-division and minimizes the occasional disintegration.

Bulstrode's case is not so calamitous as Dickens had made Jasper's
because George Eliot manages to absorb her rival's single-minded study of
the interiority of evil into her multiplot novel: the banker's downfall
becomes just one of three major story lines. The genesis of Eliot's novel was
twofold in a way that went beyond simply adding Lydgate's story to
Dorothea's. First, evolution of character proceeds apace through fortunate
exchanges of personality traits, a vindication of *Felix Holt*. Second, the
additional matter of Bulstrode's duplicity, which the community is strong
enough to withstand, eradicates the horror of Jasper's.

Although George Eliot conceived the Vincy/Featherstone parts as
early as 2 August 1869, Joan Bennett writes that a separate story about
"Miss Brooke" did not develop until 2 December 1870, nearly six months
after Dickens's death. [1] Bennett adds that the "original subject," the frustration by circumstances of a gifted young doctor, was planned in "considerable detail" before Eliot realized how thoroughly Dorothea's adventures
"related" to it. The eventual successful fusion of the three principal stories,
well under way during the summer of 1871, had Eliot's rivalry with
Dickens as an unnamed catalyst: she had determined that the limiting of
Lydgate and Dorothea by their environment and the limited impact of
Bulstrode's hypocrisy upon that same environment could be made to work
well not only together but simultaneously a second time as a redoing of
Dickens's last novel, which she, not Wilkie Collins as had been rumored, in
effect would finish for him.

Middlemarch coruscates with literary rebuttals. Among the novel's
neglected charms are not just its benevolent adaptations of Wordsworth but
the sharp correctives it administers to several eminent Victorians—Carlyle
and Arnold, for example, besides Dickens and Collins. George Eliot

directs her satire against characters who expect too much from life, but it falls heaviest on writers who commit the same error, particularly forerunners of the phenomenon elsewhere described as the modern satirical novel.[2] Her strategy is to redo scenes and characters from Dickens as a way of parodying pessimists in general. Dickens stands for all writers who, finding life fundamentally unsatisfactory, respond far too critically. He also allegedly palliates his displeasure by creating episodes that are unrealistic (that is, sentimental) compensations.

Middlemarch is never modern and satirical simultaneously. Unlike Dickens's satire, George Eliot's is best described as pro-Victorian and, in that sense, anti-modern. Not only are satirists satirized in *Middlemarch*, but the validity of all social criticism that is not sufficiently improvement-oriented is disallowed. Otherwise, Eliot could not reestablish her assertion that personal relations and their formation of personality will continue to flourish in a society she considers advantageously secularized. The essential point to remember about George Eliot's masterpiece is that nearly twenty years after *Bleak House* and *Little Dorrit*, the society it depicts still works. Characters mature, society will be reformed, and novels are made by a process Lydgate calls "arduous invention" (MM, 122).

In the memorable passage outlining Lydgate's commingled notions of scientific research and great literature, George Eliot does three things at once: discounts satire, devalues Dickens, and demonstrates the superiority of her own realistic techniques. Lydgate laments that

many men have been praised as vividly imaginative on the strength of their profuseness in indifferent drawing or cheap narration. . . . But these kinds of inspiration Lydgate regarded as rather vulgar and vicious compared with the imagination that reveals subtle actions inaccessible by any sort of *lens*, but tracked in that outer darkness through long pathways of *necessary sequence* by the inward light which is the last refinement of *Energy*. . . . [For Lydgate] was enamoured of that *arduous invention* which is the very eye of research, provisionally framing its object and correcting it to more exactness of relation; he wanted to pierce the obscurity of those minute *processes* which prepare human misery and joy, those invisible thoroughfares which are the first lurking-places of anguish, mania, and crime, that delicate poise and transition which determine the growth of happy or unhappy consciousness. [MM, 122; italics added]

Lydgate subsequently objects to stories featuring "very poor talk going on in distant orbs" or "Lucifer coming down on his bad errands." But Dickens's outdated concerns, not Milton's, make George Eliot's archrival the chief culprit among Lydgate's "many men."

Good writing for George Eliot draws closer to scientific experiment in

Middlemarch than in *Felix Holt*. The more insistently she endorses Lydgate's scientific rigor, the stronger is her implication that Dickens's satire, founded on discontent with man, society, and life itself, must be too splenetic to be reliable. Eliot enlists for her art a researcher's eye so sensitive that no lens yet in existence can compete with it, certainly not her rival's perspective. If the Victorian artist is as methodical as the scientist, Eliot's analogies suggest, no counterpoint between art and life is possible, no animosity of artist to any subject matter that is properly understood.

Along with Darwin and T.H. Huxley, George Eliot pursues truths too "subtle" for the naked eye, actions "inaccessible" to the less observant, "minute processes" protected from scrutiny by their "obscurity." These processes, synonymous with life's secrets, must be magnified, but not exaggerated, until the workings of provincial Middlemarch illuminate the macrocosm. Arduous research and the inspiration that comes only after much preliminary tracking—these have always been and will remain Eliot's prerequisites for the realistic exploration of character, not the careless drawing, "cheap" and shallow, that results in the complaining so displeasing to her in Dickens.

One concludes that George Eliot finds "vulgar" and "vicious" any broad indictment of the life process because she believes it cannot be based upon absolute exactitude. In her opinion, satirists like Dickens and Collins are impatient realists who do not search correctly for the finer points essential to a truthful overview. Only a novelist who thinks life is basically sound, however, operates that way in quest of hidden laws. Writers who follow Lydgate's prescription are virtually barred from writing most varieties of satire, especially the kind found in the modern satirical novel. There, because the human condition appears deplorable, something irreversible is said to have gone wrong in the very nature of things. Satirical novelists who criticize the workings of life, George Eliot would argue, distort rather than magnify in order to expose largely superficial twists and warps. They have slight interest in correcting a provisional framing until it is "more and more" exact, the way one adjusts a lens; on the contrary, they pile enormity upon outrage.

Lydgate's views have an unmistakable positive bias that is ultimately as conservative as it initially sounds aesthetically and scientifically experimental. George Eliot speaks about her craft through a scientist and in scientific terms to intimate that science and sociology do not mix with a penchant for satire. Research implies discovery. The effort expended may be painful, "arduous," but never the results. Lydgate reveals George Eliot's sense of exhilaration at the prospect of piercing life's obscure but essentially commendable processes. That piercing is the only cutting she allows.

Unlike Emma Bovary, Dorothea Brooke will not end by exclaiming that nothing works. She will not demand to know why life is "so unsatisfactory." She will not find that everything she leans on crumbles instantly to dust, so that "nothing was worth looking for: everything was a lie."[3] These sentiments, however, would not be out of place in the third-person narrative of *Bleak House*, and they would easily fit into Jasper's outburst about the soul-grinding drudgery of his daily round. George Eliot's ambition is to negate such sentiments, which she considers unfair or unrealistic responses to life. Although origins and ultimate causes may be microscopic, "processes"—a term germane to chemistry and manufacture—connote purposiveness, positive movement. This is very different from Evelyn Waugh's depiction of the secular world's comic absurdity or Aldous Huxley's sense of society as fragmentation. Such negative visions, like Emma's depressing epiphany, seem closer to Dickens's fears of "the perpetual stoppage" (BH, 157), an antilinear, nonprogressive phenomenon whereby reform and societies themselves periodically stagnate.

Instead of tracing "necessary sequences" like a laboratory scientist, modern satirical novelists fashion satirical images for life to express their disillusionment. Huxley's impossibly complex "human fugue" of "eighteen hundred million parts" conjures up pictures of uncontrollable multiplicity. Waugh compares life to a wheel of fortune like the crazily spinning disk, an amusement ride, that one can attempt to remain perched on at Luna Park. Anthony Powell's image is an interminable dance, the steps for which one can only guess. Monstrous cacophony, pointless circularity, endless gyration—by comparison with these images of breakdown and futility, George Eliot's metaphor for life is flowing water. It is with the idea of society as progressive flux that the aptly named reformer, Miss Brooke, finally allies herself, however modestly. In modern satirical novels, characters never get in tune or in step with life's baffling sequences.

Middlemarch betrays no suspicion of an underlying barbarity on which civilization and human nature precariously rest. It wants to keep such suspicions from surfacing by parodying as unscientific the novelists who entertain them: namely, Dickens and Collins. In George Eliot's rendition of the world, momentum, no matter what the pace, is always forward. Middlemarch society, she demonstrates at novel's end, is entering the age of reforms, from the midst of which the novelist is writing. Given such beginnings, communities cannot be shown sliding back into primal slime as the era continues.

The sense of pervasive corruption and decay issuing from the crypts of Cloisterham's cathedral makes that symbolic edifice as central as Chancery to the London of *Bleak House* but an even more moribund institution.

Whether sacred or secular, Dickens charges, Victorian institutions have become oppressive holdovers because they remain unaware of or indifferent to people's needs and failings, both of which they consequently exacerbate. With Middlemarch poised on the brink of the greatest era of reform in centuries, George Eliot implies that satirizing cathedral towns is even less pertinent than scoffing at archaic legal systems. She reflects the shift in perception among enlightened, doubt-free Victorians from a predominantly religious view of the world to an outlook more tentative, highly secular, less spectacular, but allegedly more accurate or scientific. Replacing Cloisterham with Middlemarch, the novelist sets out to prove that she is the true expert on shifts in perception, the true sociologist of provincial life, knowledgeable about changes in its rhythms and in those of life in general.

In *Bleak House* Dickens's world is run by Dedlocks and Smallweeds, fossils and predators. Jasper hovers over Cloisterham and Rosa Bud like a giant vampire bat. Dickens's animal imagery invests his novels with a skeptical mistrust of evolution and history that foreshadows the modern. Anti-evolutionary satire in Dickens anticipates Aldous Huxley's zoological fiction and the derisive animal imagery one discovers as a hallmark of most modern satirical novels.[4] Throughout *A Dance to the Music of Time*, for instance, Widmerpool, Powell's idea of the new type of powerseeker, is consistently shown as a large esurient fish. Lucy Tantamount, the modern *femme fatale* in Huxley's *Point Counter Point*, resembles a crocodile whenever she smiles. The modern revaluator posits a retrospective double vision: if Dickens is seen looking forward to Huxley, then Lydgate's conceptions of the manner in which character should be analyzed can be construed as an effort to prevent prefiguration of the scientist-novelist as a satirical zoologist of fiction.

Life is not working itself out smoothly in Dickens's novels, and some punitive act of God or nature—flood, fire—is needed to clear the ground. Instead of pursuing reform, society's equivalent of biological evolution, Cloisterham is going downhill, just as Jasper's personality is disintegrating. In *Middlemarch*, however, flowing water replaces the primeval mud engulfing London and the floods that threaten Chesney Wold. Also, a reclaimable Bulstrode—his name suggests an ordinary farm animal that has acquired an unhealthy swagger—is brought to heel. Dickens calls for divine judgments to be carried out by biological processes. This is not only unscientific but not far removed, Lydgate insinuates, from Milton's fascination with a fantasy world of divine wrath and infernal errands.

Many powerful people, Dickens says in *Bleak House*, do not "receive any impress from the moving age" (BH, 157). Such impress is George Eliot's bailiwick, the steady bringing to bear upon character of ordinary causes. In *The Mystery of Edwin Drood*, Dickens substitutes an oppressive society and Jasper's repressed second self for the impression process celebrated throughout *Felix Holt*. Showing how unscientific Dickens was became a way of identifying the era's most powerful novelist as one on whom new and progressive ideas had made little impression.

George Eliot revalues Dickens parodically simply by endorsing Lydgate's restrained use of scientific imagery to describe creative endeavor. Such images come directly from Darwin and the researcher's laboratory. An irresponsible, melodramatic Dickens, by contrast, is shown to tincture his scientific imagery with prophetic and apocalyptic qualities that identify him as biblicist rather than scientist. George Eliot employs "arduousness" as a code word for an exacting mimesis; "inventiveness" is her slightly misleading term for careful observation and research. When she credits Dickens with profuse imagination, that is her ironic euphemism for writings created out of thin air, like Milton's cosmogony.

Reproaching Dickens again six years after *Felix Holt* did not seem redundant to George Eliot. *Middlemarch* became her most concerted attempt to rescue contemporary science from subversive refashionings of its findings into a satirist's weapon: Dickens's devolution instead of her evolution. George Eliot maintains she is just as progressive an evolutionary humanist as she seemed six years before. Regardless of Dickens, Will and Dorothea inhabit an ameliorable world in which Tennyson's single, far-off event, the perfectibilitarian's idea of a joint goal and climax, can still be foreseen. Most of all, George Eliot wants the philosophy of life and human nature in Dickens's unfinished novel consigned, along with his earlier masterpiece, to the allegedly inferior, pre-Darwinian epoch.

Admittedly, Dickens's apocalyptic tone, his sense of judgments to be rendered at appointed times, and his preoccupation with eruptive inner darknesses (man's and society's) leave his world suspended between Deluge and Armageddon.[5] A world of this kind, however, often seems more modernist than George Eliot's, despite her strictly Darwinian scientific imagery. Determination to bring life under the artist's microscope is an antisatirical, Victorian impulse; it rests on the euphoric conviction that society, like the natural world, develops by discoverable laws and ascending stages. When the modern revaluator of hidden rivalries substitutes double vision for George Eliot's lens, she seems more modern than Dickens for her times, the better-informed Victorian, yet less modern than her more satiric archcompetitor in our own.[6]

In *Bleak House*, readers once drawn into Chancery's labyrinth have to search with Bucket and the novel's amateur detectives for concealed relationships that impede meaningful community. Characters in Dickens's novels who develop do so mainly with the help of inner resources superior to the obstacles life offers, obstacles insurmountable by the majority. Inherently static, most of Dickens's characters indirectly disclose his antievolutionary bias. John Jasper's dual personality aggravated that bias. Warring elements within the murderer-choirmaster appear to be splitting further apart as *The Mystery of Edwin Drood* proceeds. Climactic reunification of Jasper's divided self, had it occurred, would probably have been fatal.

The strengths of those who triumph in *Middlemarch*, as in *Felix Holt*, receive support from other members of the community-at-large, so that Will and Dorothea find in society ample room for exercise and growth. George Eliot repeats her earlier revision of the perversions of social intercourse Dickens satirized in *Bleak House*. Unrealistic complaints then, she argues, are equally so now. Failures meet defeat in *Middlemarch* through insufficient internal fortitude, through a lack, which is not as negative an idea as evil's presence. In response to Dickens, there is greater awareness of frustration and failure than in *Felix Holt*; nevertheless, Eliot manages to subsume success and defeat under the same affirmative biological analogy.

When she introduces Lydgate or any other major character as someone "at a turning point"—that is, "still in the making"—she divulges her evolutionary definition of character as "a process of unfolding" (MM, 111). This is how society and individuals advance. Unfolding also has affinities with the way research problems are solved. Even an individual's failure, George Eliot instructs Dickens, ought to be classified as an "unfolding," an instructive manifestation of maturation processes at work. Deficiencies in human nature should not be enlarged melodramatically by confusing them with a deepening interiority of evil, a phenomenon which, she charges, has been largely invented by Dickens and Collins.

The modern revaluator notes in retrospect that personages in nineteenth-century forerunners of the modern satirical novel frequently "are characterized by structural tension between impulses to associate and to disassociate public and private realms of experience."[7] They are not only characterized by such tensions but defeated by them. In Thomas Hardy's last novel—in many ways the last Victorian novel—the author forfeits at a stroke the audience that Dickens's last novels had already unsettled. The purpose behind *Jude the Obscure* (1895) was to "pierce" the "obscurity" of the kind of "minute processes" Lydgate talks about. But Hardy desires to learn what keeps Fawley "obscure," invisible to others and incomprehensible to himself. Hardy's un-Eliotic conclusion is that the individual is no longer sustained by society but frustrated by it and consequently alienated.

As a split man, one who seeks to join but is kept apart, Jude also seems torn between conflicting demands of flesh and spirit: personal goals and ideals on one hand, recalcitrant external reality on the other. Rather than becoming a steadily more integrated personality, the stonecutter who aspires to be a scholar is not only at odds with society; half of himself is at odds with the other half. Starting with Dickens and Collins and then accelerating in Hardy, the modern satirical novelist's image for secular life as division and fragmentation develops into one of self-division as both a reflection and root cause of other breakdowns. Passion against reason becomes the rule in nearly all of Huxley's characters throughout his early novels. In Powell, where division is an accomplished fact, characters are walking halves: either they are ineffectual creatures of the imagination or they exhibit relentless will power. Waugh's characters divide neatly into "static" and "dynamic," victims and victimizers in a secular society without adequate restraints.

George Eliot returned to the parodic revaluation of satirists of the Victorian ethos because Dickens, improving upon Collins, had fabricated a prototype for a new satiric metaphor for breakdown, collapse, and disintegration. In *The Mystery of Edwin Drood*, Dickens added the split personality to his panoply of satiric metaphors in *Bleak House* and *Little Dorrit*: life as an interminable law case, or society and one's self as a prison. Adaptations of this new metaphor subsequently proliferated in Hardy, Robert Louis Stevenson, Joseph Conrad, and other early moderns.

Lydgate concedes that the scientific realist, too, travels the thoroughfare of human failure—"anguish," "mania," "crime"; indeed, his listing catalogues the stages of Jasper's disorder. But reasons for such miseries become clearly discernible, and the satisfaction of discernment, Lydgate insists, leaves no room for disapproval, much less general disappointment with life.

The superior realist, George Eliot maintains through Lydgate, does not create or evoke darknesses in order to spread fear or dim hope. Instead, he or she dispels them, as befits a bringer of understanding. Like Lydgate, George Eliot feels obliged to show herself no stranger to "outer darkness" (inner recesses), those long-forgotten events or interior "lurking-places" where, invisibly, frustration, self-delusion, and even crime originate. But again like Lydgate, the scientific sociologist shines an "inward light" upon them, a penetration of more useful intensity than the facile attempts at psychological realism in Collins and Dickens. As George Eliot envisions it, genuine realism absorbs man's shortcomings into the daylight, communal world. It tries to be reconciled with deficiencies that Dickens, extending Collins, promoted into subversive energies capable almost indefinitely of subterfuge and sabotage.

A late-century variation occurs on the tension within Victorian realism between the utopian and the dystopian as realism's leading exponents divide over how to handle life's divisions. Does the novelist better serve community by underlining, perhaps widening, existing gaps to be sure they are recognized? Or is he or she obliged to be a healer who narrows gulfs, possibly even proposes realistic paradigms for bridging them? Opting for the first, Dickens employed imminent divorce throughout *Hard Times* as his metaphor for the widening split between men and masters in industry, Fact and Fancy in British society; Jasper's dual personality in *Edwin Drood* epitomizes division within the self and of the self from community.

George Eliot revalues Dickens by taking up where Mrs. Gaskell left off. The latter joined North and South, business and the aesthetic sensibility, Thornton and Miss Hale. In *Middlemarch* the former tries to cap the union of an artisan and a lady (in *Felix Holt*) through the fusion of Dorothea's spiritual aspirations, the relic of a former dispensation, and Ladislaw's savvy regarding practical reforms in the newly secularized world.

Always society's servant, the Victorian realist saw him- or herself primarily as either a critic who disturbed or a sage who solved. The gap between these roles became virtually identical with that between satires and solutions. George Eliot wanted to elevate the offering of solutions by connecting her concerns with science and sociology; her spokesman in *Middlemarch* is not merely a scientist but a member of the healing profession.

Illumination via "inward light," George Eliot's antidote for the deepening interiority of evil that worried Dickens, has gratuitous religious connotations, as if it were a grace that shines on those afflicted or driven to crime. Mainly, however, this light is not a Rhadamanthine providence but a scientific and sociological force: "the last refinement of Energy." In other words, through the services of the authentic sociological and psychological realist, the community's cohesiveness is shown to be more potent than any "darkness" or void that materializes. The "last refinement of Energy" finds nothing so deep or mysterious that it cannot be corrected to "more exactness of relation." Thus, says Eliot, it is more powerful than the satirical impulse that must cower in despair before the blacknesses it angrily, sensationally, yet helplessly uncovers.

Bulstrode has been called "a serious study of hypocrisy (different in kind from, for instance, Dickens's epitomizing of that quality in Pecksniff)."[8] More accurately, he is George Eliot's revaluative revision of the hypocrites abounding in the later fiction of her melodramatic competitors: Sir Percival Glyde, Mrs. Catherick, and Godfrey Ablewhite in Wilkie Collins, and, principally, John Jasper in Dickens. Eliot believes she must confront the impression one gets from these figures that duplicity is becoming epidemic in Victorian England. She wants to eliminate the argument that such a counter-evolutionary state of affairs exists. Her strategy is to show that an instance of hypocrisy in a community slowly stirring toward reform is neither a product of community nor proof of inextricable evil in human nature and society; it need not amount to catastrophe for the life process.

Middlemarch is set earlier than *The Mystery of Edwin Drood* to preclude it: having the unmasking of Bulstrode take place prior to the Reform Bill is a way of asserting that communities can handle cases of division within the individual self without losing their forward motion. Owing to Bulstrode's fall, *Middlemarch* strikes a somber note toward its close, unlike *Felix Holt*, which ends on an upswing. But it is as if George Eliot were familiar with Dickens's plans for *The Mystery of Edwin Drood* as confided to Forster and is writing, in effect, to rule out the even darker conclusion Dickens might have composed. Collins could not outdo what Dickens had left undone, but Eliot's brand of parodic revaluation still works because she accommodates Dickens's darkest material without having to come to similarly sour conclusions.

It is easy to forget how much of the final third of *Middlemarch* is taken up by Bulstrode's virtual murder of Raffles and his efforts to justify this crime, along with his past transgressions, to himself. As Lydgate struggles against debt and Ladislaw strives to win Dorothea, one must realize that disclosure of the banker's past and society's expulsion of him from its councils are central to the final chapters. Read in light of *The Mystery of Edwin Drood*, *Middlemarch* becomes as much Bulstrode's story as it is Lydgate's or Dorothea's. George Eliot studies the different fates of these three as variations on the theme of self-division.

Dorothea's rebound from Casaubon to successful marriage with Ladislaw, Bulstrode's collapse and expulsion, and Lydgate's quieter but self-enlightening failure are commentaries on the difficulty of keeping one's inner or personal life and one's outer or public role in harmony. The three characters are no longer vital parts of Middlemarch by novel's end, yet they have all been made or broken by it, sent on to larger things or retired from life's fray. This shows, Eliot argues, that nothing has happened to approximate the disaster Jasper constitutes for polite society at Cloisterham.

A murderous choirmaster, harboring a secret self within, symbolizes an inherent duality in human nature, contrary to George Eliot's definition of personality as a continuous opening-outward. A man with a "skeleton" in his closet—the sinister side of Jasper's nature—is Dickens's final satirical metaphor for a life process that remains tragically split between good and evil, that is not evolving constantly toward greater good. Bulstrode's story revalues Jasper's with a psychological portrait that is always more sympathetic. A devoted husband, a supporter of local charities, and an advocate of hospital reform, Bulstrode has good points that persist in his character. Jasper's secret hatred of his nephew nullifies his outwardly avuncular behavior.

George Eliot humanizes Bulstrode to minimize the hypocrisy that Dickens demonized. She dramatizes Bulstrode's losing battles with himself at length and without rancor. Dickens could not have done this with Jasper until the climax in the choirmaster's prison cell—a scene destined to remain unwritten.

Nicholas Bulstrode is not a con man like Pecksniff or Ablewhite, not one of those "coarse hypocrites, who consciously affect beliefs and emotions for the sake of gulling the world" (MM, 453). George Eliot concedes that such persons may exist but apparently doubts it, since Bulstrode is so emphatically "not one of them":

He was simply a man whose desires had been stronger than his theoretic beliefs, and who had *gradually* explained the gratification of his desires into satisfactory agreement with those beliefs. If this be hypocrisy, it is a *process* which shows itself *occasionally* in us all, to whatever confession we belong, and whether we believe in the future perfection of our race or in the nearest date fixed for the end of the world; whether we regard the earth as a putrefying nidus for a saved remnant, including ourselves, or have a passionate belief in the solidarity of mankind. [MM, 453; italics added]

This passage is central to George Eliot's creation of Bulstrode as an anodyne for Jasper. She argues that Bulstrode's wrongdoing is due to human frailty, not to perversity, such frailty also being more complex than sheer malevolence would be. Indeed, she appears to define evil not as an independent force—the rival of goodness in some sort of perennial Manichean split—but as weakness or inadequate goodness. Jasper is hopelessly flawed; Bulstrode, in sharp contrast, is not quite good enough. He is not so much man's fallen nature as a man who falls short, his "desires" proving "stronger than his theoretic beliefs." Even so, he succumbs "gradually," slipping deeper into hypocrisy over the years, rather than erupting dramatically, as happens repeatedly with Jasper when his violent-erotic second self takes control. The difference is between analyzable "process" and unnatural outbreaks that are as unpredictable as an earthquake.

George Eliot pretends to be unsure whether Bulstrode's conduct can be called "hypocrisy." Is it really, she asks Dickens's readers, a virulent component in a new type of man in whose dual personality evil has reached a new pitch in response to an oppressive Victorian society? Or do failings like Bulstrode's, which are truer to life than Jasper's, manifest themselves "occasionally in us all"? Eliot is determined to dismiss Dickens's venture into psychological portraiture as the rantings of an extremist. If "all" men are only occasionally like Bulstrode, they can never resemble Jasper: he is highly exceptional, not a pardonable exaggeration of the universal condition. Bulstrode, says George Eliot, is already such an exaggeration. His personality results from the steady development of tendencies "occasionally in us all," and still he is not the harsh indictment of polite society that Jasper represents. For parodic revaluation to succeed, Bulstrode must seem more intricate than Jasper yet more truly representative.

One should not miss George Eliot's attempt to cancel duplicity as an issue in her debate with Dickens. She caricatures the opposition between her position and his: her confidence in "the future perfection" of the race is pitted against his predictions of imminent apocalypse. His view of earth as purgatory, an unwholesome breeding place ("putrefying nidus") for those few who are destined to enjoy salvation elsewhere collides with her "passionate belief" that redemption lies in increasing "the solidarity of mankind." If the "process" going on in Bulstrode occurs to some extent, but only "occasionally," in utopians and dystopians alike, it cannot be used to validate either frame of mind, hers or Dickens's. Since Dickens tried to use Jasper's duplicity in a way that cannot possibly count, he alone loses by its disqualification as an objection to her world view. The emergence of John Jasper's dual personality in *The Mystery of Edwin Drood* is thrown out as evidence; it is neither here nor there as a detriment to the philosophy of life previously expounded in *Felix Holt.*

The Middlemarch banker is driven to deceit by a mistaken belief in himself as an "instrument of the divine glory" (MM, 453), an agent of providence like the self-appointed Walter Hartright in *The Woman in White* or Dick Datchery, ostensibly the avenging angel in *The Mystery of Edwin Drood.* A kind of self-promotion, sanctioned at times by Dickens and Collins, becomes fundamentally hypocritical in *Middlemarch*, thus a source of the problem rather than a cure. Hartright and Datchery operate with a scrupulosity that George Eliot suggests is unrealistic. Bulstrode, by contrast, reconciles himself to questionable acts because he believes that "his serviceableness to God's cause" must be preserved whatever the cost. He lacks the disinterestedness that Felix Holt and Dorothea Brooke work to acquire before enlisting as lieutenants of reform, society's equivalent for changes in the natural world.

Bulstrode is not done in by an overly uprighteous society whose repressed energies he embodies to assault respectability itself. On the contrary, George Eliot says that hypocrites are usually too righteous for their fellow men: a "saintly Kill-joy" is Mr. Hawley's epithet for Bulstrode; "Pharisee" is the community's (MM, 535, 91). Hypocrites, George Eliot advises Dickens, are rarely victims of a community they have either been denied a role in unjustly (Glyde, Mrs. Catherick) or by which they feel unnaturally constrained (Jasper). Realistically presented, these masters of deception fail their communities, not vice versa. Mistakenly, they set themselves too far above the common lot.

Mr. Vincy accuses Bulstrode of "wanting to play bishop and banker everywhere" (MM, 97). Unlike the drives fueling Jasper's repressed self, this desire to have both monetary and moral say-so is implicitly a vindication of community; it stems from eagerness to earn the respect of society and wield its authority. The deceiver, says George Eliot, does not deserve preeminence but pays tribute to society by yearning for it. Unlike Jasper, Bulstrode does not subvert or undermine his community; that would be self-destructive if he hopes to fatten upon it. Eliot readjusts the vampire imagery that accumulates around Dickens's choirmaster, correcting the idea of the way a double-dealer preys upon the lifeblood of his fellows. Bulstrode's declared purpose in gaining "as much power as possible" is to "use it for the glory of God" (MM, 115). Many "crass minds" in Middlemarch insist that "he must have a sort of vampire's feast in the sense of mastery."

Crassness in Middlemarch means not being convinced of Bulstrode's altruism. The irony indicates that Geoge Eliot writes from the community's point of view, even though she pities the banker and probes his failure sympathetically. Dickens speaks more from Jasper's viewpoint than from the community's. He identifies with the inner dissatisfactions of this outwardly respectable malcontent. In George Eliot's opinion, Bulstrode is not just an unworthy success; he is a burden upon society, not vice versa. Jasper's secret, antisocial self wants to break free of society's restraints but can only doom itself in the process without improving the general condition. George Eliot questions the reality of such an impossible situation from which so little can be gained. She considers Bulstrode oppressive, a restraint Middlemarch must throw off for its own good and for his.

Besides the allusion to vampires, Bulstrode is connected to Jasper by another verbal echo of Dickens's novel: the banker is pictured as a choirmaster presiding over his own shortcomings. As Bulstrode struggles not to wish Raffles dead, George Eliot recounts the "strange piteous conflict in the soul of this unhappy man, who had longed for years to be better than he was—who had taken his selfish passions into discipline and clad them in severe robes, so that he had walked with them as a devout quire, till now that a terror had arisen among them, and they could chant no longer, but threw out their common cries for safety" (MM, 517). Bulstrode's "selfish passions" have been disguised as "a devout quire" of austere practices to deceive Middlemarch. Now, like so many independent selves within him, these passions fear they will perish along with their host when seen for what they really are.

Personifying Bulstrode's failings and making their "clamorings" audible seems rather fanciful and melodramatic. But the image of man's interior as a discordant choir is hardly catastrophic compared with internal revolutions that alternate a respectable choirmaster with a lustful murderer. George Eliot alludes to Jasper's occupation to imply that she, not Dickens, knows what happens when personality disintegrates. Bulstrode's passions savor their virtuous appearance and dread losing it; Jasper's second self finds its coverings necessary but hateful.

The young Bulstrode would have preferred to become a preacher full time. As Mr. Dunkirk's confidential accountant, however, he had to countenance the pawnbroker's receiving of stolen goods. Like Miss Twinkleton, who has "two distinct and separate phases of being" (ED, 53), "Bulstrode found himself carrying on two distinct lives" (MM, 451). Wemmick's solution, in *Great Expectations*, is to lead each life separately. This is also Ablewhite's strategy in *The Moonstone*, although the philanthropist in his case is actually in thrall to the philanderer. Bulstrode discovers that "his religious activity could not be incompatible with his business as soon as he had argued himself into not feeling it incompatible."

Hypocrisy, George Eliot admonishes Dickens, is invariably conscious and voluntary, resulting from an act of the will. The goal of the individual with a dual personality or a double life, she continues, is to make the baser self seem to be serving the nobler, contrary to the unrealistic inversions of this pattern in Ablewhite's case and, more remarkably, in Jasper's, where the darker, inner self wants to assume control. Hypocrisy involves self-deception. In Eliot's opinion, this is its most difficult aspect. Bulstrode is thus truer than Jasper to the way all men sometimes behave, but the degree of self-deception he accomplishes seems harder to duplicate than the choirmaster's split personality, of which the one half need not constantly justify the other. Bulstrode is consequently both more representative than Jasper and less threatening to polite society.

Bulstrode's case reaffirms the rule that whenever one locates a hidden rivalry—revisions of another novelist's themes, characters, or situations—a recurring Victorian anxiety is certain to emerge. The extent of duplicity— also defined as doubleness and hypocrisy, the need for secrecy or a second self to cope with society's demands—was clearly one such cause for concern from 1860 on. It marks a curious beginning for the modern conviction, expressed in a variety of ways by figures as different from each other as Conrad, Freud, and Mrs. Woolf, that man's interiority, his inner life, has more to tell about him than his outward, verbal, conscious self.

Dickens and George Eliot disagree as to whether duality is a criticism society imposes upon itself. Dickens maintains that it is if he can prove that the Victorian social system creates a monster like Jasper or aggravates the perennial split in man's nature between his good and evil impulses. Bulstrode's gradual surrender of principle to selfish passion and the unspectacular manner in which his day of reckoning arrives readily combine to defuse the explosiveness of Jasper's violent-erotic self. The unmasking and downfall of Nicholas Bulstrode scarcely permit George Eliot to claim that life, the human condition, has been gradually getting better from 1832 to 1872; Dorothea's story, the subject of editorializing in the novel's "Finale," does that. Bulstrode is Eliot's way of removing Jasper as an insurmountable, scientifically unfounded obstacle to the more promising outlook the rest of *Middlemarch* conveys.

Opium and an inheritance play parts in Bulstrode's fall from prominence and perhaps in Jasper's. If the choirmaster is Drood's older stepbrother, Edwin's prerogatives should have been his; if Jasper has killed Drood and broods over it whenever he takes opium, the drug might be used to trick him into leading Edwin's friends to the body. Bulstrode marries Dunkirk's widow and then diverts to himself legacies intended for her daughter, who becomes Ladislaw's mother. When Raffles, whom Bulstrode has paid to keep silent about Will's mother's whereabouts, is seriously ill from alcohol poisoning, Bulstrode fails to prevent Mrs. Abel from allowing the sick man brandy in place of the "extremely moderate doses of opium" prescribed by the doctor (MM, 517).

Ladislaw spurns Bulstrode's offer of restitution, and opium is *not* administered—George Eliot reuses drugs and money anticlimactically to parody their melodramatic importance to *The Moonstone* and *The Mystery of Edwin Drood*. Unlike Rachel Verinder in *The Moonstone*, who accepts the accursed diamond her uncle stole, Will wants nothing from a man who has made his fortune disreputably. As easily as that, George Eliot argues, one can disassociate oneself from an unwanted past and any wrongdoing in which a relative was even indirectly involved. Esther Summerson, Arthur

Clennam, and Charles Darnay are made to seem to have agonized excessively.

Opium helps Franklin Blake to redeem himself in *The Moonstone*. In *The Mystery of Edwin Drood*, the lustful murderer within the choirmaster has an addiction that could be manipulated to bring about his detection. But the drug is negated in *Middlemarch;* it is shown to have no control per se over good or evil, no link with either. The crucial moral struggle occurs in Bulstrode's conscience as he tries to decide whether to follow doctor's orders. And Raffles's ravings (about Bulstrode's past) the few times he *is* given opium are less coherent, hence less useful, than Jasper's during his visits to the opium den.

Bulstrode carries on "two distinct lives" throughout the novel: he is outwardly Middlemarch's banker, its most influential citizen, but inwardly he knows himself to be a thief and a fraud. He takes care of Raffles as if from charitable motives, yet he hopes for and finally conspires to gain "deliverance" (MM, 516) through the death of this blackmailer. The extent of Bulstrode's culpability in Raffles's death is questionable but the fact of it is never a question mark, like Jasper's responsibility for Drood's disappearance. Even so, George Eliot constantly makes Bulstrode less sinister than Jasper and easier to sympathize with. She stresses his private anguish, which never permits him a moment's peace. Rosa Bud lives in fear of Jasper; Drood clearly should have. In *Middlemarch*, it is Bulstrode who dreads being "disclosed," who shrinks from becoming "an object of scorn" (MM, 449).

The banker's impression of the newly returned Raffles as "an ugly black spot on the landscape at Stone Court" (MM, 389) tells the modern revaluator how squarely George Eliot has the diminishing of Jasper's villainousness in mind. This description recalls Rosa's abhorrence for her tutor, who leans against the sundial at the Nuns' House, "setting, as it were, his black mark upon the very face of day" (ED, 228). The banker is not less odious than Jasper makes himself in the garden scene but seems less harmful because, in the interview at Stone Court, he is the persecuted instead of the persecutor.

When first cornered by Raffles, Bulstrode experiences severe shock. His "usual paleness" takes on "an almost deathly hue," and his impression of the world alters: "Five minutes before, the expanse of his life had been submerged in its evening sunshine"; now, Raffles blocks out the sun (MM, 384). George Eliot wants to rewrite more realistically the scenes in which Jasper's darker self materializes. At such moments the choirmaster-murderer suffers severe changes: bodily rigidity, heavy perspiration, "a sharp catch of his breath" (ED, 47). Although hardly as grotesque as the shifts from Jekyll to Hyde, Jasper's transformation is far more traumatic than Bulstrode's and totally incredible in Eliot's opinion.

George Eliot parodies the outlandish idea that the closet a skeleton comes out of is the innermost recess of the self. She uses Raffles as an externalization of what Dickens overly internalized. The advent of the blackmailer does not merely cause more believable alteration in Bulstrode than Drood brings on for Jasper; it also discredits the notion that the skeleton in the closet is a recalcitrant impulse toward evil buried deeply within every man and likely to transform his world into a personal hell at any moment. Had Raffles not appeared, Bulstrode would never have experienced that eclipse of the sun. Eliot is determined to rule out the crescendo of catastrophes with which *The Mystery of Edwin Drood* apparently would have concluded; she redoes, as it were, the sensational scenes Dickens previewed in the letter he wrote John Forster about the outcome of his novel.[9] *Middlemarch* is a parody of Dickens's unfinished work in that Bulstrode's story finishes it for him but in a way very different from what he apparently intended.

Bulstrode has Raffles removed to prevent "the mournful perception" of "certain facts of his past life" (MM, 449) by his fellow citizens. But the drunkard's death is gradual, the result of conscious omission rather than commission. Then the "haunting ghost" of Bulstrode's past, the skeleton in his closet, comes out anyway—not with a bound but virtually by accident, after Bulstrode has already decided the danger is over. When Bambridge went to nearby Bilkley to purchase a gig-horse, he heard "a fine story about Bulstrode" from "an old chum" of the banker's named Raffles (MM, 525). Having just returned to Middlemarch and not yet aware that Raffles is dead and buried, he is reminded of the story only when his acquaintances observe Bulstrode riding by.

Instead of involving an action-packed capture sequence, possibly including Jasper's being chased to the top of the cathedral tower, the suspense in George Eliot's redoing is mostly mental, a matter of gauging emotional tensions and registering a cruel irony. Bulstrode unwittingly comes to a meeting called to cope with an outbreak of cholera; his accusers denounce him publicly and remove him from all civic commissions. His soiled past is proclaimed during a "sanitary meeting" (MM, 536), at which the community cleanses itself of his presence.

In *Edwin Drood*, the focus would be on Jasper's pursuers as they expunge him from their midst; the mental state of the choirmaster-murderer's double personality would not be studied in depth until he is locked up and his suppressed self relives the murder. George Eliot not only records the mixed motives of Middlemarch residents as they topple the man who has unjustifiably behaved like a lord over them; she also concentrates on the confusion, both physical and internal, of the denounced man. She stipulates that the banker's fall from prominence blend pathos with tragedy while excluding the sensation of terror; it must be piteous as well as a purging, the cornering of a man who is *not* a monster.

Once Bulstrode forced his business for Dunkirk into compatibility with his religion, "the train of causes in which he had locked himself" simply "went on" (MM, 451). George Eliot's "train of causes" sounds like Marian Halcombe's "conviction of an unseen design in the long series of complications" that have "fastened round" her and Laura Fairlie (WW, 305). Actually, it is very different from providential supervision; it is secular, less mysterious, and furnishes proof of Eliot's wisdom in relying on ordinary rather than exceptional causation—on gradualism rather than sudden disaster or extraterrestrial interference—to explain how life works.

Years pass between the payoff and the moment when Raffles, back from America, spies Bulstrode's signature on a "folded paper" (MM, 304), and decides to blackmail the man who once bought his silence. This is how "The Dead Hand" of the past reaches into the present, says George Eliot. It happens in a roundabout way, without "unseen design" or a "long series" of complications. To discredit Dickens's melodramatics, she intentionally overdoes it in the opposite direction: her causation is so ordinary and coincidental as to become a parody of uncommonness.

Lady Dedlock's agitation at the sight of Hawdon's handwriting on one of Tulkinghorn's documents is the sensational antecedent in *Bleak House* that George Eliot rewrites. It is Bulstrode, not the novelist, who goes in for resurrection imagery: he complains that his past has "risen" into a "second life" (MM, 450). But the return of Bulstrode's past is deliberately not on a par with Dr. Manette's summons back to life in *A Tale of Two Cities*, nor are the consequences of a "folded paper" meant to match the retribution that overtakes the St. Evrémondes, in the person of Darnay, from the letter Manette wrote about their crimes while he was prisoner in the Bastille.

The introduction of Hawdon's script spells disaster for Lady Dedlock; it leads to exposure of her secret, then to disgrace and death. When Defarge produces Manette's letter, it causes a sensation. The revolutionary court has to impose the death sentence. Raffles picks up the paper to wedge the glass of his flask firmly into its leather covering, enabling George Eliot to put Bulstrode's resurrection imagery in sharp contrast to the commonplace causes of his downfall. As Bulstrode becomes more pitiable and the explanation of his unmasking unremarkable, Jasper is supposed to disappear as a challenge to gradualism, evolution, and the inevitability of progressive reform—three associated ideas in Eliot's philosophy. She distinguishes Bulstrode's misfortunes from those of Lady Dedlock, Darnay, and Dr. Manette to broaden her parody of Dickens's fondness for catastrophes.

The novelist's finest moment as a revaluator of *The Mystery of Edwin Drood* is her revision of Dickens's projected scene in "the condemned cell," where Jasper would recount the murder "as if" another person had committed it.[10] At first, George Eliot appears to omit a comparable scene entirely, so understated is her reworking of Dickens's contemplated climax. But her lower-case version parodies Jasper's confession scene by leaving out every sensational element Dickens would have exploited, including the actual confession, and concentrates on pathos and understanding instead. Being anticlimactic is her final way of being anticatastrophic.

Returning home from the public meeting, Bulstrode enters his version of a prison cell by "shutting himself up in his private room" (MM, 546), declining the company of his unsuspecting wife and daughters, none of whom has witnessed his disgrace. The final pages of Chapter 74, among the best in the novel, contain no shattering moments of epiphanic self-discovery, no head-on confrontations. When Mrs. Bulstrode finally learns of Nicholas's "odious deceit," she enters his room and rests "her hands and eyes . . . gently on him." He bursts out crying, and the author tersely relates that "they cried together" (MM, 550). Mrs. Bulstrode longs to be told the charges are "only slander and false suspicion," and he would like to say "I am innocent" (MM, 551), but both realize this is impossible. Bulstrode's "confession was silent"; so too is his wife's "promise of faithfulness." Ultimately, it is Dickens's satire and sensationalism that George Eliot wishes to silence. His view of hypocrisy as proof of an ineradicable duality in human nature is overruled by her portrait of the contrite Bulstrode as a crushed hypocrite, a portrait that is almost tender.

Surveying three cases of the divided self, George Eliot maintains, is more scientific than generalizing from one extreme instance. The two other major figures in *Middlemarch*, Dr. Lydgate and Dorothea Brooke, experience problems with self-integration, but their fate is kinder than Bulstrode's and thus appears designed to make Jasper's even more inconceivable; Dickens's choirmaster-murderer exists well beyond the outer limits that Eliot uses Bulstrode to establish. Man's dual nature, it follows, is not the all-encompassing anti-evolutionary dilemma that Dickens considered it. Studying duality in triplicate suggests to George Eliot that all Victorians, as proto-moderns, may be plagued by self-division to some degree, but none to the extent that Jasper is.

Initially, Dorothea cannot find in the real world a mission exalting enough to satisfy her aspiring soul or inner self. At the root of her character lies a timeless yet acutely Victorian problem: she cannot connect her spiritual life with her earthly existence. As crumbling orthodoxies increase the gap between spiritual and secular, George Eliot realized, the latter must not be made to seem banal and pointless. Dorothea, she observes, "could not reconcile the anxieties of a spiritual life involving eternal consequences, with a keen interest in guimp and artificial protrusions of drapery. Her mind was theoretic, and yearned by its nature after some lofty conception of the world which might frankly include the parish of Tipton and her own rule of conduct there; she was enamoured of intensity and greatness, and rash in embracing whatever seemed to her to have those aspects" (MM, 6). Miss Brooke's dilemma is a parodic variation on Jasper's warning to Drood about the consequences of "a daily drudging round" (ED, 48).

Redoing Jasper's bitter frustrations as the romantic yearnings of a young, inexperienced girl deprives his discontent of much of its meta-physical impact. His is a common complaint, says George Eliot, and not impossible to cure—which is very different from presenting it as a peren-nial quandary, a burden upon all of Adam's children. Her argument is complicated but not self-contradictory: Jasper suffers from a common complaint that Dickens allegedly diagnoses so unrealistically that the choirmaster becomes not just exceptional but incredible.

George Eliot believes that Dorothea's dissatisfaction with Mid-dlemarch is largely her own fault, the result of a failure in perception. The novelist proceeds to prove this by subtly enhancing, one could say roman-ticizing, events and locales at first trivial and unappealing to her heroine. Dorothea avoids becoming a second Madame Bovary by learning to recog-nize the legitimate opportunities offered by her spot in time and space. Expecting life to conform to one's personal designs for achieving sainthood, instead of putting oneself into harmony with its rhythms and patterns, emerges as a variation on Bulstrode's view of himself as God's chosen instrument. It is not unlike Dickens's disdain for a world that is neither as perfect as he would prefer nor improving as rapidly as he wishes. That such ridiculous expectation, if unrevised, might lead to disappointment and catastrophe, Eliot concedes, is hardly surprising; it is not, however, an indictment of the human condition so much as a failure to understand ordinary life and the genuine possibilities it still offers in a secular, scien-tific age.

To elevate "arduous invention"—in effect, a definition of realism—over Dickens's satiric imagination, George Eliot reworks in *Middlemarch* several scenes and situations from his earlier novels, *Bleak House* especially. These revaluations take place concurrently with Dorothea's conversion, her progression from outmoded ideals to an appreciation of a profane world that needs her assistance. Revaluation and conversion, the latter in itself a revaluation of temporal existence, combine to Dickens's disadvantage: both support the case for Dorothea's growth and development in contrast to Jasper's disintegration.

In all instances where George Eliot attacks Dickens, she wants to narrow the gap between "spiritual life" or "eternal consequences" and daily rules of conduct for Tipton parish. Rewriting selected pieces from the Dickens canon, bringing together her rival's earlier and later errors, re-emphasizes her overall cancellation of dichotomies: wrong before, Dickens cannot be another dichotomy by being correct now. Eliot finds Boz either too cynical and satirical to be realistic or else grossly sentimental—seemingly opposite failings (another superficial dichotomy) that stem from his reluctance sufficiently to admire life as found.

Dorothea's "lofty conception of the world," utopian and impractical, reflects Louisa Gradgrind's "struggling disposition to believe in a wider and nobler humanity than she had ever heard of" (HT, 127). Initially, Dorothea is on the side of Sissy Jupe and the adherents of Fancy, but George Eliot strongly disapproves. Miss Brooke's imagination is always ahead of the facts, which is not how "arduous invention" (realism) works. For Eliot, the fanciful are idle dilettantes whose dissatisfaction, an end in itself, never takes life forward. Thus Mr. Brooke and Sir James must curtail Dorothea's enthusiasm for building tenants' cottages by reminding her that she knows nothing of economics.

A fox-hunting man, Mr. Brooke warns Dorothea that her enthusiasms "may carry [her] too far—over the hedge in fact." His reminder that "life isn't cast in a mould—not cut out by rule and line" (MM, 12-13,30) makes him thoroughly non-Gradgrindian. George Eliot rewrites a scene from *Hard Times* in which the father-villain personifies a ruthless practicality, while Louisa, his daughter, senses within herself a suppressed capacity for imaginative life and warm physical relationships. Dorothea's uncle objects to all molds which the mind imposes upon life, including unrealistic romantic frameworks that can be as confining as Utilitarian ones. His warning ought to have deterred Dorothea from a marriage generated by religious-romantic fantasies that proves as cold as Louisa's. In *Middlemarch*, the equivalent of fact accumulation and dry-as-dust statistics is a classi-cist—Dorothea's first husband—whose studies of mythologies have no practical bearing on the problems that secularized society faces.

To George Eliot, Dorothea's case seems more realistic than that of a healthy young girl frustrated by parental Benthamism. Fancy is something that Dorothea must integrate with real life and fruitfully utilize, just as

Dickens needs to curb his much too vivid imagination. Mr. Brooke's cautionary words undermine the Shelleyan pursuit of false universals in *Middlemarch*: Dorothea's for a vague ideal or too lofty conception, Casaubon's for the key to all mythologies, perhaps even Lydgate's for the primary tissue. These pursuits are misguided efforts to find in the extremely relative temporal world equivalents for the vanishing general truths once inculcated by the major religions.

Since the imagery associated with Dorothea's spiritual aspirations always comes from religion and the Bible, she is attracted to Casaubon, a writer of religious history. Unfortunately, she does not see him any more clearly than Emma Bovary initially sees Charles. Dorothea describes her future husband, who is quite ugly, as a "modern Augustine" and decides that living with him would be "like marrying Pascal." From the moment she confesses that she would like to have married Milton, one knows she will accept Casaubon: he has bad eyes. "The really delightful marriage," Dorothea reflects, "must be that where your husband was a sort of father, and could teach you even Hebrew, if you wished it" (MM, 8). George Eliot's deluded heroine can envision her husband only in terms reserved for God; she is linked mock-heroically with the Virgin, and the marriage she longs to duplicate—including the Hebrew tutorial—is not unlike the one heralded by the Annunciation.

Regrettably for Dorothea, Casaubon is constantly associated with death.[11] His classicism, like her aspiring romanticism, is left over from another age. Their marriage parodies the symbolic fusion of eras and temperaments that Goethe achieved by wedding Faust to Helen. Externally, Casaubon classifies scholarly material; internally, cut off from life, he resides in the tomb of his own self-doubt. He begins to rely on Dorothea only when his physical death is imminent; ironically, he starts to emerge from the grave shortly before his death. This abortive resurrection, a negative comment on the sensational recalls to life received by Laura Fairlie and Dr. Manette, unsatisfactorily approximates the godlike capabilities with which Dorothea foolishly invests him. Casaubon expresses the hope that his key to mythologies, hardly the document required for a time of impending social change, will stand as a "tomb" (MM, 362) to his memory.

When Will Ladislaw's artist-friend asks Casaubon to pose for a painting of the head of Thomas Aquinas, nothing could have pleased Dorothea more, George Eliot notes, "unless it had been a miraculous voice pronouncing Mr. Casaubon the wisest and worthiest among the sons of men" (MM, 159). Dorothea hopes for a repetition of the biblical scene in which the heavens open and God pronounces Himself well pleased with His Son. Parodies of biblical scenes in *Middlemarch* do not merely satirize Dorothea's delusions; they firmly separate the real Victorian world, in which one must live and toil, from poetic accounts of past eras, when interpenetration of temporal and supernatural was evidently still credible. Eliot also parodies the biblicist in Dickens for masquerading as a scientific sociologist. His novels, she implies, teem with the kind of scene Dorothea is laughed at for imagining. Confronted with a secularized world, George Eliot tries not to equivocate as noticeably as Dickens sometimes did; she expresses her preference for what remains and is to come over what has been lost.[12]

The 1830s, in which *Middlemarch* is set, and the 1870s, when it was published, were the two decades of the nineteenth century most synonymous with reform. The events of these decades were real and challenging for George Eliot; partings of the heavens and annunciations were not. Unlike Evelyn Waugh's novels, in which the profane world becomes a parody of its formerly more religious self, *Middlemarch* parodies the sacred to enhance the secular. Life's unwillingness to duplicate scenes from the New Testament compromises the relevance of that text; the real world is not discredited.

Dickens successively commissioned Pickwick, Oliver, and Nell as Principles of Good, thereby endowing them and their opposition with cosmic alignment. He wished to determine whether the pseudoreligious qualities they personified had any survival value in an increasingly corrupt secular world. George Eliot responded with anti-Dickensian experiments conducted in novels she considered more relevant, hence more realistic. She wished to determine whether a Dorothea Brooke could convert nebulous romantic longings, pseudoreligious qualities, into the practical activities a secular, confining, but improvable society demanded.

The central event in the widowed Dorothea's reorientation is her love for Will Ladislaw. Although Will commences as a somewhat shiftless Romantic, he becomes a useful, if minor, advocate of reform. At first, Will is waiting for some indication of what profession to choose. Genius, Ladislaw says (in a prosaic paraphrase of Wordsworth's "wise passiveness"), "may confidently await those messages from the universe which summon it to its peculiar work, only placing itself in an attitude of receptivity" (MM, 61). The link between Casaubon and Dorothea is a mutual desire for the dead past, but Dorothea and Will discover in each other a mutual appreciation for current life and future prospects. Ladislaw's summons comes jointly from society and Dorothea; there are no climactic equivalents of the Annunciation for him either.

No longer a case of aspiration without suitable purpose, Dorothea furnishes Ladislaw with stability, and he awakens in her a practical emotional life. Dorothea moves from transcendental to more secular concerns, from the "vividly imaginative" life of a Sissy Jupe to a more commonplace yet exhilarating existence based on untiring individual effort. Will and Dorothea help to unfold each other's personality as efficaciously as Adam Bede and Dinah Morris, or Felix Holt and Esther Lyon. Each furnishes the other with character traits necessary for betterment and completion—unlike the uncle who seems to have strangled his nephew in *Edwin Drood*. What Adam Bede called sincere converse[13] remains a necessary concomitant of the evolution of character.

When Dorothea defends Lydgate against the charge that he conspired with Bulstrode in the death of Raffles, and gives the doctor enough money to erase the debt that ties him to the banker, she performs a generous action that is frankly monetary and more practical than the good deeds Dickens's ministerial angels perform for their consort-patients. More demonstrably than Esther Summerson, Dorothea is filled with "the idea of some active good within her reach": "There is nothing better that I can do in the world," she remarks (MM, 559). Unlike Sydney Carton's "far, far better thing," her decision is not melodramatic, and it is definitely this-world oriented. Lydgate concludes that Dorothea "has a heart large enough for the Virgin Mary" (MM, 563). Her association with the Virgin, like her resemblance to Saint Theresa, is taken seriously once she has scaled down or secularized her grandiose expectations; that is, once she has stopped complaining, as a satirist might, and become involved.

For George Eliot, the extravagant hopes an exemplary Victorian must guard against are generally spiritual, not monetary. Believing one is on an errand from God or that one merits providence's undivided attention—these aberrations form the truly unrealistic mentality in a progressively secular age, not the comparatively minor mistake, on Pip's part, of confusing wealth with gentility.

Dorothea's new concern for the world around her prompts her to study economics, and interest in this discipline signals her liberation from the impractical. It also takes the story of Dorothea's development strikingly in the opposite direction from that of Louisa and Tom Gradgrind, or from J. S. Mill's and Teufelsdröckh's. To her capacity for feeling (formerly wasted on airy enthusiasms), Dorothea adds a working knowledge of things. Fortunately, opting for the facts of daily life in place of poetry brings a heightened sense of the latter as well. Looking out the window at Lowick, Dorothea notices "on the road . . a man with a bundle on his back and a woman carrying her baby; in the field she could see figures moving—perhaps the shepherd with his dog. Far off in the bending sky was the pearly light; and she felt the largeness of the world and the manifold wakings of men to labour and endurance. She was a part of that involuntary palpitating life, and could neither look out on it from her luxurious shelter as a mere spectator, nor hide her eyes in selfish complaining" (MM, 578). Her eyes are no longer as bad as Casaubon's and clearly much superior to Mrs. Jellyby's. Dorothea observes and accepts what George Eliot extols as the romance of real life.

Vital words here are "largeness" and "manifold." Stripped of its metaphysical extension, the world becomes larger, not smaller. "Labour and endurance" become agreeable values, quite modern ones in fact, but not absolutes or consolations. Dorothea considers herself at one with the world in a sense that is provisionally Wordsworthian but also entails a reformer's involvement. The "luxurious shelter" she abandons is not merely the tranquil life she has led up to this point; it is also the veil of disengagement that the unfounded idealism of a "mere spectator" can place between the self and life's remediable ills. It is admittedly a mundane, low-key epiphany, but that is its point.

Dorothea's name means "gift of God." As for Stephen Dedalus, another convert to profane beauty, the clue to vocation is in the name all along. James Joyce's young hero will transubstantiate life into art; Dorothea will change the bad or insufficient into workable good. She need not look beyond her own inestimable abilities for proof that this world and human endeavor were made for each other—the truest of the marriages in the book, one that makes Dorothea's suitability for Lydgate irrelevant. A novel expressing greater confidence in the efficacy of human effort is difficult to imagine. Although the day of supernatural revelations is over, the life process remains benevolent: Dorothea is Will's summons from the universe and he is hers.

By mentioning the scene's "palpitating life," Dorothea reveals how much of Ladislaw's Romantic outlook she has incorporated. The palpitations, however, are "involuntary," not indications that Nature is God's living garment. What happens to the pulsations of a world now seen to be excitingly alive is strictly up to human determination. One of the day's "manifold wakings" has been Dorothea's. Less climactic than the Ancient Mariner's blessing of the water snakes or Carlyle's progression from indifference to affirmation in *Sartor Resartus*, the passage stands as another Victorian experience of conversion, one that in both mood and content rebuffs the social satirist in Dickens.

The passage is also an amazing blend of modern and Victorian elements. It marks the birth of Dorothea's social consciousness and thus of a good Victorian. It also pinpoints an important stage in the modern triumph of secularity. By adapting Wordsworth to a new set of circumstances, it voices an acceptance of life that empowers the Victorian Sibyl to talk back to the greatest Victorian Sage: Dorothea's yea-saying, unlike Carlyle's, confirms the value of work without positing an invisible spiritual reality which the material phenomena of the world conspire to conceal.

At the end of a Dickens novel, a character like Oliver Twist comes into his inheritance; Dorothea forsakes hers to marry Will. Ignoring the boundaries set for her by the restrictions in Casaubon's codicil, she forgoes outmoded ideals and a guaranteed income to commit herself to the life process here and now. The better it becomes, the better will be the quality of her life. Dorothea comes into her true inheritance: she inherits the earth. As George Eliot modifies Wordsworth and rebukes Dickens, she also rewrites the Beatitudes: the committed and the aware are earth's true heirs, unlike Oliver, who will forfeit his legacy if he is sullied by too much contact with the world.

George Eliot is determined to have the last word on the phenomenology of inheritance, even refurbishing Mrs. Gaskell's conclusion to *North and South*, in which Margaret Hale gives her legacy from Mr. Bell—a dilettante rivaling Casaubon—to Mr. Thornton for modernization of his factory. Unlike Sir Percival Glyde in *The Woman in White* and the almsmen of Hiram's Hospital in *The Warden*, who want more, Dorothea learns that it is more important to leave something to posterity, to make some improvement in the quality of life, than to come into money.

Although a secular experience, inheriting money can have religious overtones in Victorian novels, as if the legatee were being received into his or her kingdom. But cultural transmission, the passing on in improved form of the best that has been thought and done, is more in keeping with an age of progressive, evolving reform. Dorothea's behavior doubly discredits the fictions of Dickens and Collins. Giving up Casaubon's legacy, she reaffirms Esther Lyon's decision to decline the Transome estate in favor of marriage to an artisan-activist. But Dorothea is not above using money to assist others, as when she erases Lydgate's indebtedness to Bulstrode. Like Mrs. Gaskell, George Eliot sees money not as the root of all evils in Victorian society but a means of providing comfort and dignity to others and achieving one's autonomy.

It is inconsequential, therefore, whether Fred Vincy, would-be owner of Stone Court, comes in for disappointments. True good fortune lies in the mutually advantageous exchange of personality traits, which is facilitated by the wealth of evolutionary energy on deposit in any community where social intercourse proceeds the way George Eliot believes it can. Ladislaw has no use for the bequest Bulstrode has kept from him, having concluded earlier that "to have within him such a feeling as he had towards Dorothea was like the inheritance of a fortune (MM, 344)."

In *Bleak House*, Esther Summerson is providentially spared marriage to Mr. Jarndyce to wed instead the capable doctor, Allan Woodcourt. Reworking this situation, George Eliot insists on the January- May marriage, then refuses to allow Lydgate to duplicate Woodcourt's role. Like many of the marriages in Dickens, however, Dorothea's have a symbolic aspect. Her shift from a mythologist husband, preoccupied with worn-out creeds, to a reformer husband involved in the needs of the present is a progression that George Eliot herself made intellectually in her views on religion and morals. She seems to recommend this progression to Dickens and her century. The new humanism of duty and practical concerns offers few transcendent goals but provides greater opportunity for individual development. The medium for "ardent deeds" is "for ever gone" (MM, 612); the medium for "arduous" ones, in literature as well as life, remains.

For all its occasional approximations of modernity, therefore, *Middlemarch* is chiefly a nineteenth-century novel, an optimum restatement of Victorian humanism that flies in the face of Dickens's increasing doubts about the redeemability of human nature. Its author possesses a distinctly Victorian sensibility. Her confidence in social relations and the advancement of society exceeds that of Mrs. Gaskell, Dickens's earlier rival on this score, and makes George Eliot less anticipatory of the modern discontent than Dickens and Collins, both of whom she parodies for being unrealistic: that is, gloomy and old-fashioned.

In George Eliot's rather romantic "Finale," a very practical Romanticism is meant to contrast sharply with the tale of Saint Theresa in the "Prelude." The author attempts a significant revision of Gray's "Elegy," which in turn leads to another assault on Dickens. The narrator asserts that "the growing good of the world is partly dependent on unhistoric acts." If things are "not so ill . . as they might have been," Eliot concludes, it is "half owing to the number who lived faithfully a hidden life, and rest in unvisited tombs" (MM, 613).

Reformers of Will's and Dorothea's caliber may not be in the same class with Mill, Bentham, Carlyle, and Ruskin, but they are equally important. They are neither mute and inglorious nor obscure, in Hardy's pessimistic use of the word, because the life process benefits from their exertions. Wordsworth maintained that the finest portion of a man's life consists of his unremembered acts of kindness and love. George Eliot's reference to "unhistoric acts" indicates that she still believes him. She rejects the Carlylean adage that history is exclusively a record of the deeds of great men and enlists Wordsworth in the cause of social activism. Pushing Gray and Carlyle aside, she reaffirms the Romantic splendor inherent in familiar things, annexes to it a Victorian sense of duty, and thus adapts the Romantic Laureate to the needs of the new humanism.[14]

Dickens's attitude toward Wordsworth also had its reformist thrust. The message of *Bleak House* and *Lyrical Ballads*, especially "We Are Seven," is basically the same: life, Dickens argues, is a matter of perception; most separations, seen correctly, are an illusion, a question of correcting one's point of view. But Dickens's version of Wordsworth, once his favorite nineteenth-century poet, was sour and embittered by the 1850s, the irony hard and caustic. It requires a minor plague from Tom-all-alone's to prove Wordsworth right in *Bleak House*. Twenty years later, however, George Eliot finds Wordsworth still easy to apply; indeed, she works to rescue him from Dickens's parodic usage.

Despite some hedging ("not so ill," "half owing," "partly dependent"), the "hidden life" Dorothea and Will elect is a viable alternative to Matthew Arnold's discontent with a "buried life" and Dorothea's initially sheltered one. Burial is a definite motif in *Middlemarch*, but ways of avoiding it prematurely or being reconciled to it at last seem numerous. When Dorothea announces her intention to marry Casaubon, Ladislaw warns that she will be "shut up in that stone prison at Lowick" and "buried alive" (MM, 163)—like Dickens's Doctor Manette, but only because she misunderstands historical process, not because she is swept up in it. Although the prophecy proves correct, Dorothea experiences resurrection and is recalled to a useful life. By contrast, Casaubon is entombed once and for all, while Manette, after being liberated, is never free from the shades of the prison-house. Only those who are converted to the reform cause, George Eliot suggests, act like the saved and and rise providentially from the dead to lead a second, more productive life.

Dorothea and Will live in a time when secular is displacing sacred, when oncoming reforms promise a future different from the past. Yet they do not walk with Arnold between two worlds, "one dead, the other powerless to be born."[15] On the contrary, they are part of a new dispensation welcome to them both: together, they are responsible for keeping the world's heart beating.

When Nell dies in *The Old Curiosity Shop*, Dickens is perplexed by the problem death poses in a secularized world deprived of its confidence in the life to come. He searches for some way to be secularly satisfied and religiously consoled. By writing Nell's death as a kind of Nativity,[16] he implies that death may be the means of rebirth into a better world but is spared the necessity of saying so. The reverse of George Eliot, Dickens tries to Christianize secularity. For once it is he, not his archrival, who tries

to minimize a split, avoid a dichotomy. He employs a religious aura
sentimentally in order to make the secular world bearable, in order to
attribute to it a metaphysical significance it can no longer expressly claim.

As Joyce does throughout *A Portrait of the Artist as a Young Man*, George
Eliot often uses a Christian aura that seems similar to the one Dickens
employs. But again like Joyce, she distinctly secularizes Christianity.
Dorothea will be an uncanonized, secular saint of the new humanism, just
as Dedalus, who chooses to become an artist instead of a Jesuit, can be
called a priest of the imagination. Eliot turns her readers from the absolute
toward a bright new world of unlimited development through personal
effort. Dickens does not want readers to lose sight of the absolute.

Resurrection is still possible in George Eliot's world, if taken to mean
reorientation of one's life from outmoded to more practical concerns.
Annunciations still call the receptive, but to worldly vocations, secular
apostolates. In *Little Dorrit*, Dickens sends Amy and Arthur Clennam
down into the roaring streets of London with little hope that they will be
leaven enough to influence the social chaos. George Eliot dispatches Will
and Dorothea from Middlemarch confident that reform or reformation will
go forward. For her it is another acceptably secular revision of a religious
phenomenon.

Unhappy with the life process, the satirist in Dickens always paves the
way for the sentimentalist, George Eliot charges. The famous passage
spoken by the schoolmaster is an attempt to ensure some kind of immortality first for the little scholar and subsequently for Little Nell:

There is nothing. . . no, nothing innocent or good, that dies, and is forgotten. Let
us hold to that faith, or none. An infant, a prattling child, dying in its cradle, will
live again in the better thoughts of those who loved it; and play its part, through
them, in the redeeming actions of the world, though its body be burnt to ashes or
drowned in the deepest sea. There is not an angel added to the Host of Heaven but
does its blessed work on earth in those that loved it here. Forgotten! oh, if the good
deeds of human creatures could be traced to their source, how beautifully would
even death appear; for how much charity, mercy, and purified affection, would be
seen to have their growth in dusty graves![17]

The "dusty graves" Dickens mentions may well have been in George
Eliot's mind when she described the final resting places of Will and
Dorothea. Both novelists are concerned with "redeeming actions" and the
possibility of exerting influence from beyond the grave in a secular age, but
George Eliot rejects the notion that idle innocence exercises any power for
good. Experience, she insists, is the only ticket. She ridicules Dickens's
treatment of Nell on grounds that one does good before one's death, not

after. Nell goes to her grave and then good deeds transpire, a clear instance of *hysteron proteron*. Will and Dorothea do good and then take an earned rest. Once they die, they are very dead indeed; however, Eliot hastens to add, the good they do is not interred with their bones. Will and Dorothea are immortal in that the benefits they conferred upon society survive long after they themselves are forgotten. Except for sentimentalists, who expect too much too soon, that is said to be immortality enough.

The society George Eliot envisions will be a better place for the persons in it even though they have no personal recollection of the Ladislaws. Saintly though they were, George Eliot stubbornly refuses them the personal immortality that canonization in the minds of others would bring. Mindful of a workable life process and characters whose personalities unfold, she need not cater to the individual ego. She must have secular saints, no matter how obscure, to confirm her judgment that Victorian humanism offers as many job opportunities as did the old orthodoxies; nevertheless, the influence such saints exert must be impersonal, or they become cult figures—like Nell—and detract from one's trust in the cumulative effect of unhistoric acts.

In *To the Lighthouse*, Mrs. Ramsay, even after her death, is so important a part of Lily Briscoe's moral consciousness that the latter woman seems to become the former and vice versa. The late Mrs. Moore, in *A Passage to India*, exercises a beneficial influence upon Dr. Assiz and also seems to attain a permanent position in Godbole's stream of consciousness. Like Virginia Woolf and E.M. Forster, Dickens needs secular saints as compensatory substitutes for all that has been lost; they help him to make the profane modern world more sacred, just as a diabolical Jasper heightens the need for a providential agency to purge the community.

When Dickens tries to make the secular more Christian and George Eliot secularizes Christianity, they come at times surprisingly close to doing the same thing: making life better than it is. At such times, both behave in ways the modern satirical novelist cannot tolerate. Dickens to the contrary, Aldous Huxley and Evelyn Waugh rule out intercession by Christlike children,[18] and the parade of heartless *femmes fatales* in their novels debunks intervention by adult angelic women, whether Dickens's Agnes, George Eliot's Dorothea, or Bloomsbury's pseudomystical pantheon of Mrs. Ramsay, Mrs. Wilcox (in *Howard's End*) and Mrs. Moore.

What looks similar to the modern satirical novelist, however, seemed a crucial difference to George Eliot. Her secularity betrays her utopian bent, whereas Dickens's vestigal Christianity often glosses over a deepening pessimism. In Eliot's opinion, Dickens's recourse to unrealistic secular saints and demonic villains is proof of the "general discontent with the universe" (MM, 473) that identifies writers of his ilk as humanists gone awry; he finds it too hard to restrict the outcome or consequences of human acts to this world. In moving from lofty conceptions to practical economics, from Carton's "better thing" to betterments nearer at hand, from Oliver's inheritance to the transmission of a richer earthly existence, George Eliot experiences little of Dickens's difficulty with temporal finality. Such transfers, besides involving parodies of scenes from Dickens's novels, eliminate the dichotomy of heaven and earth by turning away from the former. More important, as evidence for the "growing good of the world," they bolster Eliot's cancellation of Jasper's dislike for his confining daily round and thus negate the resulting separation of his inner from his outer self.

If Dorothea is George Eliot's model for success, Lydgate is her story of how not to do it. The new Middlemarch doctor consistently fails to apply his scientific ideals to everyday life; he cannot bring his outer and inner worlds together. Lydgate never matures as a medical reformer because his public and private lives are constantly at odds: "that distinction of mind which belonged to his intellectual ardour, did not penetrate his feeling and judgement about furniture and women (MM, 111)." Dorothea requires a public outlet for her native acuity, whereas Lydgate cannot use privately his professional acumen.

In neither case is duality as painful for the individual or as disastrous for the community as the division within Jasper. By adding Lydgate's story to Dorothea's, however, George Eliot admits that it may be harder to apply professional skills to private life than to translate misdirected private aspiration into lasting social achievements. Still, like the creation of Bulstrode, this concession makes Jasper's disappointments—his frustration with Rosa Bud fueling his despondency as cathedral choirmaster—seem an unpardonable exaggeration. *Middlemarch*, one can argue, revaluates *The Mystery of Edwin Drood* by means of progressive concessions. Dichotomy can develop between inner needs and external possibilities, but Dorothea solves the problem, Lydgate fails to, and Bulstrode refuses to. Eliot follows the account of Bulstrode's downfall with the conclusion to Lydgate's story and the "Finale" for Dorothea's. Having confronted the worst without becoming Dickensian, the author escorts her readers back up the scale of humanistic possibility as if returning from the borderlines of fabrication to the realm of fact.

From the time Lydgate pursues Laure, a French actress, until his marriage to Rosamond, he is conscious of having "two selves within him" (MM, 113): the public self is a careful, scientific researcher; the more private self is emotionally impulsive, a poor judge of character. The second makes Lydgate "prone" to a "fitful swerving of passion" (MM, 112). Whenever it assumes control, the doctor diverges from his goals with an abruptness resembling "the sudden impulse of a madman." Yet even this lunatic behavior, George Eliot insists, is explicable as human error and can be accepted and forgiven. It does not amount to a major indication of the unsatisfactory nature of things or proof that man is mismade.

Lydgate is neither unaware of his "two selves," as Jasper apparently is of his darker half, nor helplessly at the mercy of a baser self, as Dr. Jekyll subsequently is. Since neither of Lydgate's selves is evil or irrevocably ill-disposed to the other, George Eliot has him decide that "they must learn to accommodate each other and bear reciprocal impediments" (MM, 113). This sounds like naive psychology on the doctor's part. Yet his duality, it appears, can be treated with humor and understanding; it need not be fatally divisive, devilish, or permanently incapacitating. Seen realistically, that is, tragicomically but without melodrama, it recedes to manageable proportions and becomes another subtle problem in human relationships.

Speaking to Lydgate, Dorothea looks back to Mrs. Gaskell and ahead to Bloomsbury's conception of heaven as good human interrelationships when she asks, "What do we live for, if it is not to make life less difficult for each other?" (MM, 537). Likewise, Lydgate's twin selves are advised to make life more bearable for each other, as if, by a process of trade-offs and compromises, Lydgate the intellectual researcher and Lydgate the passionate lover could school each other, imitating Esther Lyon and Felix Holt. George Eliot's more modest explanation revises Lydgate's in order to cancel Dickens's idea of Jasper: like many others, Lydgate does not actually have "two selves" but "alternate" conceptions of himself, in one of which, unfortunately an infatuation, he orchestrates his rival tendencies. But even as he muses, his "persistent self" (MM, 113), not alien, powerless, or ignorant, always knows his limitations. On the other hand, revealing the irony in its name, it continually fails to live up to Lydgate's higher vision, much as Bulstrode is insufficiently good rather than evil and Dorothea must be herself and not a sixteenth-century saint.

Dorothea's love for Will and her social idealism can be conveyed by the same imagery: she is always saint and apostle but learns effectively to secularize these roles. The split in Lydgate between public life and private concerns is not a matter of sacred versus secular but of passion against reason, and less easily resolved, a realization that is reflected in the tension between images of him as a lover and as a potential Columbus. The inadvisability of his marriage to Rosamond appears the more striking because Lydgate is already figuratively married to his profession. Once involved with Rosamond, his private life as a lover interferes with his public endeavors to become the Columbus of modern pathology.

Lydgate and Dorothea both marry twice. But both of her unions are expressions of her aspirant nature, while his first allegiance—the figurative wedding to science—is superior to his second and undermined by it. Dorothea successfully transfers the energies behind her private fantasies to the public arena she belatedly discovers. Similarly, George Eliot argues, Lydgate ought to have brought to his private life the sagacity he prizes as a scientist—a harder task, Eliot concedes, but she uses parallelism to control the variation in degree of difficulty; it is supposed to keep one instance from seeming too good to be true, the other from being discouraging or unfair.

As debt encircles Lydgate, the doctor compares himself to Vesalius, who began a new era in anatomy but "got shipwrecked just as he was coming from Jerusalem to take a great chair at Padua." After Lydgate and Rosamond have ceased to love one another, they are "both adrift on one piece of wreck" (MM, 335, 554). Comparisons with Columbus and the shipwrecked Vesalius allow George Eliot to color Lydgate's pretensions and soften his defeat with a comic irony as subtle as anything expended on Dorothea's eagerness for martyrdom. Lydgate's story is not quite the tragedy of a man made for better things; it is more the tragicomedy of a man who thought he was made so.

In addition, Lydgate is made better in the course of his misfortunes, and his fate is alleviated by the opportunity his distress provides for Dorothea's development. Through contact with her the physician is purged of his "spots of commonness" (MM, 111), especially his insistence on having it known he is better born than most country surgeons. Dorothea's generosity lets Lydgate attain a glimpse of true nobility; his personal need awakens her to a sense of the practical good to be done near at hand—an exchange through social intercourse that is of greater value than an exchange of marriage vows.

Woodcourt in *Bleak House* and Collins's Ezra Jennings are like modern physicians of the post-1860 variety. But the former is a two-dimensional figure and the latter, although instrumental in redeeming Franklin Blake, not much rounder. George Eliot demonstrates the higher caliber of her realism by filling in gaps in Dickens and Collins with a full-scale portrait of problems in a practicing doctor's professional and private life. Ironically, the novelist with the greatest confidence in reform denies her doctor the success enjoyed by his predecessors in the works of her rivals.

Lydgate goes backwards as he unfolds: he begins as a researcher-reformer and ends as a gentleman doctor, more decorative than useful. He is not to remain one of the new doctors in Victorian fiction—a physician concerned with public health—but becomes a practitioner among the rich with some expertise on gout, an ailment monopolized by the wealthy.[19] Significantly, Lydgate, not George Eliot, regards himself "as a failure": "he had not done what he once meant to do" (MM, 610). This is precisely the state of over-expectancy Jasper epitomizes—he lists "ambition, aspiration, restlessness" as causes of his "dissatisfaction" (ED, 49)—and that George Eliot deplores not just in her major characters but in disappointed estimators of society's progress. Still, heaping restrictions on Lydgate is part of Eliot's strategy for retaining the reader's trust in the life process. Lydgate's conversion in reverse, from hospital reformer to medical dilettante, is hardly the secular miracle that conversion from the sacred to the profane was for Dorothea, yet both protagonists expand by shrinking, even if the curtailing of Dorothea's aspirations paradoxically enlarges her world. Lydgate's achievement of greater self-understanding aside, the causes of his professional decline are as traceable beneath the author's lens as the reasons for Dorothea's rise. Instead of sparking an adverse criticism of life, his story complements hers the way a pathway to be avoided makes the right path appear more plausible.

Lydgate's marriage to Rosamond parodically devalues Jasper's obsession with Rosa Bud. George Eliot claims to depict, more realistically than Dickens can, a professional man's unhappiness at the hands of a pretty woman whose primary occupation is the self-centered examination of her own emotional life. Conversely, Dorothea's union with Casaubon shows what befalls the aspiring activist's temperament if it submits to an irrelevant, purely scholarly intellectualism. Since Dorothea errs in one direction and Lydgate in the other, Eliot implies the existence of a midpoint or norm, even though only Miss Brooke finds it.

Though a serious failure in judgment, Lydgate's passion for Rosamond is not like Jude Fawley's subsequent weakness for Arabella. It does not prove that man's susceptibility to passion, at odds with his respect for reason, places him beyond hope of unifying such diverse urges. George Eliot uses Rosamond to suggest that Jasper overestimates Rosa Bud's philosophical importance, just as Dickens exaggerates the lack of suitable outlets for the choirmaster from drudgery and monotony. It is as if George Eliot, not Dickens, draws the moral from the latter's disappointments with Catherine Hogarth and Ellen Ternan. It is not failure to attain Rosamond that frustrates Lydgate; being denied one's choice, George Eliot maintains, is a less serious problem than failing to choose wisely. The difference is between a world in which individuals are denied their fondest desires or cannot shape their destinies and a more realistic one in which, for better or worse, they must.

Through the image of a rosebud, Dickens suggests frustrated promise for Jasper, unfoldings withheld. But Rosamond's name deflects such criticism from the social order by suggesting that Lydgate has world enough and time to regret his choice. George Eliot relates Lydgate's unhappy married life with Rosamond as a comprehensible domestic tragedy with unfortunate professional consequences for the young doctor. She disarms the charge that the unfulfilled desires of the lustful murderer within Jasper reveal Victorian society's irresponsible ignorance of human nature's darker side. Lydgate's miseries, illuminated by the novelist's "inward light," have no darkly mysterious dimension. The research scientist is not destroyed by the repression of an inner, passionate self; on the contrary, he is blamed for failing to teach that inner self better judgment. So there is no calamity inescapably in store for society from the tensions between rational conduct and passionate impulse within man's twofold nature.

The "old drama" in which Laure, a Provençale actress, was appearing had a "new catastrophe" the night Lydgate, then studying in Paris, attended the theater: "At the moment when the heroine was to act out the stabbing of her lover. . . the wife veritably stabbed her husband, who fell as death willed" (MM, 112). The event can be construed as George Eliot's parodic response to the penchant for reenactments in the novels Dickens and Collins penned in the 1860s. Unlike the contemplated sequence in which Jasper might have relived the murdering of his nephew, this reenactment has a new twist that makes the action real for the first time.

George Eliot forces a comparison between melodrama and reality by piling a seemingly real "catastrophe" upon the theatrical one. Later, Lydgate learns from Laure that the stabbing was not a "dreadful stroke of calamity," caused by a slip of the foot, but her premeditated removal of a wearisome spouse. The incident is employed to compromise and discredit catastrophes altogether: the "old" one, acted nightly, becomes a "new" one that is actually explainable in terms of time-worn human motivations. The young medical student's infatuation with the self-serving Laure, who discourages his attentions by confiding that she is a murderess, fails as a preventative; it does not deter the Middlemarch doctor from succumbing to Rosamond, the perpetual thespian of private life.

The discreditable Parisian episode is unlikely to come out after Lydgate takes up his new position: "No one in Middlemarch was likely to have such a notion of [his] past" (MM, 114). Only Lydgate reflects upon the skeleton in his closet: with his "mind glancing back to Laure while he looked at Rosamond, he said inwardly, 'Would *she* kill me because I wearied her?' " (MM, 432). When the impulsive "madman" inside the arduous researcher marries Rosamond, Middlemarch is unaware that it is witnessing a virtual repetition of his earlier enslavement to an illusion. George Eliot parodies Dickens's belief that a self-combustive Krook will reform the Lord Chancellor or that a novel about France's revolution will stop one from happening in England. Progressive reform, it follows, not accounts of disaster, prevent disasters from occurring or recurring.

Jasper's violent-erotic desire for Rosa Bud is replaced by the meticulous scientist's martyrdom with Rosamond. She destroys him, not he her, and does it anticlimactically by degrees, without actually desiring to ruin a career. Dorothea's marriage to Ladislaw, however, is not a repetition of her earlier disaster with Casaubon. George Eliot uses multiplicity at Dickens's expense: in one case but not in another, history seems to repeat itself. When it does repeat itself, no one, unfortunately, is the wiser; Lydgate sees the point only after it is too late. Still, Dorothea's successful avoidance of previous error compensates for the repetition.

The chief victim in the Laure-Lydgate-Rosamond story is the concept of "catastrophe" in the novels of Dickens and Collins. George Eliot informs Dickens that there is no such thing except on stage. By allowing Dorothea to marry Ladislaw after Casaubon's death, she dismisses the contention that recurring catastrophes form the most significant pattern one can discern in human affairs. Lydgate's poor judgment in marrying Rosamond shows that even an apparent disaster in the early life of a scientist cannot make disasters as credible scientifically as are less exceptional causes.

Not surprisingly, the rising tide of reform is a metaphor the conclusion of *Middlemarch* purposely eschews. Change no longer suggests to George Eliot a flood like the one that demolishes St. Oggs and drowns Maggie and Tom Tulliver in *The Mill on the Floss*.[20] George Eliot's masterpiece does not repeat but revises, indeed retracts, her one use of a sensational ending. Dorothea's "strength" is reported to have been less turbulent than a "river," thus nothing like the Floss. Her reformer's energy, split up into countless parts, has widespread consequences. It "spent itself in channels" (MM, 613); the improvements it is responsible for are nearly invisible because "incalculably diffusive"—that is, gradual and antidramatic, contrary in both respects to the "old drama" Lydgate witnesses and Dickens specializes in.

George Eliot explores in *Middlemarch* the dominant dichotomies to be found in the human condition: aspiration versus frustration (Dorothea), reason against passion (Lydgate), and good versus evil (Bulstrode). The collisions that Maggie Tulliver attributes to a "contrast between the outward and inward"[21] are never fatal or as traumatic as they appear slated to be in *The Mystery of Edwin Drood*. Her approach to life's counterpoints is conciliatory.

In *Edwin Drood*, perhaps because it had to be left unfinished, one notices a paucity of the kind of counterbalancing that permits Esther Summerson to attain happiness despite the degenerating condition of England that her satirical co-narrator anatomizes. Doubleness is the paramount theme dealt with through multiples (Jasper's dual personality, Miss Twinkleton's two phases, the Landless twins). Dickens conveys a general sense of life splitting up, coming apart. Whether or not he intended to abandon the multiplot novel entirely, George Eliot's rejoinder is an expansion designed to thin out her rival more effectively than Trollope could scale him down; she uses multiplotting to multiply examples that cancel Dickens's obsession with the multiple self. The more instances of self-division she scrutinizes, the less cause for concern she discovers.

Throughout *Middlemarch* George Eliot relies on double vision to debunk Dickens's unfinished novel with her own version of reality, using three different case studies to his one. *Middlemarch* is the culminating or summary instance of parodic revaluation: an extensive and unique combination of undoing *and* outdoing. Mindful of Collins's failure with *No Name*, George Eliot apparently understood that a second redoing of a competitor could not simply repeat earlier objections. It had to be broader (if a restatement) or new and more severe (if an extension). *Middlemarch* was meant to be both.

Unmasking a hypocrite of thirty years' standing makes the tragic duplicity of Dickens's choirmaster, who is still under thirty, seem both too spectacular and too easy. Pathetic and broken in the novel's final pages, Bulstrode, although "odious," is hardly a terrifying monster whose deceitfulness has anti-evolutionary implications. A would-be latter-day saint and the potential Columbus of modern pathology are trapped in an environment as uncongenial as Jasper's: Dorothea is "spiritual grandeur ill-matched with the meanness of opportunity" (MM, 3). But just because the modern, secular dispensation obviates saintliness in the traditional mode or discovery on the continental scale, George Eliot argues, does not mean it must produce malcontents and devils. Since all three of George Eliot's major characters reduce, if not belittle, the catastrophic proportions of Jasper's duality, she expands upon Dickens only in order to diminish him. In the process, she, not her rival, allegedly emerges as the authority on such interrelated matters of theme and technique as dualism, multiplotting, and counterpoint.

The position that George Eliot's characters in *Middlemarch* possess an evolutionary force that urges them to realize their potentialities is not invalid but incomplete.[22] This force is not entirely self-generating, not purely internal, not exhausting itself; it is still abundantly at large in the society George Eliot bears witness to even after the publication of fifteen Dickens novels, most of which argued to the contrary.

George Eliot stresses the importance of adapting oneself to the community, which results in acquisition or aggrandizement even if it also means pruning aspirations to accommodate local values. Consider Mr. Farebrother's declaration, made appropriately to Lydgate: "I used often to wish I had been something else than a clergyman, . . . but perhaps it will be better to try and make as good a clergyman out of myself as I can" (MM, 375). This is different in tone from Flaubert's lament that all fall below their expectations: "There isn't a bourgeois alive who in the ferment of his youth, . . . hasn't thought himself capable of boundless passions and noble exploits. The sorriest little women-chaser has dreamed of Oriental queens; in a corner of every notary's heart lie the mouldy remains of a poet" (MB, 329). Farebrother only appears to settle for less; actually, from contact with Lydgate comes the novel's salvationary advice that makes Farebrother the exemplary minister he aspires to be. The resolution to capitalize on existing possibilities is precisely what Lydgate needs. For "clergyman" in Farebrother's short sermon, one can read not just provincial doctor but local mediatrix (Dorothea) and cathedral choirmaster (Jasper).

The traits needed for a character's self-realization in *Middlemarch* are evolved in the sense that they are often borrowed from another character or activated with another's help by a kind of natural selection as if from an extant communal pool. Preserved in *Middlemarch* and magnificent to watch is George Eliot's abiding belief in the worth and beauty of social intercourse, a process as important to her for human development as sexual fulfillment becomes in the novels of D.H. Lawrence. To reprimand Dickens's insensitivity to the wonder of this process, George Eliot built into her masterwork most of the criticisms of Dickensian realism that G.H. Lewes was simultaneously voicing in such Victorian journals as the *Fortnightly Review*.[23]

When George Eliot's researcher's eye compels provincial Middlemarch to yield up its secrets—such as the reasons for Dorothea's success, Lydgate's failure, and Bulstrode's downfall—a life process is revealed whereby characters complete, improve, or reprove one another to the mutual benefit of themselves and the community.[24] The process is society's primary tissue. Not only is permanent stoppage a lie, but, paradoxically, change (or interchange) is a constant, a universal. Social intercourse furnishes George Eliot's characters with the degree of clash and convergence needed either to repair one another's personalities or to add finishing touches.

Thanks to the intercourse of character, George Eliot, modern in many ways for her times, can also be seen as a holdout against modernity, one of the last great champions of viable society and the most sanguine advocate of secularization her century produced. After her, only the Bloomsbury Group has been able even to approximate her faith in social intercourse and personal relations. From her viewpoint, Dickens's imperfect humanism seemed to be holding back due recognition of society's advances. From a modern perspective, however, he seems to prefigure the kind of vision that abounds in modern satirical novels. George Eliot believed she was ushering in a new era, but, in retrospect, she also appears to have been staving off its sharpest critics: her confident secularization of communion as community failed to prevent Kafka and Beckett. Dickens's fictions formed a barrier between Victorian readers and the evolving better world that George Eliot foresaw. Her parodies of his novels were efforts to bar from consideration the modern-sounding objections he foreshadows.

Gordon S. Haight asserts that Bulstrode "might easily have qualified as a major villain in a novel by Dickens," had George Eliot been less compassionate.[25] This is one of numerous comments that point toward recognition of hidden rivalries in Victorian fictions without suspicion of their scope or intensity. Eliot's preoccupation in *Middlemarch* is to prevent the banker from developing into a Dickensian villain so she can disqualify her rival as a realistic social critic. As she replaces Jasper with Bulstrode, she concludes a series of conflicts between two professed realists that began in the mid-1860s. Her revaluation of Dickens in *Middlemarch* is both the last phase of the century's most heated rivalry and of such rivalry in the Victorian novel generally, the final chapter in the realism wars that swirled around Dickens from the 1850s until well after his death.

Although a suspension of hostilities followed Dickens's death, one should not overlook shifts toward his perspective over the next several decades and just prior to World War II. In the present century, moderns have admired the Dickens whom Trollope and Mrs. Gaskell rewrote, but they have reacted to the so-called Victorian side of Dickens more skeptically than the Victorians responded to his bitterly satirical, proto-modern aspects. For George Eliot, Dickens's weaker, sentimental side was a consequence of his ill-tempered pessimism. In *Middlemarch*, the "Dead Hand" of the past reaches out for Bulstrode at the same time that a spirit of reform begins to spread over the land. With Dickens gone, George Eliot hoped to convince readers that reform and retribution are twin processes, both of them slow-moving but ameliorative.

Dickens's unfinished novel revolves from "The Dawn" of Chapter 1 to "The Dawn Again" of Chapter 22. The suggestion is one of cycle, repetition, and perhaps resurrection—if not for the missing Edwin Drood, then for the lives and loves of his friends, which cannot be resumed until his disappearance has been solved. With the title for Book Eight of *Middlemarch*, "Sunset and Sunrise," George Eliot claims for life a forward motion, despite ups and downs. Lydgate and Rosamond are on the descent, and Bulstrode's sun is setting, but Dorothea and Will Ladislaw and the reform movement as well are in the ascendant.

George Eliot believed that Dickens's sun was also sinking as hers continued to rise at his expense. Her "Finale" does not merely conclude a novel; it signifies the end of further need to reply to Dickens, since his unfinished novel—which was shaping up as a rebuttal to anti-Dickens parodies in *Felix Holt*—has been demolished.

Realizing how artfully *Middlemarch* defends and expands the conception of social process that premiered in *Adam Bede* and *Felix Holt* is absolutely essential. The modern revaluator is able to testify to George Eliot's continuing confidence in her brand of realism: she remained as indebted to Wordsworth, for example, as she had become to Darwin. Incorporating Lydgate's failure, Dorothea's initial mismatch, and especially the downfall of the hypocritical Bulstrode, she planned to confound Dickens's supporters by bringing darker elements into her fiction without significantly dimming the "kindly" manner in which "the light of heaven falls on" life's everyday realities (AB, 177).

Felix Holt is a more sophisticated work than *Adam Bede*, and the conception of organic society in *Middlemarch* is more complex still. This should not be attributed mainly to George Eliot's increasing reliance on G.H. Lewes's social theorems in place of Auguste Comte's; nor is it sufficient to speak of her discovery of inadequacies in the realism of her earlier novels, as if her social vision, like Dickens's, got progressively darker. She matured without departing from her original position or despairing over growing discrepancies between her ideals and the realities of English life.[26] Differences in tone can best be explained in terms of hidden rivalries. One finds more conflict and competition in Middlemarch than in Treby Magna, more there than in Hayslope, because George Eliot wanted to absorb Dickens without leaving a trace, to show how many of Dickens's objections to Victorian society she could encompass without fundamentally altering her philosophy of life. Movement from Hayslope to Treby Magna to Middlemarch is not from lesser to greater disappointment, as in Emma Bovary's moves from Tostes to Yonville to Rouen; rather, provisional framings are being made more exact.

Felix Holt, besides parodying *Bleak House* extensively, cannibalizes *A Tale of Two Cities* to obtain a riot sequence that George Eliot can neutralize.

Although change is sometimes violent or threatening, she claims that stability persists as the greater reality. She reconciles her continuing interest in reform as movement and remaking with her stabilizing conception of civilization as continuity. *Middlemarch* cannibalizes *The Moonstone* and *The Mystery of Edwin Drood* to secure double selves, divisions between inner and outer, for Lydgate, Bulstrode, and Dorothea. But the author insists that one can still resolve the conflict between individual desire for self-fulfillment and society's demand that everyone contribute to its harmonious development.

From one point of view, George Eliot was arguing that her realism could accommodate Dickens's satirical vision without blinking. From a second perspective, however, the ever larger amount of Dickensian material that she felt obliged to incorporate and defuse can be interpreted as a concession to the obtrusive power of his social criticism.

Felix Holt is entitled to persist as the classic instance of revaluative parody in Victorian ficiton. It remains the purest instance of a double-barreled novel that stands on its own yet rephrases a rival work. Nevertheless, *Middlemarch*, George Eliot's finest novel, can also be read as an intricate multipurpose work, even if its reply to *Edwin Drood* and *The Moonstone* has remained better hidden from modern readers than its author's initial redoings of *Bleak House*. Since *Middlemarch* both repeats and extends an earlier revaluation, it strikes the modern revaluator of hidden rivalries as having been more "arduous" for George Eliot to compose than her previous anti-Dickens "invention."

Chapter Eight

Conclusions: Realism, Revaluation, and Realignment

A RECOGNITION of hidden rivalries in Victorian fiction necessitates a realignment of the major novelists. Thackeray can hardly be considered Dickens's archrival. His objections to Dickens, although consistent and pervasive, seldom resulted in the meticulous rewriting that one finds in Trollope, George Eliot, Mrs. Gaskell, or Collins. Any of these—especially George Eliot, his prodigious foe, and Collins, his too ardent admirer—can stake a greater claim than Thackeray to be considered Dickens's nemesis. Michael Slater contends that Dickens had "no . . . reservations about women's writing *per se*,"[1] yet *Hard Times* is so contrary to *Mary Barton* and *North and South* as to suggest that Dickens considered women novelists unqualified to understand the masculine public world of strikes, factories, and economic theory.

To Dickens and Thackeray, outdoing chiefly meant outselling the other.[2] On the other hand, Thackeray published *Novels by Eminent Hands* the same year *Vanity Fair* appeared. The novelist can be said to have cleared the way for himself by parodying popular writers of the day, principally Bulwer, a plausible stand-in for the Dickens mode. In the 1850s, when competition between realists was heating up, Thackeray's parodies were already in print as a sort of guidebook. But Thackeray employs traditional literary parody to subvert even further those novels he believes prominent hands have already mismade. Taking writing that is allegedly already bad and doing it even worse was rarely Trollope's tactic; he employed it only in the chapter of *The Warden* in which he pretends to quote from Mr. Popular Sentiment's new novel. Thackeray's parody of Bulwer fails to explain the subtler redoing of Dickens throughout Trollope's first important work.

Nor does it look forward to the kind of correctives George Eliot applied; the goal of her ameliorative parodies was to make bad novels better. George Eliot's activity as a parodist scarcely differs from Dorothea's as a reformer. Dickens's more determined rivals learned almost immediately, but not from Thackeray, to rewrite an "inimitable" novelist while also presenting their own perspectives, one operation overlapping and reinforcing the other.

Thackeray does not fit comfortably with Trollope, George Eliot, Mrs. Gaskell, and other so-called anti-sensationalists. Distinguishing melodramatic realists from their less melodramatic peers, therefore, is not an infallible method for grouping Victorian novelists or analyzing Victorian realism, even if it clearly separates Dickens and Collins from George Eliot. That Dickens and Thackeray both possessed an essentially satirical frame of mind seems more important for purposes of alignment.

Generally Horatian, the satirist in Thackeray seems sadly resigned to the prevalence of human folly and, conceivably, is even less hopeful than Dickens. His satire is Juvenalian, bristling with outrage, yet skeptical about the likelihood of taking great strides forward. In both novelists, one encounters a mental disposition quite foreign to George Eliot, Trollope, or Mrs. Gaskell whenever they consider society's fundamental worth. As a satirical metaphor for life, *Vanity Fair* is just as depressing as *Bleak House*.

These metaphors reveal an inclination to deplore temporal existence: it brings persistent social injustice in Dickens, futility or inevitable disappointment in Thackeray. In both but especially in Dickens (despite his fondness for the Beatitudes) there abides an Old Testament sense of morality that rejects a secularized universe. Each novelist writes a very different kind of novel from the other, but both require the life process to administer periodic comeuppance to the individual (Thackeray) or society (Dickens) if either mistakes the present situation for the eternal and behaves as though there were no day of reckoning.

So fundamentally critical a conception of the human condition— bleakness in Dickens, *vanitas* in Thackeray—could not but disquiet George Eliot, for whom the interlocking ideas of evolution and social reform promised steady amelioration, if not an earthly paradise. George Eliot repeatedly lambastes art that "leaves the soul in despair"; it has mainly a "laming" influence.[3] Her contempt for satire as a counterproductive force implies that the nay-sayer is always a setback for civilization, a brake upon its progress.

By fostering doubts, harping on shortcomings, George Eliot seems to think, satire saps the general will; it ruins the exhilarated state of mind vital for ongoing reform. Dickens, it follows, overly accentuates the negative. He threatens to cripple life's inherently forward motion. Consequently, much of the parodic revaluation in Victorian fiction seems anticritical even as it criticizes, for it aims at reducing the harm supposedly caused by excessively trenchant outbursts of social satire. Thackeray could never have become Dickens's main competition because his world view, at bottom, is too dystopian. His fiction is temperamentally and philosophically closer to Dickens than George Eliot feels to either of these competitor-allies.[4]

Dickens did intend *David Copperfield* to eclipse the popularity of *Pendennis*, just as Thackeray issued *Vanity Fair* to prove ostentation more rampant than pride (*Dombey and Son*). *David Copperfield* and *Pendennis* were serialized contemporaneously, yet the modern revaluator does not detect in them the incessant mutual recrimination so pervasive in the conflict between *Hard Times* and *North and South*. Beginning in May of 1849, six months after Thackeray, Dickens finished in November of 1850, one month earlier. These circumstances made mutual revaluation less feasible on a steady basis than it was for Dickens and Mrs. Gaskell, whose novels were published in close succession.

Conceivably, Dickens may have begun *Bleak House* in conscious repudiation of *Vanity Fair*. In both novels, an orphan leaves finishing school for a new residence and possibly marriage: Becky departs Miss Pinkerton's with Amelia, whose brother she tries to entice into matrimony; Esther is taken from Miss Rachel's by Jarndyce, who later proposes. Dickens shows a guileless heroine threading her way toward happiness through a labyrinth populated by grotesques whom Thackeray would consider a distortion of Victorian society. *Vanity Fair* depicts an unscrupulous operator climbing upward to eventual defeat in a world that finally frustrates the entrepreneur as effectively as it ignores passive suffering like Amelia's. Dickens may have felt that Thackeray's drawing rooms and their pitfalls originated, as did Becky Sharp's name and personality, in Restoration comedy rather than in Victorian England.

The journeys that Esther and Becky undertake are nevertheless complementary variations on John Bunyan's *Pilgrim's Progress*. Whether the pilgrim is innocent or conniving, the novelist's purpose is to excoriate a corrupt society, to unveil a fallen world, not to justify the nature of things or forecast their improvement. Dickens and Thackeray expose an unregenerate reality from different angles; their public rivalry is ultimately a form of hidden, indirect cooperation. Dickens and Mrs. Gaskell systematically revise each other's characters and situations to reach startlingly different conclusions, but Dickens and Thackeray corroborate each other in that they create congruent moral visions.

Their interplay at first seems to resemble the contests involving Dickens and Wilkie Collins. On closer examination, however, Dickens-and-

Collins proves to be more complicated than Dickens-and-Thackeray. The latter provides an example of open competition that conceals temperamental affinities; the former reveals a case of deceptively congenial emulation that is actually a form of intense rivalry. Collins, too, belongs above Thackeray on the roster of Dickens's major competitors.

Dickens and Thackeray, wrote David Masson in 1859, are "so closely associated in the public mind, that whenever the one is mentioned the other is thought of. It is now Dickens and Thackeray, Thackeray and Dickens, all the world over"; a "debate" rages "as to [their] respective merits."[5] Doubtless this discussion of comparative strengths will continue.[6] Still, if one employs double vision to review the facts in more than one light, Masson's conception of these two novelists as "opposites of each other" seems to have been both premature and yet already out of date.

Like Dickens, Thackeray came on the scene with a parody of the Newgate novel. *Catherine* appeared in 1839, two years after Dickens had tried, in *Oliver Twist*, to displace romantic renditions of life in the underworld with an account of criminals as they really were. One notes further remarkable overlappings whenever Dickens and Thackeray detect a new instance of social inequality, another adverse trend, or a form of transgression brought on by either. Old Osborne in *Vanity Fair*, for example, has been called "a new kind of portrait" yet "not less complicated than Dickens's portrait of another hard businessman [Mr. Dombey] whose adventures were being issued in installments at the same time."[7]

In March 1848, both novelists, having flirted with the subject of adultery, settled scores with would-be adulterers. Rawdon thrashes Lord Steyne in *Vanity Fair*; Carker is destroyed by a railway engine in *Dombey and Son*. Dickens paralleled Edith Dombey's outwardly respectable marriage to Mr. Dombey (or to his money and station) with the downfall of Alice Marwood, James Carker's former mistress. But Edith's prostitution of herself on the marriage market compares more readily with Becky's schemes to sell herself to a succession of suitors. In the England of the 1840s, both novelists simultaneously recognized, the only form of ruin to be dreaded even by a young woman was financial. Money, not romantic love—which is an illusion—governs the world: such is the bitter lesson of *Vanity Fair* and the precept Mr. Dombey and his ilk live by. Dickens, however, went on to depict business losses as a less serious disaster than the emotional bankruptcy they help Dombey to recognize and recover from.

It is as though each author announced himself with an anti-Newgate novel to illustrate their common commitment. Novelists who glamorized the criminal world did worse than misrepresent hard facts; their glossy books catered to audiences unwilling to address society's ills. Between 1837 and 1839, Dickens and Thackeray declared their mutual repugnance for sentimental views of the world's deficiencies. Neither English society nor the nature of things, they would always maintain, is ever as good as their rivals among popular novelists pretended.

Perhaps Thackeray based his "protest" against Dickens's novels on a dislike for his contemporary's use of melodrama. Yet more than one of the installment endings for *Vanity Fair* show Thackeray to have been attentive to the value of surprise, suspense, and delay. Becky's refusal of Sir Pitt's proposal with the disclosure that she is "married already" ended one month's number; Rawdon's discovery of her with Lord Steyne another. The jewels and rings, presents from Steyne, which Rawdon has Becky remove and discard; the diamond ornament he flings at that nobleman; the cut Steyne receives from it so that he "wore the scar to his dying day"; Becky's sole utterance ("I am innocent"); and the information that Rawdon "left her without another word"—all combine to make this scene as stagy as any in *Dombey and Son*.

Despite Percy Lubbock's classic distinction between "picture" and "drama," of which Thackeray is said to prefer the former, one can discuss the dramatic aspect, indeed the melodrama, of *Vanity Fair*, just as it is possible to chart Dickens's increasing disenchantment with romantic love. That is the last illusion to crumble, the final vanity to be exposed, in Thackeray's best novel. But the dispirited union of Dobbin and Amelia is also the reduced state of affairs Dickens came to: if not with Arthur Clennam's belated appreciation of Amy Dorrit, who is much superior to the docile Amelia, then with the reunion of a chastened Pip and a subdued Estella in the alternative ending for *Great Expectations*.

Aside from the Brontës, Thackeray had the shortest career of any major Victorian novelist. The span between *Pickwick* and *Edwin Drood* is more than twice as long as that separating *Vanity Fair* from *Denis Duval*. Furthermore, Thackeray did his best work within an even shorter period. Few of his contemporaries "had anything, much less anything good, to say of his work written after 1855."[8] That is precisely the time Dickens's real difficulties with rivals began, the year Trollope parodied him in *The Warden*, and Mrs. Gaskell went on the offensive with *North and South*.

To whatever extent it was ever "Dickens and Thackeray, Thackeray and Dickens," the rivalry, largely without steady, parodic revaluations of each other's work, ended just as the major realism wars began. Masson's judgment now seems outdated because in 1859 he was unknowingly summing up a contest that was already virtually over. That summation, one can argue, has helped to keep hidden the subsequent rivalries that would alternately annoy or preoccupy Dickens from the mid-1850s until his death. From another standpoint, Masson's coupling of Dickens and Thackeray as "opposites" was premature. The Victorian critic was actually standing at the starting place of several graver conflicts. These ensuing rivalries, although unacknowledged by the participants, grew larger and went on longer than the highly visible and quite audible public "debate" in the 1840s between Dickens's supporters and Thackeray's.

Pitting Thackeray against Dickens instead of exploring hidden rivalries is a less grievous misalignment, one concludes, than calling one school of Victorian realists more scientific than another. Nevertheless, belief in a scientific social realism, purportedly the creation of a select group of anti-sensational Victorian fictionists, dies hard. A. Dwight Culler sounds like G.H. Lewes, fulminating against Dickens all over again, when he equates *gradualism*—Charles Lyell's foremost geological principle for explaining alterations in the natural world—with George Eliot's method of developing character and plot.

Culler parallels George Eliot's desire to "show the gradual action" upon personality of "ordinary causes rather than exceptional"[9] with the passage of the Reform Bill. This legislation, says Culler, indicated England's choice of gradualism over *catastrophism* as its mode of effecting political change.[10] In George Eliot, individuals and societies, despite abundant evidence of fallibility in both, improve themselves gradually, the way the natural world continuously reshapes itself. It follows that melodramatic novels like *Bleak House* and *A Tale of Two Cities* must be unscientific and therefore unrealistic. The first is built around Krook's calamitous demise, which represents that of England's legal system and life-consuming bureaucracies in general. The second involves the re-creation of a historical event that violently overturned France's social order. Dickens's radical warnings about the fate of moribund institutions and corrupt, irresponsible societies are, by implication, out of step with the cadence of progressive reform, a rhythm of life that George Eliot is said to have captured structurally and thematically in the pace of her novels.[11]

Passage of the first Reform Bill, however, did not win permanent victory for gradualism over catastrophism as the only suitable metaphor a novelist could borrow from science to depict social change. Although electoral procedures were improved broadly in 1832 without much bloodshed, "growing tension and unrest" characterized the later 1830s.[12] The ensuing decade, roughly coinciding with Victoria's first ten years on the throne and Dickens's rise to world fame, was "the most harrowing and dangerous of the entire century," mainly because of the Chartists, who led the first sustained working-class uprising in modern history and aroused the nation's "vestigal dread of Jacobinism."[13]

When Lyell published *Principles of Geology* (1830-33), his account of gradual change in the natural world seemed in step with oncoming reforms, each giving added impetus to the other. Instead of arguing that cataclysmic occurrences remade the earth at fairly regular intervals, Lyell saw planetary changes happening gradually over extended time periods. This idea provided Darwin's theory with geological underpinnings. But in 1837, as working-class agitation increased, Carlyle's *History of the French Revolution* appeared to be just as timely as any interpretation of social change based upon Lyell; so, too, did Dickens's reconsideration of the Gordon Riots in *Barnaby Rudge* four years later.[14]

Tess Cosslett decides to omit Dickens (and never contemplates including Collins) when surveying "scientific Victorian culture."[15] Applying the scientific spirit to life, she explains, "goes along with a 'realist' approach," which Dickens lacked. George Eliot easily gains admittance to the pantheon of forward-looking Victorians who substituted scientific views for outmoded religious beliefs. But Dickens "leans more towards a 'countertradition' of fantasy, which went against the mainstream of Victorian realism." This erroneous alignment works only if one forgets that Dickens's satires against society came first, and that many of his contemporaries formed their ideas about realistic social analysis in reaction to his popular success. Defining purposeful exaggeration and satirical severity as "fantasy" is no less one-sided than enshrining the use of inherently positive metaphors from the rapidly advancing biological sciences as the only "realist" approach.

The Victorian era virtually commenced with a rivalry between gradualism and catastrophism, scientific theories that could each be applied analogously, indeed poetically, to recent events in the political and sociological spheres. This rivalry percolated throughout the 1860s in the novels of Dickens and George Eliot as passage of the second Reform Bill (1867) neared. The modern revaluator avoids false oppositions between realists and a "countertradition of fantasy," reestablishing instead the two formidable encampments or alignments that perceptive Victorians saw: on one side Lyell, gradualism, Darwin, the Reform Bills of 1832 and 1867, George Eliot, G. H. Lewes, and novels like *Felix Holt*; on the other Carlyle, catastrophism, Chartists as a reminder of the French Revolution, Dickens, Collins, and novels like *Bleak House* and *A Tale of Two Cities*. Each novelist took from the science of the time whatever he or she needed to support a point of view, a philosophy of life. They looked to different authorities and emphasized different historical or current events to corroborate whatever scientific and sociological theories each imposed on reality to explain the events.

Being sent to work at Warren's Blacking as a child made Dickens acutely sensitive to traumatic moments that redirect one's life. George Eliot's maturation into one of the period's eminent philosophical novelists was not without intellectual crises, but she seems to have suffered none of the startling shocks or unanticipated turns of events that Dickens felt could alter an individual's career or the fate of a nation. Traumatic moments in Dickens's fiction and in Collins's are meant as close-at-hand equivalents of larger disturbances that influence the course of history. Magwitch leaps out at Pip and changes his life forever. Anne Catherick accosts Hartright, and he is never the same afterward. Krook's combustion, Sir Percival Glyde's incineration, flare-ups by Jasper's murderous second self are all true to life; all supply reminders, as does the French Revolution when it envelops Darnay, that long periods of oppression and neglect—and the frustrated discontent they cause—always prove convulsive.

Novels like *Bleak House, The Woman in White, A Tale of Two Cities,* and *The Moonstone* investigate the paradox underlying the use of catastrophe in melodramatic realism: appointed times and the end of roads that have been traveled in darkness always arrive suddenly for the irresponsible and unaware. They are then called catastrophes and invested with unearthly significance, even if, upon reconsideration, they are seen by the novelist familiar with the ways of providence to have been inevitable and long overdue. Dickens and Collins emphasize the long-term consequences of seemingly hidden designs that work themselves out gradually enough but are as invisible to the eye, while doing so, as the webs of affinity that George Eliot discovers by putting Middlemarch under her microscope. Results that look exceptional, Dickens and Collins assert, often only appear to have extraordinary causes.

Dickens and Collins did not write novels as steeped in the thought and diction of Victorian science as George Eliot's, but their work is neither unscientific nor antiscientific. Both writers deliberately capitalized on surprise and sensation in order to counteract the more placid view of human events suggested by gradualism. Their novels either begin with a sudden intervention, a turning point that transforms a character's life, or proceed toward a sensational cataclysm that catches most of the characters unaware but ought to have been foreseen.

Given the Russian Revolution, two world wars, and the development of nuclear fission—this last raising the possibility that the universe could end with an explosion rivaling the one it reputedly began with—catastrophism has become plausible again, modern, realistic, and scientific once more. An essential part of the basis for one species of Victorian realism, it now seems far from absurd, either as a prognosis of things to come or as a reassertion of the way the world has always been. Not surprisingly, several twentieth-century scientists favor a hybrid theory for the life process, combining gradualism with elements of the catastrophism that Darwin and Lyell wanted to discard permanently. The new approach states that the earth, although generally changing according to Lyell's explanation, has also been subjected to catastrophes at remarkably regular intervals.[16]

Evidence for periodic mass extinctions in the natural order implies an extraterrestrial mechanism, possibly a barrage of comets or asteroids striking the earth at intervals of roughly twenty-six million years. One of the more sizable bombardments, some scientists now think, may have made dinosaurs extinct: dust clouds, raised by killer stars crashing into this planet, could have veiled the globe in darkness, lowering temperatures and destroying most of the dinosaurs' food supply as the dust eventually settled over the land.

The opening chapter of *Bleak House* describes startlingly similar conditions. "Michaelmas Term" is "lately over"—hardly a phenomenal turn of events, but the scene suggests the consequences of some floodlike disaster or barrage from outer space. Dirt and darkness, mud and fog, force the narrator to wonder "if the day ever broke" (BH, 3). A "soft black drizzle" is falling, "with flakes of soot in it as big as full-grown snow-flakes." London seems to have "gone into mourning . . . for the death of the sun." Uncannily, Dickens even allows his narrator to imagine meeting a Megalosaurus "waddling like an elephantine lizard up Holborn-hill" in search of something edible.

Later, Krook's spontaneous combustion makes the neighborhood, in Mr. Snagsby's words, "rather greasy" (BH, 421). Inside Krook's shop, it inspires Guppy to exclaim: "See how the soot's falling" (BH, 426). The missing Krook has been converted into a kind of fallout that leaves "a dark greasy coating on the walls and ceiling" (BH, 430). When Krook goes up in flames as a proxy for the country's corrupt systems of government, Dickens purposely duplicates details from the novel's opening chapter. The repetition suggests a heedless society not yet recovered from one catastrophe but primed for more of the same.

Recent theorizing about the periodicity of catastrophes in the world of nature rehabilitates Dickens's poetic use of science, his reliance on fear of impending disaster to spur a sluggish reform movement. Novels that build toward sudden explosion or the onset of violent revolution are not necessarily false to the shape and tempo of the nature of things. If catastrophes do not strike at random in the natural world but are cyclic, Dickens and Collins stay within the bounds of poetic license by making them seem fated to happen, as if they were providential judgments, periodic purgings. The modern interest in catastrophism does not obviate George Eliot's approach to life, but it does suggest that her scientific metaphor for it, a steady, organic "unfolding," was no less imaginative (or poetic) than Dickens's. Through the conformation and patient development of her novels, which foster a general confidence in reform, she discourages extremism. She demonstrates the sufficiency of nonviolent change, as though it has always been nature's way. Instead of a clash between science and fantasy, the modern revaluator discovers rival motivational techniques, different didactic strategies.

That *A Tale of Two Cities* was being serialized in the same year *The Origin of Species* appeared is, therefore, not an ironic overlay, embarrassing to Dickens. At the moment Darwin was reinterpreting the world's past, Dickens was not archaically attempting to reapply one of its catastrophes to the present. On the contrary, he was asking, as did Collins, whether life has ever been gradualistic to the exclusion of being, more importantly at times, melodramatic and sensational. The argument is ultimately not over which is true, although it has regularly taken that form, but over which is truer, which the greater reality or more determinant force: periods of drastic upheaval or the stretches of apparent stability or gradual modification that separate and surround them.

In *A Tale of Two Cities*, Dickens finds the idea that everything is constantly changing slightly—perhaps getting always better overall—a misreading of life. His strategy is to test this concept against a historically verifiable turn for the worse. The French Revolution occupies a crucial place in the evolution of Dickens's philosophy, comparable to the Lisbon earthquake for Voltaire in *Candide*.

Like the mass extinction of dinosaurs, the French revolution calls into question the concept of natural selection, the very foundation of evolutionary biology. In George Eliot's benevolent version of the competition between species, characters interact socially in order that the best or most promising specimens in the community can acquire from one another the traits needed to complete their personalities. Mass killings, whether of dinosaurs or French noblemen, challenge the idea that society is a self-perfecting organism. They open up an array of niches—ecological in one case, political in the other—in which creatures flourish without necessarily excelling those they replace.

The modern revaluator, observing that *A Tale of Two Cities* and *The*

Origin of Species both date from 1859, should view the overlap the way George Eliot did: not as an automatic indication that Dickens's fiction was unscientific but as her call to arms to prove it so. Consequently, she uses the short-lived riot sequence in *Felix Holt* to contend that every manifestation of a potential for violence in a group of English workmen is not another outbreak of Jacobinism. It helps to concentrate on a disturbance in the country rather than on a country's disturbances. Nevertheless, participation in an unruly mob, an apostate moment that leads to a jail term, does not redirect Holt's life the way Pip's changes after Magwitch extorts his help. Resuming his labors as educator of the working classes, Felix pledges himself anew to "the gradual operation of steady causes"; he predicts that the "structure of the old" will be "gradually altered" (FH, 615-16).

When Jasper teases his nephew about skeletons in the closet, Dickens broaches an anti-evolutionary theme full of potential for the sudden, catastrophic disclosures George Eliot abhorred: "There is said to be a hidden skeleton in every house; but you thought there was none in mine, dear Ned" (ED, 47). No exception to life's rule, Jasper is an aggravated example from a pattern in which some grievous transgression in mankind's past incriminates all men. Instead of pertaining solely to events in the house of Drood, the "skeleton" acquires poetic extension as an ominous reference to humanity's unacknowledged darker side.

Before mentioning skeletons, Jasper undergoes a transition from one self to the other that Grewgious later witnesses in severer form. Looking, in Edwin's words, "frightfully ill" and with "a strange film come" over his eyes, Jasper "sits for a few moments rigid, and then, with thick drops standing on his forehead . . . becomes as he was before." He touches his nephew with "a tender hand" but speaks about skeletons in a manner unusual for him, "with something of raillery or banter in it." Jasper becomes "as he was before," the same to all appearances, but internally he has experienced a revolution. His antisocial interior self succeeds the choirmaster and continues in control for the brief yet crucial remainder of Chapter 2. It is this second, murderous self who deplores the "cramped monotony" (ED, 48) of Cloisterham life and advises Drood to take the expression of discontent as "a warning" (ED, 49). When Jasper's violent-erotic other self depicts himself as a "skeleton" in the closet, he employs paleontology satirically. Admittedly sinister, this sudden interest in skeletons contradicts Felix Holt's borrowings from biology to characterize England's social system as a gradually maturing organism.

The contention behind Jasper's duality, that man's nature is deeply, indeed tragically, split between good and evil, works as contrary to gradualism as did the intimation in *A Tale of Two Cities* that one benighted society might repeat the errors of another. Showing the human personality divided against itself does to gradualism at the psychological level what describing the Circumlocution Office (in *Little Dorrit*) accomplished at the political. Self-division, like circularity, is antilinear, an impediment to proceeding forward in a straight line.

Dickens planned to outdo Collins as a scientific realist by putting "Doctor Elliotson's Human Physiology" to fuller use.[17] He would have mesmerized the imprisoned Jasper and, going deeper than Collins did with Franklin Blake, laid bare modern man's innermost self. The choirmaster's subconscious, teeming with repressed desires, would seem more dangerous to polite society than the resentment of the downtrodden of Saint Antoine for their rulers. Jasper's violent-erotic nature would burst forth from the incarcerated choirmaster with the kind of power of upheavals in nature and within unregenerate nations when periodically they disrupt the illusion of life's steady advance. *The Mystery of Edwin Drood*, begun in the second year after the second Reform Bill, indicates that Dickens still put little stock in gradualism as a realistic political science. The unfinished novel was to be his vehicle for saying that he was neither passé nor unscientific; he would not recant, or apologize for publishing *A Tale of Two Cities* the same year Darwin's *magnum opus* appeared.

The suggestion that Darwin derived his narrative techniques from reading Dickens points to one of the century's finer ironies. The "relations of structures in Darwin's work" are said to "draw on orderings of experience learnt from . . . a form of plotting crucial to Dickens's work"; throughout *The Origin of Species*, the "sense that everything is connected, though the connections may be obscured," gives "urgency" to Darwin's "enterprise of uncovering such connections." Similarly, in *Bleak House*, "the fifty-six named" characters "all turn out to be related either by way of concealed descent . . . or of economic dependency," even if the relation is between parasite and host. Whether in Darwin's natural world or Dickens's labyrinthian London, what initially "looks like agglomeration" proves to be "analyzable connection."[18] Darwin evidently appreciated the manner in which obscured relationships, connections that exist in spite of themselves, emerge from Dickens's fiction as the organizing principle beneath life's apparent chaos.

From a novel like *Bleak House* came Darwin's image of himself as scientist-detective, the Bucket of biology. Whenever Darwin uncovers undetected connections in the natural order, Dickens's narrative techniques receive an affirmative revaluation. The biologist implicitly endorses the kind of world those techniques reflect. Surprising nature's secrets and exposing society's turn out to be analogous activities. Methods used by Dickens and Collins to incriminate their era are not without a scientific parallel, if only because the century's most celebrated scientist borrowed some of them. From Darwin, George Eliot extracts support for her notion of society and human personality as evolving entities, each reliant upon the other for consequent mutual growth. But novels such as *Bleak House* share with Darwin an impression that the world is often more like a puzzle than an organism.

In the same year Dickens implied that Victorian England still had much in common with prerevolutionary France, Darwin also explored a host of previously unsuspected connections, including the disconcerting bond between men and apes. From one point of view, the 1850s saw the rise of a scientific realism (founded on gradualism) as an aesthetic ideal. But from another, one concludes that *The Origin of Species* was among the most sensational publications in a decade that also produced *Bleak House*, *A Tale of Two Cities*, and *The Woman in White*.

Reread in light of Darwin's conception of himself as another Bucket, Lydgate's preference for "arduous invention" over profuse narration, which was discussed in the previous chapter, becomes George Eliot's attempt to put herself, instead of Dickens, into creative affinity with Darwin. A scientist like Lydgate or an artist like George Eliot "reveals subtle actions" that are "inaccessible" to the eye. They can only be "tracked" by an "inward light," a special kind of "Energy" to be utilized even in "outer darkness" and over "long pathways of necessary sequence." The "very eye of research," George Eliot has Lydgate maintain, can "pierce the obscurity of . . . minute processes." It permits the meticulous scientist and the exacting social realist to travel "those invisible thoroughfares" that are "the first lurking-places" of human misery and joy (MM, 122). The diction in Lydgate's thinly disguised encomium to George Eliot's idea of scientific realism—especially references to "invisible thoroughfares" and "lurking-places"—flirts with the melodramatic. She edges closer to the Dickensian in Darwin in order to offset any suggestion of the Darwinian in Dickens.

Along with Collins, Dickens, one decides, came to occupy a makeshift middle ground, definitely not post-Lyell but no longer strictly biblical.[19] Although he stopped short of converting providence into a natural force as impersonal as evolution, he was equally reluctant to equate it emphatically with God. In *A Tale of Two Cities*, providence becomes "the great magician who majestically works out the appointed order of the Creator" (TTC, 473). Prestidigitation still originates with the deity, who determines the sequence of events, but providence is the executor. Dickens's "great magician" is a poetic fabrication intended to preserve an inherent principle of

justice without totally surrendering the anthropomorphic deity of traditional Christianity. Lest he seem old-fashioned or unscientific, Dickens
disguises his position by attempting to sound as timeless as a Greek
tragedian.

When Felix Holt urges listeners to provide "a home" within themselves
for the "outside wisdom which lies in the supreme unalterable nature of
things" (FH, 626), he sounds like Dickens talking about "the Creator."
"Unalterable" and "supreme" are divine attributes. Holt's words have
reverential connotations because he is trying to seem inspirational while
George Eliot discusses secular progress through social reform. Holt ex-
horts readers to internalize life's forward drive, to domesticate it, using
their bodies as its "home" and thereby participating in evolution. In order
not to appear overly secular and unorthodox, Holt falls back on the
language of a parson when he recommends aligning oneself with an impersonal tendency toward improvement that is allegedly indigenous to life
itself.

George Eliot's strategy is no less evasive than Dickens's and hardly less
poetic: he credits "the appointed order" with a necromancer's powers; her
subtler anthropomorphism imputes an ingrained "wisdom" to the world's
capacity for change. Dickens and Eliot put rival trends in the scientific
culture of the time to different poetic uses in the service of their conflicting
social philosophies; they do this just as imaginatively as Darwin discovered
a scientific use for some of Dickens's narrative techniques.

The rivalry between gradualism and catastrophism presented yet another crux for realism. Was it more realistic to continue interpreting the
present by bringing the past constantly to bear upon it, or periodically to
revalue the past—in effect, overturn it—in light of the present? Carlyle
typified the first approach in the philippics of *Past and Present* (1843): he
juxtaposed the well-run Bury St. Edmunds, a twelfth-century Benedictine
abbey, and modern, leaderless England. Lyell's hypothesis, buttressed by
Darwin's theory, utilized newly discovered processes to reinterpret the
past, which was then seen as prelude to the present moment and its inferior
antecedent.

In the novels of Dickens and Collins, stress falls upon the idea of life as
a concatenation of events, with the current moment as the last link in a long
chain. The melodramatic realist shines a light backward to the point from
which his sequence began. From there he looks forward to the present,
revaluating every link in the chain. Past events clarify what present developments from them mean; in turn, these developments tell what will
happen again if similar circumstances are allowed to play themselves out in

much the same way. Krook's combustion is both an outcome and a prediction because he and "all Lord Chancellors in all Courts" where "injustice is done" die "the same death eternally" (BH, 431). Catastrophism is relentlessly consequence-oriented.

George Eliot defines the past in *Felix Holt* as society's cultural inheritance, a kind of bank deposit, compounded daily, for the present to build upon. It is always the present moment that seems most propitious and has greatest value. Gradualism is chiefly future-oriented, looking hopefully toward the next step. A culmination of all that went before rather than a consequence, no next step can literally repeat triumphs or mistakes from the past. Not surprisingly, although George Eliot rewrites Dickens constantly, she displays scant interest in the device of reenactment that Collins employs suspensefully in *The Moonstone* and Dickens would have used in *The Mystery of Edwin Drood*, a device symbolizing the possibility that history repeats itself.

For George Eliot, the present, illuminating the past, enables one to understand the past fully for the first time. Darwin's theories of 1859, for instance, are applied to her reconsideration of the years leading up to the first Reform Bill. This happens in 1866 (*Felix Holt*) and again but with greater assurance after the second Reform Bill in 1872 (*Middlemarch*). George Eliot maintains that events in provincial centers like Treby Magna and Middlemarch, during and prior to 1832, were indications at the social level of the processes Darwin subsequently described as having been at work over centuries in the animal kingdom and the natural world. His ideas help her to analyze changes in the recent past which, seen in retrospect, also vindicate his ideas.

The paradox behind gradualism is that novelists who follow the dictates of Darwin and Lyell seem more willing than sensationalists to countenance drastic alteration. If one believes George Eliot, our conception of human nature changed decisively in 1859, not in 1910, as Virginia Woolf later claims. That is one reason why Eliot's Esther Lyon is so different from Dickens's Esther Summerson: she is freer to grow, less burdened by her past or any sense of original sin, hence (in Eliot's opinion), new or modern. If deserving, George Eliot's characters are mostly in the ascendant; even when meritorious, Dickens's have a stronger sense of themselves as descendants upon whom the past often cruelly imposes.

Regarding the present as the future that identifiable past events have brought to pass is one perspective on reality. Looking backward and forward from a seemingly all-important moment, be it 1859, 1832, or 1867, is another. To term the latter strategy an application of the scientific spirit to life and, consequently, the more realistic approach for a novelist seems a matter of personal preference rather than objective judgment. To think of the present moment and the society in which one finds oneself as culminant is surely a modern tendency. This attitude is to be expected whenever a country is expanding its empire or advancing technologically, or can point to some political improvements. On the other hand, satires of a society's belief in the moral superiority of the historical moment it occupies are almost equally modern. Placed in less flattering contexts, one's age becomes part of a cycle of rises and falls (catastrophism), not the finest apex to date (gradualism). In *Heart of Darkness*, for example, ivory-traders are either Europe's cultural emissaries, "bearers of a spark from the sacred flame" (HD, 4), or proof that countries which were once provinces of Rome are now exploiting colonies of their own.

The strictly scientific argument between gradualism and catastrophism, formerly considered a Victorian controversy, now engulfs astronomers, paleontologists, and astrophysicists—not just evolutionary biologists—and shows signs of spreading to the public forum.[20] England escaped revolution, but engagements with the Boers, Kaiser Wilhelm, and the Führer make it clear that the country had no power to choose gradualism over catastrophism for good and all in 1832 as the inevitable means of bringing about change in individuals and society. Otherwise, as late as 1872, with Dickens already dead, George Eliot would not have labored so diligently in *Middlemarch* to prove that it had so chosen.

Looked at from a twofold perspective, Victorian realisms, never strictly scientific, were always also poetic. Arguments from science were put forth poetically: that is, by analogies. Society in *Felix Holt* and *Middlemarch* resembles a maturing organism. The disintegration of a corrupt civilization, Dickens argues, although it seems late in coming, happens suddenly and violently, like spontaneous combustion. The worlds of *Bleak House* and *Middlemarch*, one determines, are so antagonistic to one another because each is colored in part after one of two Romantic poets—in each novel, the one who better suits its Victorian author's mood and moral purpose.

In 1798, two different ways of pursuing "the truth of nature,"[21] the same quest undertaken from different angles, yielded what Victorian novelists came to see as two surprisingly different universes, of which one proved darker than the other. The implications of this discrepancy were deemphasized at the time Wordsworth and Coleridge were collaborating to publish *Lyrical Ballads* but something similar happened later on a larger scale when Dickens and Mrs. Gaskell assessed the impact of industrialism on human nature, and when he and George Eliot explored the Victorian community for signs of brotherhood. Ostensibly working in concert,

Wordsworth and Coleridge laid the groundwork for opposing vehicular modes; these proved helpful to novelists expressing attitudes toward life that were more widely apart than the two Romantic poets ever desired their outlooks to be.

Poetry achieves "novelty" by casting over truthfulness "the modifying colors of imagination" (BL, 2:5).[22] But Wordsworth and Coleridge asked for trouble by taking "truth of nature" as an absolute. In a more secular age to follow, fidelity to the nature of things became relative, a matter of personal perspective and thus harder to agree upon. Victorian novelists accused one another of lying because the colorings or emphases they put on events virtually became the different realities they saw.

The challenge for Wordsworth, Coleridge recalled, was to make "ordinary" subjects, "characters and incidents . . . found in every village," seem splendid. His job was to impart "the charm of novelty to things of every day," to unveil "the wonders of the world before us" (BL, 2:5-6), so that simple people and diurnal occurrences would create as much pleasurable excitement in the reader's mind as something patently "supernatural." From this approach, George Eliot derives popular emotional support for observing the "gradual action" of "ordinary causes" that make the "slow-growing system of things" seem "wonderful" in *Felix Holt* and *Middlemarch*.

Paradoxically, this brand of realism becomes more romantic the harder it tries to remain realistic: it wants to show how the ordinary can be just as marvelous as the spectacular, indeed more engrossing. Such an approach is not only likely to adopt an approbatory outlook on life and human nature but also to cultivate caution and prescribe restraint when change is at hand. Its radicalism will be of a milder hue because the novelist is persuaded that the world he or she is dealing with has always been inherently attractive. George Eliot extols "unhistoric" actions to show that dividends from them, although nearly invisible, eventually accumulate. Similarly, Wordsworth, throughout *The Prelude* (1850), described the steady growth of his mind in what could be taken as a poetic paradigm for the essentially benevolent forward motion of the life process.

To Coleridge's lot fell "persons and characters supernatural, or at least romantic" (BL, 2:6), whom he had to make seem natural or convincing. "Excellence" would "consist in" the "dramatic truth of such emotions, as would naturally accompany" sensational or extraordinary "situations, supposing them real. And real in *this* sense they have been," he adds, "to every human being who, from whatever source of delusion, has at any time believed himself under supernatural agency" (BL, 2:5). Wordsworth's partner was to extract from the unusual, the deceptively exceptional, an insight into the everyday. No matter how unique the happening, it would be made to yield, more impressively than possible otherwise, fundamental precepts about human nature. These universals would be useful to all readers even if their personal experience of the "supernatural" and "romantic" never went beyond the vicarious.

The paradox implicit in the kind of "interesting of the affections" Coleridge prefers, as Dickens and Collins realized, is that situations unusual enough to appear "supernatural" are frequently required in order to jar the community into realizing deficiencies that should have been self-evident. These jarrings, the paradox continues, are less rare than they appear and never as improbable as anti-sensationalists think. Lacking the contagious fever Jo carries to Esther Summerson, the brotherhood of high and low in *Bleak House* might have become totally obscured. Dickens and Collins, one concludes, evolve a valid conception of realism by refining elements from what could be called the Coleridgean mode. Their strategy is to include startling incidents conveyed with a wealth of convincing description. They not only insist on the validity of traumatic, calamitous events but rely even more firmly than Coleridge on the access these provide to facts of life otherwise unattainable.

Ideal for shock tactics and delivering rude awakenings, a poetic realism indebted to Coleridge invited luridness; it tolerated occasional lapses into caricature but more than compensated for them by enfranchising satire. It enabled satirical novelists to criticize the Victorian scene, often by parodying Wordsworth: that is, by redoing famous sequences from his poetry in a sensational manner. This alone must have seemed sufficient provocation for George Eliot to regard her parodies of Dickens as rallies to Wordsworth's defense.

In *The Woman in White*, Collins repeatedly tries to outdo the parodies of Wordsworth that occur throughout *Bleak House*. The church at Old Welmingham is Sir Percival Glyde's Tintern Abbey. On his first visit to its vestry, he keeps his baronetcy by forging a record of his parents' marriage in the register. This action brings him "life and food / For future years,"[23] but not in the spiritual sense of sustaining impressions absorbed from nature. Revisiting the scene of the crime years later, Glyde hopes to fortify his original transgression, but he knocks over a light and is consumed in raging fire that results. On a par with Krook's spontaneous combustion, the scene is an attempt to outstrip Dickens and parody Wordsworth simultaneously. Collins's false knight will have no "after years / When these wild ecstasies [the furor of the crowd attempting to quell the blaze and rescue him] shall be matured / Into a sober pleasure" ("Tintern Abbey," lines 137-39).

The woman in white accosts Hartright, Pip is seized by Magwitch, and the ancient mariner "holds" the wedding guest "with his glittering eye"[24]—none of these encounters resembles Wordsworth's fortuitous meeting with the Cumberland Beggar, from whose benign presence—and the implications of his snug place in nature—the poet draws conclusions that reaffirm his satisfaction with a benevolent, well-made world. Pip, Hartright, and the wedding guest become embroiled in mysteries. Disoriented, they must alter their plans and eventually their philosophies.

Dickens and Collins seek to disable Wordsworth's belief in the discovery of fructifying truths through painless providential encounters, but such encounters can be seen as forerunners of character formation through beneficial social intercourse in George Eliot's fictions. To Dickens and Collins, the garrulous mariner's tale of sin, hardship, and onerous salvation comes closer to the tenor of human existence as they wish to present it than the reassuring messages allegedly contained in the beggar's voluminous silence.

The beggar's life, Wordsworth decides, is proof of the basic wisdom in "Nature's law":

> That none, the meanest of created things,
> Or forms created the most vile and brute,
> The dullest or most noxious, should exist
> Divorced from good—a spirit and pulse of good.
> A life and soul, to every mode of being
> Inseparably linked.[25]

Here is practically the identical lesson the mariner at last learns when he atones for having killed the albatross by blessing the water-snakes: "He prayeth well, who loveth well / Both man and bird and beast" (*Ancient Mariner*, lines 612-13). The sanctity and interdependence of all living creatures is also the moral that Victorian London is supposed to gather from the sadly neglected Jo; the travels of this urbanized parody of Cumberland's mendicant bring infections from Tom-all-alone's into the Jarndyce household, thereby reasserting the fraternity of man, "every mode of being inseparably linked" through the "most noxious."

By contrast, the scene a widowed Dorothea beholds from the window at Lowick delivers messages in a rehabilitated Wordsworthian vein. Dorothea is heartened by the tranquil harmony of the vista and by the liveliness and vitality of several figures who could have stepped out of a Wordsworth ballad: "a man with a bundle on his back," a "woman carrying her baby," a "shepherd with his dog" (MM, 578). They speak as silently yet eloquently to Dorothea as the beggar to Wordsworth. Despite a disappointing marriage and recent bereavement, she senses that she will always be part of the world's "palpitating life"—in Wordsworth's words, its "spirit and pulse of good." The world Dorothea enlists in contravenes the one the repentant mariner rejoins. It is a healthier, more inviting place, full of favorable prospects.

In short, Wordsworth and Coleridge become stand-ins for the real issues. Without the former, Dickens and Collins surmise, belief in the steady evolution of society loses a valuable corroborative antecedent. If the Victorian world has become more like a Coleridge poem, then cries for its radical overhaul and warnings of impending disaster are harder to ignore. The success of George Eliot's contention that gradual improvement is the essential rhythm of Victorian life rests on her ability to persuade readers that events since 1798 have proved Wordsworth's philosophy to be still correct. Besides invoking him for support, she looks back to commend his percipience.

Dickens and Collins write as if they think Coleridge the greater prophet and want the status of the two Romantics reversed. Collins reuses for *The Woman in White* the scene in which Geraldine manifests herself to Christabel. Like the apparition that astonishes Hartright, Geraldine materializes in "the middle of the night," and she is "drest in a silken robe of white."[26] Christabel admits the lady to her father's castle as a secret sharer, and Geraldine hypnotizes Christabel so that she will not be able to speak of what follows. Then, lying down by her benefactor's side, she embraces her until daylight. Having slept, the visitor seems "fairer yet" ("Christabel," line 374). Despite being compared mainly to serpents, she has renewed herself as a vampire might. In *Edwin Drood*, a vampirelike Jasper exercises a similar power to keep Rosa silent about his desire for her. If Geraldine is an aspect of Christabel which the latter has ignored or does not recognize, a second self trying to fasten upon her, Dickens and Coleridge both take an interest in split personalities and endow an outwardly respectable personage with a malevolent darker side that is presented to others as if it were a demon lover. Dickens extends the curious affinity between Geraldine and Christabel beyond the doubling of Anne Catherick for Laura Fairlie; in his hands, it comes to foreshadow Jasper's split personality.

Showing darker sides to both Jasper and Cloisterham readily develops into a parody of Wordsworth's efforts to strip the "film of familiarity" from life, to remove the "lethargy of custom (BL, 2:6)." Do so, Dickens maintains, and it will not be "the loveliness and the wonders of the world before us"—Wordsworth's specialties—that emerge with greater clarity but, instead, the "skeleton" in humanity's closet, trailing clouds of mystery and the odor of well-concealed horrors. The lustful murderer within the choirmaster despises "custom" and "familiarity," Coleridge's words for Wordsworth's domain.

Instead of proving that every "life and soul" is "inseparably linked," the choirmaster-murderer is at cross-purposes with society and within himself. As director of the choir, he is "constantly exercising an Art" that brings him into "mechanical harmony with others," while "the spirit of the man" is "in moral accordance or interchange with nothing around him" (ED, 264). Dickens inverts Wordsworth's discovery of the highest truths in one of society's lowest figures. Even a nonentity like the Cumberland beggar could illustrate "Nature's" finest "law" of universal communion, but the secret sharer in Jasper proves that the "meanest" and "most vile" aspects of human nature can be found in the highest or most respected places, "linked" in other words "to every mode of being."

The Victorian world, Dickens and Collins argue, is stranger, more extraordinary, and far less pleasant than its veneer of prosperity and propriety suggests. Their framing of reality aspires to capture not only its underlying strangeness but the contrapuntal tension, fundamentally anti-Wordsworthian in texture, between that strangeness and the superficial impression of normality.

Throughout *The Prelude*, Wordsworth's poetic intelligence nourishes itself on "the life / In common things—the endless store of things, / Rare, or at least so seeming, every day / Found all about me in one neighbourhood." The poet never tires of praising "life's every-day appearances." They show him "a new world," full of "spiritual dignity," and foster the sort of "ennobling interchange / Of action from without and from within"[27] that George Eliot finds so congenial.

Sentiments of a Wordsworthian sort seem to have been on her mind in the virtual preface she incorporates into *Adam Bede*.

As its title indicates, Chapter 17 in Book Two is one "In Which the Story Pauses a Little" so that George Eliot can interpolate an essay on realism that updates the Wordsworthian mode. Her novels will paint "faithful pictures of a monotonous homely existence," which has been the fate of the majority (AB, 176). She will eschew alike the extremes of "pomp" and "absolute indigence." Her brand of realism will exclude "heroic warriors" and "world-stirring actions." Instead, she resolves to emphasize "an old woman bending over her flower-pot." This woman's "spinning wheel" and "stone jug" symbolize "all those cheap common things which are the precious necessaries of life to her" and which the Wordsworthian realist considers major clues to what life is about for most people much of the time.

The "way in which I have come to the conclusion that human nature is loveable," the narrator of *Adam Bede* explains, "has been by living a great deal among people more or less commonplace," people "of whom you would perhaps hear nothing very surprising if you were to inquire about them in the neighbourhoods where they dwelt" (AB, 182). Therefore, novelists must always be "ready to give the loving pains of a life to the faithful representing of commonplace things"; they should "see beauty in these commonplace things, and delight in showing how kindly the light of heaven falls on them" (AB, 177).

In 1859, as George Eliot was making these pronouncements, Dickens was using *A Tale of Two Cities* to improve upon *Barnaby Rudge* with a fuller study of cataclysmic disturbances that can befall the corrupt societies of an unregenerate world. An exercise in self-justification, George Eliot's unofficial preface comes fully into focus as a competitive document only after one has witnessed the subsequent attacks on Dickens in *Felix Holt* and *Middlemarch*, which implement the 1859 policy statements.

Adam Bede is not "a world of extremes" because it avoids both "pomp" and "indigence." These are the two levels on which Dickens moves back and forth from aristocrats to citizens in *A Tale of Two Cities* and, in *Bleak House*, from the Dedlocks to Jo. George Eliot may have had the illiterate crossing-sweeper in mind when she complained about novelists who deal in "sentimental wretchedness," a misunderstanding of the commonplace person that perverts the "deep human sympathy" Wordsworth felt for figures like the Cumberland beggar. The Romantic poet could still see the beggar's "spiritual dignity" despite the old man's reduced circumstances. Dickens, George Eliot implies, claims the reader's sympathies by emphasizing Jo's loss of those very attributes. Thus Dickens's parodies of Wordsworth are failures of moral perception, insults to his characters and readers alike.

When George Eliot assails *Bleak House* directly in *Felix Holt*, old Tommy Trounsem, the "bill-sticker" and the "last of a very old family-line," is more clearly her parodic revaluation of Jo. Trounsem ought to emerge from the novel's equivalent of the Jarndyce versus Jarndyce case as heir of Transome Court. Instead, he is trampled to death by a rioting election-day mob after falling "drunkenly" near the entrance to the Seven Stars (FH, 433). Unlike Jo, who has no place, Trounsem is entitled to the grandest place in the neighborhood but never sets foot in it. Jo is Wordsworth's mendicant urbanized and a parody of the precocious child in such poems as "We Are Seven" and "Anecdote for Fathers." In *Adam Bede*, George Eliot denies the "wretchedness" in the depiction, without dignity, of persons like Jo; in *Felix Holt*, her account of Trounsem ridicules the sentimentality.

In keeping with George Eliot's internal preface, Hayslope peasantry closely resembles characters in Wordsworth's poems from *Lyrical Ballads*. Both groups have little in common with their bloodthirsty French counterparts in *A Tale of Two Cities*. The inhabitants of the little village near Monsieur the Marquis's chateau no doubt struck Eliot as outlandish. Although completed before Dickens's novel began appearing, *Adam Bede* contains no "heroic warriors" or "world-stirring actions" to match those in Dickens's novel because they would seem far-fetched in a realistic (i.e., Wordsworthian) English context, Eliot believes.

Much of the writing in this unofficial preface becomes tongue-in-cheek after one has read *Felix Holt* and can imagine George Eliot not yet ready for extensive parodic revaluations but with Dickens already on her mind. She does not think the "cheap common things" she concentrates upon either "cheap" or "common." The implication is that sensationalism always deserves these adjectives in their derogatory sense. In George Eliot's fictions, "common things," as Wordsworth says, are "rare, or at least so seeming," not "cheap" but "an endless store" of valuable material. Thus "a monotonous homely existence" is not really either if all the merits and moments of crises associated with it are carefully weighed.

In *Bleak House* and *A Tale of Two Cities*, the reader is constantly hearing "very surprising" things—about Esther's parentage, for example, or Krook's manner of dying, or Darnay's responsibility for the injustices his father and uncle committed against Manette, or Carton's redemption through self-sacrifice. If one hears nothing equally "surprising" about either Adam Bede or Mrs. Poyser, the implication arises, it is because one has already heard too much of this sort of thing about a rival's characters. Their exaggerated capacities for both good and evil allegedly cast doubt upon Dickens's love for humanity, which he can never accept as is.

That "human nature is loveable" becomes a proposition one assents to with difficulty after reading *Bleak House* or *A Tale of Two Cities*. Does it extend to the Smallweeds, Vholes, Madame Defarge, the rioters resharpening their blood-stained weapons? Live long enough among the "more or less commonplace people," George Eliot reminds satirists like Dickens, and one's opinion of humanity will be corrected for the better. The very preponderance of the "more or less commonplace" will overwhelm the would-be realist with its truth. It will cancel out or push aside such misleading extremes as Madame Defarge's unquenchable thirst for revenge and Carton's sacrifice.

The "delight" that George Eliot takes "in showing how kindly the light of heaven falls" on the "beauty in commonplace things" is her rendition of the "modifying colors of imagination" that Wordsworth and Coleridge agreed to cast over nature in *Lyrical Ballads*. But it is closer to the former's interest in bringing out "charm," "novelty," and especially "loveliness," a virtual synonym for her own word for humanity: "loveable." The secular realist's job is to demonstrate that the world retains the splendor it possessed when poets formerly saw it as a product of divine creation rather than of evolution and reform. Eliot expects the "light of heaven" to make molelike and myopic the "backward light" Dickens told Collins he had employed in *A Tale of Two Cities* to prove that retribution comes slowly but inevitably in an unjust world.

When Wordsworth insisted in 1798 that poets speak "the language of *real* life," the phrase *"real* life" had the ring of an objective standard, a visible referent against which to measure art's accuracy. Coleridge considered it "an equivocal expression." In *Adam Bede*'s Chapter 17 more than half a century later, George Eliot equivocates indeed. Her "faithful account" will be of "men and things" not per se but as they have "mirrored themselves" in her mind. Her title to objectivity, she insists, is genuine, but it rests on the confidence she puts in her subjectivity; she declares that her mind is a superior reflector of reality. The switch from *"real* life" to a mirroring of it, whether fully deliberate or not, virtually requires that George Eliot offer proofs of objectivity. She must give evidence that her artistic sensibility is subtler, a more impressionable surface than any rival's.

Trollope's internal preface in Chapter 15 of *The Warden*, also a short treatise on realism, may have schooled George Eliot for her defense of the Wordsworthian mode, since it preceded *Adam Bede* by four years. When John Bold, the Barchester reformer, reads the opening installment of *The Almshouse*, he objects to the "absurdly strong colouring of the picture" (W, 149). Mr. Popular Sentiment's "eight paupers" are innocent, angelic victims of a mismanaged charitable institution that is a metaphor for the unjust scheme of things. The sometimes petty but allegedly more realistic almsmen Trollope presents could have appeared in *Lyrical Ballads* or, subsequently, at Hayslope.

Bold thinks the absurdity produced by an overly colorful imagination should "disable the work from doing either good or harm." But, Trollope interjects, he "was wrong." The novelist "who paints for the million must use glaring colours, as no one knew better than Mr. Sentiment when he described the inhabitants of his almshouse; and the radical reform which has now swept over such establishments has owed more to the twenty numbers of Mr. Sentiment's novel than to all the *true* complaints which have escaped from the public for the last half century" (W, 149-50; italics added). Trollope's satirical interjection sounds resentful. Dickens and the reading public are presumed to be a conspiracy, making it imposible for a beginning realist like Trollope to tell the truth about society's problems because Dickens's captivating distortions have been accepted in place of life itself.

Trollope places his hopes for a favorable reception in the reader discerning enough to appreciate the ironies in Bold's discomfiture and in an authorial observation that at first sounds almost like a compliment. The "radical reform" that invariably follows Mr. Sentiment's outcries is not prompted by the "true complaints" the public makes and therefore cannot be solutions to those complaints. Instead of doing neither "good or harm," Sentiment's excesses bring about the second in the guise of the first. Thus Harding's resignation, an apparent victory for reform, rectifies what may have been a minor injustice by leaving the paupers worse off than before.

A "quiet town in the west of England" (W, 9), Barchester seems in keeping with Wordsworth's preference for "ordinary life": that is, "characters and incidents" to be "found in every village." Yet the town also serves as Trollope's crucible for a struggle between the forces for quick change and supporters, like himself, of the status quo. The outcome has reverberations across what Tom Towers calls "the whole system" (W, 144). Trollope throws ordinariness into high relief by accentuating the grotesqueness of those who fail to appreciate it. Although he stands for fidelity to the real, he paints Dickens (as Mr. Popular Sentiment) and Carlyle (as Dr. Anticant) in the "glaring colours" Sentiment uses on Mr. Harding. Trollope enlarges the failings of these writers while toning down the kind of social abuse they supposedly magnify.

Inveighing against the disadvantages under which Dickens places the would-be reporter of "true complaints" could be misconstrued as a concession speech from a novelist who envisions himself and his brand of realism being forever in the minority. George Eliot decides not to use Dickens's strong colors against him and to exude more confidence. In the internal preface to *Adam Bede*, she speaks as if her perspective represents the majority's; what she means is that she expects it soon will.

In contrast to George Eliot's apparent overconfidence, diffidence impairs the introduction Wilkie Collins penned for *Basil* (1852). His explanation of how the Coleridgean mode could be applied to a realistic Victorian fiction is feebly presented; it survives as a truncated rationale for strategies Collins used more competently in *The Woman in White* and *The Moonstone*.

Collins communicates his attitude toward the fictionalizing of real life in the fewest possible sentences:

I have not thought it either politic or necessary, while adhering to realities, to adhere to common-place everyday realities only. In other words, I have not stooped so low as to assure myself of the reader's belief in the probability of my story, by never once calling on him for the exercise of his faith. Those extraordinary accidents and events which happen to few men, seemed to me as legitimate materials for fiction to work with, when there was good object in using them, as the ordinary accidents and events which may, and do, happen to us all.[28]

Only by "appealing to other sources (as genuine in their way)" but "beyond" the reader's "own experience," Collins continues, could he "hope to fix his interest and excite his suspense, to occupy his feelings, or to stir his thoughts." Calling on the reader for "the exercise of his faith" is Collins's inferior translation of Coleridge's "poetic faith": "that willing suspension of disbelief for the moment" which the Romantic poet considered essential for the success of *The Rime of the Ancient Mariner*" (BL, 2:6).

The sensational realist will not use events that never happen or that are impossible, but Coleridge is the unnamed authority for permission to employ those rarer happenings that only a "few men" experience. Collins ought to have emphasized that such materials are "genuine" whenever they reveal general truths, primary laws, the propounding of which is presumably the novelist's "good object in using them." Like Coleridge, Collins means no disrespect to "everyday realities." He is simply not interested "only" in them, as Wordsworth was. Instead, he is also concerned with those times when the ordinary intersects with the extraordinary, with accidents and events outside the reader's personal experience but able to put that experience in a new light.

In his four-paragraph preface to *The Moonstone*, even less eloquent than the introduction to *Basil*, Collins proposes to trace the "influence of character on circumstances." Preparing for *Middlemarch*, George Eliot responds by insisting that the influence of incident on personality is the truer concern. Emphasizing circumstances rather than personality, she implies, is sensational; taking character as a constant is anti-evolutionary. Collins, although writing before her, sounds as put-upon as Dickens defending Krook's spontaneous combustion: he states that "the story of the Diamond" is "founded, in some important particulars, on the stories of two of the royal diamonds of Europe."[29] He ought to have maintained that man's character is indeed constant in the sense that it is irreparably flawed, like the diamond, and continually threatened by its darker aspects.

Collins avoids the singular in the note to *Basil*: he adheres to "realities," of which there are said to be many. The idea of life as multiple realities becomes clearer in the fragments of a total vision related by Collins's several narrators in *The Woman in White* and *The Moonstone*. Regrettably, the novelist failed to pursue his idea of a multiplicity of universes and attendant realisms beyond the subordinate clause in which it occurs in 1852. As a result, he seems to minimize "common-place everyday realities" instead of stressing the way "extraordinary accidents" can influence them. He appears to be saying that he has "not stooped" to commonplace things. Revised only slightly, "common-place everyday realities" is the phrase George Eliot seizes upon for a battle cry in *Adam Bede*. Instead of placing unrealistic demands upon the reader's "faith," she will give "faithful" accounts, not probabilities but "the exact truth." While Collins confesses he is "appealing to other sources" than personal experience, George Eliot insists her stories are of "men and things" her own mind has "mirrored."

Dickens's 1853 preface to *Bleak House* outdoes Collins at bungling opportunities. It especially misses the chance to reply effectively to G.H. Lewes, who had disputed the scientific truth of spontaneous combustion.[30] If Krook's manner of demise is pseudoscientific, Lewes wanted to suggest, then the argument that society is seething with internal corruption and could destroy itself from within also collapses. George Eliot's more attractive idea that civilization is gradually improving through steady reform can then be put in its place. Logically, no ironclad connection exists of the sort Lewes implies. One can hold unproven or outdated scientific opinions and still write reliable satiric critiques of a nation's judicial apparatus. One can even make that system an analogue for all of society's imprisoning systems, moral and mental as well as political.

The 1853 preface spends too much space justifying the factual trappings—the "thirty cases of spontaneous combustion" on record—of Dickens's poetically scientific metaphor for revolution. As with his use of Jarndyce versus Jarndyce, the prevailing idea here is that realism is the setting-down of actual facts, which is a much narrower mandate than telling the truth about life through a convincing impression of tendencies for good or ill in the nature of things. Dickens cites Bianchini and Le Cat, virtually the same sort of evidence—popular, topical, journalistic—for exploding Krook as can be located in Carlyle for letting Jo infect Esther and Charley. A contagious Jo and a combustible Krook—each was an amply documented possibility.[31]

Only in the third sentence from the end of the preface does Dickens declare that he has "purposely dwelt on the romantic side of familiar things." Then he declines to explicate what could have been the most important bit of literary criticism he ever wrote. Despite Dickens's reticence, the modern revaluator concludes that the novelist hoped to fuse his emphasis on the topical with a satiric perspective (or coloring) derived, in part, from Coleridge. This coloring reveals how strangely transformed the ordinary world, so-called, quickly becomes if seen aright. The correction of perspective occurs if one integrates the normal, everyday life one is accustomed to see with the unpleasant, disconcerting situations that government, politicians, masters of deportment, and the moral codes of polite society frequently conspire to play down or ignore. While Woodcourt teaches the dying Jo to pray, Dickens writes, "The light is come upon the dark benighted way" (BH, 611). That the world is essentially a "benighted way" which the realistic novelist brings to light—a harsh, satirical light, not George Eliot's "kindly . . . light of heaven"—is the impetus behind Dickens's borrowings from the Coleridgean mode.

Stressing the "romantic side of familiar things" sounds Wordsworthian but can be so only parodically. In an unsatisfactory social system that is said to be going rapidly downhill, the phrase no longer means finding splendor in the commonplace; it must now pertain to the unusual, unattractive aspects that people and places, once taken for granted as humane and benign, have increasingly begun to assume.[32] Melodramatic realists, Dickens ought to have continued, borrow from Coleridge in two ways simultaneously: they use the extraordinary to show the inadvisability of seeing only the usual and, more important, to argue that the usual is becoming progressively stranger, more problematic and unacceptable. Paradoxically, the extraordinary is now more and more commonplace yet never becomes less disconcerting. In the London of *Bleak House* the Coleridgean mode encroaches upon the Wordsworthian, crowding it out. Esther Summerson grows up in a fantastic London, contemporary yet biologically prehistoric. Besides a guardian angel like Jarndyce and eventually a husband in Woodcourt, it contains monkeylike moneylenders and vampires disguised as members of the bar. Few of the marvels the ancient mariner chronicles are more astonishing.

Recalling the "fog and mist" predominant in parts of *The Rime of the Ancient Mariner*, Dickens's third-person narrator shrouds all London in "rawest," "densest" fog. When confusion reigns, mysteries proliferate and responsibilities go unacknowledged; foul weather from Coleridge rather than fine, didactic landscape from Wordsworthian Cumberland determines (or colors) the moral climate: "Fog everywhere" (BH, 4). The third-person narrator insists that meeting a Megalosaurus "would not be wonderful" (BH, 3), not romantic or supernatural at all, given the rate at which Victorian society is retrogressing.

George Eliot painstakingly removes the negative emphasis Dickens imparts to "the romantic side of familiar things." Even the image of a Megalosaurus is reused good-naturedly in *Felix Holt*.[33] Sir Maximus Debarry, who represents ultraconservative interests from Treby Manor, is "like those antediluvian animals whom the system of things condemned to carry such a huge bulk that they really could not inspect their bodily appurtenance, and had no conception of their own tails: their parasites doubtless had a merry time of it, and after did extremely well when the highbred saurian himself was ill at ease" (FH, 182).

Unlike Sir Leicester Dedlock and the politicians who succeed one another as interchangeable do-nothings in *Bleak House*, Sir Maximus is a comical holdover, no cause for alarm. Meeting this throwback in Treby Magna would not be "wonderful" either. That adjective must be reserved for "the system of things," which phases out the unworthy, along with his parasites whose "merry time" upon his carcass will not last. Thanks to the in-built wisdom of this system, the endangered species Sir Magnus represents will soon be extinct—proof that Darwin's theory applies to social change and a jocular contradiction of Dickens's fossilized institutions that persist until blown up.

Regretting "the great division" in Victorian fiction, Trollope finally called for novels that would be "at the same time realistic and sensational," after the fashion of life itself.[34] By the time he made this plea, the major hidden rivalries in Victorian fiction were literary history; Dickens and Eliot were dead. Reconsidered from a twofold perspective, most Victorian realists are seen to have combined the ordinary and the wonderful but in rival ways. They emphasized the marvelousness of the everyday or the increasing pertinence of the extraordinary in what were frequently equally poetic expressions of competing philosophies.

Walter Kendrick maintains that sensationalists fell victim to a "double urge" toward conventionality and innovation, that they indulged in sensation but demanded to be read as if they were realistic.[35] On the contrary, the phrase about "familiar things" having their "romantic side" suggests that they insisted on both. In quieter ways, it bears repeating, George Eliot obeyed her own version of a twofold urge: she wanted art to mirror not only the everyday but the heavenly splendor shining both upon and from it. The "double urge" in Dickens, Collins, *and* George Eliot is better termed another form of double vision, no matter how different for each. Ultimately, the modern revaluator decides that pitting scientific realism, so-called, against the melodramatic or sensational variety is an exercise in imprecision. He opts for terms like *realistic romanticism* for the Coleridgean strain and *romantic realism* for the Wordsworthian. Denominations of this sort emphasize the importance of philosophical disposition and vantage point instead of instigating a quarrel between truth and falsity.

Wordsworth and Coleridge, one decides, drove one of the first sizable wedges between sacred and profane, thereby setting the stage for the era of competing secular realisms synonymous with Victorian fiction. Inadvertently, they gave a boost to secularization long before George Eliot declared herself its champion. As the "ordinary" became sufficiently wonderful per se, it diminished the need some Victorian novelists felt for an external, spiritual order. Eventually, Stephen Dedalus would consider the celebration of earthly beauty—the transformation of the profane into art—the only worthwhile form of transubstantiation; Virginia Woolf would call herself and James Joyce "spiritualists" mainly because they "look within . . . an ordinary mind on an ordinary day" and find its incessant activity, the myriad of impressions it receives, "the proper stuff of fiction."[36]

Walter Hartright in *The Woman in White* and Esther Summerson in *Bleak House*, like Franklin Blake in *The Moonstone* or Pip in *Great Expectations*, appear to live in a universe that frequently resembles a Coleridge poem. They confront what that poet called "the riddle of the world" and must attempt to "unravel it." Dorothea Brooke, by contrast, seems to inhabit a world that recalls Wordsworth's poetry and operates in respectful obedience to allegedly scientific updatings of its positive themes and principles. The creators of these characters drew on poems familiar to the general reader in order to ratify further their rival impressions of the kind of place Victorian society had become.

Are daily incidents, when punctuated by the exceptional or startling occurrence, less valid or less instructive than happenings whose beauty and didactic value lie mainly in their wonderful ordinariness? Is life more like a tale told by the ancient mariner or the lessons silently communicated by Wordsworth's aged beggar? Clearly, Wordsworth and Coleridge did not ask each other such questions. Theirs was not a rivalry, hidden or otherwise. Victorian novelists, one concludes, posed such questions as a means of challenging one another's credibility. Another way they became protomodern was by reexamining their Romantic heritage. Their parodies of one another's works demonstrated that the concept of objectivity as intersubjectivity or consensus had become more problematic in the 1850s and '60s than anyone had imagined possible in 1798.

To the modern revaluator of Victorian fiction, *Lyrical Ballads* furnishes an unintentional parody of the phenomenon that structuralists call dialogical or deconstructive: one work composed from two perspectives which, contrary to plan, seem to begin interrogating each other. In 1798, however, the rival attitudes belonged to two different authors who downplayed their differences. What happened to the partnership of Wordsworth and Coleridge in the 1850s and '60s was a direct result of the rivalries between novelists that it can be used to prefigure. *Lyrical Ballads* is no justification for the postmodernist argument that Dickens unwittingly pits Esther's storytelling against the third-person narrator's observations or that

Thackeray talks at cross-purposes in *Vanity Fair. Lyrical Ballads* does not deconstruct of its own accord any more than *Bleak House* does, nor do Dickens and George Eliot in effect deconstruct it. More precisely, Wordsworth and Coleridge, formerly poet-allies, were transformed into mutually antipathetic tendencies by their respective intellectual heirs. For Eliot, upgrading Wordsworth was akin to borrowing metaphors to describe the life process from Darwinian science. To Dickens, dismissing Wordsworth was not very different from Eliot's subsequent attempts to consign *Bleak House* to the era of pre-Lyell paleontology. Each novelist sought to establish a useful philosophical alignment in defense of his or her idea of realism while depriving a rival of similar support.

Any disquisition on realism in the nineteenth-century novel that omits the arguments realists conducted with one another—both about particular issues and, building upon them, the overall nature of things—is a fruitless quest. Only the modern Casaubon, one concludes, should undertake it. One candidate for the job defines realism as the acceptance of what is, without prejudice on the author's part: the novelist lets data speak, with a minimum of direction or interference.[37] This approach overlooks utopian and dystopian tendencies in competing novels like *North and South* and *Hard Times*. Another maintains that a novel is realistic to "the extent that all points of view summoned by the text agree": that is, as long as they "converge upon the 'same' world."[38] This definition neatly sidesteps the lack of consensus between rival Victorian novels: when George Eliot rewrites *Bleak House* in *Middlemarch*, she summons Dickens's point of view into her novel, where it is ridiculed for not describing the world as she sees it. One cannot speak of "the genial consensus of realistic narration" within a given Victorian novel as if it "implies a unity in human experience which assures us that we all inhabit the same world."[39] Most of the rivalries between great Victorian multiplot novels and the many worlds (not the "same world") presented in them imply exactly the opposite. In short, there were as many realisms in the nineteenth century as there were realists, and few common denominators were as omnipresent as rivalry. Victorian realism can virtually be redefined as the bravura assertion, by a prominent novelist or one who would soon be so, that his or her perspective was more realistic than any other, especially Dickens's.

Martin Price talks of supremely realistic moments in great novels when characters are observed "coming to reality."[40] At such moments of "unselfing," the reader perceives depths or layers as the character's outer self gives way to a deeper, other self. This insight ignores one of the most important layers of meaning or thematic significance that many characters in Victorian novels steadily possess: besides being forms of life, they are reforms of it, redoings or corrections of allegedly shallower characters whom they replace on every page with their fuller, more realistic selves. Correcting Dickens's Mr. Bounderby is part of Mr. Thornton's purpose in living and breathing.

In 1889, Wilbur L. Cross suggested that the English novel had developed "in clear cycles or reaction against the ascendant mode."[41] Scott and Austen revoked the Gothic mode; the Brontës and Dickens replied to Scott; and Thackeray and George Eliot wrote "in open dissent from the school of Dickens." This correct identification of Dickens as the pivotal figure in Victorian fiction neglects his replies to revaluations of his work by rivals. Much of the process of attack and counterattack was not "open" but hidden, that is, concealed beneath a veneer of cordiality, and several of the major competitions took place *within* the so-called ascendant mode, such as that between Dickens and Collins. The history of Victorian realisms from midcentury onward reveals extensive philosophical disagreements behind the aesthetic differences separating rival modes. Finally, if seen with double vision, all sides in the realism wars seem to be simultaneously on the attack and the defensive. There is constant warfare, in other words, but no "cycles." Trollope and George Eliot rewrote Dickens because they felt overwhelmed by his popularity. Dickens and Collins saw themselves beset by charges of sensationalism; critical of the social system, they were made to feel unscientific and irrelevant in an evolving community. When Dickens's rivals multiplied dramatically in the late 1850s, he must have considered himself outnumbered rather than "ascendant."

Despite Erich Auerbach's thesis,[42] the long drive toward mimesis has never been completed; it was disrupted by dissensions at the moment of alleged apotheosis. In nineteenth-century realistic fiction, the first serious challenges to the concept of realism itself began to appear. These have steadily multiplied ever since. The process of secularization that entitled each individual to his own perspective in effect guaranteed that no two perspectives would be identical and that one would often seem fabulous to another. Strictly speaking, there never was a Victorian realism: that is, a codified set of strategies and beliefs on which consensus had been explicitly reached. Rival novelists disagreed not only about how best to present reality but about what was real and what was not. To acclaim *Vanity Fair* (or any other Victorian novel) as "the outstanding example of English realism" is the sort of critical outburst one must learn to regard with a wary eye.[43]

The theory that all realistic fictions are fictions about realism and the conclusion that realism itself constitutes a fiction become less perturbing when one recognizes the fierce rivalries between one professed realist and another. Postmodern fiction and the criticism supporting its uses of literature against itself lose much of their luster if seen not as a new phase, a drastic breakaway, but as a parodic taking-to-extremes; it carries too far a modern process that began to accelerate when the nineteenth century passed its midpoint.[44] Skepticism about art's capacity ever to tell the whole truth about things as they are can be traced, in retrospect, to the onset of hidden rivalries at a time when life was daily becoming irreversibly more secularized. Questioning a rival's talent for mimesis, never one's own, started in the heyday of representationalism and should be considered virtually synonymous with it.

Despite the resulting divisiveness, rival novelists in nineteenth-century British fiction became caught up in a new collectivity as redefiners of reality and each other. Pervasive revaluation can be perceived from a double perspective as both a consequence of the secularization of experience and a counterstroke to overcome or at least offset the pluralism caused by that phenomenon. From one point of view, the process of Victorians reconsidering Victorians resulted from the collapse of orthodoxy, the loss of consensus, and was a harbinger of worse disagreements. From another, however, it became the new norm; by comparison with it, subsequent departures appear increasingly self-parodic and soon prove self-defeating.

Jonathan Culler's argument that "to speak of the meaning of the work is to tell the story of a reading"[45] means that there is no meaning, only one story told by the author and another by the critic. This position takes to extremes, thus unintentionally parodies, the valid realization that the writing of a Victorian novel was frequently also a rewriting of a rival. It perverts a competitive relativism by reducing the conflict between partial truths about perceived realities to a succession of self-referential stories about storytelling.

Some semioticians carry too far the suggestion that texts shed light on other texts: they argue that reciprocal illuminating is all that texts do, as if there were no books but only relationships between them. Where Victorian novels are concerned, rivalries between texts are part of the motivation behind a given work's inception, never the whole story. Such rivalries help to establish the meaning of both the target novel and its revaluator without superseding the texts themselves, which become richer and multipurpose. Intertextuality does not prove that a work of literature is principally reflexive in the sense of pertaining only or chiefly to other literature rather than to life. Hidden rivalries in Victorian fiction show that literature pertains to both, at times scrutinizing the two almost equally in what amounts to another exercise of double vision. Victorian novels are always about society and frequently about each other. Disagreement over the nature of things, particularly the condition and direction of civilization from 1850 onward, produces the intertextuality. Being about each other's perceptions and ideas, therefore, was ultimately yet another way in which Victorian novels were about life.

Novelists involved in the realism wars were not anxious to get out from under the troublesome influence of a great artist who overshadowed them from the past; they wanted to further themselves and their perspectives on life by preventing a contemporary's technique or philosophy from attaining a reputation they thought incommensurate with its merits. To grasp competitive Victorian realists fully, one travels through their novels again by following the parodic revaluations of other novels that they often contain. These are maps of clever, parodic rereadings based on intellectual disagreements, not misreadings.[46] Victorian novelists rewrote one another to correct a rival's misprisions of reality—a dangerous undertaking because the rival in question, alive and in full stride as was Dickens, was likely to strike back.

The 1850s, when the realism wars commenced, and the 1860s and '70s, in which pitched battles were fought, saw a critical nexus form: (1) progress, (2) reform, (3) industrialization, (4) expansion of empire, (5) secularization, and (6) biological evolution (defined as having to do with modification and perpetuation of organic beings)—each of these was both an idea and a process for the Victorians. Aligned, they were mutually reinforcing ideas, especially because the last could be said to objectify all the others by bringing them into accord with natural law. Without actually saying so, these interlocking ideas forecast a splendid future.

The question of who was a realistic novelist and who was not often hung on how much of the Victorian mid-century nexus a novelist's fictions endorsed. George Eliot championed the first, second, fifth, and sixth of the aforementioned ideas; Mrs. Gaskell the third. Trollope despised Dickens's handling of the first and second. Dickens challenged the steadiness and inevitability of the first process, doubted polite society's desire and capacity for the second, disliked the third intensely, equivocated (according to Evelyn Waugh) on the fourth, and satirized the sixth.[47]

Novelists as unlike as Dickens and George Eliot or as similar in some ways as Dickens and Collins were thus always considerably more intellectual than modern novelists of ideas (Aldous Huxley, for example) have been willing to concede. Granted, Victorian novels were not primarily constructed to be exploratory vehicles for philosophical inquiry, but the extent to which they measure up on all counts has been obscured because the rivalries they contain were seldom underlined. When Waugh has Tony Last read *Bleak House* aloud to Mr. Todd, he tips one off to parodies of

Dickens throughout *A Handful of Dust* more straightforwardly than Trollope does for *The Warden* by allowing Bold to read the opening number of
The Almshouse.

Rival Victorian novels seen side by side or read in conjunction look
very different than each does standing alone. Different, too, becomes the
world that hidden rivalries preview: a decentered universe formerly considered a much later and more modern perception. Perusing either *Bleak House*
and *Middlemarch*, or *Hard Times* and *North and South*, is clearly not the same
as reading William Faulkner's *The Sound and the Fury* or Alain Robbe-
Grillet's *La Maison de rendez-vous*. In the two moderns, problematic versions
of reality proliferate until each book is ultimately about the proliferation.
But each time the Victorian reader reexamined either half of either nineteenth-century pairing, he should have rethought the other half in order to
fully understand the text in hand.

The modern revaluator concludes that novels like *Felix Holt* and *Bleak
House* remain self-contained classics but can never again be read completely
if taken separately, as they were before one realized how thoroughly
George Eliot is redoing Dickens. Parodic revaluations that link two or more
Victorian novels become part of the total meaning of each novel involved.
Thus Esther Summerson is not just Esther Summerson any more than
Esther Lyon is merely Esther Lyon: each is also the other Esther.

Moreover, without hidden rivalries, many of these major Victorian
novels would have been not just different but, one decides, not nearly as
good. Aesthetically considered, rivalry was highly profitable. None of the
novelists who fought in the nineteenth-century realism wars would have
achieved as much creatively or financially without the stimulus provided
by intellectual and artistic competition. Edgar Johnson speaks of Scott
wielding a "golden pen."[48] The remark applies even better to Dickens. His
pen not only made possible the purchase of Gad's Hill while sustaining
himself and his various publishers; it also contributed to the livelihood of
numerous rivals and the upkeep of the houses that published them.

There is nothing to rival the hidden rivalries in nineteenth-century
British novels, neither the clash between Henry Fielding's *Shamela* and
Samuel Richardson's *Pamela* in the eighteenth century nor that more
recently between Mrs. Ramsay from Virginia Woolf's *To the Lighthouse* and
Arnold Bennett's hypothetical Mrs. Brown. In the present century, however, revaluing Dickens has again been a preoccupation for novelists intent
on smoothing the way for their own vision. But moderns parody Dickens
differently: when his peers compared his novels with reality, they generally
found life more acceptable than he recorded, more agreeable in virtually

every way; for moderns conducting a similar experiment, the status quo often seems distressingly worse.

Evelyn Waugh typifies the negative side of the modern response: he goes hardest on what he regards as Dickens's unfounded belief in the enduring value of humanistic virtues. He assails Dickens's secular humanism as a self-defeating watering-down of the traditional Christianity the Victorian novelist could neither defend adequately nor fully repudiate. In *A Handful of Dust* (1934), Waugh suggests that trying to apply Dickens's positive values to chaotic modern situations is as pointless as reading the Victorian novelist's complete works to a madman—which, in fact, is the fate reserved for Tony Last, the novel's nonhero.[49]

George Eliot contended that Dickens never took the crucial jump forward from the world view of pre-Lyell paleontology to the new era of evolutionary progress that she expected Darwin's theory to launch. Waugh also claims that Dickens faltered at the critical juncture between Victorian and modern, but he chastizes the Victorian novelist for not fending off more forcibly a secularization process that he believes ushered in the unsatisfactory present, a time marked by insufficient moral restraints. Instead of impeding the onrush of secular philosophies, says Waugh, Dickens tried to minimize the extent of the danger, as if the moral climate could be new and secular yet life's ethics remain largely the same. For Waugh, the Dickens who wanted the emotional consolations and ethical admonishments of organized religion without the religion itself appears more culpable than such clear-cut defectors as George Eliot and Matthew Arnold. *A Handful of Dust* can be reread to advantage as an even less sympathetic retrospective on Dickens than *Middlemarch* was, but for nearly opposite reasons.

From one point of view, George Eliot can be seen trying to stave off the modern satirical vision of *Bleak House* and *Edwin Drood*; from another, Waugh's Dickens can be observed failing to prevent a phenomenon that Eliot's novels embraced: the ascendancy of the profane. It culminates, Waugh thought, in the works of his own immediate predecessors, especially Lawrence and Joyce, whom he attacks (along with Dickens) in *Decline and Fall* (1928).[50]

Ironically, the outlook Waugh detests in Dickens—Huxley called it "vulgarity"—often seems stereotypical of the optimism and complacency that the cynical, satirical side of Dickens disliked in his less radical contemporaries. Trollope called Dickens "Mr. Sentiment," but it was the radical reformer he distrusted. George Eliot complained about "sentimental wretchedness," but the "wretchedness" perturbed her more than the alleged sentimentality. Dickens presented figures like Jo as helpless victims of hardhearted neglect, instances of the breakdown of community rather than as deficiencies in a social webbing not yet made good. In modern fiction, the Dickens who is too much the Victorian humanist for Waugh but not humanistic enough for some of his peers succeeds the Dickens who was always too melodramatic for Eliot yet never sufficiently satirical and sensational to please Wilkie Collins.

With a downward spiral as a metaphor for life in the twentieth century, *A Handful of Dust* is an excellent example of the modern satirical novel. This is the format that *Bleak House* foreshadows but also the outlook on the nature of things that George Eliot tried to forestall. That Waugh takes Dickens as one of his major targets for parody stands as the crowning irony to a history of Dickens and revaluation in which ironies abound. More tellingly than Wordsworth, whom Dickens parodies in *Bleak House* for being outmoded in a Victorian context, Dickens could be used after World War I to symbolize the naiveté of a bygone age. This is clear from Waugh's attempts to reinforce his own view of decline in the human condition by scuttling the brighter sides to Dickens's philosophy.

The novelist whose interest in catastrophism was often a satirical ploy for keeping proponents of reform in motion was done in, for a time, by the first great modern catastrophe. A disillusioned postwar generation, having lost the values on which it grew up, knew that the challenge to its general mood did not come from *Bleak House, Hard Times,* or *Our Mutual Friend*; modern poets and novelists borrowed from these freely. It came, instead, from the Dickens uppermost in the writers' childhood memories: the author of *Pickwick Papers* and *A Christmas Carol.* This is the Dickens whom moderns regularly called vulgar and sentimental as a way of repudiating their own fathers and bemoaning the collapse of an allegedly more comprehensible past, one that they had come to suspect was a lie. They routinely ignored Dickens's preoccupation, in *The Mystery of Edwin Drood,* with the darkness within men's hearts. Dickens and Wilkie Collins outdid each other trying to anticipate Conrad and preclude Stevenson as experts on self-division, a primary form of the modern discontent. But Waugh focuses on a Dickens whose secularized Christianity purportedly leads to a frayed humanism in Conrad and an effete aestheticism in Joyce that are not convincing as guides to conduct.

Not inappropriately, Edmund Wilson redirected attention to Dickens's unfinished novel at the start of a second, larger catastrophe for the modern age.[51] Historians still see World War II as a contest pitting the forces of light within civilization against those of darkness, and Jasper's Manichean split personality epitomizes such a struggle. Dickens's skeptical, satirical vein and increasingly dystopian frame of mind was similar to that of many moderns in the 1920s and '30s, but the link became clearer toward the end of those decades than it was at the start. Some of the delay can be attributed to ambivalent modern responses, such as Waugh's twofold ability to emulate Dickens—Fagin and Squeers compounded as Dr. Fagan, the unscrupulous schoolmaster in *Decline and Fall*, for example—while also using him to symbolize an ineffectual Victorian humanism.[52]

Parodists usually push beyond reason a piece of writing they consider already false to the point of becoming ludicrous. Dickens's Victorian revaluators submitted allegedly credible renditions of episodes in his novels that are supposed to become ridiculous immediately upon comparison with a more convincing substitution. Both varieties of parody accuse the author under attack of being false to life, but one does this by being even falser (exaggerating the falsity); the other redoes the falseness, exposing or curing it by showing what ought to have happened.

The latter type is more serviceable when the work being revaluated has been judged too severe or too narrow (George Eliot on Dickens). The former type is handier for suggesting that a novelist has glossed over unpleasant realities, including harsher implications within his own material (Waugh on Dickens). That Dickens was subjected mostly to the first kind of parody in the nineteenth century and to the second during the first half of the twentieth distinguishes Victorian from modern in him and in general. It also reveals how many of Dickens there are.

The modern revaluator, exploring the many worlds of Victorian fiction, should expect to meet more than one Dickens. A study of hidden rivalries uncovers a multifaceted author who takes on different colorings depending on whom he is revaluing or which novelist is parodying him. Positioned next to Collins, Dickens becomes ultra-Dickensian in an effort to remain inimitable. To Trollope he seems the overly persistent, radical reformer. But Mrs. Gaskell and later George Eliot bring out the antiperfectibilitarian in his makeup. It seems clear that in Dickens the temperament of a radical was joined to an increasingly anti-utopian frame of mind. The social satirist never ceased to attack widespread evils, but as these became even more widespread and interconnected in his perception of them, he grew pessimistic about improving human nature generally or upgrading the life process as a whole.

No matter how many of Dickens there were, an impressive consistency can also be demonstrated. In *Oliver Twist* and *The Old Curiosity Shop*, Dickens states his conviction that adverse social conditions prove detrimental to the human spirit. This position evolves logically into the contention that the remedies his more sanguine rivals propose for curing society's ills are unrealistic. The question Dickens asks in *Pickwick Papers* and *Oliver Twist* is whether a principle of goodness can survive in a fallen world so false and uncharitable that reconstituting it by flood or by fire often seems the wisest course. Despite two reform bills, Britain's expanding empire, and social theories with optimistic forecasts based on borrowings from the new science of biology, Dickens in 1870 sardonically rephrases—one could say replays or revalues—the question with which he started out: he ponders whether the element of evil within man and in society is ineradicable.

The novelist who began by showing the Fleet to Mr. Pickwick, Quilp to Little Nell, and the world of Fagin and Nancy to polite society went on to show Bounderby to Mrs. Gaskell and Magwitch to Pip. He concluded by bringing Jasper's dark side to the attention not just of the respectable choirmaster but of Trollope and George Eliot as well.

Wherever feasible, economical and readily available editions of Victorian novels have been chosen. These are cited with full bibliographical information only once in the notes; subsequent quotations are identified by an abbreviation and page number, as are multiple references to the works of a few non-Victorians. The following abbreviations are used:

AB   George Eliot, *Adam Bede*
BH   Charles Dickens, *Bleak House*
BL   Samuel T. Coleridge, *Biographia Literaria*
D   Bram Stoker, *Dracula*
ED   Charles Dickens, *The Mystery of Edwin Drood*
FH   George Eliot, *Felix Holt*
GE   Charles Dickens, *Great Expectations*
HD   Joseph Conrad, *Heart of Darkness*
HT   Charles Dickens, *Hard Times*
MB   Gustave Flaubert, *Madame Bovary*
MM   George Eliot, *Middlemarch*
MS   Wilkie Collins, *The Moonstone*
NS   Elizabeth Gaskell, *North and South*
RLS *The Great Short Stories of Robert Louis Stevenson*
TTC Charles Dickens, *A Tale of Two Cities*
W   Anthony Trollope, *The Warden*
WW   Wilkie Collins, *The Woman in White*

CHAPTER ONE

1. See Jerome Meckier, "How Modern the Victorians? A Plea to Have It Both Ways," *Dickens Studies Newsletter* 8 (Dec. 1977): 109-18. This is a review-essay on Jerome Buckley, ed., *The Worlds of Victorian Fiction*, Harvard English Studies 6 (Cambridge, Mass.: Harvard Univ. Press, 1975).

2. Quoted by Walter C. Phillips in *Dickens, Reade, and Collins: Sensation Novelists* (New York: Columbia Univ. Press, 1919), 22.

3. F.R. Leavis, the expert on revaluation, defines the critic's duty as an obligation to see the literature of the present as "continuation and development"; that is, he explores sameness and difference at once; see *Revaluation: Tradition and Development in English Poetry* (London: Chatto & Windus, 1936), 1-2. David Cecil (*Early Victorian Novelists: Essays in Revaluation* [New York: Bobbs-Merrill, 1935], 14-15) states that re-

valuation is passing judgment on a previous age once one's antipathies to its outdated values have quieted down. Actually, revaluation is always an updating and should begin again whenever apparently final decisions have been reached.

4. Consult the interview with John Fowles in *Saturday Review*, October 1981, p. 39.

5. For Ian Watt's definition of "formal realism," see *The Rise of the Novel* (Berkeley: Univ. of California Press, 1959), 32.

6. James Sutherland's pioneering chapter on satire in the Victorian novel treats Dickens, Thackeray, and others as occasional satirists whose targets did not include each other; see *English Satire* (Cambridge: Cambridge Univ. Press, 1962), 122-32. Jerome Buckley's statement that Victorians possessed "an unequaled talent for parody" becomes even truer if hidden rivalries are made public. (*The Victorian Temper* [New York: Vintage, 1964], 5).

7. Huxley said as much to George Wickes and Ray Frazer; see "Aldous Huxley" in *Writers at Work: The Paris Review Interviews*, 2d ser. (New York: Viking, 1963), 198.

8. See Michael Timko's essay by that title in *New Literary History* 6 (Spring 1975): 607-27.

9. See Jerome Meckier, "Double Vision versus Double Logic," *Dickens Studies Newsletter* 14 (March 1983): 14-21, and 15 (June 1983): 51-57. This review-essay discusses the postmodernist approach to Victorian fiction as represented by Peter K. Garrett, *The Victorian Multiplot Novel: Studies in Dialogical Form* (New Haven, Conn.: Yale Univ. Press, 1980). M.M. Bakhtin's views, on which Garrett relies heavily, can be found in *Problems of Dostoevsky*, trans. R.W. Rotsel (Ann Arbor, Mich.: Ardis, 1973), and Michael Holquist, ed., *The Dialogical Imagination: Four Essays by M.M. Bakhtin*, trans. Caryl Emerson and Michael Holquist (Austin: Univ. of Texas Press, 1981).

10. *The Unnamable*, in Samuel Beckett, *Three Novels* (New York: Grove, 1965), 414.

11. Richard Alter's efforts (*Motives for Fiction* [Cambridge, Mass.: Harvard Univ. Press, 1984]) to find out why mimesis has become problematic miss the key point: it was always a problem. Realism was a constant source of irritation and argument for major Victorian novelists.

12. Malcolm Bradbury selects these dates in a study edited with James McFarlane, *Modernism* (Harmondsworth, Eng.: Penguin, 1976),. 178.

13. See Kathleen Tillotson, *Novels of the Eighteen-Forties* (Oxford: Clarendon Press, 1954).

14. Catherine Gallagher accounts for the novel's Dickensian elements with the improbable thesis that George Eliot's theory of realism had changed since *The Mill on the Floss*; see "The Failure of Realism: *Felix Holt*," *Nineteenth-Century Fiction* 55 (Dec. 1980): 372-84.

15. George Eliot, *Felix Holt*, ed. Peter Coveney (Harmondsworth, Eng.: Penguin, 1977), 581 (this edition is cited hereafter as FH).

16. Coveney summarizes this argument in Appendix B, "A Note on the Law of Entail in the Plot of *Felix Holt*," ibid., 629.

17. See Appendix A, "Address to Working Men by Felix Holt," ibid., 609. One should regard this "Address," although written subsequently, as part of the novel.

18. Charles Dickens, *Bleak House*, ed. Duane DeVries (New York: Crowell, 1971), 824 (hereafter cited as BH).

19. See Thomas Carlyle, "Shooting Niagara: And After?" in Frederick William Roe, ed., *Victorian Prose* (New York: Ronald Press, 1947), 73.

20. Wilkie Collins, *The Woman in White*, ed. Julian Symons (Harmondsworth, Eng.: Penguin, 1977), 575 (hereafter cited as WW).

21. In addition to Julian Huxley's book-length studies, see his introduction to Pierre Teilhard de Chardin, *The Phenomenon of Man* (New York: Harper, 1959), 11-28.

22. Robert L. Caesario agrees and calls *Felix Holt* a conscious critique of Dickens's kind of plot; see *Plot, Story, and the Novel: From Dickens and Poe to the Modern Period* (Princeton, N.J.: Princeton Univ. Press, 1979), 97. Earlier, M.H. Dodds ("George Eliot and Charles Dickens," *Notes and Queries* [6 April 1946]: 143) noticed Mrs. Transome's resemblance to Lady Dedlock but decided against any "connection between the two" Esthers. Edward Stokes (*Hawthorne's Influence on Dickens and George Eliot* [Queensland, Austrailia: Univ. of Queensland Press, 1985]) unconvincingly derives most of *Bleak House* and *Felix Holt* from *The Scarlet Letter.*

CHAPTER TWO

1. Robert M. Polhemus admires Trollope's "witty parodies" of Dickens and Carlyle (see *The Changing World of Anthony Trollope* [Berkeley: Univ. of California Press, 1968], 29), but C.P. Snow disagrees: "His attempts at jocular attacks on Carlyle . . . and Dickens . . . make one squirm to this day" (*Trollope: His Life and Art* [New York: Scribner, 1975], 76).

2. Anthony Trollope, *The Warden* (New York: Signet, 1964), 139 (hereafter cited as W).

3. Ruth apRoberts selects *The Warden* as the logical starting point for Trollope's oeuvre: see *Trollope: Artist and Moralist* (London: Chatto & Windus, 1971), 34. Previously, Trollope had written two novels set in Ireland and a historical romance.

4. Lionel Stevenson identifies this article as a source for Trollope's novel; see "Dickens and the Origin of *The Warden*," *Trollopian* 2 (Sept. 1947): 83-89.

5. R.B. Martin, *Enter Rumour: Four Early Victorian Scandals* (New York: Norton, 1962), 182-83.

6. See Trollope's account of the novel's conception and development in *An Autobiography* (London: Oxford Univ. Press, 1961), 80-83.

7. For detailed accounts of proceedings at St. Cross and Rochester, consult Martin, *Enter Rumour.* Less convincing is Carol H. Ganzel's thesis that Trollope's novel was influenced by six letters Sidney Godolphin Osborne wrote to the *Times* (28 July–9 Sept. 1853) about simony at St. Ervan's in Cornwall; see "*The Times* Correspondent and *The Warden*," *Nineteenth-Century Fiction* 21 (March 1967): 325-36. G.F.A. Best discusses several ecclesiastical scandals that were available to Trollope; see "The Road to Hiram's Hospital," *Victorian Studies* 5 (Dec. 1961): 144-47. An earlier version of "The Cant of Reform" appeared in *Studies in the Novel* 13 (Fall 1983): 202-23.

8. Trollope, *Autobiography*, 84.

9. Topicality remains a source of strength that critics regularly attribute to Dickens, the classic example being John Butt and Kathleen Tillotson on *Bleak House* in chap. 7 of *Dickens at Work* (London: Methuen, 1957).

10. Trollope, *Autobiography*, 81.

11. Ibid., 81–82.

12. The flaw in Trollope's argument is that without agitation from reformers, sinecures are seldom abolished.

13. Dickens, preface to *Bleak House* (BH, 828).

14. Sherman Hawkins misreads Hiram's Hospital as a microcosm for the Anglican Church; see "Mr. Harding's Church Music," *English Literary History* 29 (June 1962): 202-23. Actually, the hospital is a microcosm within another microcosm (Barchester), but both are Victorian society in miniature.

15. Geoffrey Tillotson discusses the David and Goliath theme in his afterword, W, 207.

16. See William K. Wimsatt, ed., *Alexander Pope: Selected Poetry and Prose* (New York: Holt, Rinehart & Winston, 1964), 87.

17. James Kincaid finds Harding saintly and approves of Trollope's separation of private conscience from public morality; see "Trollope and the Tradition of Realism," in *The Novels of Anthony Trollope* (Oxford: Clarendon Press, 1977), 97, 101.

18. David Skilton, *Anthony Trollope and His Contemporaries* (London: Longman, 1972), 148.

19. The same year *The Warden* appeared, Dickens dedicated *Hard Times* to Carlyle.

20. George Ford gives Lewes credit for using the term first; see *Dickens and His Readers* (New York: Norton, 1965), 131.

21. This is Percy Lubbock's criterion for what a realistic novel ought to be; see *The Craft of Fiction* (New York: Viking, 1966), 9.

22. F.S. Schwarzbach, e.g., insists that Dickens could "evoke in his writing a world as close to that in which he lived as one ever could in words" *(Dickens and the City* [London: Athlone, 1979], 4).

23. Ford, *Dickens and His Readers*, 82.

24. Ibid., 100.

25. Patrick Brantlinger discusses the politics of realism in the chapter titled "Realisms" in *The Spirit of Reform: British Literature and Politics, 1832–1867* (Cambridge, Mass.: Harvard Univ. Press, 1977), 207.

26. This, says George Ford *(Dickens and His Readers*, 131), is what the novel proposed to provide when it originated in the eighteenth century.

27. Dickens quotes Shakespeare in his preface to *Bleak House* (BH, 828).

CHAPTER THREE

1. See Charles Dickens, *Hard Times*, ed. George Ford and Sylvère Monod (New York: Norton, 1966), chap. 5 of bk. 2 (hereafter cited as HT); and Elizabeth Gaskell, *North and South*, Dorothy Collin (Harmondsworth, Eng.: Penguin, 1970), chap. 15 (hereafter cited as NS).

2. Mamie Dickens and Georgina Hogarth, eds., *The Letters of Charles Dickens* (London: Macmillan, 1893), 333.

3. Esther Alice Chadwick states that "Dickens sent his story, before publication, to Mrs. Gaskell, asking for her judgement about his new venture in writing of something outside his own experience, but distinctly in Mrs. Gaskell's province"; see *Mrs. Gaskell* (London: Pitman, 1910), 302.

4. This is according to Angus Easson, *Elizabeth Gaskell* (London: Routledge & Kegan Paul, 1979), 86-87.

5. A.B. Hopkins, *Elizabeth Gaskell: Her Life and Work* (London: John Lehmann, 1952), 144. Hopkins also quotes a letter enlisting Mrs. Gaskell's services for *Household Words* in which Dickens calls *Mary Barton* "a book that most profoundly affected and impressed me" (p. 137). For more on Mrs. Gaskell's difficulties with Dickens during the serialization of her novel, see Dorothy Collin, "The Composition of Mrs. Gaskell's *North and South,*" *Bulletin of the Rylands Library* 54 (1971): 67-93.

6. Easson, *Gaskell*, 88.

7. Aldous Huxley, *Brave New World* (London: Chatto & Windus, 1932), 171.

8. Vineta Colby, *Yesterday's Woman: Domestic Realism in the English Novel* (Princeton, N.J.: Princeton Univ. Press, 1974), 222.

9. Deirdre David makes this observation in *Fictions of Resolution in Three Victorian Novels* (New York: Columbia Univ. Press, 1981), 41.

10. Edgar Wright thinks Frederick's story is not essential, "pure plot-spinning"; see *Mrs. Gaskell: The Basis for Reassessment* (Oxford: Oxford Univ. Press, 1965), 144-46.

11. This is according to Collin (NS,27), who also speculates that Mrs. Gaskell "may have spent some time revising" the second edition, which, however, appeared a short four months after the first; it is the text Collin adopts. Hopkins (*Gaskell: Life and Work*, 143) blames the disagreement with Dickens entirely on the unsuitability of *North and South*, "by its very nature," to "the form of serialization followed in *Household Words.*"

12. E.M. Forster, *Howard's End* (New York: Vintage, 1961), 27.

13. E.M. Forster, *A Passage to India* (Harmondsworth, Eng.: Penguin, 1961), 51. Curiously, Catherine Gallagher *(The Industrial Revolution of English Fiction, 1832-1867* [Chicago: Univ. of Chicago Press, 1985], 148-49) reads *Hard Times* and *North and South* as if *both* were prefigurations of Bloomsbury. They fail to be "realistic," she argues, because they recommend, but fail to prove, that relations between the classes should be modeled on "the cooperative associations of family life."

14. As Dorothy Collin notes (NS,538), this is a quote from Wordsworth's "The Old Cumberland Beggar," line 153. It is also an attempt to prove that life in Milton-Northern does not nullify established adages from the less industrialized past. Mrs. Gaskell quotes this line and the half-dozen before it as early as 1838 in a letter to Mary Howitt; see J.A.V. Chapple, ed., *Elizabeth Gaskell: A Portrait in Letters* (Manchester: Manchester Univ. Press, 1980), 22-23.

15. D.H. Lawrence, *Lady Chatterley's Lover* (New York: Signet, 1959), 142-49.

16. Ibid., 147, 142-43.

17. Carol A. Martin discusses Mrs. Gaskell's knowledge of the pre-1859 debate about evolution and assesses the impact of Darwin's ideas on her novels; see "Gaskell, Darwin, and *North and South,*" *Studies in the Novel* 15 (Summer 1983): 91-107.

18. Forster, *Passage to India*, 68.

19. Lacy's Acting Edition of Edward Sterling's *The Old Curiosity Shop; or One Hour from Humphrey's Clock*, a two-act drama, survives in the Huntington Library. Dickens saw the stage version on 9 Nov. 1840, according to Edgar Johnson, *Charles Dickens: His Tragedy and Triumph* (New York: Simon & Schuster, 1952), 1:304.

20. From a letter written c. Feb. 1849; see *The Letters of Matthew Arnold to Arthur Hugh Clough*, ed. Howard Foster Lowry (London: Oxford Univ. Press, 1932), 99.

21. Quoted in Park Honan, *Matthew Arnold: A Life* (Cambridge, Mass.: Harvard Univ. Press, 1983), 196.

22. Lawrence, *Lady Chatterley's Lover*, 126-27.

23. Cf. Arnold's definition in *Culture and Anarchy*, in R.H. Super, ed., *The Complete Works of Matthew Arnold* (Ann Arbor: Univ. of Michigan Press, 1960–77), 5:87-88.

24. Although Dickens seems to be on the offensive against industrialization, Susan Sontag's remarks on the Snow-Leavis debate apply: "The literary men, whether one thinks of Emerson and Thoreau in the 19th century, or of 20th century intellectuals who talk of modern society as being in some new way incomprehensible, 'alienated,' are inevitably on the defensive. They know that the scientific culture, the coming of the machine, cannot be stopped" ("One Culture and the New Sensibility," in Gerald Howard, ed., *The Sixties* [New York: Washington Square Press, 1982], 294). According to Philip Collins, however, Dickens not only realized that industrialism was here to stay but indicated that his hopes lay with its future ("Dickens and Industrialism," *Studies in English Literature* 20 [Autumn 1980]: 651-73). By contrast with Sontag, Collins's conclusions seem only half right.

25. Paul Edward Gray, ed., *Twentieth Century Interpretations of Hard Times* (Englewood Cliffs, N.J.: Prentice-Hall, 1969), 9.

26. John Updike quotes Bowen and Green in his introduction to *Loving, Living, Party Going: Three Novels by Henry Green* (Harmondsworth, Eng.: Penguin, 1978), 7.

27. K.J. Fielding, "The Battle for Preston," *Dickensian* 50 (Sept. 1954), 159-62. In addition, see Geoffrey Carnall, "Dickens, Mrs. Gaskell, and the Preston Strike," *Victorian Studies* 8 (1964): 31-48.

28. Ivan Melada agrees that the popularity of Burke's genealogies during Victoria's reign stems from a desire of aristocrats to keep the attainment of gentility out of reach of the new industrialists—they, in turn, strongly aspired to be considered gentlemen; see *The Captain of Industry in English Fiction 1821–1871* (Albuquerque: Univ. of New Mexico Press, 1970), 164–66.

29. Michael Wheeler, *The Art of Allusion in Victorian Fiction* (London: Macmillan, 1979), 62. John Lucas says Mrs. Gaskell knew more about working-class Manchester than Engels did *(The Literature of Change* [Sussex: Harvester Press, 1977], 55). W.A. Craik finds her more realistic than Kingsley and Disraeli *(Elizabeth Gaskell and the English Provincial Novel* [London: Methuen, 1975], 82). But Stephen Marcus decides that "what Mrs. Gaskell does have to say in large measure and at almost every critical juncture confirms what Engels had said before her" *(Engels, Manchester, and the Working Class* [New York: Random House, 1974], 49n). H.I. Dutton and J.E. King find Dickens "a poor historical source," whereas Mrs. Gaskell is said to be "more realistic" about strikes than *Hard Times* is, and her characters, too, are "far more real" *("Ten Per Cent and No Surrender": The Preston Strike, 1853-1854* [London: Cambridge Univ. Press, 1981], 198-220).

30. Gray, *Interpretations*, 5.

31. To assess the impact of *Hard Times* on modern dystopias, see Jerome Meckier, "Dickens and the Dystopian Novel: From *Hard Times* to *Lady Chatterley's Lover*" in R.G. Collins, ed., *The Novel and Its Changing Form* (Winnipeg: Manitoba Press, 1972), 51-58. Readers should also consult my essay "Dickens Discovers America, Dickens Discovers Dickens: The First Visit Reconsidered," *Modern Language Review* 79 (April 1984): 266-77. Dickens's anti-utopian tendencies date from his first trip to America: his hopes for a strikingly better future, through across-the-board changes, perished when the only ideal republic he could imagine failed to meet his specifications.

32. George Eliot, *Middlemarch*, ed. Gordon S. Haight (Boston: Houghton Mifflin, 1956), 613 (hereafter cited as MM).

33. See Jerome Meckier, "Boffin and Podsnap in Utopia," *Dickensian* 77 (Autumn 1981): 154-61.

34. George Levine, *The Realistic Imagination: English Fiction from Frankenstein to Lady Chatterley* (Chicago: Univ. of Chicago Press, 1981), 8.

35. David, *Fictions of Resolution*, ix, xi.

36. See the letter of 27 January 1855 in M. Dickens and Hogarth, *Letters of Dickens*, 354-55.

37. Dickens blamed a decline in sales of his periodical *Household Words* on Mrs. Gaskell's "divided, wearisome" novel. See Norman Page, *A Dickens Companion* (London: Macmillan, 1984), 33.

CHAPTER FOUR

1. See Dickens's letter for 6 Oct. 1859 in Walter Dexter, ed., *The Letters of Charles Dickens* (Bloomsbury, Eng.: Nonesuch Press, 1938), 3:124-25.

2. K.J. Fielding, *Charles Dickens: A Critical Introduction* (Boston: Houghton Mifflin, 1964), 198.

3. *A Tale of Two Cities* (New York: Dell, 1963; hereafter cited as TTC) commences with Darnay being tried in England on suspicion of being a French spy. He is subsequently arrested twice in Paris and tried two times for offenses his father and uncle committed.

4. Throughout, this essay incorporates material from Jerome Meckier, "Wilkie Collins's *The Woman in White*: Providence against the Evils of Propriety," *Journal of British Studies* 22 (Fall 1982): 104-26.

5. John R. Reed indicates the widespread popularity of providence as a novelist's helper in *Victorian Conventions* (Athens: Ohio Univ. Press, 1975), 132-37. Ian Ousby concludes that Collins's use of providential patterns rests on no firm intellectual commitment and merely serves to link him with lesser writers of the age; see *Bloodhounds of Heaven* (Cambridge, Mass.: Harvard Univ. Press, 1976), 127. Omitting Collins, Thomas Vargish views the Victorians' use of providence as a cooperative effort, begun by Charlotte Brontë, perfected by Dickens, and brought to a close by George Eliot; see *The Providential Aesthetic in Victorian Fiction* (Charlottesville: Univ. Press of Virginia, 1985), 89-162.

6. Thomas Carlyle, *Past and Present*, in the centenary edition of *The Works of Thomas Carlyle* (New York: Scribner, 1899), 10:8.

7. Ibid., 12.

8. Ibid., 14.

9. Ibid., 9.

10. One should not overlook Collins's personal problems with propriety. His un-Victorian life-style, particularly his unofficial families by Caroline Graves and Martha Rudd, caused him to be ostracized socially. Still, the argument of Collins's finest novel transcends personal grievance.

11. Collins's intellect has been underrated ever since Swinburne regretted the "evil day" the novelist decided to correct abuses and advocate reforms; see William H.

Marshall, *Wilkie Collins* (New York: Twayne, 1970), 17. Clyde K. Hyder insists that Collins "belongs among the great story-tellers rather than among the great novelists" ("Wilkie Collins and *The Woman in White*," *PMLA* 54 [1939]: 297-303). Bradford C. Booth recommends Collins to all who "have not lost their appetite for sheer, one might even say, mere, story telling" ("Wilkie Collins and the Art of Fiction," *Nineteenth-Century Fiction* 6 [1951]: 131-43). Harvey Peter Sucksmith calls *The Woman in White* "the greatest melodrama ever written" (Sucksmith, ed., *The Woman in White* [London: Oxford Univ. Press, 1975], xxii). Robert Ashley finds it a masterpiece, judged by standards of melodrama, "the only standards by which it is fair to judge it"; more to the point is his subsequent view of Collins as a "serious novelist," a "rebel who rather subtly attacked the most cheerful foundations of Victorian respectability" ("Wilkie Collins," in George Ford, ed., *Victorian Fiction: A Second Guide to Research* [New York: Modern Language Assoc., 1978], 228-29).

12. See James Laver, *Manners and Morals in the Age of Optimism 1848-1914* (New York: Harper & Row, 1966), 40-45; and Buckley, *Victorian Temper*, 116-17.

13. Asa Briggs, *The Age of Improvement* (London: Longmans, Green, 1959), 465.

14. Walter E. Houghton, *The Victorian Frame of Mind, 1830-1870* (New Haven, Conn.: Yale Univ. Press, 1957), 394, 397.

15. Dougald B. Maceachen credits Collins with advocating five reforms of the legal system, four of which were adopted; see "Wilkie Collins and British Law," *Nineteenth-Century Fiction* 5 (1950): 121-39.

16. Symons (WW, 20) grants Collins some of Dickens's talent but asserts that "a powerful symbolic image was beyond him."

17. Ousby, *Bloodhounds of Heaven*, does not include Walter prominently in his survey of detectives who are heaven's agents.

18. An early tipoff to Fosco's vulnerability is his extraordinary interest in learning whether any "Italian gentlemen" are settled in the vicinity of Blackwater Park (WW, 245).

19. Peter Caracciolo hunts down Collins's allusions to Dante in "Wilkie Collins's '*Divine Comedy*': The Use of Dante in *The Woman in White*," *Nineteenth-Century Fiction* 25 (1971): 383-404. Pesca's employer, "the golden Papa," epitomizes the denial of the natural in favor of the artificial when he proclaims, "We don't want genius in this country, unless it is accompanied by *respectability*—and then we are very glad to have it, very glad indeed" (WW, 41; italics added).

20. The woman in white accosts Walter early the same day on which he later travels to his new post at Limmeridge House. The next morning, at breakfast, he encounters Marian.

21. Marshall *(Wilkie Collins*, 64) thinks they are. Of similar opinion is A. Brooker Thro in "An Approach to Melodramatic Fiction: Goodness and Energy in the Novels of Dickens, Collins and Reade," *Genre* 11 (1978): 359-74.

22. U.C. Knoepflmacher typifies prevailing opinion when he speaks of Collins's "asocial energies," his "trademark" allegedly being "sympathetic treatment" of villains ("The Counterworld of Victorian Fiction and *The Woman in White*," in Buckley, *Worlds of Victorian Fiction*, 353, 361, 368-69). Winifred Hughes argues that Collins, unlike Charles Reade and Dickens, wrote morally ambiguous sensation novels *(The Maniac in the Cellar: Sensation Novels of the 1860s* [Princeton, N.J.: Princeton Univ. Press, 1980], 138-45).

23. Collins called Fosco "a clever devil" in "How I Write My Books: Related in a Letter to a Friend," *Globe*, 26 November 1887, reprinted in Sucksmith's edition of *The Woman in White*, 596.

24. See Robert Louis Brannan, *Under the Direction of Charles Dickens: His Production of "The Frozen Deep"* (Ithaca: Cornell Univ. Press, 1966), 3.

25. In Ibid., 39-49, Brannan comments on Dickens's revision of the Wardour role.

CHAPTER FIVE

1. J.W.T. Ley, "Victorianism," *Dickensian* 28 (1932): 66.

2. See Earle Davis, *The Flint and the Flame: The Artistry of Charles Dickens* (Columbia: Univ. of Missouri Press, 1963), 183-96.

3. See Sue Lonoff, "Charles Dickens and Wilkie Collins," *Nineteenth-Century Fiction*, 35 (Sept. 1980), 158-59.

4. Nuel Pharr Davis states that Dickens was extremely jealous of the success of *The Moonstone;* see *The Life of Wilkie Collins* (Urbana: Univ. of Illinois Press, 1956), 257. Except for the letter to Collins on providence, Dickens's correspondence was thus less than candid. On 29 July 1860, he wrote to congratulate Collins on "having triumphantly finished your best book," *The Woman in White*; later, he found *No Name* superior (Lawrence Hutton, ed., *Letters of Charles Dickens to Wilkie Collins* [New York: Kraus Reprint, 1969], 96, 112).

5. Dickens, *Great Expectations* (New York: Signet, 1963), 83 (hereafter cited as GE).

6. Collins also borrowed the reemergence of a document written long before as a pivotal point for his plot: Manette's letter in "One Hundred Five, North Tower" becomes the marriage register at Old Welmingham. Secret societies whose victims are marked for extermination no matter how long it takes—the Brotherhood and the Jacquerie—appear in both novels as well.

7. Harry Stone calls Collins's novel "the final impetus" for the creation of Miss Havisham. It was probably also the strongest. See "The Genesis of a Novel: *Great Expectations*" in E. W. F. Tomlin, ed., *Charles Dickens 1812-1870* (New York: Simon & Schuster, 1970), 130. Philip Collins detects hints for *A Tale of Two Cities* and *Great Expectations* in Dickens's prior writings but overlooks Wilkie Collins. See "A Tale of Two Novels: *A Tale of Two Cities* and *Great Expectations*," *Dickens Studies Annual*, 2 (1972), 336-51.

8. Collins's one-page preface appears without a page number in a recent reprint of *No Name* (New York: Stein & Day, 1967).

9. Ibid.

10. See Philip Collins, *Dickens and Crime* (London: Macmillan and Co., 1965), 206.

11. Collins, *The Moonstone* (New York: Harper & Row, 1965), 305 (hereafter cited as MS).

12. Mark M. Hennelly, Jr., stresses the "polar symbology" of the moonstone and Collins's symbolic gemology in "Detecting Collins' Diamond: From Serpentstone to Moonstone," *Nineteenth-Century Fiction* (June 1984): 25-47.

13. Chap. 6 of the "Seven Sketches from Our Parrish" in Dickens's *Sketches by Boz*.

14. Sue Lonoff explores this point in *Wilkie Collins and His Victorian Readers* (New York: AMS Press, 1982), 210.

15. See Joseph Conrad, *Heart of Darkness; The Secret Sharer* (New York: Signet, 1958), 24.

16. When the captain abets Leggatt's escape, he is setting his secret sharer free, not dispatching part of himself.

17. The first two volumes of Browning's *The Ring and the Book* appeared in 1868.

18. "Godfrey" means "peace of God." "Ablewhite" suggests ability and integrity or, more precisely, the competency of white, Anglo-Saxon integrity. "Ezra" means "help."

19. John R. Reed discusses society's mistreatment of the Hindoos in "English Imperialism and the Unacknowledged Crime of *The Moonstone*," *Clio* 2 (1973): 281-90.

20. In *Liittle Dorrit*, however, the circumlocutionary speech habits of Dickens's characters point inward to prevalent attitudes of mind. Such habits help to account for the avoidance of hard truths and hard work throughout the novel. See Jerome Meckier, "Dickens's *Little Dorrit:* 'Sundry Curious Variations on the Same Tune,' " *Dickens Studies* 3 (May 1967): 51-63.

21. Cf. Collins's acceptance of Blake and Charlotte Brontë's approach to Jane Eyre. According to Elaine Showalter (*A Literature of Their Own* [Princeton, NJ.: Princeton Univ. Press, 1977], 118), Rochester's insane wife, the mad woman in his attic, is Jane's darker, sexual self. If so, this inner reality seems permanently foreign to the daylight self.

CHAPTER SIX

1. Charles Dickens, *The Mystery of Edwin Drood*, ed. Arthur J. Cox (Harmondsworth, Eng.: Penguin, 1974), 53 (cited hereafter as ED).

2. Dickens's letter is quoted by Angus Wilson in his introduction, ibid., 17; or see John Forster, *The Life of Charles Dickens* (New York: Scribner, 1899), 2:452-53.

3. See chap. 52 of *Oliver Twist*.

4. My comments elsewhere about Dickens "outgrowing his early Manicheanism" do not overlook Jasper. The point was to stress Dickens's greater awareness, in the so-called darker novels, of life's diversity. Also, the Manicheanism in *The Mystery of Edwin Drood* is more complex than it was in *Oliver Twist* or *The Old Curiosity Shop*. See my review of *Charles Dickens' Sketches by Boz* in *Criticism* 18 (Spring 1976): 198-202.

5. Bram Stoker's novel appeared in 1897; page numbers refer to *Dracula* (New York: Bantam, 1981), hereafter cited as D.

6. See "Chapter the Last" in *The Old Curiosity Shop*.

7. This is Edmund Wilson's position in "Dickens: The Two Scrooges" (1941), in *The Wound and the Bow* (New York: Oxford Univ. Press, 1965), 14-15.

8. Harry Levin enumerates "The Uncles of Dickens" in Buckley, *Worlds of Victorian Fiction*, 1-35.

9. See *Oliver Twist*, chap. 22.

10. William Blake, "The Sick Rose" in Northrop Frye, ed., *Selected Poetry and Prose of William Blake* (New York: Modern Library, 1953), 42.

11. Masao Miyoshi, *The Divided Self: A Perspective on the Literature of the Victorians* (New York: New York Univ. Press, 1969), 278.

12. Charles Forsyte, *The Decoding of Edwin Drood* (New York: Scribner, 1980), 104.

13. See *The Great Short Stories of Robert Louis Stevenson* (New York: Pocket Library, 1957), 38 (hereafter cited as RLS).

14. Joseph Conrad, *Heart of Darkness*, ed. Richard Kimbrough (New York: Norton, 1971), 12 (hereafter cited as HD).

15. Angus Wilson bases his interpretation of Dickens's last novel on the letter to Forster, which he quotes in his edition of the book (ED, Introduction). Andrew Sanders looks mainly to *A Tale of Two Cities* and *Our Mutual Friend (Charles Dickens: Resurrectionist* [New York: St. Martin's, 1982], 198-218). Jerome Meckier recommends studying Nell's stand-ins for the key to her fate ("Suspense in *The Old Curiosity Shop:* Dickens' Contrapuntal Artistry," *Journal of Narrative Technique* 2 [Sept. 1972]: 199-207).

16. Nevertheless, considerable use has been made of Felix Aylmer, *The Drood Case* (New York: Barnes & Noble, 1965); Leon Garfield, *The Mystery of Edwin Drood* (New York: Pantheon Books, 1980); and Forsyte, *Decoding*.

17. Robert Patten, *Dickens and His Publishers* (Oxford: Clarendon Press, 1978), 323.

18. A. Wilson, ED, 27.

19. E. Wilson, "Dickens: Two Scrooges," 71.

20. Aylmer, *Drood Case*, 20.

21. Earle Davis, seconding Aylmer, argues for Drood's return as "a sudden and surprising conclusion which would startle the reader as *The Moonstone* had done"; see *Flint and Flame*, 194.

22. Ezekiel 18:27. The first words are "intoned" by Jasper's choir as Chapter 1 ends (ED, 40). In Garfield's continuation (*Mystery*, 320), Jasper, already on the scaffold, sees his other self, the murderer or "wicked man," turn toward the choirmaster and repent.

23. Quoted in Wilson, ED, 17.

24. Ibid. Forster's account of what Dickens told him: "discovery of the murder," identification of "the person murdered," the "locality of the crime," and the name of "the man who committed it" would all be discovered by "means of a gold ring which had resisted the corrosive effects of the lime" into which the killer "had thrown the body."

25. Forsyte *(Decoding*, 214) theorizes that she is Rosa's former nurse.

26. ED, 53. Cf. this passage with one from *The Moonstone* in which Jennings shows Blake an anecdote from "Doctor Elliotson's Human Physiology" about "an Irish porter to a warehouse, who forgot, when sober, what he had done when drunk; but, being drunk again, recollected the transactions of his former state of intoxication. On one occasion, being drunk, he had lost a parcel of some value, and in his sober moments, could give no account of it. Next time he was intoxicated he recollected that he had left a parcel at a certain house, and there being no address on it, it had remained there safely, and was got on his calling for it" (MS, 382-83).

27. Edmund Wilson ("Dickens: Two Scrooges," 76), misjudging the nature of hidden rivalries, rules out a crucial role for opium in Dickens's novel on grounds that Collins had already made sensational use of the drug in *The Moonstone*.

28. Neville could plunge to his death from the cathedral tower prior to Jasper's capture, especially if the murderer he is pursuing turns out to have a vampire's superhuman strength and climbing ability. Only in the verbal reconstruction of the crime would Jasper claim his victim, either strangling Drood or pushing him off the tower (or both), then hiding the body in the crypt or the Sapsea monument.

29. Jasper's drug habit is of English origin and does not predate the disintegration of his personality. "When you first come," the Opium Woman reminds Jasper, "you was quite new to it; warn't ye?" (ED, 268).

30. Fred Kaplan puts the case for Jasper as mesmerist in *Dickens and Mesmerism: The Hidden Springs of Fiction* (Princeton, N.J.: Princeton Univ. Press, 1975), 131.

31. The murderer inside the choirmaster offers this self-description to Crisparkle during the death-cell sequence in Forsyte's persuasive continuation (*Decoding*, 194). Jasper tells of hating Drood yet being simultaneously drawn toward him until these diverse feelings brought about a split in his personality. For Aylmer's rendition, see *Drood Case*, 53ff.

32. Richard M. Baker, e.g., argues that Jasper is the younger brother of Drood's mother. See *The Drood Murder Case* (Berkeley: Univ. of California Press, 1951), 75.

33. Charles Dickens, *David Copperfield*, ed. George Ford (Boston: Houghton Mifflin, 1958), 41, 44, 47.

34. Note a similarity in the names: jasper is hard, dark green stone.

35. Johnson, *Dickens: Tragedy and Triumph*, 2:1119.

36. Edmund Wilson ("Dickens: Two Scrooges," 71) says Jasper "is supposed to be a member of the Indian sect of Thugs." His statement relies on Howard Duffield, "John Jasper—Strangler," *American Bookman* 70 (1930): 581-88.

37. Wendy S. Jacobson's attempt to demolish Wilson and Duffield makes one more convinced by the pair than before; see "John Jasper and Thugee," *Modern Language Review* 72 (July 1977): 526-37.

38. The French writer Jules Verne, sending an Englishman around the world in 1872, felt obligated to have him pass near the stronghold of a Thugee chief; see *Around the World in Eighty Days* (New York: Bantam, 1984), 37.

39. Stoker's vampire possesses "a pair of very bright eyes" which seem "red" in lamplight and "sharp-looking teeth, as white as ivory" (D, 10).

40. Sanders, *Dickens: Resurrectionist*, 207. Angus Wilson reminds readers that contemporary reviewers compared *The Mystery of Edwin Drood* with Trollope's clerical novels (ED, 14).

41. Everett F. Bleiler writes that "the forename Septimus seems to have been a second thought for Dickens. . . . There seems to be no obvious reason for Septimus." See "The Names in *Drood* (Part Two)," *Dickens Quarterly* 1 (Dec. 1984): 137.

42. Dickens wrote Forster that "Rosa was to marry Tartar, Crisparkle the sister of Landless."

43. Baruch Hochman finds George Eliot's sense of her characters inadequate "as they undergo the process of their unfolding": she "fails to explore the darker side of their selves" (*The Test of Character: From the Victorian Novel to the Modern* [Rutherford, N.J.: Fairleigh Dickinson Univ. Press, 1983], 45). This was precisely Dickens's objection.

44. Neville, Forster recalls Dickens telling him, was "to have perished" in the unmasking and capturing of Jasper.

45. Johnson, *Dickens: Tragedy and Triumph*, 2:1113-14.

46. Raymond Fitzsimons, *Garish Lights: The Public Readings of Charles Dickens* (Philadelphia: Lippincott, 1970), 146ff.

47. Lonoff, "Dickens and Collins," 168.

48. Edgar Johnson traces the growth of the idea for readings without connecting it to Dickens's entanglements with rivals (*Dickens: Tragedy and Triumph*, 2:601, 904-5).

49. That Dickens and Collins "may have been in hidden competition" is as far as Sue Lonoff ("Dickens and Collins," 169) will go, and the concession is contrary to the direction of her essay.

50. Davis, *Flint and Flame*, 303.

51. Kenneth Robinson, *Wilkie Collins: A Biography* (London: Bodley Head, 1951), 259.

52. Davis, however, suggests *(Flint and Flame*, 289) that Collins's novelette *The Dead Alive, or John Jago's Ghost* (1873) uses the "same ingredients" one finds in *The Mystery of Edwin Drood*. Actually, this short, half-hearted attempt demonstrates that Collins realized the rivalry had ended.

53. Lonoff, *Collins and His Victorian Readers*, 221.

54. George Orwell, "Charles Dickens," in *Dickens, Dali and Others* (New York: Harcourt, Brace & World, 1946), 5. Unlike Charles Reade, says Orwell, Dickens realized that "given the existing form of society, certain evils *cannot* be remedied."

CHAPTER SEVEN

1. Joan Bennett discusses the decision to combine "Miss Brooke" with the Lydgate material; see *George Eliot: Her Mind and Her Art* (Cambridge: Cambridge Univ. Press, 1962), 160–63. Gordon S. Haight also recreates the genesis of the novel in *George Eliot: A Biography* (New York: Oxford Univ. Press, 1968), 432. The fullest account can be found in Jerome Beaty's *Middlemarch from Notebook to Novel* (Urbana: Univ. of Illinois Press, 1960). Although Bulstrode appears in the stalled novel that was put aside in 1869 (chapters 11-16 or 17 in Haight), most of the scenes involving him were written or revised after 19 March 1871, the date by which Eliot had on hand the present chapters 1-18 plus 23, having joined "Miss Brooke" (chapters 1-9) to the Lydgate story with chapter 10 as the bridge; see Beaty, 38-42, 131-32.

2. See Jerome Meckier, "The Case for the Modern Satirical Novel: Huxley, Waugh and Powell," *Studies in Twentieth Century Literature* 14 (Fall 1974): 21-42.

3. Gustave Flaubert, *Madame Bovary*, trans. Francis Steegmuller (New York: Modern Library, 1957), 322 (hereafter cited as MB). The consensus has been that George Eliot never read Flaubert. Leslie Stephen recognizes her as the founder of English naturalism but argues that "sympathetic treatment of the commonplace and the ugly . . . preserved her . . . from the scorn for the *bourgeois*" that is "the weak side of Flaubert's *Madame Bovary*" (*George Eliot* [London: Macmillan, 1904], 111). The extent to which Eliot is against Dickens, however, also puts her against the French novelist, in whom drab realities and romantic illusions undercut one another, the former deflating the latter, the latter exposing the former's banality. To champion George Eliot along with Flaubert as inventors of the modern novel—the argument Barbara Smalley makes—seems a mistake; see *George Eliot and Flaubert: Pioneers of the Modern Novel* (Athens: Ohio Univ. Press, 1976). Eliot is closer to Walter Scott's *Waverley* than to *Madame Bovary* in her belief that illusions can be outgrown because an acceptable reality exists to be put in their place. Disagreements between Eliot's and Flaubert's novels— which are subtitled, respectively, *A Study of Provincial Life* and *Patterns of Provincial Life*— were featured prominently in an earlier version of this essay; see Jerome Meckier,

" 'That Arduous Invention': *Middlemarch* versus the Modern Satirical Novel," *Ariel* 9 (Oct. 1978): 31-63.

4. See Jerome Meckier, "Quarles Among the Monkeys: Huxley's Zoological Novels," *Modern Language Review* 68 (April 1973): 269-82.

5. See William F. Axton, "Religious and Scientific Imagery in *Bleak House*," *Nineteenth-Century Fiction* 22 (March 1968): 357. For a full discussion of George Eliot's imagery, see Barbara Hardy, *The Novels of George Eliot: A Study in Form* (New York: Oxford Univ. Press, 1963), 218-26.

6. This position runs contrary to Henry Auster's in "George Eliot and the Modern Temper," Buckley, *Worlds of Victorian Fiction*, 75-101.

7. Catherine Gallagher, *The Industrial Reformation of English Fiction 1832-1867* (Chicago: Univ. of Chicago Press, 1985), 149.

8. Bennett, *George Eliot*, 171.

9. Forster's recollections of Dickens's letter are quoted by Angus Wilson in his introduction to Arthur J. Cox's edition of *The Mystery of Edwin Drood*; see ED, 17.

10. Ibid.

11. Casaubon admits that he lives "too much with the dead" and is "buried" in his books (MM, 13, 28). The name of Casaubon's estate, Lowick, is a tag name as blatant as Bounderby. Doubtless, it describes Casaubon's capacity for physical ardor.

12. While living a quiet provincial life, George Eliot researched the origins of Christianity and concluded that miraculous interventions were not to be expected in the course of nature. See Asa Briggs, "Religion and Science" in Richard A. Levine, ed., *Backgrounds to Victorian Literature* (San Francisco: Chandler, 1967), 89-90.

13. George Eliot, *Adam Bede* (New York: Signet, 1961), 18 (hereafter cited as AB).

14. Throughout *Middlemarch*, George Eliot revises Wordsworth, but more is at stake than what Michael Squires calls a post-Wordsworthian pastoralism in which realism is brought to bear upon rural life. This is the argument of *The Pastoral Novel: Studies in George Eliot, Thomas Hardy, and D.H. Lawrence* (Charlottesville: Univ. Press of Virginia, 1974), see p. 72.

15. See lines 85-86 of Matthew Arnold's "Stanzas from the Grande Chartreuse," in Jerome Hamilton Buckley, ed., *Poetry of the Victorian Period* (Chicago: Scott, Foresman, 1965), 492.

16. Malcolm Andrews offers this accurate observation in the introduction to his edition of *The Old Curiosity Shop* (Baltimore, Md.: Penguin, 1972), 29. Nell perishes in a little country town after a hard journey. It is midwinter. Their belated arrival identifies Kit, Mr. Garland, and the single gentleman as Dickens's secular Magi, guided to Nell by "one single solitary light," which substitutes for the biblical star.

17. Ibid., 503-4; the passage is rephrased by Dickens after Nell's death (p. 659).

18. See the gruesome deaths of little Phil in Huxley's *Point Counter Point* (1928) and young John in Waugh's *A Handful of Dust* (1934).

19. George Eliot brushes aside Dickens and Collins as experts on changes in the medical profession; she claims to know, better than they, a given doctor's merits and the difficulties that prevent society from recognizing them. Ezra Jennings's skills in Collins's *The Moonstone* unite physiology, psychology, and pharmacology. He is the physician new-style, but Mr. Candy, who represents the old guard, recognizes his genius. Lydgate is highly trained compared to the other Middlemarch doctors, who nevertheless oppose him. He has studied in London, Edinburgh, and Paris. Thanks to a

cosmopolitan air and a sense of superiority, Lydgate remains more of an outsider in provincial Middlemarch than Jennings is at Frizinghall, where his outlandish physical appearance belies his inner worth. See C. L. Cline, "Qualifications of the Medical Practitioners of *Middlemarch*," in Clyde L. Ryals, ed., *Nineteenth-Century Literary Perspectives: Essays in Honor of Lionel Stevenson* (Durham, N.C.: Duke Univ. Press, 1974), 278-79.

20. The flood has been interpreted as a "metaphor for the sweeping progress of history," a step forward rather than a purging. It also demonstrates that the sufferings of victims and martyrs are never in vain: they contribute to the advance of mankind. So argues U.C. Knoepflmacher in *George Eliot's Early Novels: The Limits of Realism* (Berkeley: Univ. of California Press, 1968), 180.

21. George Eliot, *The Mill on the Floss* (New York: Pocket Library, 1960), 251.

22. This is the major thesis in Bernard Paris, *Experiments in Life: George Eliot's Quest for Values* (Detroit: Wayne State Univ. Press, 1965).

23. Reviewing the first volume of Forster's *Life of Charles Dickens* in the *Fortnightly Review* for February 1872, Lewes stressed Dickens's intellectual limitations: his mind allegedly "never passed into ideas." Unlike Dickens's other rivals, George Eliot had the advantage of a literary critic to defend her practice, if only by announcing shortcomings in others. George Eliot and G.H. Lewes were a formidable alliance, on a par with Dickens and Forster.

24. Suzanne Garver is the latest to argue that George Eliot's fictions are "committed" to a "renewal of community," the idea for which derives from biological science and leading nineteenth-century social theorists. In George Eliot's world, says Garver, society goes forward through the "psychological and moral evolution" of its citizens; see *George Eliot and Community* (Berkeley: Univ. of California Press, 1984), 28, 34.

25. Haight makes this comment in his introduction (MM, viii).

26. Sally Shuttleworth proposes all of these except Dickens as reasons for changes in George Eliot's realism; see *George Eliot and Nineteenth-Century Science* (London: Cambridge Univ. Press, 1984), xi, 171-74.

CHAPTER EIGHT

1. Michael Slater, *Dickens and Women* (Stanford, Calif.: Stanford Univ. Press, 1983), 318.

2. Robert L. Patten chronicles the struggle for sales in "The Fight at the Top of the Tree: *Vanity Fair* versus *Dombey and Son*," *Studies in English Literature 1500-1900* 10 (Autumn 1970): 759-73. On the other hand, Myrick Land considers Thackeray's quarrel with Dickens "the greatest of the Victorian literary feuds" (*The Fine Art of Literary Mayhem* [San Francisco: Lexikos, 1983], 92). But the disagreement was personal, not literary centering as it did on Thackeray's remarks about Ellen Ternan.

3. Quoted by Peter Coveney in his introduction to *Felix Holt* (FH, 58).

4. G.H. Lewes's reservations about Thackeray resemble George Eliot's rationale for parodying *Bleak House* and *Edwin Drood*: Thackeray's "scepticism is pushed too far." He needs, Lewes contends, a more generous view of humanity, a larger admixture of good with evil (quoted in Geoffrey Tillotson and Donald Hawes, eds., *Thackeray: The Critical Heritage* [London: Routledge & Kegan Paul, 1968], 46).

5. David Masson's essay, from *British Novelists and Their Styles*, 1859), is reprinted in George H. Ford and Lauriat Lane, Jr., eds., *The Dickens Critics* (Ithaca, N.Y.: Cornell Univ. Press, 1966), 26. Masson assigns Thackeray to "the Real school" and Dickens to "the Ideal, or Romantic school," categories that will not work to distinguish them from each other or, later, Dickens from George Eliot.

6. See Carol Hanberry MacKay, "Surrealization and the Redoubled Self: Fantasy in *David Copperfield* and *Pendennis*," *Dickens Studies Annual* 14 (1985): 241-65.

7. G. Armour Craig discusses similarities between old Osborne and Mr. Dombey; see "On the Style of *Vanity Fair*," in Harold C. Martin, ed., *Style in Prose Fiction* (New York: Columbia Univ. Press, 1959), 107.

8. Arthur Pollard, "Thackeray," in A.E. Dyson, ed., *The English Novel* (London: Oxford Univ. Press, 1974), 169.

9. Gordon S. Haight, ed., *The George Eliot Letters* (New Haven, Conn.: Yale Univ. Press, 1954-56), 5, 168-69.

10. A. Dwight Culler, *The Poetry of Tennyson* (New Haven, Conn.: Yale Univ. Press, 1977), 15.

11. Sally Shuttleworth argues that "scientific ideas and theories of method affected not only the social vision but also the narrative structure and fictional methodology" of George Eliot's novels. Eliot, she maintains, "brought to her writing a breadth of knowledge of contemporary social and scientific theory unmatched by any of her peers" *(George Eliot and Science*, ix, x).

12. Richard Altick, *Victorian People and Ideas* (New York: Norton, 1973), 89.

13. Ibid., 92.

14. For a discussion of *Barnaby Rudge* as Dickens's Chartist novel, see Thomas J. Rice, "The Politics of *Barnaby Rudge*," in Robert Giddings, ed., *The Changing World of Charles Dickens* (London: Vision Press, 1983), 51-74.

15. Tess Cosslett, *The "Scientific Movement" and Victorian Literature* (New York: St. Martin's, 1982), 5.

16. Two recent studies in favor of catastrophism are David M. Raup and J. John Sepkoski, Jr., "Periodicity of Extinctions in the Geological Past," *Proceedings of the National Academy of Sciences* 81 (Feb. 1984), 801-5; and Walter Alvarez, et al., "Impact Theory of Mass Extinctions and the Invertebrate Fossil Record," *Science* 223 (16 March 1984): 1135-41.

17. In *The Moonstone*, Ezra Jennings adopts this text as the basis for experiments on Franklin Blake (MS, 382). Collins tries to give the most sensational episode in his novel a scientific foundation. Indeed, as Ira Bruce Nadel has observed, Collins's lifelong interest in science prompted him to provide rational foundations for mysteries in his fiction; see "Science and *The Moonstone*," *Dickens Studies Annual* 11 (1984): 239-57.

18. Gillian Beer, *Darwin's Plots: Evolutionary Narrative in Darwin, George Eliot and Nineteenth-Century Fiction* (London: Routledge & Kegan Paul, 1983), 8.

19. The "dreadful hammers" of geologists clinking away at "every cadence of the Bible phrases," Edgar Johnson writes, perturbed Ruskin yet held "no terrors for Dickens." If so, it was not because the world according to George Eliot or Mrs. Gaskell held many attractions. As Johnson notes, *The Origin of Species* was "greeted in *All the Year Round* with an article of lucid and respectful exposition calling attention to the far-reaching implications of its theory" *(Dickens: Tragedy and Triumph*, 2:1132). But the "implications" discernible in *North and South* and *Felix Holt* were not favorably received by the author of *Hard Times* and *The Mystery of Edwin Drood*.

20. The renewal of interest in catastrophism is not confined to scholars. For a popularization of the findings cited in n. 16, above, see "Did Comets Kill the Dinosaurs? A Bold New Theory about Mass Extinctions," the cover story in *Time*, 6 May 1985, 72-83.

21. S.T. Coleridge, *Biographia Literaria* (1817), ed. J. Shawcross (London: Oxford Univ. Press, 1962), 2:5 (hereafter cited as BL).

22. Also see the emphasis on "the primary laws of our nature" in William Wordsworth, "Preface to *Lyrical Ballads*," in *Prose of the Romantic Period*, ed. Carl R. Woodring (Boston: Houghton Mifflin, 1961), 51. Wordsworth's and Coleridge's activities in 1798 included "The Old Cumberland Beggar" (which Wordsworth could have inserted in the first edition of *Lyrical Ballads* even though, like "Tintern Abbey," it is no ballad) and "Christabel" (which Coleridge did not complete in time for inclusion in the volume but later stated "would have more nearly realized" his "ideal").

23. William Wordsworth, "Lines Composed a Few Miles above Tintern Abbey," in Mark Van Doren, ed., *Wordsworth: Selected Poetry* (New York: Modern Library, 1950), lines 64-65 (subsequent quotations from Wordsworth's poetry are taken from this edition and cited by line number).

24. S.T. Coleridge, *The Rime of the Ancient Mariner*, in R.C. Bald, ed., *Samuel Taylor Coleridge: Selected Poems* (New York: Appleton-Century-Crofts, 1965), lines 9, 3 (subsequent quotations from Coleridge's poetry are taken from this edition and cited by line number). Richard Haven ingores the use of Coleridge's poem in Victorian novels; see " 'The Ancient Mariner' in the Nineteenth Century," *Studies in Romanticism* 11 (Fall 1971): 360-74.

25. Wordsworth, "The Old Cumberland Beggar," lines 73-78.

26. Coleridge, "Christabel," lines 1, 59.

27. William Wordsworth, *The Prelude*, I, lines 108-11; XIII, lines 368-76).

28. Technically, Collins wrote a "Letter of Dedication" instead of a prefatory essay to *Basil*; see *The Works of Wilkie Collins* (New York: Peter Penelon, n.d.), 10:5.

29. Preface, MS, xvi.

30. The authoritative article on the controversy is Gordon S. Haight, "Dickens and Lewes on Spontaneous Combustion," *Nineteenth-Century Fiction* 10 (1955-56): 53-63.

31. Trevor Blount treats spontaneous combustion as a "documented" phenomenon in "Dickens and Mr. Krook's Spontaneous Combustion," *Dickens Studies Annual* 1 (1970): 183-211. For evidence in support of a contagious Jo, see the account Carlyle took from William Pulteney Alison's *Observations on the Management of the Poor in Scotland* (1840) in *Past and Present*, 10:149.

32. Robert Newsome's thesis that Dickens was interested in tensions between romantic and familiar and in the possibility of seeing each in the other tends to make him Wordsworth and Coleridge combined; see *Dickens: On the Romantic Side of Familiar Things* (New York: Columbia Univ. Press, 1977), 7.

33. Instead of a zoo, George Eliot's world in *Felix Holt* is an aviary. Esther Lyon laughs as sweetly as "the morning thrush" and resembles "a white new-winged dove" (FH, 603, 599). The males in her life are no fiercer than household pets: Felix, after marriage, is "a sleek dog," and little Harry emits "puppy-like noises" (FH, 606, 582).

34. Trollope, *Autobiography*, 194.

35. Walter Kendrick, "The Sensationalism of *The Woman in White*," *Nineteenth-*

Century Fiction 32 (June 1977): 18-35. Kendrick rephrases the sensationalist's "double urge" in postmodern jargon: "exploitation of textuality runs counter to the achievement of mimesis" (p. 34).

36. Virginia Woolf, "Modern Fiction," in Mark Schorer, ed., *Modern British Fiction* (New York: Oxford Univ. Press, 1961), 4, 6, 7.

37. George J. Becker, *Master European Realists of the Nineteenth Century* (New York: Frederick Ungar, 1982), 4, 6.

38. Elizabeth Deeds Ermarth, *Realism and Consensus in the English Novel* (Princeton, N.J.: Princeton Univ. Press, 1983), x.

39. Ibid., 103, 66.

40. Martin Price, *Forms of Life: Character and Moral Imagination in the Novel* (New Haven, Conn.: Yale Univ. Press, 1983), xi, xvi, 43.

41. Wilbur L. Cross, *The Development of the English Novel* (New York: Greenwood Press, 1983), xi, 196. Unsuccessful attempts to codify realisms include Michael Bell, *The Sentiment of Reality* (London: Allen & Unwin, 1983); Chris Brooks, *Signs for the Times: Symbolic Realism in the Mid-Victorian World* (London: Allen & Unwin, 1984); John Vernon, *Money and Fiction: Literary Realism in the Nineteenth and Early Twentieth Centuries* (Ithaca, N.Y.: Cornell Univ. Press, 1984); and John P. McGowan, *Representation and Revelation: Victorian Realism from Carlyle to Yeats* (Columbia: Univ. of Missouri Press, 1986).

42. Erich Auerbach concludes that modern realism, particularly in nineteenth-century France, "completed a development which had long been in preparation" *(Mimesis* [New York: Doubleday, 1957], 489-90).

43. Joseph Warren Beach bestows this accolade in his introduction to *Vanity Fair* (New York: Modern Library, 1950), xi.

44. Gerald Graff blames structuralism and deconstruction on William Blake and the New Criticism. See *Literature Against Itself* (Chicago: University of Chicago Press, 1979), 35 and passim. Meckier, "Double Vision," pt. 2, defends the New Criticism against postmodern criticism, which is seen as a self-defeating parody of it and thus an additional stage of the modernist movement that undermined its Victorian forebears.

45. Jonathan Culler, *On Deconstruction: Theory and Criticism after Structuralism* (Ithaca, N.Y.: Cornell Univ. Press, 1982), 35. See also Culler, *The Pursuit of Signs: Semiotics, Literature, Deconstruction* (Ithaca, N.Y.: Cornell Univ. Press, 1981), 35-43.

46. See Harold Bloom's theories about poets misinterpreting their illustrious predecessors in *A Map of Misreading* (New York: Oxford Univ. Press, 1975), and his earlier study, *The Anxiety of Influence: A Theory of Poetry* (New York: Oxford Univ. Press, 1973).

47. Dickens may have intended to use the double thesis that foreign is not evil and evil is not foreign more dramatically in *The Mystery of Edwin Drood* than Collins had in *The Moonstone*, a thesis that can be construed as an oblique hit upon England's moral fitness for supremacy as a world power.

48. Edgar Johnson, *Sir Walter Scott: The Great Unknown* (London: Hamish Hamilton, 1970), 2:888.

49. See Jerome Meckier, "Why the Man Who Liked Dickens Reads Dickens instead of Conrad," *Novel* 13 (Winter 1980): 171-87.

50. See Jerome Meckier, "Cycle, Symbol, and Parody in Evelyn Waugh's *Decline and Fall*," *Contemporary Literature* 20 (Winter 1979): 51-75.

51. E. Wilson's "Dickens: Two Scrooges" was published in 1941. See pp. 69-85.

52. The Circumlocution Office from *Little Dorrit* influences the circular structure of Waugh's novels and may be responsible for the many satiric symbols of pointless circularity they contain.

Index

Browning, Robert, 140
Buckley, Jerome Hamilton, 1
Bud, Rosa (*Edwin Drood*), 155, 158, 160, 162, 181, 187, 195, 217, 235
Bulstrode, Nicholas (*Middlemarch*), 206; dual selves of, 217, 232, 242; as hypocrite, 210-20, 238; vs. Jasper, 201-02, 212-15, 240
Bulwer, Edward Lytton, 3, 124-25, 243
Bunyan, John, 245

Candide (Voltaire), 252
Can You Forgive Her? (Trollope), 8, 10
Capra, Fritjof, 24
caricature in Victorian fiction, 90
Carlyle, Thomas, 19, 23, 27, 30, 148, 226-27, 228, 269; catastrophism of, 249, 256; "Dr. Pessimist Anticant," 36, 267; Eliot on, 202; Trollope's disapproval of, 40; on workings of providence, 96-98, 100, 101
Casaubon, Edward (*Middlemarch*), 211, 222; associated with death, 223-24, 229
catastrophism: and evaluation of past, 256-58; modern theories of, 250-52; vs. gradualism, 248-54, 256
Cathedral Trusts and Their Fulfilment (Whiston), 30
Catherick, Anne (*Woman in White*), 103-04, 111, 127, 172, 196; and Laura Fairlie, 104, 106, 120; and Miss Havisham, 127
Catherick, Mrs. (*Woman in White*), 104-05, 109, 127-28, 211
Catherine (Thackeray), 246
Charles Dickens: The World of His Novels (Miller), 1
Charterhouse, 28, 29, 43
Chartists, 248-49
Chatterley, Clifford (*Lady Chatterley's Lover*), 67, 80
Chatterley, Connie (*Lady Chatterley's Lover*), 18, 70, 89
"Christabel" (Coleridge), 262
Christianity, 229; of Dickens, 278; Eliot on, 229-31; secularized by Joyce, 230
Christmas Carol, A (Dickens), 67-68, 279
Clennam, Arthur (*Little Dorrit*), 216-17
Cloisterham: Dickens's use of, 189-92, 205
Coketown: as industrial setting, 77-80

Coleridge, S.T., 40, 226; and Collins, 262, 267; and Dickens, 262, 269-70, 272; and Victorian realism, 5; and Wordsworth, 258-73
Collins, Wilkie, 2, 20, 243; arousal of Dickens by, 188; clues for ending of *Drood* in, 169-74; and Coleridge, 262, 267, 272; contrast of two cultures in, 249-52; evaluation of past by, 256-58; failure in *No Name*, 128-32; flawed individuals in, 146-49; foreignness in, 139-86; goals of, 132-37, 152; on illegitimacy, 110-14; melodrama in, 130; *Mystery of Edwin Drood* as Dickens's final response to, 195-200; outdistanced by Dickens's readings, 197; outdoing of Dickens by, 93-121, 152, 245-46, 274; parodies of Wordsworth by, 260-61; on providence and propriety, 101-08, 111, 115-18; science in, 250, 252, 254, 255; on secret selves, 145; secrets in, 15-16, 108-10, 130; as social critic, 113; vs. Stevenson, 163-69; on workings of providence, 96-101, 113, 118
commonplace: changing views of, 270; Collins on, 263, 267-69; Dickens on, 262, 265, 269; Eliot on, 261, 263-65; Wordsworth and Coleridge on, 258-60. *See also* realism
Comte, Auguste, 241
Confessions of a Thug (Taylor), 186
Conrad, Joseph, 11, 138, 147, 148, 164, 279; on duplicity, 216; on split personality, 209
Cosslett, Tess, 249
Cross, Wilbur L., 274
Cuff, Sergeant (*Moonstone*), 134, 139, 141-42, 158
Culler, A. Dwight, 248
Culler, Jonathan, 275
Cumberland Beggar, 261, 264

Daily News, 29
Dance to the Music of Time, A (Powell), 12, 206
Daniel Deronda (Eliot), 14
Dante, 110, 117
Darnay, Charles (*Tale of Two Cities*), 98, 119-20, 136-37, 217, 220
Darwin, Charles, 148, 204, 249; on

vs. solution in Victorian fiction, 210
science: of Dickens and Collins, 250-54,
262; extolled by Thornton, 71; and
realism, 5; and Victorian novelists,
248, 258
scientific social realism, 248-54
Scott, Sir Walter, 71, 274, 277
secrecy: Collins's use of, 108-10; Dickens
on, 122; lack of surprises in *No Name*,
130
secret selves: of Blake, 137-38, 139, 145;
of Jasper, 189; of Rosanna Spearman,
145. *See also* duality
Secret Sharer, The (Conrad), 138, 147, 148
secularization, 276; and redefinition of
reality, 275; by Wordsworth and
Coleridge, 271-72
self-made men: Dickens vs. Mrs.
Gaskell on, 73-76
sensationalism: Collins vs. Dickens on,
94-97, 126, 268; Trollope on, 271; vs.
realism, 27
sentimentalism: Eliot vs. Dickens on,
230-31
sex: frustration of, as motive, 159-60,
162
Seymour, Robert, 196
Shakespeare, William, 145
Shamela (Fielding), 277
Sharp, Becky (*Vanity Fair*), 9, 245, 246
Shaw, G.B., 22
Shelley, Mary, 138, 155
Signs of the Times (Carlyle), 40
Sketches by Boz (Dickens), 196-97
Skilton, David, 37
Slater, Michael, 243
Snow, C.P., 12, 22
Social Darwinism: of Mrs. Gaskell, 61
social interaction: emphasized by Eliot,
202, 239, 241
society, Victorian: Collins on flawed
individual in, 147; competition in
depiction of, 2-4; depiction of familiar
things in, 270; Dickens and Collins on
Wordsworth's view of, 263; Dickens on
origins of evil in, 183, 192-93; Eliot's
view of, 207, 214, 228, 238;
Englishness of ills of, 179-80; Hardy
on, 208; as "multiverse," 1-2; social
consciousness in Dorothea, 226
Sound and the Fury, The (Faulkner), 277
Spearman, Rosanna (*Moonstone*), 145-46

Sterling, Edward, 76
Stevenson, Lionel, 28, 29
Stevenson, Robert Louis, 163, 279; and
Dr. Jekyll vs. Jasper, 164-69; on split
personality, 209
Stoker, Bram, 156, 164, 174
Stone, Harry, 127
*Strange Case of Dr. Jekyll and Mr. Hyde,
The* (Stevenson), 164, 169
Strangers and Brothers (Snow), 12
Summerson, Esther (*Bleak House*), 8-9,
10, 93, 216, 225, 245, 272; as
autobiographer, 111; counterbalance
in, 238; marriage of, 228; vs. Esther
Lyon, 13-15, 18, 182, 257, 277
surprises: lack of in *No Name*, 130; use of
in *Woman in White*, 108-10, 130
Surtees, Robert, 197
Swift, Jonathan, 36
symbols: used by Collins, 133, 135, 146

Tale of Two Cities, A (Dickens), 4, 97,
109, 193; and catastrophism, 249,
252-53; Collins on, 93, 113-14, 146,
147; contrast of cultures in, 149-52;
Eliot on, 241-42; ending of, 163; role
of propriety in, 106; as stimulus to
Collins, 123; use of secrecy in, 108
Tao of Physics, The (Capra), 24
Taylor, Philip Meadows, 186
Teilhard de Chardin, Pierre, 24
Tennyson, Alfred, 207
Ternan, Ellen, 157, 235
Teufelsdröckh (*Sartor Resartus*), 225
Thackeray, William Makepeace, 2, 9,
273; congruent moral visions of
Dickens and, 245-46; and Dickens, 3,
243-44, 245-48; length of career, 247;
parodies by, 243-44; on propriety, 102
Thornton, Mr. John (*North and South*),
50-51, 52, 56, 60; described, 69-71;
development of, 67; and evolution of
personality, 61; innovations by, 67-69;
in interacting trio, 62, 63, 66; as self-
made man, 73-76; significance of
manliness of, 70-73; on utopia, 87; vs.
Jasper, 187
Thugs: Dickens's use of, 184-86, 192
Times (London), 29
"Tintern Abbey" (Wordsworth), 260
topicality: of hasty journalism, 35;
individual's ethical choices, 37;